J. W. Alexander.

The Life of J.W. Alexander

Forty Years of Familiar Letters

Edited by the Surviving Correspondent, John Hall, DD

Volume 2
1844–1859

Audubon Press
& Christian Book Service

AUDUBON PRESS
2601 Audubon Drive
P.O. Box 8055
Laurel, MS 39441-8000   USA

Orders: 800-405-3788
Inquiries: 601-649-8572
Voice: 601-649-8570 / Fax: 601-649-8571
E-mail: buybooks@audubonpress.com
Web Page: www.audubonpress.com

ISBN # 978-09820731-0-0

Original Publication:
In Two Volumes
Volume 2

New York:
CHARLES SCRIBNER, GRAND STREET
London:
SAMPSON LOW, SON & COMPANY
1860

Original Publication Layout and Typography:
John F. Trow
Printers, Stereotypers, & Electrotypers,
50 Green Street, N.Y.

CONTENTS OF VOLUME II.

CHAPTER IX.

LETTERS WHILE PASTOR OF DUANE STREET CHURCH, NEW YORK.

1844—1849.

NEW YORK, *October* 4, 1844.

I WAS licensed just nineteen years ago, this day. Last evening I was installed. My father preached. Dr. Potts gave me a good charge, very kind, but somewhat laudatorial. Dr. Krebs charge to the people. Mr. Greenleaf presided. Dr. Spring made the last prayer, in a very memorable manner; it was a prayer of great pathos. The house was full. The presentation to the people was long, wearisome, exciting, but accompanied with such circumstances as cheer and humble me. I slept little and am tremulous with a cup of unwonted coffee. Till advised, address J. W. A., " Care Hugh Auchincloss & Sons, 49 Beaver Street. " [1]

NEW YORK, *October* 10, 1844.

Where shall I begin about this Babel? I ought to begin by expressing my thanks to benignant Providence for the pleasantness of every thing, and especially the warm reception I have had. We are not yet admitted to our new house, but remain with our good friends [the late Mr. Hugh Auchincloss] in Barclay St. We hope to set up our tent this week. I have the back room, 2d story, for my study, which I regard as the chief room in a parson's house. Ours is only a two-story house. From my window I have a constant view of the "Tombs."

---

[1] Dr. Alexander preached his first sermon, after the instalment, October 6th, from Psalm li. 12 ; and in the afternoon from Matthew xi. 16–19.

I preached all day, on Sunday; and Monthly Concert on Monday. Attendance good, but nothing which need cause any resort to the police, as yet. As for myself, the worst I have experienced is bodily fatigue. Running all day, and dead sleep all night. Yesterday I attended my first funeral, and my first clinical case. In the evening, Mr. Auchincloss took a raft of us to the Tabernacle, to see and hear the Campanologians. They are really Tyrolese, and in costume. It passes belief. They are seven, and the music is as exact as a Geneva box. I wished for Dr. Ewing. *Inter alia*, they gave the overture to Fra Diavolo, with every rapid and every chromatic passage perfectly, and all the varieties of pianissimo and fortissimo. The bells, on a rough count, are 30—40. Each man has a cluster before him. But they do not stick to this arrangement, but snatch up one another's bells with the rapidity of lightning. At a distance, exactly like common table or hand-bells, the largest about three pints measure. On examination, the handles are leathern, stiff and elastic, and within are cushions so that no shake but in a certain plane will give a sound. I presume the vibration is checked by a slight twirl of the wrist, such as throws the clapper against the cushion. The audience about 4,000. I saw the Rev. Symmes C. Henry and daughter there. My sexton is a treasure; both intelligent and pious, and withal as humble and "bid-able" as a Helot. His name is Peter Tarlsen, from Mandel, near Christiansand, in Norway. Of course his vernacular is Danish; but he has twelve years' worth of English. He is my man Friday, and does all manner of chores for me, being this moment toting my books from the basement. We have the Croton, but no bathroom. Indeed, New York is immeasurably behind Philadelphia in all that concerns neatness &c. *E. g.* we have no back alley; nor has one house in a thousand. I told you I have the house where Dr. Romeyn once was. I have found out a number of very agreeable neighbours. We have every thing near. Centre Market is about three Philadelphia squares off; Broadway, seven doors; the Harlaem railway-route, about two squares. The market folk send every thing home for you, and all sorts of trades-people come to one's house, on receiving a note through the Despatch-post. The thing which most strikes me, is the loss of time by the immense distances. For instance, Presbytery met at Chelsea, three miles from the Battery. One hundred guns this afternoon in the park. These are days of general muster. Presented one bag of coffee and one box black tea; one barrel flour, one do. sugar; item, one rocking chair, and one arm ditto. Stolen, one pile of boards from the "stoop." I wish you to say to my Trenton friends, especially in your street, that, in the extraordinary hurry of departure, having one house dismantled, and the other unfurnished, I was barely able to say adieu to my Princeton friends; nay, one or two of them I had to leave ungreeted. The processional politics of New York amounts to a furor. Thousands must be spent on banners and music alone, not to speak of drink and time. I think I have spent half a dollar a day on omnibuses. The weather has been delightful. Unless I err, there is a great desire for real pastoral attention, and for Christian profit.

NEW YORK, *October* 23, 1844.

I verily believe the exchange is against Trenton; but, for an ensample, I write. Last night, or this morning, was allotted [by the " Millerites "] for the day of doom. Some went out and encamped at Harlaem. On Monday evening I heard the Rev. Mrs. Bishop, of the True Israelites persuasion, at the Tabernacle; which is now "a house of merchandise." Her delivery, grammar, Scripture-citation, &c., excellent. Her main point was the exaltation of woman. This day has been one of great hubbub: the Young Whigs' celebration. A live eagle; three live coons; procession of trades; cavalcade of some thousands; bands and banners sans number. Nothing gratified my eyes so much as the Boston delegation, amounting to hundreds: fine fellows all. Willis has started a daily; and for New York gossip and idle, but witty badinage, it deserves well. Kirk called yesterday. I have, in my flock, Mrs. Renwick, the " Jane " of Burns: she knew the poet well. The New Yorkers mean to have a new paper: both new and old synods have jumped together in this, and in assaulting the American Tract Society, about Merle's book.[1] I find myself in a very central situation for my charge. The church and lecture room are easy to speak in. Mr. Andrew and two daughters, of my parish, have just arrived from England. Capt. Auchincloss is every day expected from Rio. My friends here have attended very properly to my wants in the grocery line. The fair of the American Institute is worth seeing. Serious talk of a railway in Broadway, to exclude the omnibuses, which peril life every moment. A member of our congregation was killed by an omnibus, some months since. Leeser called on me, on Sunday; he had been supplying the pulpit of Rabbi Lyon in Crosby Street. Rabbi Isaacs lives just round a corner from me; and two synagogues are near. The omnibuses of the better sort are lined with velvet or plush, spring cushions, some

[1] Dr. Merle d'Aubigné's History of the Reformation, which had been slightly altered in the republication.

of them having mahogany arms dividing seat from seat. Wainwright and Richmond's edition of the Potts controversy is mean beyond common meanness. The annotator is bold in billingsgate. Our door bell hardly ceases to vibrate. I have laid my people under an injunction to furnish me in writing, with their respective names and number of house. Dr. Potts has not yet elected elders. I hope you will come on very soon; bed and all ready; the "Tombs" in the rear; I am in the "bloody Sixth Ward."

Yours most interruptedly.

NEW YORK, October 30, 1844.

Last night, after my return from lecture, who should come in but Packard, on his way to Boston. On Saturday night I heard the guns announcing the Great Western; these big things are now quite punctual. Smyth [of Charleston] came in the Western, bringing $1,500 worth of books with him. He was called up, impromptu, in the Farewell Missionary meeting, on Sunday, and made an admirable address. Brown (for China) sailed yesterday. Mr. Masters [an elder of Duane street] is ill with fever. Mr. Auchincloss had a touch of illness on the 28th. Mr. Hinsdale has left us for Brooklyn. Mr. Beers, our only remaining elder, is up the river. On Monday evening I heard Major Mordecai Manasseh Noah, on the Restoration of Israel; an hour and a half: rain, but full house. Doctrine: the Jews are to be restored to their own land. Inference: Christians should aid, by procuring for Israelites a secure tenure of land in Palestine. He proposed to the Society for Conversion of Jews, to deliver several lectures under their auspices. The outcry against Merle's History as altered by the Tract Society is very absurd. The book is exactly what it was, to all intents and purposes: and its influence is rendered a hundredfold greater by the Society taking it up. I have carefully collated all the passages in question; and while I think the alterations needless, I would not give one cent for the difference. Certain New School men are bent on awakening a New School sectarism, as against all Union Societies. They mean to have a Publication Board. These jealousies are horrid. I do not wonder that some pastors feel themselves at length constrained to do all their works within their own parish. I cannot but think that spiritual religion is at a low ebb in our churches in this city. Never have I heard, in the same amount of visiting, so little savoury discourse. I believe Puseyism triumphs, (not because Presbyterians fight so little, brag so little, and stickle

so little; so saith ——,) but because our actual state, in Presbyterian churches, *has so little to awaken and fill the affections.*
Old spiritualism (Pollockism) [i. 199] is no more. Revivalism
is no more. The only activity visible is a mere business bustle
in regard to organisms and agencies. Must we not go deeper
than we have gone? I am deeply affected with a sense of this.
But how to begin? *At home,* we need most of all. I have shut
up books, and live in the streets and houses, all the available
hours of the day. Bush is out with his anti-resurrection book.
☞ Expect him to turn Swedenborgian. [This took place.]
—— and family in the Great Western, from third visit abroad.
He says he saw much of Carlyle. C. and Tennyson had a night
with him just before he left London. Pipe-smoking, with
wash-basin on table for spittoon. Carlyle is in talk as in his
books; only "more so." As Addison is printing [Isaiah]
with Wiley & Putnam, I have the entrée there, and enjoy a
grand gloat on the arrival of each steamer. The English
books are reaching a sumptuosity which constitutes a branch
of *luxe* quite new in the world; *e. g.* Murray's 4to edition of
Byron. While I write, the grand Whig procession is advancing:
Vanitas vanitatum. The under-current of religious activity in
this city strikes me with unexpected force, as strong and branch-
ing into a vast number of charities. I did not conceive that so
much was effected in regard to seamen, tract distribution, and
care of poor. The increase of foreigners is amazing: I perceive
it in the increase of foreign newspapers in New York, signs of
stores, and lingos in shop and market. Liveries are all the go
again: everywhere coachmen with white neckcloths, of true dissenting cut. I am just called down to talk with a man from
Rome (N. Y.) who heard me preach on Sunday, and is under
great distress of mind.

NEW YORK, *November* 18, 1844.

Mr. Masters was buried on Thursday. The body was
brought to our church, contrary to New York usage. Dr. Potts,
and Dr. Cummins of Florida, an old friend, assisted. I spoke
from John xvii. 24. Large assembly, including some of the
chief merchants of New York. We have lost the leading mind
in our church. In the use of his pen, Mr. Masters took rank
with scholars. As a merchant, he was sagacious to a remarkable
degree. I have now but two elders; and old Mr. Beers [since
deceased] is out of town nine-tenths of the time. I catechize
every Saturday from nine to ten. My lecture is on Tuesday
evening, half-past seven, in the basement. Last Thursday (which

is our prayer-meeting) we had the Rev. John Macnaughton of Paisley. You may remember the long debate in the Free Assembly of '43, which resulted in refusing to translate him to N. Leith, on account of the resistance of his flock. He has been on a special mission to Canada, and sailed on the 16th in the Hibernia. He has preached much oftener than once a day, in America; on several Sabbaths four times. Young, ruddy, handsome, uncommonly plain in dress, and a most eloquent preacher. He never uses a note, and says "reading sermons is almost exploded in the Free Church." None of the Scotchmen come near him for unction, elegance of diction, and Summerfieldian soaring of imagination. In the Native American procession, among abundance of Bibles and Bible-banners, I read, with my own eyes, the following, on a large canvas, and most prominent place : "By the eternal, we must and shall"—I presume the last word was "rule." I regard the outcry against the Tract Society's edition of Merle d'Aubigné as factious and wicked. For all the ends, the mutilated book is not one stiver worse than the other. The New School men are intent on having a sectarian Board of Publication. They are angry with the Tract Society for being so old-fashioned in doctrine. In two years, the Society would have had 100,000 copies all over the land. Now they are paralyzed, not only in regard to this, but all their operations. All this, while I think the alterations should have been first submitted to Merle. I fully agree with you about Polk; he never fought a duel; that is something : Ezek. xxii. 6. A visit from you will be truly acceptable. If at any time you find us full, your kin will receive you ; here are the names and residences, in full, viz. : [Here a list of "Halls" from the Directory.]

My prospects of a full house are certainly not less than I expected. All our down-stairs pews are sold, but there are *seats* offered to let. Gallery-pews are not sought. I have not visited ——, lest I should seem to be canvassing ; the name has not been given to me, as among our hearers, and my time is unequal to the search for such as are. Several cases of awakening are known to me. It is generally believed that no church in New York has so many young men. They have a monthly association, which I have attended. Kidder has put out a valuable translation from the Portuguese, on Celibacy : see this week's Observer. I have met him twice. *Me judice*, the Methodists are doing more than all of us, in evangelizing this Sodom. The monthly visits of the City Tract Society's distributors, is the most wonderful and blessed agency ; the half had not been told me. Burns has determined to settle at Toronto. A visiter told me this of —— which follows : He was presented to the Governor of New Brunswick. After he had blathered away, as he is wont, for about an hour, the Governor rose and said : " As I find no opportunity to say any thing, I will take my leave." The Scotch Publication scheme is grand ; they will have no lofts filled with unsold books. It is this : No books are in market, nor any printed, but for subscribers. *All the money* goes to cheapen the books. Each subscriber, who at first received two bound vols. per annum for 4*s.* sterling, now receives four bound vols. for the same. Subscribers now, 40,000. This ensures their being read, and they are cheaper than our " cheap litera- ture." In all our operations here, I am afraid much of the water runs beside the mill-wheel ; *e. g.* the millions of " winged mes- sengers " which fly into waste-paper-deposit. But let's not croak : for croaking is already hindering half we attempt. I wish Willis was not so incorrigibly and laboriously frivolous. His " Mirror," now daily, gives the best daguerreotype of this frivolous city. —— is to be the editor of the New School paper, " and to party give up, what was meant for mankind." My people will not stand up in prayer. Some pastors have used pains to introduce what Dr. Cox calls a " sedentary reclina- ture." I hope they will not introduce berths, for repose in devotion.

NEW YORK, *December* 2, 1844.

Your thoughts about the Sabbath Convention show how well you have succeeded in picking up my views, probably from my old parishioners. Beware how you use " my thunder." Our ponderous fire-bell is telling of fire. Though we hear the tocsin at least daily, I have never seen an engine, nor met with that sort of hubbub which agitates all Philadelphia at once, on such occasions. The reason perhaps is, that the law forbids engines to go out of their own district, unless a special call be made for more help. I have a choking new cold ; yet I preached twice yesterday, and was at a funeral to-day : Dr. Milnor, Dr. Snod- grass and I. Fourteen white scarfs, of fine twined linen. Burial in vault in Trinity-yard, where Milnor officiated, after my ser- vice at the house. The old Doctor is right hale for 72. [He died April 8, 1845.] He tells me he practised law, actively, twenty years. Morse, after long silence, is editorializing about Merle's history. The life of McCheyne humbles me. What zeal and faith ! what a proof that Old Calvinism is not insusceptible of being used as an arousing instrument ! Macnaughton seems to be of the same school. The book is open to an objection, conveyed in an anecdote told me by a nice Scotswoman, the other day. Dr. Chalmers said of Burns jr., McCheyne, McDonald, &c. : " These young brethren are doing a good work ; but I wish they would have done with their *nursery endearments.*" Noah is repeating his lecture this evening. Potts has been challenged by Richmond, to discuss prelacy in an oral way. This, you remember, was Potts' proposal to Wainwright. " And," Richmond adds, " as you are well prepared, let us begin to-morrow." The November number of the " North British Review " is good. Leading article by Chalmers. One on Davy, by *Carlyle ;* one on America, by Cunningham ; admirable. One on somebody's telescope, by Brewster. The best is on Backhouse (quaker)'s missionary visit to Africa ; developing the principle of a book called " Good—Better—Best." Among all my catechumens, I find but two who know the whole Shorter Catechism. I find it my pleasantest hour in the week. Much talk in Princeton of the amazing genius of a young poet. He belongs to the set which may be said to constitute the " New America." They go for metaphysic, Coleridge, almost for Spinoza. They laugh at Locke, Reid, Stewart, &c. They undervalue Newton and Bacon. They applaud Plato. They care less, than they once did, for prayer-meetings, missions, &c. Keep your eye on this. How much we need to stick by the plain declarations of the written word ! Reading McCheyne makes me feel how defective we ministers are, in helping one another in the main point. It is a great thing to have one to go to in a soul-trouble. Bustle, bustle. It was temperance— it is now the Sabbath. I am trying to fall in with a good little Moravian, named Bigler, who is said to preach the old gospel with much unction. Some of the Methodists preach delightfully ; and when they all sing together, it leaves the orchestral style far behind. I am anxiously concerned about new elders, having only Messrs. Auchincloss and Beers. I have never had any one to pay a visit of introduction with me ; still I am getting on. I lecture on Hebrews, and wish I could do nothing but expound. I read one sermon a week ; with a growing persuasion, that written sermons have undoubted points of superiority ; but that these are all *worldly.* I more and more believe (my practice belies it) that (1) constant Bible-study, using Scripture to explain itself, and (2) culture of the heart, by prayer, &c., are the great preparation for the pulpit. O for a generation of the old sort of preachers ! Matt. Henry, Newton, Cecil, &c. We are dying of *Moderatism.* Listen to the talk of our divinity-students ; it is of Coleridge, Emerson, &c. In New York, the result of the former exciting revivals is seen, even in good men, in the making all religion consist in evangelical *effort.* Some are very busy saving souls, with all the dialect and levity and coarseness of Maj. Downing. I feel my own defects. I desire to be a parish-minister, wholly, and with all my soul.

NEW YORK, *December* 9, 1844.

I think we are at cross-purposes about the "old sort of preachers." I meant such Presbyterian pastors and preachers as were known to our fathers. I would not demand that any of us should adopt those peculiarities which belonged to the age and fashion of the Puritans; their "pun-divinity," as Charles Lamb called it. Nor do I deny that they sometimes introduced inconvenient niceties of distinction. Yet even in respect to these, I believe it may be taken as universally true, that every distinction arises from some new error to be opposed. The Apostles' creed sufficed, till Arianism arose. Sabellius made other distinctions necessary, and so on to the end of the chapter. Some of the distinctions of the Reformed Theology, and even of our Confession, have become obsolete, but new ones have taken their place, and the number does not seem to be lessened. But the technical formulas of these nonconformists and Scotch Presbyterians are not the things I would imitate. One good characteristic, however, of this whole class, I do wish we had in greater measure; they not only held Scripture truth, but they associated it with Scripture *language.* Their writings teem with Bible phrase and Bible figure; a necessary result, in any age, of affectionate devotion to the book. For this I love them; and, in my best moods, in this I feel myself sliding into imitation of them. I do *not,* I own it, think even the Puritan writers, as a body, chargeable with overlaying the truth, or complicating its simplicity. True, they pursue doctrines into minute ramifications; the necessary consequence of their dwelling so profoundly on them. The *general* statement of a doctrine is, I know, true; it is, also, more intelligible, and more fit for a beginner; but the fault of modern divinity is that it too seldom gets beyond these generalities. *Jay* represents such a truth as this, "Christ died to save us," in a thousand ways, and each of them coloured with some Scriptural phrase, figure, or example. Some of us, if we taught the same, would scrupulously avoid every such vehicle, and would translate the Bible-diction into that of philosophic elegance. The former I think most luminous, most interesting to common minds, and most safe. It is a great merit of this way, that it is prized by our Stuarts, Pollocks, and Woodruffs, [humble parishioners.] It is the way which made them just what they are. If all our youth were bred in this way, all our old folks would relish it, as the Scotch peasantry actually do. The reverse method, though simpler, and less liable to the charge of cant, has never produced as desirable fruit. And we must not take as our model the way which pleases such as are, by the supposition, uninstructed. We must interpose some long words in the child's lesson, or he will never know any but the short ones. And I cannot help thinking it one of the chief faults of the New School or revival era, that its plan of teaching had respect too exclusively to the initiation of new converts. One thing I more and more feel, the excellency of figures and illustrations and examples drawn from the text of the Word. To aim at either simplicity or elegance, by avoiding these, leads either to vagueness or dryness. Hence I never could get along with this rule of Dr. —— : "if you have a figurative text, explain the figure, *and then dismiss it.*" It is the secret of the good Doctor's tameness. By this rule, all sermons on *Faith* will be the same sermon. I will send you shortly two numbers of "Punch." Though the old Adam in me relishes his passes, yet I agree in what a very poor editor lately said of him, that it is bad, week after week, to undermine the *veneration* of a people. We are too fond of laughing at every thing. On the 4th I was at a soirée, at ——. He is a McElroyalist; and is eldest of eight sons of a late clergyman of Glasgow. One of the ablest lay-talkers on theological matters. I met there Hugh Maxwell, Esq. Our host had that same day entertained Dr. McLean, husband of Miss Landon, L. E. L.; and Governor of Cape-Coast-Castle ; said castle covers several acres. Said governor is autocrat ; and has condemned as many as eleven to death ; he also buries and baptizes. A parishioner of mine spent some time in Madeira. He knows good Dr. Kalley. I have before me two of his letters ; date 1840. Facts from them : He was bent on China, to join Dr. Parker, as an M. D. Wife's health prevented, and took him to Madeira, October 1838. In 1839 he went home and was ordained ; independently, though a Scotch Calvinist. The London Missionary Society would not, however, take Madeira as a station. The Continental (now the European) Society also refused. He began as M. D., gave medicine gratis, prescribed. "During the last twenty-five days, I have come into contact with 112 individuals as patients ; and during the last eight days, forty-five besides patients have had opportunity to hear more or less of the word of God." "When the room is filled, I take the Bible and read a few verses," &c., &c. He mentions in detail different classes during each week. "One of the most regular attendants is a schoolmistress, who has 130 scholars." "One old woman has a family of six, but till lately has had nothing of the Scripture of God in her house. I gave her a Testament. Next day she returned, inquiring about the reward people receive, who love to pray that they may be seen of men, and various other questions about prayer. She said she had spent many hours in saying *rezas,* but never felt as if speaking to God; and asked very earnestly what it is to pray. Another day she complained that, though she felt a *toca di Dios* (touch of God) in her heart, while she prayed, it went away when she got home to her family and *fazenda ;* and wished to know if that were sin." He mentions numerous cases of persons dying in lively faith.

Tuesday 10.—This morning I married two of my Sunday School teachers; this evening another couple. The savour of the old old-schoolism is not good here. Many have never seen old-schoolism allied to any zeal, and have all their early associations connected with new measures. Such a character as McCheyne would be to them as out of nature as a Centaur, a Sphynx, or a Griffin. The new school of Scotland, predominant in the Free Church, gives some occasion to Chalmers's censure of their " nursery-endearments of style." They have also much to learn about the evils of unseasonable meetings, outcries, &c. But they are in earnest, and they exalt Christ. I am convinced you are right about the place ministers seek to occupy in society. One loses nothing, either, by being behind the fashion. Paul, or Luther, or Swartz, would perhaps have been poor Mentors about a visiting card, or a sack-coat. Their tea-service was perhaps humbler than a Methodist's. If we had more men, we ought to have more and smaller churches, and smaller stipends. I have seriously proposed to our clergy, as we have no night-meetings for the young and strangers, that the Presbyterians of New York buy the Broadway Tabernacle, and have first-rate preaching Sunday evenings all the year round. It holds 3,000, and has always 2,000, *whoever preaches.* The site is incomparable.

NEW YORK, *December* 18, 1844.

I expect to be here all the holidays. The custom is for the congregation, one and all, to call on the pastor on New Year's Day, to eat a morsel, &c.: I must of course be in place; and I shall be glad to have you to do some of the pump-handling for me. You will be particularly welcome. If the worst comes to the worst, and company from Princeton should be here, I know my deacon and deaconess will give you a chamber in ditto [Chambers] Street, and I can answer for their pie: *probatum est.*

A sermon in your pocket will celebrate Tuesday evening, if they have a meeting. I regret to say that my attic-room has but a dormouse-window, but otherwise it is as good as any we have. Any how, come on. The "Tombs" I now see, as I write; admission free, and company sociable. My mother went this morning. I write merely to tell you to come, wherefore adieu, and love to all, and all friends, with "Merrie Christmasse."

NEW YORK, *January* 10, 1845.

Van Rensselaer is working here, [for endowment of Princeton Seminary.] He will have to work hard to get the $40,000 he has assessed on our island. Dr. Phillips's church has given him $13,000. When the new railway to Boston, viâ New Haven, is done, it will be a great thing. They say already that its terminus will be where the Brick Church stands. To-day I attended the funeral of the only surviving child of a new-comer. I was trying to light a lamp at an expiring fire, when it breathed its last. This evening I preached a preparatory lecture, from Cant. iv. 16. Seven on profession, twelve on certificate. The apostles have sold the copyright of the trial, [of B. T. Onderdonk,] which is *sub prelo*. Berrian has a manual, "Enter into thy Closet," from the prayer-book, and "ancient litanies:" some beautiful prayers in it. I always admired the Latin collects of the Catholics. The lapse of ages has given some of these old prayers a polish, and rotundity, and denseness, such as pebbles get in a river-bed. The rhythm of the almost metrical Latin is exquisite, and untranslatable. Most of them, however, are idolatrous. Dr. Hawes has published a very simple, touching sermon, on the death of his missionary daughter, Mrs. Van Lennep. Williamsburg has 8,000 inhabitants; and Paul Stevenson, late of Staunton, is gathering a first Presbyterian church there. I am appalled at the extent to which our city churches have become machines for raising money. Every month a stated collection, and almost weekly calls between-whiles. Now, aside from any selfish feelings, is this right? Is it the ideal of a true gospel state? Is not most of these sums given by worldlings? Is not the pecuniary association kept rankling, to the hurt of piety? These are questions more easily asked than answered. Ecclesiastico-politico-economy wants an Adam Smith. More equalization is certainly one thing we ought to aim at.

It is rumoured that the Episcopalians are meditating a revolt against the Episcopal degradation of Onderdonk; but *que faire?*

Do you know that Sue's "Wandering Jew" is aimed at the Jesuits? It is an awful book, and its principles are clearly anti-christian. Hordes of scavengers do not remove the ordure and smell of our streets. We have none of the great sewers of Philadelphia.

I see a new book on the Ruling-Elder, by King, of Scotland. He seems to adopt the view of a bench of Presbyters, some of whom preach. Thornwell is out with a volume against the Apocrypha; it looks very learned, and is no doubt able. He has certainly touched the right string. The Jews are evidently very uneasy. Witness Leeser's "Occident," and others summoning them to defensive efforts; Noah's Lecture; the reforms in Germany; the prevailing and admitted rationalism; the forsaking by many of their belief for ages in a personal Messiah.

I want to preach a sermon on this subject, viz., Men of Business live in a perpetual hurry, scarcely taking time to refresh nature. This keeps out thoughts of God. This spell must be broken. *For such men*, stated inviolable periods of devotion are therefore necessary. Apply to closet-prayer, family-worship, and especially the Sabbath. I feel the evil as I never did before. Broadway is a spectacle these sunny mornings. I sat by ——, [a fashionable author,] in an omnibus, to-day; black, shaggy sack, plaid pants, gaiter-boots, blue and red neckcloth, crook-dangling curls like a Miss, face of a vinous character. I have always felt serious concern at the evident repugnance of a friend of ours to the Tract Society. It is unfortunate, for the principle of compromise in the two charities is identical. And the only privilege of the S. S. Union in the event of disaster, will be that of "being devoured last." I am loth to say it; but to this I apprehend it will come. Even the New School, who spread wide their no-sect flag in '37, are now moving every thing to be as sectarian as possible—newspaper, Board of Publication, complaint about suppression of Calvinism, &c. A great protraction of meetings and revival reported at Sag Harbor, L. I., (Old School.)

NEW YORK, *January 30, 1845.*

I have just returned from my weekly prayer-meeting. Prayer-meetings are like Jeremiah's figs. Where gifts are rare, and graces are small, the edification, and certainly the comfort, are accordingly. One of our men is ill, I fear dying. It is a case in which severe remedies afford the only hope; but he has two Homœopathists. Contrary to every principle avowed, and all their denunciation of " Allopathic" means, they are now, when he is moribund, giving strong medicines. The more I see of them, the more am I confirmed in my belief, that their pretensions are those of systematized charlatanry. Bush is going over fast to the New Jerusalem, [Swedenborgian.] In the Tribune, he challenges all the world to prove the resurrection. He has a book coming out on the " Soul." He practises Mesmerism. He told me of a lady who can read any one's character by feeling a paper on which he has written : and read me a copy of his own character thus deduced. His talk is mild, self-complacent, learned, and fascinating. He has a man translating the German account of the famous Clairvoyante of Prevorst. You can imagine nothing of the sort too big for his swallow. The coalition between Mesmer and Swedenborg is becoming patent : both affect to see things beyond the vulgar ken. You have read the account of young Dr. Bodenier's extirpation of a glandular parotid tumour, from a woman, during magnetic sleep, in presence of Mott, Rodgers, Doane, Delafield, &c. Come on and be mesmerized. I am strangely obtuse, for I can't wake up enough to see these things in the favourable light. That they can put people asleep, I believe : but so can I. McCartee is called to the Canal Street church. You see that Texas is all but annexed, and the " area of *freedom*" widened : N. B. *area* is the Latin for " threshing-floor." I am heretic enough to believe, in very earnest, that this very enormity will be overruled to the good of the negro. It will drain Maryland, Virginia, Kentucky, and Tennessee of their slaves. It will push the slave-mass towards the tropics. There they may physically thrive ; there they are always happiest. There they will outgrow their white holders. There they will be in the region which is exempt from the real hinderance to their freedom, the prejudice of colour and caste. In Mexico, Central America, and Colombia, black is almost as good as white. Half the Mexican officers of the two steamers. whom I saw, were one-half or two-thirds Africans. Amalgamation, say what they please, can go on, does go on, and will go on. The longer we put off the national break, the greater will be the Free America. All this, I think, leaves the emancipation question just where it was. But leave this out of view, and what becomes of our negroes, slave or free ? Those called by mockery free people, are a race of Helots or Yahoos, in our estimation. We do not give them our dinners, or our daughters ; we debar them from pulpits, pews, and omnibuses ; we deny them actual citizenship. We smell their rancid odours, and hustle them off our streets more vehemently now that they are free, than when they were slaves. Educate them, and this prejudice makes them miserable. Look at ——, a sensible, travelled, pious woman yet hanging between the two races.

New York, *February* 10, 1845.

Your letter of 8th to-day. When the House of Representatives assents to the new and reasonable postage, [it was then ten cents a sheet,] we can write more fully. I lament with you our friend's troubles, and feel sure you have traced them to their true source : only physical derangement is usually the cause of the depression. I also agree with you as to what would be best. A southern or a foreign trip would probably cure. Such cares cannot be thrown off at home : every domestic association forbids it. Travelling is beyond all things the best remedy. Nolens volens, the patient becomes filled with new objects. I wish you would tell me when and how I could render any aid, in a case where I am so truly interested. Good old Mr. Fenton ! [a pious bookseller in Trenton,] I doubt not he rests in peace. We have a letter telling us of Mrs. Le Grand's death. I suppose I had no better friend on earth. Mrs. Le Grand has been an extraordinary woman. Her views of her own religious state were always dark : on every other point, no one could be less morbid, or more clear of sight. Her conscience and intrepidity exceeded all I ever read in books. I do not believe the human being lived to whom she durst not speak her mind. Her beneficence, for sixty years, has been, so far as I know, unexampled. Like most planters she had little ready money ; but she has been a perennial fountain of good works. She has washed the saints' feet. Her notions of plainness were extreme. Her personal attire was little above that of her servants, in expense. She loved all, of every sect, who loved religion ; and such as did not, she exhorted and warned, in a way which shames me when I write. She was distressingly exercised about slavery. But what could she do ? She often asked me, but I was dumb. She had as many as possible taught to read, and this up to the present time. A large number of her slaves are real Christians, not to speak of perhaps a hundred who have gone to heaven. I fully believe that more of them have secured eternal life, than would have been the case in any freedom conceivable. And surely, if eternity is more than time, this is a consideration to be pondered. But she saw no escape ; individual opinion was inert. She greatly opposed the acts of '37, in the church, and was therefore called New School, but adhered to the church. Several fires last night ; and they are serious things, now that the streets are so filled with snow. It is scarcely safe to cross Broadway. Every thing on runners; six pair of horses in some cases, and such a din of bells, and bellowing of drivers, and mad rush of cutters and horses, as confounds one. The Moravians had their last αγαπη and service, yesterday, in their meek little chapel in Fulton street, before migrating up-town. Arnold's Life is a bonne-bouche. Latitudinary, but O, how fresh, original, vigorous, increasingly Christian, Catholic, anti-puseyite, scholarlike![1] Our travelled merchants say our new Post Office is the best in the world. You find yourself in a well-warmed colonnade, and see into the interior hall and proceedings. I do not know the number of private boxes, but the number I saw was somewhere about 3,000. The exterior is squat and Dutch. One of our clergymen, a paralytic, goes about the room, but is said to be a speechless infant, though comfortable. I can never forget seeing another minister in the same case: "And Swift expires, a driveller and a show." Not only "I would not live alway," but I would humbly pray not to live thus. Yet let us say, *fiat Voluntas Tua.* I see a desert place within; but I think eternity is oftener in my mind than it was. For pleasant views, one must look at some thing more organized than this world.

NEW YORK, *February* 17, 1845.

Speaking of Plutarch, I think him the best story-teller out of Scripture. His universal popularity shows this. Our English translations are vile and paraphrastic. G. Long, Prof. &c., of London, has just issued, as one of " Knight's Weekly Volumes " a shilling volume of Roman Lives from Plutarch. The version is literal, strong, vivacious; and the book delightful. It is good for a boy. Two-thirds of all we believe about the Roman Commonwealth is out of Plutarch, including all our famous anecdotes. Forgive what is egotistic in the following incident, for the sake of the little romance about it, a quality not rife in New York. This morning I was at the Sunday School Depository in Nassau Street, when a little old woman, cleanly, but poor, came in, and in German-English asked for half a dollar's worth of my *Infant Library.* I found they knew her, and was surprised to learn that she was in the habit of *giving them away.* I talked with her in such German as I could produce, and found her a warm-hearted, overflowing Christian—a Lutheran — worshipping in Columbia street. But the thing

[1] Stanley's Life of Dr. Arnold, reviewed by him in Repertory, April, 1845.

which struck me was, that she pointed out to me her aged blind
husband, at the door, holding a harp, on which he plays for his
livelihood, while she leads him about. They play chiefly in
families. The husband, before his blindness, was a man of some
education. My young people have agreed to support an Evangelist in France, $250. The snow is rapidly going from our
broadways. Omnibuses on wheels to-day, for the first. We have
no further news from Charlotte, [Mrs. Le Grand's death.] The
more I reflect on it, the more I feel the solemnity of our good
friend's departure. My father lived under her roof several
years; so did I, thirty years after. My first interview with
my wife was there. There also was my first ministry. A longer
course of good doing (εὐποιΐα, Heb. xiii.) I never knew. The
executive part of Christianity seemed almost perfect in her.
Frugal and self-denying, laborious, constant, independent, fearless, tender, and sympathizing. Yet I have to add this remarkable fact: during all her life, she knew nothing of *comfortable
frames.* She was always panic-struck, in view of the standard
she had set up; and so she judged others. Her mind was
always under the stress of *obligation.* Yet a more operative
religion could scarcely be pictured. She was always the same—
always taking the religious view of things—sober, vigilant,
looking to the judgment. No man seemed to have left such an
impress on her as her old pastor, John Blair Smith; and he
was a John the Baptist; opposite, in all but eloquence, to his
brother S. Stanhope Smith. This grave, somewhat hard and
unforbearing type of religion, appears in all the fruits of the
great Revival, which founded our church in that part of Virginia. Plainness in dress, expenditure, and manner, was indispensable to the Christian character.[1]

NEW YORK, *February* 27, 1845.

My boys are both in bed with the measles. The younger
has a very bad cough. In these circumstances I am a nursing
father, and have risen from a bed of small slumbers. This
always depresses my animal powers. Some things in my
labours are encouraging. Three are propounded for communion, on profession of faith. A few are under concern
of mind. Seven female Sunday School teachers, who meet
for prayers, seem well exercised. One of them, besides regular Sunday School duty, has all her class, two hours, every

[1] Among other legacies Mrs. Le Grand bequeathed $2,000 to the Union
Theological Seminary of Virginia, and $1,000 to Mr. Alexander.

Saturday, for instruction. For five years she has taught a class of six poor girls, from 9—12, *five days in the week*, at her own house. On my proposing that our young men and young women should sustain an Evangelist in France, she raised $164 in a week.

I have lectured to Heb. iv. 11. The next passage is a *crux interpretum*. I spent a pleasant evening with Bro. ——, the Moravian. About 37; healthy, ruddy, vivacious, with that happy "no manner," which is common to Moravians and noblesse, and that absence of sanctimony which is uncommon among Puritan Christians; more marked by quickness and hilarity, than tenderness or pensive gravity. He was a missionary in Antigua. One of our pastors tells me that he does not pretend to visit any but emergent cases. I see more and more how naturally and necessarily a man comes to this. I have been engaged, late and early, every day, and have not yet effected a thorough visitation, though I have, for this, sacrificed almost all writing of new sermons. One of our ministers avows the opinion, that, in such a society as ours, the pulpit is the great engine. Accordingly, he spends every day from 8—3 in his study, not answering knocks before 1. Most of this time he is sermonizing. He writes one fresh sermon every week, and says he has not failed to have it done by noon, on Saturday, once in ten years. He has a series of sermons, on the system of doctrines, which he has delivered three times. He is always catering for a sermon; all his conversation is on the topic he is about, and it is therefore stimulating and instructive. He has had an unparalleled hold on his people, and influence over them. They visit him a good deal in his study. He is the airiest, youngest man, of his years, I know anywhere. Another pastor always goes out (when well) on Monday, Tuesday, and Wednesday. On these days he has no fire in his study. The remaining days he sees no one; gives himself to study; but never writes any. Did I tell you that I was copulpited with good Mr. [the late Dr. John] Johnston, who preached the installation sermon? It was read, every word, 40 minutes, and filled just $\frac{13}{16}$ of a sheet like this! S—— is a grand fellow, good sense, gravity, suavity, independence, honesty, kindness, every thing but animation. Consternation in our church, by reason of a *base-vile*, last Sabbath. O that we could chant the psalms, in a selection, as they are! Jacobus [Brooklyn] does it, at times. C. S. Stewart is very active. As many as 100 converts among sailors reported this winter. Good text, 1 John iv. 5.

NEW YORK, *March* 10, 1845.

How do you feel this morning, after the unrest of the Sabbath? I own to a little megrim, for yesterday was our Communion. Three on confession, of whom one, a painter, and the other a lithographer; both born in England, as was the third also. The book-cheapening business is poor here. I miss two of my old pleasures, (1) shops like Redman's, [a second-hand book shop in Philadelphia,] and (2) rows of old standard books. The auctions have revived the first, and the two weekly steamers the other. Ask for such a book as Witsius, and the answer is: "No, but we will take your order, and have it in a month." Kernott (Wiley's factotum, a Pater Noster man) says: "We try to *have* all fresh works, but to *keep* none." After twenty years, I say decidedly, "No comment, no lexicon, like a Greek concordance;" *i. e.* if you ponder the contexts. Take such a word as μετανοια, or μυστηριον; and how the conventional meanings fly away! How odd that we learn to write English from Scotchmen; viz., Kaimes, Campbell, and Blair. After teaching them ten years, I am just learning how they have betrayed me. Fear of provincialisms drives them (as us Americans) into prudery; just as parvenus dare not dress plain. Think of Blair's nonsense about the evil of ending a sentence with a particle! E contra, read Shakspeare's "ills that flesh is heir *to*," or the sentence cited by Lord J. Russell, "Shall there be a God to swear *by*, and none to pray *to*?" Pascal had the courage to break through the French rules of his day. He says, (golden words!) "Masquer la nature, et la déguiser: plus de 'roi,' de 'pape,' d'évêques, mais *auguste monarque*, etc. Il y a des lieux où il faut appeler Paris, Paris; et d'autres où il le faut appeler capitale de royaume." And better still, about having the same words over again: "Quand, dans un discours se trouvent des mots répétés, et qu'essayant de les corriger, on les trouve si propres qu'on gaterait le discours, *il les faut laisser*." Macaulay has found this out. Johnson and Gibbon ruined us about this. After all the thousand disputes about 2 Pet. i. 20, I think all difficulty removed, by translating ἰδίας literally: "no Scripture-prophecy is of *its own* interpretation;" *i. e.* it does not explain itself. And see how exactly this suits the context: "FOR prophecy came not by *man's will* (as if the prophet so originated it, as to give us means of exposition in his words) but by *God's will*—by the Holy Ghost." Even the Vulgate has "propria interpretatione." Apropos of which, the collation of the Vulgate is useful, to show us traditional errors in our interpretation. I find no common error more growing among our young people, than that men are not responsible for what they believe. This is the dogma of Brougham, Mackintosh, and Bailey. We should preach against it: Prov. xiv. 12. If Lalor lives, give him my love, and please to read John xvii., or a part, to him, as my best message. Also, in regard to his being cut off from expected earthly service, dwell on the word " serve," in Rev. xxii. 3.[1] A unitarian pair have been offended, and walk no more with us. Qu. *Up to what age* should we baptize children of parents coming into the church? The usage of this church answers, *To seven years.* Potts and I exchanged on the 2d. His church to be done inside in May. It is a beautiful interior. Capt. Auchincloss sails on the 12th for Tarragona. Our clerical meeting goes on; a Question and skeleton each time. Thus far, Spring, Snodgrass, Potts, Lowrie, Krebs, Jacobus, and Stevenson.

NEW YORK, *March* 19, 1845.

I have been at a wedding; but do not ascribe any subsequent brilliancy to the potations, for the lemonade was very thin. They waited for me to give the signal; so we sat a good hour; I thinking every creaking of the door would bring in the pallid pair. At length one of the children of the bridechamber set me right, and I summoned the parties. As you anathematize ——'s wrappings, while you wear gum shoes yourself, so I detest his a-thé-ism, while I repudiate coffee most virtuously. I hope you will button up till you get quit of your cold, for the March is searching. The rise of Pennsylvania-fives has killed Sidney Smith. Buxton is no more. Wellington has lost his brother Mornington. Smyth's book against Confirmation is nearly out; with an Appendix, almost as long as the book, defending the public aisle-profession, and anxious-stand, of new-communicants. I have thought, for a good while, that any Christians might lawfully celebrate the Communion; though, as a municipal regulation, a restriction like ours seems needful, to repress bold spirits and promote discipline. I thought you would like Arnold. The account of his death is graphic. I long to read his histories. He has shown how great a study history may be made. If he had lived a little longer, I think he would have got better. His portrait is noble. My lectures on Hebrews give me more and more comfort; and I am pleased to observe an increased attendance of men. Looking back—for I have now passed the XL—I lament many things in my preaching; and among these that I have not from the beginning aimed at the *greatest subjects.* Two

---

[1] Jeremiah D. Lalor, a candidate for the ministry. He had died in Trenton two days before this message was written.

things keep us from this : 1, a diffidence about treating them, because they are great ; 2, a dislike to topics which seem so familiar. By the great topics, I mean, not the outworks of Christianity, but the citadel ; the Fall, the Atonement, Faith, Judgment. The same remark applies to the famous parts of Scripture, the Crucifixion, the Good Samaritan, the Ten Virgins, &c. We are in danger, from neglect of this, of passing our short lives in frittering away at the appendages of the Gospel. I am much delighted with old John Brown's Explanation of the Catechism. My catechetical class delights me more and more. I wish I could hope as much from my sermons. When I compare professor with professor, what a difference between those who were taught early, and those who were not! I am much touched at reading in Socrates's Ecc. History, the old story, remembered from my childhood, of Origen's father, who used to uncover the bosom of his sleeping boy, and kissing it, say, "It is a temple of the Holy Ghost." Insert in your Almanac, (for May and onwards,) *about this time expect a display of gown—and—bands.* The Church of the Pilgrims, at Brooklyn, is to have (on dit) a series of painted windows, representing the "gests" of the paint-hating pilgrims. Day by day do I quakerize about these things, priesthood, paraphernalia, pomps. But riches begets ceremony, as surely as dung begets weeds, and blue flowers among the wheat. Would the apostles know their own children? Would that by some turn of the wheel we could see a Puritanism without sanctimony, without stickling, without fierceness, and without bigotry! I sometimes think, with Arnold, that Christ will throw all our exciting church-forms into the crucible, to produce a new form out of the molten mass. Before I got your rescript, I had baptized the girl (æt. 13½) against the immemorial usage of St. Duane; especially moved to it, as the child had been withheld from her right by the pressing of a false scruple, a scruple inconsistent, I think, with our hypothesis of household baptism. But O how we neglect that ordinance! treating children, in the church, just as if they were out of it. Ought we not daily to say (in its spirit) to our children, " You are Christian children, you are Christ's, you ought to think and feel and act as such!" And, on this plan, carried out, might we not expect more early fruit of grace, than by keeping them always looking forward to a point of time at which they shall have new hearts and *join the church?* I am distressed with long-harboured misgivings on this point. Read our Directory, chap. ix. § 1, what a dead letter! I fear thousands perish, indirectly, from within the communion, from our and their overrating the church-judgment of their piety ; and from confounding full communion with experience of renewing grace. All the epistles seem written *to the church;* yet how full of searching tests, as to personal piety. When a preacher addresses (1) saints and (2) sinners, all of the former is commonly taken by professors, as such. There seems really to be a great revival of the old seed, in Holland. Ferris told me some pleasant things about this. I had a present to-day of a share in the Society Library, where, a few steps off, I can see all the periodicals, home and foreign, and a tolerable collection of books. Take care of your cold, and believe me yours, JAMES DUANE.

NEW YORK, *April* 2, 1845.

I have had a turn of vertigo, which would not have deserved mention, if it had not seized me in the pulpit. I was myself again for the afternoon, and am much as usual; though I think I have run rather too long without considering the need of a breathing-spell. Your argument against systematizing I do not admit; I mean that from the truth that all the Bible runs up into two great principles: for it is the glory of all systems to admit this; and it is as true of astronomy, and other sciences; and it proves too much, for it would not only destroy systems, but sermons and the Bible itself. I have at last been reading " Froude's Remains." He is the true leader of the Newmanites; but one thing explains all, he had no glimpse of true religion. His whole diary contains no allusion to Christ! Newman, the Editor, admits this; and expains it in some transcendental way. *Bush* has preached for *Bellows;* his name will consort with the other fuel—*Greenwood, Sparks, Burnap, Furness,* &c., [all Unitarian preachers.] He leans most, however, to the New Jerusalem. Cheever begins to coruscate in the Evangelist; he will not join against the Tract Society, with Cox, Patton, McLean, Eddy & Co. I am about to get Carter to print McCheyne's scheme for reading through the Old Testament once, and the New Testament twice in the year. It includes family worship as well as private reading, and the table will do to hang up, or paste in a book; though as he issued it, it is a pamphlet, with remarks. Wayland has, you know, had a controversy on slavery, with Dr. Fuller of S. C. It is out in a brochure, and is very readable. We have had many rebuffs, in seeking new members of session. It will probably stand thus: Elders— Mr. Walker, Mr. Jennings, and Dr. McLean; Deacons—Mr. T. U. Smith, Mr. Burchard, and Mr. Greenough. Having gone over all the accessible members of my charge, in visiting, I have a *residuum* of 30—40, concerning whom I can scarcely get any information. Every week brings in some new family, or individual to increase the task. At my lecture, the number of *men* greatly preponderates ; young men chiefly. My catechizing class holds at about 50. Our collections are encouraging, but not a tithe of what is due. Since I came, we have received about $900 for foreign missions. —— is our chief-giver ; he is a broker, and knows how to let money go out gracefully. I have not met five undeniable Quakers among the world of people in my walks ; one would think Philadelphia visiters would furnish more than this. I am *au desespoir* about psalmody. The best I ever heard was in a German church, hard by, where every man, woman, and child joined *con fuoco*. I am in favour of chanting prose-psalmody, *without repeats;* they do it at Jacobus's. Also, I am more in the notion of a plain, unartificial, somewhat slow, chant-like music. Even the best choirs I hear, affect me thus : my mind is too much attracted to the individual, or insulated performance. Seriously, I hope for nothing in our day. What they call fine music here, is orchestral. The Methodists sing all, but then I am put out with the jiggish melodies. I wish we had the Apostles' Creed in our Liturgy, as we have it (though nobody seems to know it) in our Confession, &c. Dr. Wilson once lectured on it ; and, if he lives, another Doctor probably will. I also wish the Lord's Prayer reinstated. I am also for a vestry, but not for vestments ; I am also for the old table in the communion. What a blessing it would be if we could have more preachers, smaller churches, and, of course, more of them ! With grief and anxiety I see that, if I do any study whatever, my utmost parochial visiting amounts to little. Our ministers must be more active in concerted plans for increasing the efficiency of church-measures, by new methods within each parish. The crying evil is, strength in the laity is not brought out ; we are an army in which all the battle is done by the commissioned officers. We are tolerably well, and send salutatories. Greet the friends by name.

NEW YORK, *April* 17, 1845.

I do not know that I have ever been in a busier week. Besides more patients than common, and usual parish cares, we have had the presbytery these three days ; have talked the ordinary twaddle on points of order, and have licensed nine probationers. Last evening, I took tea with Mr. Griffin, and met Mr. Bremmer, (?) late Mayor of Boston, and Mrs. Sigourney, who is sojourning with the Griffins. She is free from any the least pretension, and shines in my eye far more in private than in her books. I have never talked with a more sensible or a more unassuming woman. Benj. Richards is here with two daughters of Gov. McDowell of Virginia. Item Dr. Sprague, item Kirk, item Mahon, item two Hammills, item Miss Reid of Va., (chez nous,) item Mr. Lacy, (chez nous,) item Miss Rice, (chez nous.) Cheever has yet to show, whether a fine essayist is necessarily a good editor. Paragraphing is an art by itself: his rhetorical circuits are, I judge, not the thing : *non tempus eget*, &c., &c. —— reappears, plenished with new layers of adipose matter. Old Mr. Johnston avers that, in Scotland, it is universally the case that a minister who demits his pastoral charge ipso facto loses his " status " in the Presbytery. The new Congregational Church of " the Pilgrims " in Brooklyn, is a noble, massive affair, with wealthy, aspiring people : it will be a great chance for somebody. The oftener I go to Brooklyn, the more I admire the site. The view from the " Heights " is, I am sure, more than Neapolitan, and the air is freshness itself. It is quiet and cool, like the country, and nearer to New York business than Bond Street, to say nothing of University Place. Therefore, name your price, abjure presbytery, take the palmer's gown and scallop shell of a pilgrim, show your descent from Jack Robinson, affect cod-fish and baked beans, keep Saturday evening, and prepare for having read to you, through spectacles, an eloquent " right-hand-of-fellowship." Bacon preached on Tuesday, in the Tabernacle, at Thomson's installation. I have been several times to see [David] Abeel, who is in the precincts of heaven, in regard to his feelings. His lungs are almost gone. Our commissioners [to General Assembly] are Goldsmith and Krebs, Platt and Baldwin. —— is just fitting out his eldest boy for a mercantile post in China. He is a faithful minister, and a most worthy companion ; unaffected, unpretending, well-informed, and judicious. I made some " improvement " of Dr. Milnor's death, and of the loss of the Swallow. Kidder is nearly out with his two volumes on Brazil. My honoured father is 73 this day. Should I say this, without adding that I know how ungrateful my habitual state of mind is, for such a favour as the preserved life of my parents, until now ? I have adopted the plan of writing a monthly letter to my associated Young Men. Should I see next year, I propose to print a little monthly sheet, to be put in the pews, containing such statements as may bear on our missions, church condition, collections, &c. ——, the poet, has a volume in the press ; I have not seen any of it. It is underwritten by ——, ——, &c., &c. Whether he will alight on Zion or Parnassus, may depend on the market he finds. Bush is in the straw, with an answer to Skinner, and a work on the Soul. He has now got Bellows to blow him up. There is no great preacher here among the Episcopalians. The last

"Punch" pictures Pusey and the Pope, in a most loving hug. The "Pictorial Times" gives serious likenesses of Pusey, Ward, &c. The Infidels are becoming bold, and have summoned an Infidel Convention, under that name. They seem to think the new Geology upsets Moses. Tayler Lewis is coming out with "Plato contra Atheos," with dissertations. I suppose he is as much steeped in the Greeks, as any man living. So poor —— has had to go. Why did he not stick to his Episcopal see at —— ? Will not —— have a sort of "proximus-Ucalegon-ardet" feeling about it? What—what is the matter? something is surely wrong with us. Is it that we are all too stiff, unreal, formal, routine-ish, in our ministry? Is it that we copy others? that we do not copy primitive ways? that we do not act out our Bible-persuasions? that we are cowardly about the world? that we seek the subordinate church and congregational ends, instead of the principal ones? Whatever it be, our churches **are** in a heavy, slow state; wheels deep in ruts and mud. Our preaching, I feel it, is too little like earnest talking; we are too unlike, in and out of the "sacred desk." Old Dr. Wilson, with "a gill of lightning into him," would be the thing for the pulpit, and Commodore Eastburn [the Mariners' Minister] out of it.

NEW YORK, *April* 28, 1845.

Monday is an ill day for letter-writing. I have no chance to say any thing. I praught for Read [Pearl Street Church] yesterday; a good quiet congregation. Thompson has immense audiences in the Tabernacle; he is said to be a good preacher, but of New Haven divinity.

There is some small-pox in town; ten cases mortal last week.

The Bowery-burning [theatre] was superb; we had a fine view of the pillar of fire.

The Anni- { domus- caput- } versaries are on the approach. I will freely say, their original interest, for me, is gone. They feel this; and *sermons* are reviving again. But even sermons, like Samsons, lose their strength. Religious showmanism is the order of the day; a church, an organ, a poll of hair, a neat stock, a ditto hand, a gown; these are thy gods, O Israel!

I am in some thought of gathering a few of the remnant of Quakerism, to form a new society. The succession may be secured through Gurney, quite as well as Abp. Parker's, at the Nag's head.

—— lectures on Babylon on Friday; a good selection; he

wili speak all the tongues, with a little original confusion of his
own *babble*. Visiters knock and ring " frae morn till e'en."
Addison says I should practise self-denial—at the door.

Yours almost in the cab.

WHITE STREET, *May* 3, 1845.

My epistolary hours must be snatches.   I am glad you have
—— with you.   I hope she will open her eye wide to all the
gracious goodness that is the very life and soul of the new dispensation.   You say right about praying for earthly good.
That is a great verse, Matthew vi. 32.   Reading a book of
prayers, (a kind of book, by-the-bye, which I find I much need,
at certain moods,) by one Hardman, and admiring the same
very much, I was struck with this in his Preface : " Should any
persons think them too spiritual, or experimental, they are requested, first, to consider, that *temporal* blessings can never be
asked for, but conditionally, and secondarily to spiritual," &c.
The article on Pascal in the April Repertory is Addison's.

I am more and more persuaded, that a man who walks " in
the Spirit," must often seem to himself and others to walk alone.
I mean he must follow leadings towards paths of feeling and
conduct, remote from the precedent and fashion even of good
people.   Don't we find things, in Christ's teachings, which, if all
our books, and human patterns, and diaries were forgotten,
would lead us further and in other directions than we have gone?
and is not this accompanied with an inward feeling, that what is
thus indicated is true, and right, and sanctifying?   In regard to
the care of souls, I am constrained, after trial, to give over wear-
ing other men's clothes, however much better than my own.   I
have found pain and barrenness in every attempt to do things
by the approved methods for getting up " an interest," &c.
Truths, found in Scripture, and affecting my own mind, freshly,
strongly, and as it were newly, I mean coming to me, after frequent perusals, as living words of God, verifying themselves in
my experience, are those which, when simply spoken or preached,
seem to reach other people.   Suppose the result is *not* the
awakening of A B, or of anybody on the spot ; suppose no revival ensues : my growing judgment is, that the utterance of
such truths will accomplish God's end on his elect : " for they
know His voice."   Surely, in our craving for effect, we lose the
value of such remarkable passages as John x. 27 ; 2 Cor. iv. 2,
3 ; 2 Thess. ii. 10.   *Simplicity*, in following Christ as a teacher,
is worthy of our consideration.

I am led to think I have erred, in the direction of ultra-prot-
estantism, in regard to *fasting ;* when I look out the connexions

of the word and thing in the New Testament. A favourite notion of mine is that a church is a school. As you may not have
Owen, let me extract a passage on Hebrews v. 11-15, which
pleased me the more from coming from a source whence I did
not expect it : " Our hearers do not look upon it as their duty
to learn to be Teachers. They think it enough for them, if at
best they can hear with some profit to themselves. But this
was not the state of things in primitive times. Every church
was then a Seminary, wherein provision and preparation was
made, not only for the continuation of the preaching of the gospel in itself, but for the calling, gathering, and teaching of other
churches also. When therefore a church was first planted by
the ministry of the apostles, it was for a time continued under
their own immediate care and inspection, and then usually committed by them unto the ministry of some evangelists." Then
overseers. " Upon their decease, others were to be called and
chosen from among themselves to the same work by the church."
" And men in those days did not only learn in the church, that
they might be able afterwards to teach in the same, but also
that they might be instrumental in the work of the gospel in
other places. For out of these churches went those who were
made use of in the propagation of the gospel ordinarily "—
" wherefore *hearers* in the church were not only taught those
things which might be sufficient unto their own edification, but
every thing also that was necessary to the edification of others ;
an ability for whose instruction was their duty to aim it."
(Owen on Heb. c. v., verse 12.) All our missionary gifts will
fall short, unless people come to give their own selves first unto
the Lord ; in some such sense. *Monday 5.*—Holy Week [Anni-
versaries] has begun. White cravats swarm ; chiefly from New
England, of which this is the capital. The Biblical Repository
for May contains a racy McClelland-like article on South, by
Withington. Henry's Calvin, which I gutted for the Repertory
years ago, is made much of in a similar article in the Repository
as bran new. Ditto of Zuingle's works, p. 402, which I long
since reviewed. So little known is labour, out of the Land of
Promise. Give me some hints towards a prayer-book for the
Navy and Marine.[1]

NEW YORK, *May 23, 1845.*

After rain and thunder in the night, we have very good
weather. My parents have been a week with us. To see my

---

[1] He prepared for the Presbyterian Board of Publication " A Manual of
Devotion for Soldiers and Sailors," comprising Prayers, compend of Bible
Truth, Shorter Catechism, and Hymns.

father so brisk and happy, at 73, is matter of thankful acknowl-
edgment. But what is this to old Mrs. Lindsay, whom I visited to-day, æt. 97! She is a native, and has lived near a century in Liberty Street, (next to the one you enter by, from the
ferry,) which was a rural suburban hill in her youth. She remembers the rector and curate of the " English church," in which
she was bred. She sits in her chair, a venerable and still fine-
looking woman, almost in full use of her mind, and full of
Christian knowledge and piety. She gave me two fine folios of
Erskine's works, for the Seminary; and bade me observe that
the shortest sermon in the book was the means of awakening
Dr. John Mason, the father of Dr. J. M. Mason: this she had
from the lips of the former. She lives with Mrs. Lowndes,
(who is the wife of her nephew,) and one of the Crowells of
Pine Street; umquhile numbered among the green-bench catechumens, *ou vous savez*, [the aisle of Pine Street church, Philadelphia.] Dr. McElroy visits this ancient woman once a week.
I felt a peculiar reverence in her presence. My election as
Tract-committee-man [American Tract Society] was unexpected.
I know not how to act. I am overladen. It is giving away
time I owe to our own schemes. Yet it is something to have a
voice in selecting religious books for so many thousands, and
standing in the gap against error. A Neapolitan gun-ship is
here. Bp. Hughes made most of the crew give up Bibles which
had been given them. They are fine fellows, swarthy, but
blooming, clean and trim, and with a jovial but temperate look.
Wm. E. Schenck has begun at Hammond Street. The small-
pox prevails fearfully in some parts of the city. Making every
allowance for exaggeration, it is formidable. The list of the
General Assembly furnishes only a few whom one could think
of for speech or action, and these all young. Of Seminarists, I
note these: Reeve, Frame, Krebs, Goldsmith, Imbrie, Davidson,
Perkins, Curran, Olmstead, Corss, Jones, Hope, Harrison,
Williamson, McMaster, Smith, Weed, Rice, Wood, Alexander,
Crowe, Montfort, Goodrich, Cowan, Dickson, Bard, Cunningham,
Edgar, Bowman, Pratt, Morrow, Weatherby, Twitchell: no
doubt others not recognized by me. In expectation of taking
the chair in '46, prepare yourself with a good Indian speech, and
wampum, for Je-chah-tu-guck-click-hoh, (Walk-in-prairie-grass,)
Chief of the Flat-noses, who may greet you as " father." As
the Assembly gave " six barrels of provisions " to " No-heart-of-
fear," it is likely we shall have a numerous council in the Xth
church-wigwam, [Philadelphia.] " Church of Trenton City,
seventeen barrels of jerked meat."

Our summer-birds are on the wing. Last Tuesday, my father

lectured. Among the hearers was the Rev. Mr. Arnott, with wife, sent to Canada for three months by the Free Church. They had not yet slept in America; and seemed melted by a service, so exactly (as they said) like their own. Lord's poems are out. Kidder's book also, [Brazil;] good style, beautiful illus-tation, and grand reading. I mean to give an article (D. v.) in Repertorio, [July 1845.] I hope the abolitionists are ready to support all the superannuated negroes, called slaves, who are living snugly in warm comfort over Jersey. How little relief has followed all their thousands yet expended! Herschell is a good speaker, and though slow yet pathetic, full of unc-tion, and abundant in apt Scripture citation such as none but a Hebrew of the Hebrews ever employs. He had several thou-sands at the Tabernacle of Witness, or House of David, (Halc.) Dr. Adams found twenty-three young Americans at Rome, in preparation for the tonsure. Our streets are cloacine, mephitic, stercoraceous, Augæan, fimous, and infamous.

NEW YORK, *June* 11, 1845.

When I examine myself, for being somewhat slack in my letter-writing, I seem to find my excuse in the thermometer. Sunday, Monday, and part of yesterday were equatorial. Mr. Hotchkin, one of my people, late from Java, says he did not suffer as much there; but this he attributes in part to their houses and their habits. I have been an hour on the battery this evening; by sunset and moonlight. A thousand people, but mostly canaille. Fashion does not acknowledge this lordly park. Wherever I saw a knot of gentlefolk I heard French, or more often Spanish. The 74 near by, the ships in the distance, the scores of small craft under gentle sail, the hundreds of small boats, the blue shores, the water, the delicious breeze, the lights among the shipping, the fine trees, the half-seen groups—end the period, according to the rule in that case made and provided. Dr. Potts's church is to be dedicated to-morrow. I would rather preach Christ, by such a history as Merle d'Aubigné's, than by many sermons; yet men judge differently, from going by names instead of things. Herschell is a fine preacher; I mean he is a good one: full of uncommon Scriptures, of unction, of force, and of Christ. He feels our climate very much. Monod and Merle have both been at Edinburgh. Dr. Phillips has a noble session-house, separate, back from street, but fronting full on the cross street. I have always considered June our health-iest month: it is so here now. Yet I cannot describe what I see in my walks in certain streets: dunghills, nakedness, dead dogs

and cats, offal, garbage, leprous folk, lazars, magdalens. The
stench, in some quarters, is mephitic. The single element of
water (nota bene, not Croton) flows, and floods, and smells in
a manner unmentionable. Cloacina herself must preside in and
about the park and its purlieus. Nobody ever cares about this
or any thing similar, for it is characteristic of a New Yorker to
feel like a stranger within his gates: no esprit de corps, no responsibility. I think Unitarianism flourishes here; also its ally
Swedenborgianism. The vast body of young New Englanders
who are here, affect the easy young-lady philosophy of these
teachers. I think there is a great deal in Hazlitt's Table Talk
which would please you; scoffer as he sometimes is. The pews
in the beautiful Jersey City Church are almost all taken. Their
steeple is commanding, and is said to be the first object, on entering the Narrows. I have some hopes of erasing my pulpit
scenery, [painted in perspective.] Sometimes I dream of resum-
ing my old plan of a Comment on the New Testament, simple
notes. Surely it is wanted. I can't feel easy under this deliverance [in General Assembly] anent Popish baptism, [as invalid.]
Perhaps it is right: but to me it savours of Succession, Braminical
orders, Puseyism, &c. Our " erring sister " is naughty enough,
but I choke a little about " Antichrist," the " Son of Perdition," &c.
Alas ! I feel my own indecision, and know my own mistiness, on
points which other men see as plain as Polus's sky-dragon: qu.
didst ever read " Polus," in Erasmus's Colloquiæ? Every day I
have to go to the pure New Testament, especially Matthew,
Mark, Luke, and John; as one goes to the hydrant, after coffee,
tea, lemonade, beer, wine, brandy, and physic; in all which,
natheless, are some true aqueous particles: βλέπομεν γὰρ ἄρτι δι
ἐσόπτρου, ἐν αἰνίγματι.   I am yours and yours's.

NEW YORK, *July* 14, 1845.

The hot weather makes the page so dripping, that epistolation
is more onerous than common. Besides, we sat ten solid days
in Presbytery; on one of these fourteen hours; on another I
was in the room from 3 till 10 P. M., after a morning session.

I am tired of my correspondence with the " Northern Warder," [1] and now propose to you to take it; which, by agreement, I
have a right to do. Terms, a column (about) a month, by the
steamer, or oftener on emergency. I will send you my files, so
that you can follow in the footsteps of your illustrious predeces-
sor. I confidently expect your acceptance by next advices.

---

[1] A religious newspaper published in Dundee, Scotland, for which Dr.
Alexander wrote as its American correspondent, a monthly letter.

Say nothing about the thermometer. I sat up much of Sunday night in Georgia summer costume. Generally towards evening there is a breeze, especially grateful down town, but it has failed us. It was our communion, and our church is very warm, and pulpit at the south end.

My mind is led a good deal more than formerly to consider the topic of gnat-filtering and camel-bolting. With all our talk about our " Pilgrim-fathers," some of the said fathers' pills are a little too grim for me. It seems to have been an indigestion of the age in England, and bred Quakerism as well as Puritanism. It rejected mince pies and the word " Sunday" as violently as crosses and bishops. Have you lighted on some " Sketches of Newburyport," &c.? In 1752 one Bartlett was " dealt with" for refusing communion with the pastor, because the latter wore a " wigg." In Judge Sewall's diary, these entries: " 1685, Sept. 13th. Three admitted to the church. Two wore periwigs." " 1697. Mr. Noyes of Salem wrote a treatise on periwigs, &c." " 1708. Aug. 20. Mr. Cheever died. The welfare of the province was much upon his heart. He abominated periwigs." John Eliot, the Indian apostle, attributed King Philip's war to a judgment on periwigs. My father remembers the birth of a calf in Rockbridge, with an extraordinary tuft or top-knot: it was voted by the good people to be a monition of heaven against a prevailing mode of dressing women's hair. A Ruling Elder, being at Saratoga, set his face very sourly against the playing of nine-pins for exercise: the camel which he swallowed was something more robust.

Clirehugh, hairdresser, is a character. I never saw a man with a more decided gentlemanly air, quiet, dignified, easy, deferential. He is a collector of coins, has a volume made of all the Tartans of the different Highland clans and families, has all the Scotch music ever issued, gives lectures on Burns, with songs, and has a world of old engravings. He cuts one's hair with the gravity of an inquisitor, and talks literature and vertu.

The modern schools are all humbugs. Teach a boy Latin and Greek; the rest will come of course. But fritter up his time on a dozen branches, and he misses the lingoes: and if he misses a fair grounding in them from 10 to 13, he never gets it. In hundreds of pupils whom I have examined and taught, I never knew an exception.

NEWARK, *August* 30, 1845.

For a time I did not know of your return, and then I was jaunting about in regions where for the most part writing facilities are not easy to get. My journeys afford no journals. The whole thing was somewhat dull, especially as the burning drought, up the North River, has been universal. They are longer about our church [painting, &c.] than I had thought, and I propose to charter the cellar [basement] after to-morrow. We have made a clean riddance of the fresco painting, which had become a Nehushtan, [2 Kings, xviii. 4,] with some of the mothers in our corner of the vineyard. I traversed the Great Britain, a wonderful piece of hardware. The British steamers are intensely filthy compared with ours; and I learn that the observation is true of all their shipping. She has twenty-four fire-places, and burns 100 tons of coal per diem. When the last touch is put on, she will have cost $600,000. I am informed by one who pretends to know, that Cogswell is going on laboriously, making out the catalogue of the great Library, which Astor is to found; after which he is to go to Europe and realize the plan. We hope to re-open our house about the 12th prox. This is a beautiful town, and, near as it is to New York, is remarkable for quiet and honesty. I am at the house of three maiden ladies, at a corner, in a thinly-built part of the town; yet they have never had any fastening to their windows, or their side-door. I have not rallied as much as I need to do, to encounter another campaign. My New York experiment is by no means tried: but as I never did any thing with more wish to do right, so I now endeavour to cast myself on the Master, for the result. Yesterday I came from Staten Island. Every time I visit that delightful isle, I perceive it to be unequalled as a summer retreat; such variety of coast and prospects, such numerous drives on roads almost uniformly shaded with rows of trees, such graceful ups and downs, and green recesses, and such a feeling of remoteness from the world, though you are but an hour from the city, that I should like of all things to have a house there, and go to town every day in summer. This is done by several scores of New York merchants, &c. I saw the coffer-dam, at Caldwell's, which they are making around Capt. Kidd's vessel; $60,000 have been expended already. I saw the ruins of Anthony's Nose; they have blown the nose so hardly, that no rhinoplastic means can ever restore it.

NEWARK, *September* 1, 1845.

I fear my letter of this morning was " as vinegar upon nitre;" for, five minutes after mailing it, I heard the news of your sister's death, and tried to get it out of the office, but in vain. Had I learnt the melancholy tidings earlier, I should certainly have hastened to the funeral: as it is, I have searched the papers in vain for the date. O what a change in your mother's household, and what a shade over her hearth! Your brothers have really lost a guardian angel, at least from this world. Anna's qualities come very freshly before me. She was certainly a marked character. I do think I never knew any person of more honesty, truth, self-denial, charity, or liberality. Her standard was high, and she judged fellow-Christians severely ; but she judged justly in this, and condemned herself in full measure. I forbear to say what you have lost, or to indulge in ordinary condolence. God grant that this renewed call on your family may be blessed to those who remain, especially to your mother.

These gathering shades on our path, as we go onward, tell us that "the night cometh." I look back to the days of *Sixth street,* [his earlier visits to Philadelphia,] and my eyes fill with unaccustomed tears. What manner of persons ought we to be, &c. ? How many of our cares and anxieties are very vain, when seen in the light of coming things ! Under a gracious influence, our character is no doubt *formed* by successive dispensations of this kind. It is a new immersion, and we come out with a graver tinge. I feel unusually serious under this sudden news ; and as yet know no particulars.

NEW YORK, *September* 25, 1845.

I should feel better and stronger, if I had taken some bona-fide distant jaunts, which the state of my family did not allow. The Boston people have the good sense to put their ministers' vacation into the call as a matter of claim. In many of our congregations there is enough of the croaking sort to grudge even that recreation to a minister, which a humane drayman would give to his horse. I have a presentation copy of [Rev. Mr.] Lewis's [of Scotland] Impressions of the American churches. He censures right and left. Our preaching, in particular, he describes as characterized by want of animation and earnestness. He is very severe on slavery and democracy. In fine, very little pleases him. There is, throughout, a very offensive air of self-sufficiency and patronage. Dr. —— thinks there never was among our churches so general an indifference ; that ministers give undue value to learning, and less than is due to piety ; that such men as Payson and Nettleton were of a generation, of whom we have not one left. Lewis speaks of the total desuetude into which pastoral visiting has fallen. Cheap literature blasts religious reading. I seldom see a young professor with a spiritual book. Church extension goes on coldly. We are not quite as far behindhand, as to new churches, as Philadelphia, but we add them by threes and fours, when we should by twenties and thirties. Vacant ministers swarm in our cities, beseeching one for places, instead of rushing into the wild West and South, as was done by the McKennies, Henrys, Blairs, Todds, Grahams, and Davieses, who founded our church. I feel the justice of Lewis's remarks on this topic, when contrasting our lethargy with the actual state of the Scotch churches. I don't wonder at the sympathy he felt with the Methodists.

New York, *October* 3, 1845.

Heavy rains. I have seen specimens of words and sentences, *printed* by the new magnetic telegraph; it works by keys, like a piano. Music is well off here; Ole Bull, Templeton, and de Meyer. One of our missionaries in India is succeeding well in teaching Hindoo boys to read the Hebrew. Its connexion with Arabic renders it both easy and desirable. Rankin, our most valuable missionary there, will have to come back; he is almost dead. Austin Dickinson thinks he has such arrangements with news-editors, as to ensure the publication of any religious paragraph, in 40,000 copies of *secular* prints. This is worth considering. He is very avid of scraps. Send me for him a bit of a sermon, and you may do good. I am just from Monthly Concert. I think our average of collection at it slowly rises. Bush goes the whole Swedenborgian figure. Some of his revelations are not so very fascinating; as of people's being conscious in their coffins, thinking themselves on earth, while they are in heaven.

One of the great Christian problems of the age seems to me to be how to carry the gospel to the thousands, in cities, who will not enter any church. Pews are high. Or they are not dressed well enough. An effort is making to establish minor religious meetings, for such purposes, here and there, all over the city. It is a fine scheme, though not a new one, being that of the old Evangelical Society of our boyhood.[1] But its simplicity and homeliness gives it a Bible-look. When shall we come down from our stilts, and be in earnest with a perishing world? Decorum and conservatism do not rank as the most needed virtues just now. Lewis justly charges our church with want of aggressive power in the cities. We have lost much by stiffness. A covenanter minister said to me, last week, and I had thought it myself, "If your church had only allowed the 'Old Psalms' and a few such things, to old-country people, on their coming here, *our* church would by this time have had no existence here." I did not hear Wines's Lectures, but he was very well patronized.

---

[1] Described in Life of Dr. Archibald Alexander, chap. xii. Dr. J. W. Alexander gave some thoughts on "Poverty and Crime in Cities," in the Repertory, October, 1845.

Dr. Spring has a very good plan for a preachers' library here. It could be easily accomplished. There is frequently a call to consult volumes, which are not to be found at all. A building is all that stands much in the way. Look out for a "Christian-Alliance man," with the cry of the daughters of the horse-leech. Could not some Christian Newton arise with advantage, and simplify our methods, indicate some gravitation, or what not? We have a wonderful diversity of methods, whereby to reach the same ends. Thus, take the one object of *European popery;* I have been solicited to open our doors to (1) this Christian Alliance; (2) to Herman Norton, well known in Trenton, but now more familiar with Trent, agent for the Protestant Association; (3) The Foreign Evangelical Society; while I prefer (4) The Presbyterian Board which we are endeavouring to aid, in this very field, by sustaining an Evangelist in France.

NEW YORK, *October* 7, 1845.

The late Free Church Assembly at Inverness fills two of the large Scotch papers pretty full. —— slips by the whole in two or three sentences, without a word of extract, and yet I have seldom read any proceedings more full of interest and edification. It is "life in earnest." This extra meeting was all in a glow. Day after day, in the absence of all ordinary business, they warmed one another up, in regard to their "schemes." That church seems to me all in one great revival. Where could one hundred and twenty ministers be found among us to engage each for a month's Missionary itinerancy? Their "pavilion" had four thousand worshippers, thrice a day. Inman says Chalmers was very charming, while sitting for his portrait, [for a gentleman in New York.] He used to go to breakfast, and family worship. He says Macaulay spoke of the American clipping of words in pronunciation : to which I rejoined, every Englishman says "Ill thenk ye for thet het." Inman is a great artist, and a fine talker. Have you seen Bailey's "Festus," a poem? A bold, irregular, but gigantic genius. Some things equal any thing I ever read. But the extravagance is wonderful, and the great aim is to enforce Restorationism. Bush is to establish Swedenborg's divine mission next Sunday. Dr. Cumming, an educated Scotchman, says, that having re-visited Scotland after the disruption, he could scarce believe the change; a spirit breathed into every thing; even drowsy country ministers roused up and elevated by zeal for a great cause. Dr. Potts's church is certainly very beautiful. As a work of art it is exquisite. They have very nobly resolved to leave no debt on the congregation. The cost is at least $80,000. One pew-sale has come off. I understand half the down-stairs pews were sold. The highest price was $1,008. I am told the purchases equal $35,000. On the 1st day of the 7th month, Tisri, or New Year's day, I attended synagogue, and saw men in their shrouds, (an old usage,) heard the ram's horns blown, &c. Saturday is the day of Atonement. I also saw the Levites pour water from a silver pitcher on the hands of the Cohens; and the latter ascend, shoeless, and bless the people, according to the trine benediction in Deuteronomy. There are now nine synagogues in this city. Neander is working away among the Jews. I saw Abeel yesterday; alive, but scarcely more; full of faith and love; going to Savannah.

NEW YORK, *October* 20, 1845.

Dr. [Kearney] Rodgers, about ten days ago, performed an operation, for aneurism, which is considered unique : the tying of the *left* subclavian artery. Sir Astley Cooper attempted it once, and failed. The man is thus far doing well. Mott, Stevens, Cheeseman, and three hundred spectators, were present.

Thus far I had written on Friday, the 19th; now, on 20th, I add that Baynard R. Hall is here, and is to preach for me to-morrow. A new book on Tobacco, dedicated by S. H. Cox, D.D., to the "*Right* Honorable" (sic) John Quincy Adams. The New School Synod are at work to-day, hammer-and-tongs, settling the mutilations of the Tract Society. Wines is here on the Hebrew Commonwealth. D. X. Junkin, in press, on the Oath. Bush has great audiences and is making converts. Bellows [Unitarian] has got into his new house. It has two conspicuous crosses in alto relievo, in front : lucus a non, &c. J. F. Clark, formerly of Flemington, has got into hot water (strange to say) at Cold Spring, by circulating some Douay Bibles among Romanists, who would receive no others. The Hydrarchos Sillimani is said to be artificial. The Mastodon is in full feather. Templeton and de Meyer are convulsing the musical world. I wish some new Whitefield or even Summerfield could rise, to carry the crowd a little that way. I believe more than I did in the need of some radical, revolutionary, aggressive action, in our Christianity. Our present method does well enough to keep what we have got. I am about to make a small Hymn Book, to contain none but *unaltered Hymns*, about two hundred and fifty.

Bickersteth on the Prophecies, though a 1000-narian book, is in a lovely Christian spirit, and is very delightful. All the delegates from the Established Church of Scotland have been here; some of them more than once. I do not know of their preaching anywhere.

NEW YORK, *November* 17, 1845.

Yesterday I compassed three services, a thing I have not done for some years. For two successive Sabbaths I have had in church, Peter R. Livingston, brother of Mrs. Armstrong, [of Trenton,] also Maturin Livingston ; and, on the 9th, the former partook of the Lord's Supper, in our church, a very pleasing sight to me. One of the most agreeable hours I spend in the week, contrary to all my expectations, is on Monday morning at the Foreign Missionary Executive Board. Dr. [J. J.] Janeway, who comes more than thirty miles, is our most punctual member. We have adopted as a missionary to Africa, *Ellis*, the learned blacksmith, of Alabama. Two synods have bought him and his for $2,500. His attainments (without a teacher) in Latin and Greek are certified to us as extraordinary. A late German has the following scheme, which is certainly ingenious. Christian doctrine has four grand epochs : 1. *Theology*, proper ; περι του Θεου. The Trinity, &c., settled in the early age ; doctrine not moved since ; this was done by the *Greeks*. 2. *Anthropology* : Doctrine of fall and grace ; the Pelagian controversy : this was done by the *Latins*. 3. *Soterology*: Doctrine of the way of salvation ; Justification controversy : this by the *Germans*. 4. *Ecclesiology* : Doctrine of the Church. In this era we now are. There is, to me, a beautiful vraisemblance in this. No. 4 is undoubtedly true of our times. Some notions have lately struck me more than ever before ; such as these : In proportion as cheap publication goes on, *books* become more and more like *conversation ;* and the attributes and laws of the latter belong to the former : this admits of being carried out to wonderful particulars. Again, the more we are flooded with bad books, the more should we read the Bible—I mean the simple text ; even of ministers, few do what they ought of this. Lest you should be overburdened, I spare you the remaining aphorisms ; which shall appear in my " Novissimum Organon, vol. iii. § ccccxcviii. *De libris supprimendis."* I heard de Meyer, [pianist ;] it was with astonishment and almost fright, but I was not touched. I have gone through seven chapters of Hebrews, [in weekly lectures.[1]] What a wonderful *abandon* in the style of Hamilton's "Life in Earnest !"

NEW YORK, *December* 2, 1845.

I lament over your provincialism, in using the word "freshet" [for fresh] as you do, in letter of October 17. Perhaps you have not met with " The New Methodist Pocket Hymn Book : " the following is from it :

[1] The series of lectures on the Hebrews extended from October 29, 1844, to February 23, 1847.

"When I was blind, I could not see,
The Calvinists deceived me ;
They, by the Scripture, strive to show,
That sinners nothing had to do :
At length I heard another preach,
Who ways of righteousness did teach :
He warned me of the Calvinist,
And how God's word they would resist."

P. 113.

I have this day had a most painful interview with a man of some note in the world of art. I talked earnestly with him about his soul. (He is, I fear, on his death-bed.) He received it well, considered as kindness ; but considered as gospel, I think he did not receive it at all. After my most serious endeavours, he very calmly changed the whole subject, and talked about his last picture, and a bas-relief for the tomb of a friend.

I believe all the pews not sold, in the lower part of Dr. Potts's church, are rented. Old Dr. Milledoler preached at the Installation : he made a prayer which I shall certainly long remember; it was exalted, scriptural, childlike, tender, and moving. The man who can so pray, (and even so preach, as he did,) is a man I should like to know better ; and I mean to seek his acquaintance, at the first opportunity.

NEW YORK, *December* 9, 1845.

Your hints about mission-efforts around our city- (you may add town-) churches are good : so much so, that I have been harping on that same string ever since I came here, and have preached one sermon very directly to that point. Our city is not altogether behind, in the matter, even now ; we have twenty city missionaries, and more than a hundred weekly meetings of the sort you mean. But this does not reach my notion, and I am not going to rest until, as a congregation, we have a preaching-place and missionary in regular operation. This, with God's blessing, I hope to set agoing, before the season is over. We already support two missionaries in the West, and one in France ; and I have this moment had a note, saying that our young women have assumed the whole charge of the last, leaving the young men (formerly associated) to give their money another direction. I am recommending the coloured people to their care.

I do not see any great exaggeration in regard to Dod.[1] It is my deliberate opinion that I never saw his superior in extent of knowledge, in exactness in certain branches, in capacity to teach, in power of colloquial argument, in generous enthusiasm.

[1] Professor Albert B. Dod died at Princeton, Nov. 20, 1845.

Just at this time, I am doubtless disposed to look at the bright side of his character, and to consider his death a very significant blow to the college. There is something very pleasing to me, in the almost universal expression of sorrow among all classes in New Jersey, and especially among his pupils. His dying exercises strike me as truly gracious.

I forgot to talk to you about——'s preposterous elocution. When warmed, he thoroughly forgets it; but he read a passage in a way which may be thus represented: "P*R*aise ye the Lo*R*d; p*R*aise ye the name of the Lo*R*d; p*R*aise him, O ye Se*R*vants of the Lo*R*d." The effect was great, and the click of the articulating wheel-work almost drove me out of the pulpit.

I spent two charming hours to-day at the Protestant Half-Orphan Asylum, where I speechified; 175 children. Wetmore, who conducts the City mission, &c., is an extraordinary man. He is ten hours every day at ironmongery, yet labours beyond every body else in religious matters, and is withal as gentleman-like a man as you will find in a summer's day. What a mean, nasty, anti-analogical word "reliable" is. Fanny Kemble laughs at "Bakery;" what would she say of "Bindery," and "Paint-ery," which I see passim. In due time, a church may be called a "preachery."

I am now in the 8th chapter of Hebrews. I have never had an exercise more acceptable. To myself, I trust, it has been useful, as leading me to dwell much on the very marrow and riches of gospel grace. One thing, to my mind, above all others, grows in centrality (ut ita dicam) among converting doctrines; the infinite, sovereign, freeness of grace, through the death of Christ. Within a few days I have been directed to several persons, who, I think, are savingly exercised.

NEW YORK, *December* 23, 1845.

I have never yet felt the argument to be demonstrative which would keep a poor bedridden creature from ever partaking of the Lord's Supper. I preached on War, at great length, a fortnight agone. Elders and Trustees were for printing it; but I was wiser than all that. South, in his sermons, constantly uses "shew" for the perfect tense of "show," (blow, blew, grow, grew, &c.;) but Sorin and Ball's edition (Phila.) constantly makes it "show," supposing it a various spelling of "show." I never have read as keen a writer as South; nor one *me judice* of better style.

Jones has made a valuable and most entertaining book.[1] I

[1] Dr. Joseph H. Jones's "Influence of Physical Causes on Religious Experience," enlarged in 1860 in his volume entitled "Man Moral and Physical."

trust you will apply the principles anent reporting, exemplified in the "slips" of your lecture, to the newspaper report of my sermon on Dod. The Observer makes me say at least ten things which I did not say, and leaves out every one of the qualifications on which I laid much stress, and my earnest attempt to withdraw notice from D.'s metaphysics to the simplicities of his dying hour.

—— makes a prayer which one feels and remembers : I think this is a point which I observe more than formerly. The Offertory [Christmas] is promising ; one turkey, two barrels apples, one do. flour, half do. sugar, one wrapper. I have preached, this evening, on Eph. vi. 19, 20 ; look at it. I used to see a number of things from Germany, at Princeton, which I miss now. It reminds me of what Lamb says, about missing the stationery of the India House : "When Adam laid out his first penny upon nonpareils in Mesopotamia, I think it went hard with him, reflecting on his old goodly orchard, where he had so many for nothing." I hope to have my father and mother here, on New Year's, when we desire our boy to be baptized. The absence of Quakers in New York is wonderful. I have never seen one in full rig, and do not meet any kind of perceivable ones more than once in a month. But we have an Armenian store, with "Notions" from Stamboul. Our confectioners and toymen are in high feather. Wild turkeys and venison abound. Gentlemen wear "shawls," London-wise, also a very thick-soled, sensible English shoe. Our Executive Committee have, for months, been anxiously endeavouring, by correspondence with our missionaries, and with other societies, to mature a plan for the education of missionaries' children. It is a painful and delicate subject. On Monday we were two hours upon it.

Sunday School Meetings are common here on Christmas. My sexton, who is here just now, says he has a brother named Ole, and that Christmas in Danish is *Yule*. The words of my good father become more and more precious to me, like the books of the Tarquinian Sibyl ; I therefore copy what follows from his last letter :

"As to the effects of the truth preached, never doubt that every faithful sermon will produce its effect ; it will not return void. Give it efficacy by prayer. If you have any persons in the church who are mighty in prayer, engage them to pray for the success of the gospel. Payson instituted little circles, called 'Aaron-and-Hur-societies,' the sole object of which was to pray every Sunday morning for the success of the word preached."

NEW YORK, *January* 16, 1846.

Knowing your dislike to thin paper, I have now provided some, which I know will suit you to a nicety. I have been sitting for my " effigies," as Cromwell calls it ; a mean business. Prof. Henry thinks the late discovery of the late Michael Faraday, of the relation of electro-magnetism to light, the greatest made in our day. He has also examined the talking-machine, [an automaton,] and pronounces it valid and wonderful.

For some time I have not had access to Inman's chamber. To-day I was sent for with a message that he was dying. He had just (vix et ne vix quidem) finished a portrait of Harper. Certainly he is great in that line. Perhaps you have seen his $1,000 full length of Bishop White. His Chalmers, Wordsworth, and Macaulay, are great. There are, I think, no services in which we need a prescribed schedule, more than those which come often, as for example, sacramental preparations : they are apt to be the same thing over and over. For many months I have been going over our Lord's own preparatory words and acts, in the Gospels. Last Sabbath four on examination, and fifteen on certificate. Three hundred dollars anonymously for Theological Seminary. In preaching on Home Missions, on " Sabbath first," I shall touch a little on War again ; text, " Righteousness exalteth," &c. Mr. [E. F.] Cooley might have gone back much further with his [edition of the New England] primer : I wait for a chance to send you an exact reprint of that of 1777 ; some of the *lectiones* are fine; *e. g.* :

C. "Christ crucify'd For sinners dy'd."
D. " The Deluge drown'd The Earth around."
E. " Elijah hid By Ravens fed."
F. " The Judgment made Felix afraid."
L. " Lot fled to Zoar, Saw fiery Shower, On Sodom pour."
T. " Young Timothy Learnt sin to fly."

Dr. Potts has one hundred at his catechizing, and sixty ladies at his Dorcas Society. I am glad S. has shown the pole-bags to be means of grace, for they have hitherto lacked due reverence of me.[1] What a euphonious title, that of his Oglethorpe University Address : " Denominational Education." I have a young merchant, in ample business, who studies the Greek Testament, with lexicon and commentaries. The abolitionists seem to have adopted a motto from Julius Cæsar : " Help, *Cassius*, [Clay,] or I sink !" The —— [a religious paper] is obviously improving. Do I err in detecting your hand in the item on " Preparing

---

[1] In the times of " Pine St. Church," the usual Sunday "collections" were taken with velvet bags at the end of long handles.

Potatoes for Stock ?" Who contributes the piece, in the same on " Save your Salt Barrels " ? I have sought for an anagogical or mystical meaning in this last. How touching the allusion to " glanders, grease, mange, blindness, coughs, and broken wind " ! What is your judgment of crib-biting ? The very violent attempts at visible Unity, as in the Liverpool Convention, savour of an unworthy suspicion that there is no Gospel Union but in protocols, and platform *accolades.* The unity (ni fallor) which the Bible enjoins, is no such thing, and is consistent with great diversity. Push a ritualist, and how little he can show for real unity. A Dominican and a Jesuit are far more asunder than Kidder [Methodist] and I, in dress, in creed, and in service. Who authorizes them to say that unity resides in swearing by one and the same pope ?

NEW YORK, *January* 26, 1846.

The evils of indiscriminate reading, even of religious books, has so weighed with me, that on Sunday I devoted both sermons to " Christian Reading." Inter alia, I gave a list of books, under these heads : 1. Explanatory of the Bible ; 2. Awakening and Inviting ; 3. Experimental Religion ; 4. Theology ; 5. History ; 6. Biography ; 7. Poetry; 8. Miscellaneous, including Periodical. Our collection for Domestic Missions=$520 ; add $100 by an individual, and $300 by Young Men=$920. I was vaccinated last spring, and had a perfect pustule ; so my Doctor says. My father's book on Colonization is out. I have preached three times on three Sabbaths this winter ; but I find it too much. Don't fail to read the articles from the " Times," on the Polk-Message, in the " Warder." I feel ashamed of our American bluster. But how plain is it, that the British dread a war far more than we ! They know better what it means. I have a let-ter from Abeel, in Savannah ; low in body, but triumphant in mind ; as he has been ever since I knew him. The sleighing has been a perfect intoxication, till the thaw came. Such a display of costly vehicles, furs, &c., is seen nowhere south of this : some had fourteen and even twenty horses. It would have been worth a visit to see the omnibus-sleighs, carrying forty, fifty, and sixty, and bedizened with all manner of pictures, &c. We have two hundred and fifty omnibuses constantly running in New York. Talk of railway in Hudson street. —— continues prolific ; but how unreadable ! a swill-tub of citations. Though given to quotation myself, I think it below the highest method. There is more in a man who spins all out *e propriis visceribus.* This has often struck me in my good father,—no scraps, no pretty " phrases," no poetry, no Latin sentences. The other way is a sign of weakness: *habeas confitentem reum.* Yet still more am I convinced that a man must be himself, and that he gains by following his bent. I have read Carlyle's Cromwell, and believe he was a converted man.

NEW YORK, *February* 19, 1846.

If my little sister Mary Ann had lived, she would have been thirty-five years old yesterday. This makes me think of the flight of time, and of the mercy of God, in that long interval, to my father's house. Mr. Lowrie authorizes me to say, that, though the knowledge of Wilson's[1] wants did not all come through himself, they have long since been supplied, as far as could be done here. His troubles, mutatis mutandis, are those of all missionaries, and such as occupy our Monday mornings, all the year. You might properly say to Wilson, that in every case he should make known his wants directly to the Board: the reasons are obvious. I am glad of your contempt of weariness, [on Mondays;] I cannot brag of the like, but still belong to the paradoxical class who find the day of greatest lassitude immediately after the day of greatest labour. The Tabernacle [Broadway] is filled every Sunday night, no matter who preaches. My church-mission-project is in abeyance, until I see how the Presbytery's plan (for the same end) turns out. I have no idea, however, of doing our work through the Presbytery: it is a slow work. After all the outcry of the Synod of Philadelphia for a " separate organization," whereby to give their benefactions to domestic missions,—just look at their amount of contributions !

One of the unreasonable demands on a pastor is, that he should like and dislike the people whom A, B, and C dislike. I try hard to let no prejudices or bickerings affect me. But oh! what a disposition, in ourselves and others, to be censorious ; to see faults before excellencies in our neighbours ; to applaud ourselves tacitly, by criticizing others openly, as to the points where we feel less vulnerable ! I know no Scripture precept harder than that, " Let each esteem other better," &c. Sometimes I am painfully affected with the consciousness that this or that duty, which I have performed, would certainly have been neglected or deferred, if no human being were to have known it. I wish I felt more the force of the phrase, " the praise which cometh from God." Protracted Meetings seem to me absolutely indifferent ; to be used, if there be cause, but not as a crack-measure to get up excitement. Where there is a hearing ear, it seems reasona-

---

[1] Thomas Wilson, a coloured man, who went to Africa under the Board of Foreign Missions, and died at his post, September 8, 1846.

ble to multiply instructions. Perhaps Edwards (on Revivals) goes a little too far; but his general views strike me as just.

I reluctantly break my rule againsst *lecturing*, in order to mendicate in that way for the Princeton church. For three weeks I have had cold and sore throat. I have lost, however, only one exercise by it, which was in the week. Kidder and I have been exchanging calls for fourteen months, but have never met in a house. The St. Valentine's day is so serious a thing here, that the city post is interrupted for three or four days; they put on extra carriers, and have a special chest in the Post Office. There are Valentines offered at $200 a-piece; being ingenious pictured integuments of gold watches, pins, brooches, &c.

NEW YORK, *March* 16, 1846.

It was only at a late hour this evening, on my brother Henry's return from Princeton, that I heard of your recent anxiety. And now I do sincerely hope that all cause of serious apprehension is removed, and that you will feel at ease to write me soon that you are giving thanks for great deliverance. I say this with the more feeling, as for a few days we have been in much fear, by reason of the sudden and severe illness of our second child. He has had a fever; and, though still confined to his bed, is greatly mended. Let the God of our salvation be exalted.

How much, in time of sickening fears, we are made to feel our need of a *direct* and *immediate* Divine influence; and how gracious is the hand which so often gives it to us! Our reasonings, even on the basis of the word, do not reach the case in such a time.

The healings, and manifold compassionate acts of our Lord, while on earth, as given in the simple narrative of the gospels, have been an unspeakable comfort to me, in days of despondency. "When my foot slipped, thy mercy, O Lord, held me up."

NEW YORK, *March* 24, 1846.

The Gospel is not attractive enough for people now-a-days. Ministers must bait their trap with something else. The old-fashioned topics are seldom heard. This diminishes one's wonder at the small progress made in spirituals. The following is taken, just as it stands, from the Journal of Commerce.[1] A

---

[1] Here followed a few advertisements of sermons on "the Holy Week at Rome," "Washington the Friend of Peace," "The Influence of Calvin," "Signs of Stability and Decay in the Government of our Country," &c.; but the custom has become so familiar since the date above, and the incongruous subjects so multiplied, that the notices pasted in the letter would not now seem curious.

sermon which I preached on the 15th, seems to have been graciously owned to the awakening of two persons. It is a sermon above all I have, remarkable for two faults : first, it is common-place; secondly, it is flowery. Mr. Begg, of Edinburgh, is to preach for us next Sunday evening. He is a very warm, interesting preacher. Like all the Scotch, he interweaves Scripture passages, out of the common line, in a way to surprise and charm. My Presbyterian folio, for the Blind, is published by the Board. It contains, 1, Prayers; 2, Hymns; 3, The Catechism; 4, A Compend of Doctrine, by my father. I have not, since McCheyne's, had such a treat as in "Housman's Life," just published by Carter. I am just about to have my favourite tract "Poor Joseph," printed in large type, with covers, for the aged and for poor readers. We collected $600 in February for Education, and about the same in March, for the Bible Society. Dr. S. has come over to our views, against public aisle-covenant, at communions, after practising thirty years the other way. Addison's first volume [Isaiah] is all "in hands," and daily expected. A stranger lately gave me $250 for colportage. Walsh's letters, in the National Intelligencer, are equal to his best days. Don't fail to read every extract in the "Warder," from the Examiner. I never saw such a sustained wit, as in the leaders of that paper. Savage Landor is said to write many of them. A Chinaman, with tails, &c., parades our streets. First fruits of our mission at Amoy, are reported. Abeel is expected here every day. In our chief churches here, the praise of God is now performed by committee, and sometimes by a very small one. In some tunes, I am sure, not more than six constitute the acting-worshippers. Why not one? *Instrumental Worship* would be a good title for an Essay. Begg says it was overwhelming, at Inverness, to hear 15,000 voices, all joining, *sub dio*, in the old psalms. O to hear it!

NEW YORK, *April* 8, 1846.

The lowest down-town church is the North Dutch, then Vande water St., (Free Episcopal,) then Dr. Spring's, then ours. I manage somehow to have a third service almost every Sunday. My article in the Repertory ["Metaphysical Theology of the Schoolmen"] has some brilliant typographic variations, as "hired for hindered." It is worth coming to New York to see the power-presses in the Bible House. One of the most learned Jews is become a Christian; to my knowledge. He does not wish it bruited till he has prepared a treatise, in German and English. He tried Unitarianism, to avoid the grand "offence"; but it would not do; he has come out a thorough trinitarian.

More of this anon. Swedenborgianism grows. Dr. Potts is the star of our pulpit-sky. Cheever is gathering a Congregational congregation at Union Square. The interior of Trinity Church is grand. The pulpit is crawled up to, around one of the pillars, as it were in a corner. A pupil of mine heard Bellows the other night, and said the substance was: "Be good; and if you can't be good, be as good as you can." I this day corrected the title-page of Addison's book. Mr. Read has a revival. I cannot dismiss the conviction, that the thing to be aimed at is a warmth which may be continued; numbers always inquiring; additions each communion; so necessitating no breach of routine in preaching. On Sunday mornings I always preach straight on in the catechism, except when my monthly collections come. I have had much hope from the effect of my last four, on "Adoption," "Assurance," "Peace," and "Joy." The new missionary map of the world, (Colton's,) 14 feet by 8, is worth having. Y.'s piece takes no account of the distinction between Assurance of *faith* and of *hope;* and hence he charges confusion on our theologians which does not exist. This is the eighteenth letter or note (some of them long) I have had to write, within twenty-four hours. If I may judge in such a case, my best effusions [in the Sunday School Journal] have been as "An Old Contributor." My weekly catechizing continues to be delightful to me. Several of the young people are very seriously inquiring. We have averaged sixty from the beginning. There is immense need of an Explanation of the Catechism, not to exceed 100 pages, and with these qualities: 1. Simplicity. 2. The breaking of the matter into short — very short questions and answers. 3. Avoiding unnecessary accumulation of texts. 4. Absence of school-divinity. A member of my church gave $1,400 to repair a country church, and has given $200 a year, several years, to the minister's salary. Another member does as much for the Thomsonville church. Would it not be a good rule, in visiting, to contrive to repeat a few verses of the Bible at every place? How much precious matter it would give the pastor, for his meditations. Again, might not a man, properly, make a point, in every prayer he offers in houses, to have a sentence or two specially bearing on his own pastoral and individual wants? By these two methods, what we lose from private culture might in a good degree be made up. I have resorted to the old plan, of carrying select tracts, &c. One who has free use of one's pen, may gain much by little notes, even to persons who are shy, unapproachable, and unfeeling. I have had more calls to converse with people on religion, lately, than ever before.

New York, *May* 11, 1846.

Your letter reveals to me that you are not altogether relieved from your anxieties. I lately preached on Mark ix. 19; a subject which I felt a good deal myself, in reference to some former domestic experiences, and which seemed to affect my people more than usual. *Direct bringing of our cares to Christ,* is a duty or privilege less practised than is thought. If we *ventured* more on Him, (unless the very term savours of unbelief,) we should doubtless have more to praise for. See Psalm xxxiv. 4—6. Is not our Christianity derived too much from report, from a sort of average, from common experience of those about us, and not from the simple Word? You will find some sweet, useful things in the " Mount of Olives," a pendant to " Life in Earnest."

Yesterday was our Communion; seventeen on certificate, and eight on examination. A Free Church minister, Mr. Stevenson, was with us, but did not partake. Another, Dr. Willis, of Glasgow, has been here. They adhere boldly to their plan of sending over settled pastors of some note, on missions of three months, to Canada. This strikes me as a noble plan, fitted to do great good, at least to the deputies themselves.

How can I pray for a blessing on our fight with Mexico! Poor creatures, they have done as little against us as we could have expected. As a Christian nation, we should have sent them the Gospel; but now, unless God interpose wonderfully, we shall rob and invade them. Who knows but that we may find ourselves engaged with a stronger than they?

I am more and more of opinion, that the great Missionary work of America should be among the two races which we have most injured, viz., the black and the red. I have misgivings whenever we send men to Northern India, (British ground,) and neglect the perfectly open field among our Indians. The government yields every facility for the prosecution of this work. To-day I heard a letter read, in which the Superintendent of Indian Affairs offers to accompany our Secretary, in a tour among all the Western Tribes. We all feel that this work presses on us more than heretofore. The intercourse of a year with ——, has led me to set him down as one of the best men living; for honesty, generosity, self-denial, greatness of love, good sense, and zeal for God. He seems to me to have the heart of a father, towards every one of the missionaries; and when he engages in the harassing labour of purchasing for China, Africa, or the Indians, does it as for dear children. Old-fashioned pastors are about as common as knee-breeches. Literary clergymen abound. Europe is like to have a full representation this summer. The question will soon be, " Who has not been in Europe?" I confess I should like to spend three months in the Free Church, to try and find out the secret of their ardour. Beyond this, the longing for Europe, which haunted me for years, is all gone.

NEW YORK, *May* 28, 1846.

I am occasionally struck with the force of a phrase in the Greek, which is lost in our own version: ex. gr. Romans xvi. 25, σεσιγημενοι.[1] That chapter is a great trap for orthoepists. Urbane ought to be Urban, as it is in the old English version, being a man's name. Andronicus, Aristobulus, and Epenetus, are seldom hit right. Next Sunday I hope to preach a Sunday School sermon. The cause needs lifting among us. My little report on Parochial schools has made a breeze in our Assembly, which I was unprepared for.[2] The resolutions appear to me milk-and-water enough for anybody. Yet I feel no zeal for them, beyond this, that I should like the skirt of the Assembly to be cast over those who are attempting church-schools. I see no proof that Onesimus ever ran away, in the technical sense, at all. I can go a peg higher than you about slavery, and fail to see the scripturalness of much that is postulated now-a-days, respecting the popular idol, liberty. As existing, slavery is fraught with moral evil; the want of marriage, and of the Bible, and the separation of families, &c., &c., are crying sins; but I am totally unable to see the relation to be necessarily unjust. The moral questions are so various from the circumstances, that each must be decided apart, *e. g.*, "Is A justifiable in holding B to service?" Our church, I am clear, ought to protest against the laws about reading, &c. As clear am I, that our States should regard slavery as a transition-state, to be terminated as soon as possible, and that they should enact laws about the *post-nati*. That the most miserable portion, physically and morally, of the black race in the United States, is the portion which is free, I am as well assured as I can be of any similar proposition. That immediate emancipation would be a crime, I have no doubt; and therefore believe there are cases in which there is neither injustice nor inhumanity in holding. I have had but eleven weddings in New York, and only half-a-dozen in my own charge. Dr. Cox once met my good Puritan brother, Greenleaf, and as his wont is, saluted him in Latin, to which G. replied, "Let him that speaketh in an unknown tongue

---

[1] In our version "kept secret;" in Wiclif's, "holden still."

[2] The General Assembly of 1844 appointed a committee to consider the expediency of establishing Presbyterian Parochial Schools. Of this committee Dr. Alexander, though not in the Assembly, was chairman. The report was not ready until the Assembly of 1846, when it was, after some debate, adopted and ordered to be printed in the Appendix to the Minutes of that year.

pray that he may interpret." Cox is fond of tinkering about the top of his house and sheds. Greenleaf, seeing him thus aloft, gave him this text to expound : " What aileth thee now, that thou art wholly gone up to the house-tops ? "

NEW YORK, *June* 15, 1846.

My father spent last week with us. Gen. Scott, of soup-memory, is now called Marshal *Tureen.* We have set up Cornish in a coloured congregation—Potts and I becoming responsible for the rent of the room. My congregation is perceptibly thinning. Our lieut.-governor, Gardiner, of Rochester, worships with us when he is in town. He is a pious man, and a zealous Sunday School teacher. If this treaty with England really goes into effect, we shall have occasion for heartfelt thanks. As to Mexico, I fear their defiles and sierras will give them opportunity to protract the war, much beyond present expectations. Five members of one family in our church are in Paris, or on the way. The Central Church committee [seeking a pastor] called here on Wednesday, on their way to Troy, as fond and avid as ever the Greeks were after Helen. Seekers of vacancies are as abundant as crows in a cornfield. I believe I am solicitor for a dozen at this moment. All make for the cities. Young probationers all hover about home. Quere : whether, in the present destitution of the West, every candidate for orders should not be compelled to do two years of missionary service ? It would be a good test. I wish I had means to draw up a schedule of the licentiates of the last five years, and where they are. Among persons who desire vacancies are four or five settled ministers. Van Rensselaer is full of a new magazine. [" Presbyterian Magazine," began in 1851.] I think I should like to write bits for such a thing, sometimes ; so would you. Though I did not doubt that Taylor would be nominated for President, I did not surmise that Trenton and Tucker would have the honour of taking the initiative. I saw a gold-headed cane, to-day, made of wood from the first Presbyterian Church in America, the old McKemie church of Accomac, Va. It was in the hands of Mr. Locke, a minister of Northampton, Va. It is marked " 1690." Trinity Church is open at 9½ and 4 for prayers, daily. This I like, Pusey or no Pusey. Yet it never comes to aught in practice. Have you read the " Fox and the Geese " ? It lacks all probability, and is in my opinion a sheer invention, to be added to the fictitious literature of the day, concerning which see " American Messenger," passim. It encourages expectations which can never be realized, of seeing elephants keeping shop, and using their trunks for dry-goods. It is erroneous in point of natural history. The goose (*anas anser*, Linn.) is not endowed with the faculty of speech, like some of the genus *Psittacus;* and to represent it as thatching its house, is absurd. But the ridiculous falsity of the book may be considered as *au comble*, when the common fox (*vulpes callida*, Linn.) is represented as carrying a torch. This in a religious age, and in the nineteenth century! [1]

NEW YORK, *June* 29, 1846.

Dr. Rice came in this evening from his mission to the Massachusetts General Association at Pepperell. He says the Congregationalists are blowing up the sectarian flame very hard, and labouring to propagate their " distinctive " principles. Congregational Puseyism is funny enough. I wish you would read *Schaff's* famous book ; ["Historical Development"?] Cry out as we may, he tells us some plain truths, and reveals things which none but a transatlantic eye could discern. It is a most exciting and suggestive volume, with a figment for the hypothesis, but great genius, learning, and truth in many of the details. I have always felt the force of what he says about the Puritans having cut to the quick, in regard to externals ; about the charity we should have for Papists ; and about the evils of innumerable sects. But he goes fearfully far, about visible unity. The dread of Millenarianism has sealed the mouths of too many of us, I think, in respect to the Second Coming. There is a great deal about it in the New Testament. If others teach a false second-advent, why should not we, all the more earnestly, enforce the true ? I have no recollection of having ever heard any brother preach on it. We have (Potts and I) at length got our Old School coloured church a-going. I have thus far failed entirely to get a room for our Duane St. Mission-Church. But there seems to be a readiness among our people. Waterbury has accepted the call to St. Bowdoin's, (I merely transpose the " St.") A very large proportion of my flock is now in rustication ; their place is very much filled by travellers. The constant presence of such, governs my preparations more than it did. Some very encouraging things have occurred, from

---

[1] This ironical notice of the objections to fables and fictions reminds one of the lines of Cowper, which the letter-writer quoted in a graver article on the same subject long before this, (Sunday School Journal, January 9, 1833.)

> " I shall not ask Jean Jacques Rousseau
> If birds confabulate or no ;
> 'Tis clear that they were always able
> To hold discourse—at least in fable ;
> And e'en the child who knows no better,
> Than to interpret by the letter
> A story of a cock and bull,
> Must have a most uncommon skull."

time to time, in regard to such drawings of the bow at a venture. I beheld the other day about 500 new army-recruits, for Mexico, a most sorry collection of ragamuffins. My proximity to the arsenal gives me plenty of this playing at soldiers. Another Free Church minister was here to-day, from Canada, where he has been preaching, almost daily, for several months in Gaelic. His name is MacTavish, from Inverness-shire : a plain, honest, warm fellow. Williamson, who preaches here in one of the French Protestant churches, is a native of London, yet speaks broken English, having been "raised" in France. He is an evangelical Episcopalian.

PRINCETON, *July* 22, 1846.

Addison is in my place in New York ; but for no reason but that of a more perfect seclusion, in order to complete his work. He has finished to the end of the 57th chap., since the first volume was published. He is almost overwhelmed by it, and I do not wonder he escapes all engagements when he can. I feel no sympathy with your Quaker propensities. There is, indeed, something good in Gurney, *videlicet*, the very part which is not Quaker, and for which his tribe are ready to abjure him. When I consider their anilities about coats, days, and grammar, and the fruits they have borne, I feel no regret that they are so near dissolution. Their way of treating death and eternal things, and their opiates to all conscience, except that of mint, anise, and cummin, make their influence a most irreligious one wherever I have met them.

NEW YORK, *August* 25, 1846.[1]

I will not inquire how you were affected by a sight of the "Falls," [Niagara.] I remember the great object, with a sort of religious awe. None of our Heavenly Father's works seems more expressive of his sublime, incomprehensible greatness. Yet, I dare say, so far as pleasure in concerned, you more value the moment in which you met with your children. There is a depth of joy in such affections, which no external objects can produce.

I am writing in my solitary house ; having returned to the city without my family. We were afraid to bring our infant back too suddenly from the purer air of the country. Of my season of holidays I spent ten days at Saratoga, with much advantage, and four or five at Long Branch, with none at all : for I took a cold and cough, under which I am still labouring. The place of our daily duties, with all its cares, is, after all,

---

[1] This letter was addressed to one of the family of the editor of the correspondence.

the place where we are usually most happy. This I feel very sensibly on my return to New York. Though almost overwhelmed with the press of matters which have been waiting for me, I am nevertheless rejoiced to be at home.

Let us be instructed by the many mercies which we receive, to trust our God and Saviour more implicitly, and to yield ourselves to his service with more entire resignation of all that we have and are. To write and to say such things is easy, but we need special grace to enable us in any degree to realize such a character of mind and life. A cheerful reliance on God, and a firm hope in his promises, are great part of our duty ; and these tempers should be encouraged in us, by every new instance of Divine compassion.

You will understand me when I say, that home is not home without my children. I am more dependent than most men, for personal comfort, on the presence of my immediate family-circle. I pray for the hour when, by God's favour, we may be gathered once more.

NEW YORK, *September* 1, 1846.

The summer is, by no means, over ; and I am not sure that I do not feel the heat more than in July ; we have, however, a very perceptible sea-breeze towards evening, and the nights are not at all oppressive. Addison finished his second volume, including a large introduction. I communicated your strictures to him. He says his own private wish always was to make a commentary of the popular sort, and that he was overruled by his friends and advisers.

Those of my people who pretend to pass the summer in the country, are still abroad. Yet our congregations have been full ; in part from other churches, in part from the hotels. I never saw the latter more overflowing. Mr. Wetmore, our indefatigable Tract-and-City-mission-man, not long since said at a meeting : " New York Christians appear to think that souls cannot be converted in the month of August." Gospel-efforts, like Oysters, are for the months which have an R in them. I have been reading John Foster's life, with more pain than pleasure.[1] A great, original genius, but too radical, too censorious, too contemptuous of his brethren, too prone to see good only in his own ways. I greatly prefer Hall, or even Jay.

NEW YORK, *September* 28, 1846.

I have been somewhat occupied in getting my family home, which is one reason why I have not written. Our police now constitute a strong body, being visible at numerous stations,

---

[1] He had reviewed Foster's Essays in the Repertory, October, 1844.

well understood, with conspicuous badges. Two fire-companies
have been disbanded, since I came here, for fighting; the only
instances of disorder in the corps. Our fires are very silent
affairs. Niblo's garden and theatre were burnt down, without
any cry in the streets. Stewart's new store is considered, and
I dare say justly, the greatest dry-goods shop in the world.
The sales, on three days, were $30,000. A withered old apple-
woman used to sit on the step of his old store. Stewart, on
removing, sent his porter for the old body's basket, and she now
graces his marble threshold. Of the returned members from
the Holy [Evangelical] Alliance, I have chatted with Forsyth
and De Witt. Both were chiefly impressed by Baptist Noel.
De Witt says it is worth a voyage to look at him, and that he
made *the* speech, par excellence. They also talk with admiration of Adolphe Monod and Tholuck. De Witt reports a few
hopeful things about the churches of Holland. Elliott Cresson
sent the Autocrat [Emperor of Russia] a copy of my father's
Colonization Book. The oldest lawyers in New York (Matthews
of Rochester) and New Jersey (Smith Scudder) have died
within a few weeks of each other.

I am very busy in looking up my people. In this long-
street-city it is no short job. This morning I had an affecting
conversation with a lady, of Quaker education, who has long
been feeling her way in the dark towards religion. Probably it
was the first conversation she ever had on the subject. Such
instances, I fear, are very numerous. It was pleasing to preach
the news of a free gospel to one who had not been hardened to
its phrases. The Free Church people of Scotland are amazed
at our Assembly's decision on Romish baptism. I have just
been down to chat with Mr. Leckie, a Scotch parishioner of
mine. His father, a secession minister of Peebles, raised a family
of ten sons and three daughters, on a stipend of £120, educated
five of them at the University, and died without owing a penny.
Bp. Howley, now Archbishop, on hearing the circumstances, gave
the widow £10. I have lately obtained the copy of Milton
which my mother's father had read to him during his blindness.
You have no idea what a place New York is for musquitoes
(moschettoes.) But the natives tell you it is nothing. It is
remarkable how generally these Scotch merchants have had a
liberal education. This is fine weather for all sorts of people,
and I hope you are all in good health. Adieu.

NEW YORK, *October* 12, 1846.
The passage[1] is in the *Punica* of Silius Italicus, (vii. 41.) It

[1] Supposed to illustrate the *yoke* of Matthew xi. 29.
VOL. II.—3*

occurs in a speech of one Cilnius to the Pœni, when about to
deal with the famous procrastinator Fabius. Speaking of the
latter, he says :

> " Nosces Fabios certamine ab uno.
> Veientum populi violata pace negabant
> Acceptare jugum, ac vicino Marte furebat
> Ad portas bellum, consulque ciebat ad arma."

There is nothing further in the context, to clear the matter.
The passage in Livy (xxxvi. 37) relates to the campaign of
L. Cornelius Scipio against Antiochus, about B. C. 190. The
words are in a reply of S. to the ambassador of A., who had
offered S. " auri pondus ingens." They concern certain offers
of surrendering cities, &c. Scipio says, " Concesso vero in
Asiam transitu, et non solum frenis, sed etiam jugo accepto, quæ
disceptatio ex æquo, quum imperium patiendum sit, relicta est ?"
The sense I take to be : " If you once let us into Asia, and thus
submit not only to restraint, but subjugation, it is vain for you
to talk of treating on terms of equality, since the controversy
is for sovereignty." Dr. Wm. Smith, in Dict. Class. Antiq.,
says : " By another figure, the yoke meant *slavery*, or the condition in which men were compelled, against their will, like oxen
or horses, to labour for others. Hence to express symbolically
the subjugation of conquered nations, the Romans made their
captives pass under a yoke," &c., *i. e.* a spear upon two other
spears placed upright.

My measure of experience teaches me, that it is God's method
never to leave me long in a season of such freedom from anxiety
as shall make me forget my dependence. You know something
of what it is to preach under such burdens, and to go home
afraid to open the door. At such times, one thought predominates : *my sin*. Is not this one chief end of trials ? I
sometimes sink, but, I think, I do not rebel. God is just, and he
is good. We, who teach others, need a peculiar discipline. I
am thankful that my domestic trials, on the review, seem all
right. Yet I confess to you, my anxieties are almost always
inordinate ; nor do I grow any wiser. It is, no doubt, wisely
ordered, that we suffer in those we love. I did not intend a
sermon ; but I have thought more of your trials, amidst my own.
Is there not a lesson in this also ? When we pray for a more
useful ministry, God answers us by stripes which we did not
expect ; but they fall from a gracious hand. I have to preach
before Presbytery, and to lecture on Tuesday. The " Great
Britain " is anxiously looked for. People seem to have misgivings about these steamers ; but it seems to me that nothing
saved the " Great Western," under God, but its engine, which

never stopped, or went awry. Some time since, being in a
pulpit with Mr. Johnstone, of Jersey City, I observed him read
from a paper, half this sheet in size. The fourth page was but
a quarter covered. He declared to me that he had read every
word, and he spoke forty minutes. It was a stenography, which
he has used forty years; his father a still longer time. This
would save paper, ink, pens, chest, and time.

October 14.—Thus far I had previously written. Our Presbytery is meeting. I gladly abdicate in favour of W. E. Schenck.
The "Great Britain" is not reported yet. An eastern storm is
beginning. Dr. Beecher is on the arena; giving the echoes of
the Alliance. The Monterey affair gives me little but pain. O
the lightness with which hundreds of men are sent into eternity!
There is a peculiar use of the word PEACE, in the Bible, which
gives it great emphasis.

NEW YORK, *November* 23, 1846.

Yours of the 2d lies unanswered. The period has been one
of much pastoral anxiety. Inter alia, one of my hearers has
been lying ill, with a rapid consumption, at Brunswick. I never
before wrote a letter to a dying man. I suppose he is dead.
Mr. Nathaniel B. Boyd, a bachelor, member of our church, was
at our lecture on Tuesday, and went home well, and spoke with
interest of the exposition. In the night he was smitten with
apoplexy; and died on the 21st. I have had for months a
case of mental anguish beyond all I ever saw described, unless
it be Bunyan's man in the cage, or Cowper's latter days. Our
Philadelphia friends fear our endeavours towards a City-Mis-
sion; but we cannot live without it. Our collection yesterday
for Domestic Missions (the general cause) was $512.30. I am
not convinced that any Episcopal element would help our church.
I am least of all convinced by the progress of Episcopalians.
What have they done, except in towns? They had the whole
South once, and where is it now? I am not convinced by the
Methodists, for the Baptists have increased as much as they.
And their episcopate is but nominal. It is their itinerancy and
lay-labour, which has pushed them on. Two of the most learned
German Jews (from Rotterdam) are studying Addison's Isaiah.

NEW YORK, *November* 30, 1846.

I have just returned from Dr. [Wm. J.] Armstrong's funeral,
and write sooner than I meant to do, in remembrance of his connexion with your church, and to give you some accounts " in
advance of the mail." Dr. A. was accustomed to go to Boston, the
last week of every month, to confer with the Prudential Committee.

He had accomplished his business, and was on his return in the steamboat Atlantic. It seems the storm had begun before he left Boston; and his friends urged him not to leave them; but he earnestly desired to be with his little family on Thanksgiving Day. You know the general course of the events. When, on Thursday, it appeared that the danger was imminent, and that no vessel could near them, Dr. A. got permission of the captain to have religious services. He gathered all the passengers below, read the Scripture, prayed, called on two other gentlemen to pray; and invited all present to spend a few moments in silent devotion, which they did. From various accounts, it appears that he was much engaged in comforting and corroborating the minds of those around him. While he was praying, a lieutenant in the United States Navy thought he recognized the voice, and on going to him, remembered him as the pastor of his infancy in Richmond. This gentleman's mother was also on board, but has perished. Her son was in church to-day. Dr. A. put on the life-preserver with which his poor wife had supplied him, and with others, at the instance of Lieut. M., tore slips of blanket and bound about the head. What a sight it must have been! They already expected to go to pieces at sunset; but they did not till 4 A. M. All night in the howling storm, the fires all out, the cold insufferable, a few biscuits, but no drink, and the bell tolling all the while. The last time Dr. A. is reported to have been seen, he was standing above, surveying the scene, perfectly calm; he then uttered these words (I think) to a hearer of mine: "I entertain hope that we may reach the shore; but if not, my confidence is firm in that God who doeth all things well, in wisdom and in love!" Surely no man in the serenity of a dying chamber could be better employed. Young C. S. Stewart (United States Engineer) who was saved, stayed by the vessel till the timbers parted, in company with Capt. Cullum and Lieut. Norton. At length, his hair and eyelashes being frozen, his hands were so benumbed, that he thought they would become useless, unless he let himself down at once, which he did. After struggling in the surf, he gained footing. Shortly after he heard Capt. Cullum's voice. Norton was lost. Charles S. was much bruised, and so exhausted as to fall down three times before reaching the house; of which they had previously endeavoured, by day-light, to fix the locality in their minds. After ten hours he reached New London, whence he had set out; he is there engaged on the new fortification. Dr. Armstrong was struck on the head a violent blow by the falling timber, which probably killed him instantly. His body was taken to Norwich, but was not recognized for some time, as the pockets had been cut and rifled of every thing. The funeral services were attended, at 11 this morning, in the Broome St. church, which was crowded, in every standing-place; hundreds could not gain entrance. The hymn, "Unvail thy bosom faithful tomb," was sung. Dr. Adams delivered a simple, touching, and admirable address; in which he did justice to the excellent character of the deceased, and applied to him with much force those words, as eminently characterizing him, "In simplicity and godly sincerity, not with fleshly wisdom, but by the grace of God, we have had our conversation in the world," 2 Cor. i. 12. The choir sang, "Hear what the voice from heaven proclaims." The pulpit was occupied by Drs. Skinner, Adams, De Witt, and Cox. Dr. De Witt offered a prayer of great earnestness and impression. The clergy of our city were very generally there, and deep emotion was manifested.

Dr. Armstrong has left a wife and five children, one a young infant. The remains are gone, to be laid by those of his venerable father, the Rev. Dr. Amzi Armstrong, of New Jersey.

You will find that our departed brother is remembered with respect in Trenton. He was an upright, believing man, and a solemn, and often pathetic preacher. Those who have often been warned and entreated by him should remember the voice of God by him.

NEW YORK, *December* 31, 1846.

Monday, which is always a day of many interruptions, has this day been busier than usual. One Mission-committee, one Seamen's-committee, one Church-extension-committee, and one prayer-meeting of ministers. The last I could not attend. Letters from China tell us that the anxiety, in consequence of the riots, is very great. I saw in my church yesterday a Dane, a Swede, and a Chinese. We have recently gained a Jew, who is a candidate for baptism. Count Zinzendorf, on one occasion, (as I find by his Life,) extemporized six hymns, during one meeting; it was his frequent practice. Most of the Moravian hymns are by him, and these are very beautiful in German, however ludicrous in the wretched English version. The fine gold has become dim. If ever there was true religion, since primitive days, it was among the Bohemian and Moravian confessors. Two of my young men have interrupted me, and taken up two hours. Yet I am not sorry. What little strength I have here, lies in this. How humiliating it is to find that I am pained, when I learn that M or N does not like my preaching, yet am so calm, when all the alphabet, for years, reject my Master's message! Our theory of a church-session is grand; but O what a practice! It is made for a church in a high spiritual state, and this I think is in its favour. One of my elders makes up to every man, woman, and child, who frequent the church. He visits as much as I do; knows every church-member; talks to every inquirer; goes often to every house; and, when I point out any place, is sure to be there within twenty-four hours. This leads me to two practical reflections: 1. How important to have a number of young men in training for such offices. 2. How desirable for a pastor so to labour, as to leave the church in the best possible state for his successor; in regard particularly to the children, youth, family-habits, &c. My latest texts have been such as have much interested me: 2 Tim. i. 19, John xiii. 36, Eph. v. 2, Matt. vi. ult., Deut. xxxiii. 1, Ps. cxix. 9, Rom. viii. 34, Matt. xxv. 10, Luke xii. 57, John xvi. 12, 13, Matt. v. 6, Heb. ii. 4, Rom. viii. 1. What we seem to want here, is not polish or literature in sermons, but something earnest, real, and affectionate; something to make the people hear as if some truth of transcendent present interest was set forth. Never was I more convinced that in order to this there is nothing so necessary as a direct and specific influence from on High. Rhetorical interest is impotent. There was great interest under the Finneyitish revivals, but it was not evangelical, and I am working among its bitter fruits every day. There is a wonderful vitality and permanency in experience which is built on the preaching of Christ. The style of sermons in the Scottish Free Church seems to be the thing. When the new-divinity-converts grow cold, they are colder than ice, nothing but a biting censoriousness. I had no idea, even in Jersey, of the modifications wrought in the religion of this city, by the overwrought revivalism of past years. Some, even of those who were once fiery, have degenerated into pulpit-metaphysicians, subtile and elegant. Vanity-Fair is beginning. New Year's day is a very carnival hereabouts. I am in despair about church-music. The nearest approach to my ideal is in the German church near me, where every creature sings, where the tunes are all slow, making up in volume for the lack of twiddle-diddle, and where they never have a new tune. In some churches here, the choir is about a pew-full, and the people use a purely vicarious psalmody. I sometimes feel a tune, in our lecture-room; in our church, never. Do we employ psalms and hymns sufficiently, as a means of grace, in our families? A poor Irishman has found, I trust, the true foundation, in his sick-room. Last night he sat up, with his popish host, till they had read over twelve or fourteen chapters of the Bible. He has been faithfully followed up by a most assiduous young man of ours. This young man spends part of every day among the poor. I fear our Whig Congress-men are going to use no general exertion for peace. I honour Calhoun for his manful resistance to both the war-measures. I am astonished at the greatness of the evangelical movement among the Papists of France, as detailed in the late French reports; whole villages reformed, assemblies of several thou-sands, &c. I wish you, beforehand, a happy New Year. Let us seek to have one of simpler walk, and higher usefulness.

NEW YORK, January 9, 1847.

I compliment you on the termination of your church-debt; we are making an effort towards ending our own " pious fraud." I hope both parsons may soon have their respective parsonages. The immigration to this port alone, last year, was 115,000; or more than 315 per diem. An effort is making to get decent Temperance-ism out of the gutter, and on its legs again. It has been sadly drugged hereabouts, and is in a state of titubation. Falstaff's regiment could not have exceeded our recruits for Mexico. My congregation is a receiving-ship for up-town. I am just setting up a converted popish book-pedler, with a basket of books for the wharfs, sloops, and grog-shops. I saw to-day a Californian paper, (Colton's,) Spanish and English. My text for the year was, " We are the Lord's." I have since seen it in a " copy of verses " <i>penes me</i>, and engraved on a (phylactery) gold-ring. As I used to remark in Trenton an endemic pronun-ciation, in the female choristers, of " mĭde " for " mãde," " tȳke " for " tãke," &c.; so here I find in the same class, " fã-er " for " fire," " tã-em " for " time." I perceive little or nothing like con-gregational devotion in psalmody, often scarcely attention. I have a trifling book in hands of Sunday School Union, which I have written out of pity for town-boys.[1]

NEW YORK, January 25, 1847.

I had to-day the offer of a ticket to the grand concert, 13th prox., for the Popish orphans. It is to surpass all ever heard " on this side." Except the operatic corps, amateurs are to do the thing. The " lady patronesses " are all Protestants. The Presbyterians make so much of a call from a congregation, and in theory are so much opposed to ordination <i>sine titulo</i>, that I lately made a search of the whole New Testament in quest of authority. I find none. I find no minister undeniably marked out as the pastor of

---

[1] " Frank Harper ; or, the Country Boy in Town."

any single flock.   I have copious notes of the results.   Mondays are much alike with me ; first our Foreign Committee, which I always meet with pleasure, and then a round of visits till three. Yesterday our Bible collection was made ; $374.   We add about $180 by female association.   One young lady in my flock does a work which is very unusual and pleasing.   She devotes about three hours a day to teaching poor girls.   Almost every one of those who have left her class, perhaps twelve, is well educated, and truly pious.   I can almost pick out her pupils in the gallery by their looks.   She also teaches in Sunday School ; is a leading Dorcas, and collects annually $250 for a French evangelist. What a change, if each of us had even six such : and does not this suggest the importance of separate and deliberate efforts to train individual helpers?   I am unspeakably blessed in several of my young men.   A, a schoolmaster, superintendent of Sunday School, is a model of modest, able, indefatigable service.   B, a dry-goods man, Sunday School teacher, is the most of a Harlan Page I ever saw ; shrewd, original, humorous, always among the poor, courageous, and prudent.   I could hardly wish him other than he is. C, teller in bank, Sunday School teacher, well-read, gentle, ortho-dox, punctual, liberal, looked up to by the others.   D, more re-served, but valuable, and always in his place, a ship-chandler.   E, lawyer, accomplished, active, a good collector, and real aid.   F, a bookseller, graduate of Princeton, ditto, ditto.   All, except the last, are New Englanders ; all are unfailing at prayer meetings, &c. Their influence on young men coming in among us is great. Nothing is more remarkable in all these, than their readiness to do any thing I propose.   It is my chief comfort.   I sensibly feel what you say about reports of sermons.   Some months ago I was shocked at the inane stupidity of a report of one of mine.   A few days after, a poor mantuamaker, not of my parish, read it in the newspaper, and found something in it the means of bringing her to Christ, after two years bondage.   I wonder whether our meanest sermons are not our best.   Loughridge's[1] death made me say to myself : " How seldom, now-a-days, does a minister die among his own people !   From this time our Board of For-eign Missions will have the annual distribution of some of the government money, for Indian Schools.   Our Choctaw Academy is quite a college ; Ramsey is a noble fellow.

NEW YORK, *January* 26, 1847.

I follow one letter with another thus soon, because I omitted what I meant to say in my last on a point of interest.   Some time ago you mentioned, in passing, a desire to have an occasional

[1] Pastor of the Fourth Church, Philadelphia.

German discourse in Trenton. There is a man here well fitted for such a work, to whom a few dollars would be a great help; if some of your people would bestow it. For a trifle more than expenses, I think, he would go on, once a month, or perhaps a fortnight. He has been taken under our Presbytery, though Lutheran by ordination. A Jew, but very long under the best Christian and University training. A learned man. As far as can be judged, warmly pious. He has preached repeatedly in the German pulpits here, and is said to be highly acceptable. He preaches every Sunday in the Almshouse, gratuitously, to the seven hundred Germans who are there. I know not what could be done in Trenton, in this regard; but if any thing is needed, you could scarcely alight on a better person for an occasional sermon and an experiment. I hope before long to get him some permanent preaching-post here; but things do not mature as fast as I could wish. He speaks poor English, but can talk French and Latin.

NEW YORK, *February* 22, 1847.

The snow has set in (like some preachers) with a codicil, after the conclusion. Broadway is beginning to ring and swarm. I can't help thinking how much better off the Southern slaves are, physically and morally, than the Irish. Who ever heard of slaves starving until the master starved? I see no trace of the modern dogmas about absolute freedom in the Bible. The wretchedest portion, by far, of the black race, is the free portion. Our New York negroes are lower than savages in many respects. I believe slavery will be abolished; and will be abolished in Mexican lands, and parts adjacent, where the climate suits, and where the taint of colour is less felt; and that all attempts to wall slavery within its present bounds, only hurts the negro and procrastinates the grand result. I am more and more convinced that our endeavours to do at a blow, what Providence does by degrees, is disastrous to those whom we would benefit. To give the gospel to the slaves, is a duty pressing above all others; and my painful and mortifying endeavours for two years to build up a black church here, and my previous preaching for six years to free people in Jersey, convince me that it is easier to give the gospel to the slaves. I am looking for a house. That in which I live has been a perpetual mortification to me: no spare room to which I may ask a friend without chagrin. I am forced to live down town; and here there are no new houses. I have inspected many houses. Scarcely five have had Croton water, and only one a bath-room. I was pleased with one in Barclay street, two stories and a half: the rent was $950. I heard Gough the other night. I never willingly miss him. His pathos and his humour and acting are beyond any thing I know of just now. What a nasty mean little squabbling your Trenton papers keep up. I have taken the Newark Daily for ten years, and have never seen a line which would apprise me of the *existence* of the rival print. In regard to correspondents, you are the only regular one I have in the world. Did you ever meet with an expression of Jane Taylor's, " Preserve me from *affrontable* people " ?

NEW YORK, *March* 5, 1847.

I am a little disturbed about our epistolary debits and credits, —so here goes. The military funeral to-day of sundry officers slain in Mexico, is holden to have been a failure. The mud and mire was such, that the "municipalities" would not "walk." The canaille were out in force, by tens of thousands. I felt it to be a bathetic affair, and no honour to the poor victims. Our church-collection, chiefly for Scotland, is a little short of $700: individual subscriptions among our people, in addition, about $1,000. Mr. G. last night, gave some of his views, as a law yer, of the evidences of Christianity. Take the following mems : " Every regeneration is a *miracle*—answers all the definitions. Most Christians, at some time or other, are sure they have been subjects of it. Suppose the affidavits of these, taken on dying-beds, were collected, (say 300,000,000,) how far ought this to go, with an honest sceptic, as *testimony?*" "Hume, &c., say a miracle cannot be made credible. But if so extraordinary a thing as a *revelation* could be proved, it might be credible that *for this* even a miracle might be wrought. I would, therefore, seek to prove a *revelation* on separate grounds. Thus : the human race is not eternal. They were created. They could not have continued in existence without some Divine instruction. *This is a revelation.*" Dr. Boardman has spent a week here. He sails for Europe proximo. Greeley said, in a speech, that this city has already made twenty-five millions by the scarcity in Europe. How our good brother —— removes the claws and horns from autocrats ! Having done that office for Nicholas, and shown that he never wronged the Poles, he has now presented the Grand Turk in the same amiable guise. Would that he had seen the Pope ! I have finished my exposition of the Hebrews; in sixty-two lectures : I trust to my own instruction at least. L——, who has just uttered a volume on the Apocalypse, (moderately millenarian,) is a retired merchant ; the same who some years ago mauled the New Havenites so unmercifully, in his periodical pamphlets, entitled " Views in Theology." He is very acute, cool, perspicuous, consistent, and erudite ; and I sup-

pose has guessed about as near as the rest. Our streets are at
the acme of filth and putrescence. The new planet, I hear, is to
be called Neptune, and its sign ♆. Dr. Cox is lecturing on it.
The next should be Vulcan ; for steam, ocean, and iron, are in the
astrological ascendant. My congregation sends a captain and a
lieutenant in the new regiment of regulars.

NEW YORK, *April* 5, 1847.

Your kind letter of the 2d was received on the 4th, and you
will accept my thanks. Our little one was a very lovely object
in our eyes; and our remembrance of him is peculiarly free from
all that could give pain. He faded away exactly like a slowly-
dying flower. Partly to avoid funeral mockeries, and partly to
have the three little graves together, for the moral influence on
my other children, I removed the remains to Princeton, to " the
plot of ground" where I shall probably lie myself.

I have this morning been furnishing New Testaments (they
cannot carry large-print Bibles) to a company of the 10th regiment. I have been stimulated by the war to prepare a manual
of devotions for sailors and soldiers, which is now complete.[1]
Bunsen is getting out the most magnificent work on Rome, pictorial and antiquarian, which has ever been made. The American Messenger (of American Tract Society) is expected this year
to rise to a circulation of 100,000. One should write for such a
paper, however slim it is, and to make it less so. I dreamed
that I heard Dr. Yeomans say these words, on hearing a Presbyterial lecture, or the like : " Yes, it is only *nonsense :* but nothing
is more damning than nonsense ; especially when it purports to
be the Word of God, in exposition." I have recovered my
father's trial sermon, preached fifty-six years ago, æt. 19.
He was very boyish, and the text was Jer. i. 7. The style is
exactly that of his present writing.

118 CHAMBERS STREET, *May* 8, 1847.

I am writing on a most shoemaking sort of paper, which
please ascribe to my study-less condition ; my work-place being
the back-parlour. Coming into a house which has been " improved" by a defaulting boarding-house keeper, we find horrid
filth, damage, and dilapidation, and are amidst a gang of glaziers,
whitewashers, plumbers, and joiners. I have gone up one story,
leaving the first-floor-back (Anglicè) for distinguished clergymen.
Your patronage is solicited. The military display to-day was

---

[1] Published by the Board of Publication in 1847. In the same year, his
" Thoughts on Family Worship " was published by that Board. The latter
work was republished in Edinburgh in 1853.

very grand : once it would have pleased me : it did not : and
the illumination, which is about to begin in a few moments, I do
not expect to see.[1] I feel like preaching on " Charity . . . . re-
joiceth not in iniquity—vaunteth not itself." Dr. Burns of
Toronto left town this evening, after a sojourn of two or three
days. He goes to Halifax about a new theological school there.
I think he has more exactness and extent of knowledge, and a
greater outpouring of it in vehement and often affectionate discourse, than any man I ever met ; unless I except Chancellor
Kent, whom he resembles in his contempt of all conventionalities.
Our communion is coming on, without one addition on examination. This causes " searchings of heart." I feel no disposition
to look at other parties' share of the blame. From my soul I
say, confitentem habes reum ! On an examination of my preaching, I do not see any thing in doctrine, topics, or application,
(notwithstanding grievous defects in zeal and faith,) which I con-
demn myself in : yet I am not " hereby justified." This day of
festivity has found me very sad, at times, in the survey of every
sort of temper almost or quite as bad as years ago. Few things
startle me more than this *permanency* of one's inward features :
the same man, the same nature, in a degree. If it were not for
other, and sometimes countervailing tendencies, I might well
doubt whether any new nature exists. If I have any experience
it fully agrees with that exegesis which ascribes Romans vii. to
a believer, who " delights in the law of God after the inner
man." Durbin's Travels in the East are full of good matter for a
preacher ; he has a knack at painting the scene to your imagination.
We cannot be too well versed in the physique of the Holy Land.

Dr. Jenks's Explanatory Atlas is the best geographical help
for a pastor I have seen. Robinson's book will be a great one.
The Conference of the American Branch of the Evangelical Alliance have been fighting several days about slavery, &c., and do
not seem to know what the aforesaid Alliance is for. A man of
prudence may be pardoned for not securing a berth until he
knows whither the ship is bound. From the pugnacity of the
crew, the " sign " would seem to be " Castor and Pollux." They
will probably succeed in creating a new anti-slavery sect. One
speaker said, if they went wrong about slavery, *a new Alliance*
would certainly be formed. Perhaps it would be as well to
have enough new ones to suit us all. Murray's Letters to
Hughes are producing a great sensation ; far beyond any thing I
can account for. They are read with avidity in kitchens, and will
sell by thousands among the Irish. The Irish abolitionists are
agitating, with tremendous fury, because the Dublin Committee

---

[1] For the victories of General Taylor in Mexico.

did not " send back the money" of the slave-holding States. So
great is their compassion for Cuffee, that Paddy may die of starvation. Poor Lichtenstein lies very low, with a fever which he
probably caught from the infected air of the almshouse. His religion shines in this affliction. Dr. Burns's son, æt. 20, is just
settled in Kingston, in one of the chief posts in Canada. An
elder son is in the ministry in Scotland. Mrs. Burns is a cousin-
german of Bonar, who accompanied McCheyne and wrote his life:
(the Latins would have avoided that ambiguity, " et *hujus* scrip-
sit vitam.")

NEW YORK, *May* 13, 1847.

I thank you for reminding me of the date of our correspondence. I feel it somewhat tenderly in connexion with the kindness you intend for us, in the naming of your boy. My tears
(I seldom shed tears) flow profusely while I think that in a sort
he takes the place of our sweet translated child. Forgive this
burst (unusual in our long correspondence, and proving, perhaps,
that I grow weaker as I grow older,) and accept my prayers for
the little one's eternal good.

Our anniversaries are as much thronged as usual, but less
and less by New Yorkers. I also perceive that the old, staid
societies, *e. g.* Bible and Tract, are forsaken by the more fiery
persons. At the Bible Society to-day, the prime thing was a
glorious speech from the delegate of the British and Foreign
Bible Society, a Londoner, Mr. Corderoy, a youngish, soldierly-
looking layman. Fine delivery, noble elocution, and that tact
and pathos which I have never found in our American cut-and-
dried speeches. Hundreds of pocket-handkerchiefs were moist-
ened, and the enormous auditory, usually impatient, would not
let him stop. I will try to send you a report, but perhaps it
was all in his manner, pronunciation, tone and *feeling.* I sat between Vermilye and Pres. Hopkins (both cool men) and both
weeping. You will see nothing in the words to account for this.
Lewis Green made an eloquent speech yesterday at the American Tract Society. Fred. Douglass is a black Demosthenes.
For the mere quality of *strength* I never heard his superior. He
has a diabolical smile, from ear to ear, which contrasts with his
ferocious, lowering brow, in an indescribable manner. It was
Catilinarian and treasonable. He said, up and down, that he
despised and hated the country and the Constitution, and in-
voked the aid of England. The Millerites, the Fourierites, and
other Bedlamites, have protracted agonisms. The Evangelical
Alliance has been sweetly pugnacious, like Gen. Scott, bent on
" conquering a peace." Like the dear Baptist brethren, they

open their arms to all Christendom, free-gratis, full admission, to the broad union-platform; only with proviso, that no one enters the door who mispronounces the Shibboleth. In their chagrin at their smallness, they anathematize all who have not sued for entrance. Is Christendom really more united than before, by such means? I trow not.

If there is such a thing as the duty of warring, I think a Mexican might assert it. Who can deny them the credit of bravery? Military martinets here, as I happen to know, are now glorifying Scott at Taylor's expense: they say Scott's way of killing Mexicans is *selon les règles*. Certainly it effuses less of our own blood. I loathe and fear this war. We shall be readier for another. Yet perhaps Popery may lose its secular hold on Mexico.

UNIVERSITY OF VIRGINIA, *May* 27, 1847.

Having done the job for which I came to Richmond,[1] I proceeded to another matter of very great moment, which has brought me here. The Assembly looks young. Scarcely any gray heads. The fathers are Dr. Janeway and Mr. Smylie. Great array of sunburnt, broad-brimmed southern and western Chorepiscopi. Some sons of Anak, noble specimens of manly beauty from the west. Thornwell is the great man of the south, and I do not think his learning or powers of mind have been overrated. His speech on taking the chair was a chef d'œuvre. His sermon (not the popery one) was ill-delivered, but natheless a model of what is rare, viz., burning-hot argument, logic in ignition, and glowing more and more to the end; it was memoriter, and with terrific "contentio laterum." The spring was very late; consequently the sudden outburst just before we came clothed every thing with beauty. The mountains are green to the very tops. Albemarle is the crack county of Virginia; and the state of the grain-market has thrown much tobacco-land into wheat. I passed numerous wheat-fields in full ear, not one of which was less than one hundred acres. The education of the gentry here has led to a brisk competition in scientific tillage; observable around the seats of such men as Mr. Rives, Col. Randolph, Gen. Gordon, Dr. Merriwether. The foreground is all arable land, one sea of grass, blossoming-clover, and wheat, slowly rising, without any visible fences or artificial demarcations to injure the landscape, and the background a chain of wooded or cultivated heights (S. W. Mountain) unequalled by any I know. I have seen hills, and I have seen farming; but I never saw them so blended. After going westward for some miles to this place, crossing a lap of

[1] He preached the annual sermon on Missions, before the General Assembly, in Richmond, May 25. The text was Phil. ii. 11.

this ridge, and skirting the Rivanna, which has craggy and precipitous banks, full of rhododendron, honeysuckle, &c., we come
to the side of Monticello, and then into this valley, over which
the long chain of the Blue Ridge begins to tower in the North-
west. Jefferson knew how to select one of the finest plateaus in
the land for this college. His antichristian plans have been
singularly thwarted every way. For example, here is a chapel,
(since I was here last;) three professors communicants, besides
Dr. McGuffey, who is a Presbyterian minister; and a proctor
and treasurer who are Presbyterian communicants. McGuffey
is a West Pennsylvanian, and is second to no man in Virginia
for fame as a lecturer and public speaker. He does not preach
here, but often in other places. I shall not be surprised if, before ten years, this rich and central institution should have on
its very grounds a Presbyterian theological school; as the law
founding the University gives leave to any Christian sect to
build, and to have a theological professor, with freedom of
library, apparatus, &c. Schele, professor of Modern languages,
is a Prussian, and a pious Lutheran. The chaplain for next year
is Gillette, a Baptist of Philadelphia, [now of New York.] I
have met with all the Professors here; they are remarkable for
their courtesy to strangers. Dr. Cabell is just closing his year
of presidentship, with some eclat. I see he is nominated in the
Richmond Enquirer to succeed Dr. Warner in the Surgical Chair.
Emery tells me their edifice (Medical College of Hampden Sydney) is the finest in the city. I think I observe more prevalence
of religious warmth here than with us. I lodged with Mr.
Beadle of New Orleans, four years Missionary in Syria; he is
fluent in Arabic. To-morrow, Deo volente, I go to Gordonsville,
to visit the house of my birth, which I have not been in for
forty-two years: this will consume one day. I hope to reach
home by Thursday or Friday night. The Charleston and Columbia folks have a refinement of manners which has always
struck me. They do not depend on Northern cities, but get
their books and fashions direct from London and Paris. It is
something new under the sun, for Virginia daily-prints to report
doings of a General Assembly. There is preaching every morning, and service every evening. Dr. Empie, formerly President
of William and Mary, (Episcopal,) opens his church, St. James's,
all Sunday and thrice during the week, for the Presbyterians.
So do all the Baptists and Methodists. Fleming James gave a
great soirée in his palatial house, to sundry of our brethren;
among whom I was present. We are revelling on strawberries,
with floods of bona-fide cream; and ice-cream is what its name
imports.

NEW YORK, *June* 15, 1847.

I have been waiting for time to fill a sheet, but cannot any longer hope for it. Till my Princeton Discourse [1] it is utterly out of my power to do any thing out of New York and Princeton, great or small. This must be my reply to your invitation, which I fully estimate, to baptize your child. There is, however, another thing : though not often moved, I am sometimes very weak, and I do not think I *could*, publicly in Trenton, pronounce the name you have given your boy [2] without a degree of pain, which I am perfectly sure you would not allow me to incur, even for the pleasure which the solemn service, thus administered, might afford your friendly minds.

LONG BRANCH, *July* 28, 1847.

I ran away from your capital, much disordered, reached New York about two yesterday; visited Junk. The Chinamen look very much like Malays; but I saw one of them writing Chinese characters. Embarked at seven this morning; cool, but fine passage; but in the outer bay a great prevalence of cascading. Found all well here. At this present I am in my pigeon-hole; our children's shakedown on the floor; voices of female and male singing on the piazza. A glorious full red moon rose out of the ocean. Bathing is cold work. I saw one of the Junk-men drunk with opium. Addison has engaged for another month at Dr. Boardman's. More than five hundred obits in New York last week : more than eighteen hundred emigrants in one day.

Love to the young and rising generation, not forgetting my godson Johanniculus, as Luther often calls his young Hans.

What a useless pest capital letters are : the ancients had none, or rather they had none other; nor were they bothered with punctuation. How I envy them. A capital plagues me so, that I foresee it with apprehension, as one foresees a mudhole in driving. i am your friend,

j. w. alexander.

NEW YORK, *September* 3, 1847.

We got home on the 1st, and are in the hubbub of fixation, and the heats of our second edition of summer. Choir and organ business, everywhere, seems fruitful of ills. Lowell Mason has now come out against choirs, but, I fancy, not against organs. My idea of psalmodic service is, that it should be : (1) universal; (2) vocal; (3) slow, (in general ;) (4) without complication

---

[1] At the Centenary of the College, June 29, 1847.
[2] John Alexander, the name of one of his deceased children.

of parts; (5) simple; (6) little varied; *i. e.* a few tunes well learnt; (7) with no prominence of individual voices, (duets or solos;) (8) without fugue; (9) without frequent repetition of words; (10) depending on volume of many voices, rather than brilliant execution of one or two. It is plain as A B C, that whole masses cannot sing, unless the tunes be familiar to a high degree. This ideal I never expect to see realized. The nearest approach is in the large Lutheran congregations, barring their harshness; but better the harshness, than the feeble warble of twenty per cent. *in vacuo.* Much illness about; chiefly dysentery. Every day some case of sorrow in my large flock attracts my feeble help. My topic for Sunday is "Sorrow is better than Laughter."

This is my fifth letter, at one sitting. The Mexicans seem to me plainly below our free blacks; except a corps of desperate military leaders, whose trade and hope have been War, nothing but war ever since they broke with Spain. Taylor's election, I judge, would be a national vote for peace.

New York, *Sept.* 20, 1847.

Elizabeth Fry's life (the large one, vol. 1) will make many quakeresses: a lovelier woman I never read of or heard of; humility, meekness, love, and sense. The "meek and quiet spirit" in such a case, looks, as it is, πολυτελές. Dictionaries and id genus being my chief helps for exposition, I have added Kitto's Biblical Cyclopedia, and find it the best thing yet, in its line: it is rationalistic and Andover-like, in many places. One of the missionaries lately sent out by A. B. C. F. M., before his going, being then at New Haven, told a friend of mine, approvingly, that Dr. Taylor said *in his lectures,* in regard to David's expression, (Psalm 51,) "In sin did my mother," &c.; that they are to be interpreted as exaggerations like that of the sailor, [who in prayer spoke of himself in a phrase of vulgar slang.] Three services yesterday. I addressed my young men and women. The city is vile with common sewers. Nathan Rice's book against Popery is good: only about two pages can I except to. Why do you not have a Reading-room in Trenton? The Newarkers have laid the corner of a grand Library. I was invited to lay it, but pleaded un-Masonic dispositions.

New York, *Sept.* 23, 1847.

Yesterday we had the O'Connell obsequies. It speaks well for the good nature of our people, that so immense a procession should have marched for miles, with effigies of the pope, &c.,

&c., yet without a word or gesture of interruption. Apropos of which, the recent site of Niblo's is occupied by the " Great Tent " of the Millerites, with a lofty flag, bearing, " Thy Kingdom come ! " Preachments, concourse, &c. Failures have occurred here, and more are looked for. Addison's popularity in Philadelphia surprises me the more, as his last summer's work here seemed to draw scarcely anybody. The sphere, I admit, is very different : a people engaged solely in trade affords small intellectual ability. I think I am not censorious, nor chagrined, in judging that religion in New York runs very much towards externals. Fine churches, pews, and music, fine sermons, fine ' enterprises,' viewed in the same light as stock-company concerns, fine collections ; such are the stimulating ideas. " Moderatism " is the *terminus ad quem*. So far as my researches go, Presbyterianism has never and nowhere made striking advances, except when the body of preachers and people has been animated with a zeal for truth and saving souls, such as at the very time has been a little too strong, methodistical, pietistical, enthusiastical, in the eyes even of many sound, good sort of brethren. When we substitute for this secular stimulants, wealth, apparatus, ritual, decorum, letters, or oratory, we find that these (at least in the apprehension of the million) exist in greater force among the Episcopalians. Nor do we mend the matter by fighting these last, on questions of difference. Our real aggression has always been by warm pushing of our evangelical tenets. Right or wrong, this has become more and more my theory : I would I could show some corresponding practice : *negatively* I think I can.

NEW YORK, *October* 5, 1847.

If these rumours of new horrors in Mexico are true, what an account will our country, and we, as claiming to be self-governors, have to render to God ! I am much impressed by Webster's speech at Springfield. It is a war of pretexts. None of the alleged causes existed. It has gone from small skirmishing beginnings to the most hideous atrocities. Never have I so much feared the judgments of God on us as a nation. Yet I am not quite clear as to the duty of individuals ; or what means are best for stopping further carnage. Who knows but our judgment will be, that our people, having tasted blood, and grown proud of their undoubted prowess, will become, as Rome became, a people with war for a trade ? Military lust for conquest is manifestly on the rise. All Mexico would not (on worldly grounds even) repay us for the American lives which have been lost. A Chinese youth, named Khur, was here to see me to-day ;

on his third voyage to America, from Amoy: wishes to go to school here. He speaks a most funny mixture of English, Portuguese, and Chinese, an almost unintelligible baby-talk. But he is acute and bright-faced. The Millerite tent, Chinese Junk, and Fair of American Institute, are all in full force. Powers's Greek Slave is only a beautiful piece of licentious nudity. Mons. Niel, a reformed French popish priest, has appeared. Old Mr. Gallatin still receives company, and takes lively interest in philological inquiries. It is a wonderful fact, that the characters on the famous stone, found at Grave Creek Mound, on the Ohio, (Virginia,) are fully proved to be ancient *Libyan*. It is the very first documentary link between the red men and the old world. No doubt of the above fact remains with our knowing ones. I am pleased that you like Simeon:[1] his influence was owing, perhaps, in no small degree, to his amazing colloquial flow, chirping oddity, and irrepressible vivacity: hence his soirées, which nobody else could reproduce. As to his dread of systems, I do not share in it; unless said systems be false; and even then I prefer methodized to immethodized statements. His own system was clear enough, though he chose not to own it. In regard to his plan of preaching both sides of questions, on which the Scriptures seem to speak both ways, no man ever did it, except on two or three picked topics. Every man's common sense teaches him that he must aim at conciliation of apparent discrepancies, or abandon inspiration. No man ever preached *e. g.* that the planet is eternal, though Scripture seems to say so. They have a noble copy of his Skeletons, twenty odd volumes, in the Seminary Library at Princeton, the gift of Wilberforce. On Sunday night I had a soirée under our church, where I chatted to fifty of our young men. I saw Addison's big congregation in pretty full review. The steamers to Bremen are quite an epoch: I hope you saw traveller Stephens's account of the jollification at arrival in Bremen. George P. Marsh (M. C.) of Vt., speaks French like a Frenchman, and Swedish like a Swede, and is thorough in Danish, German, and Spanish; yet he has never been abroad. He is associated with Gallatin, Robinson, Turner, Gibbs, Salisbury, &c., in the Ethnological Society. The modern books of note on Arithmetic, such as Davies's, adopt the French billion, which makes the whole series go homogeneously by threes, (000 000 000 000.) A six-story house in my daily walks seventy-five feet long, which had been completed to cornice, has just been taken down brick by brick to the very ground from fault in the foundation: it filled me with thoughts every day as I passed.

[1] Life of Rev. Charles Simeon, of Cambridge.

NEW YORK, *October* 27, 1847.

When the demission business was sent down to the presby-teries some years ago, I voted against it. Since then I have doubted. The demission takes place all over the land, *de facto :* the question seems to be, how to legalize what we already allow, and avoid the evils of our " anomalous condition." But *curia vult avisare.* Before I look for your extension-table, let me say an experience of one of the crack (not cracked) ones is unfavour-able. Madame says the old way, of annexing a common table, in case of clerical invasions, is better. Our extension-table is too heavy, on the floor, as a fixture; hurts carpets, and is hurt by hoofs of youth, &c. If one is used, the one we have *quà ex-tensio,* is admirable. It is, however, paying for a daily encum-brance, in view of an occasional need. I went to Astoria yester-day, to see my landlady and parishioner, who is dying with con-sumption; a fine specimen of old-fashioned Presbyterian religion; all the doctrines turned into experience; full of calm hope and wisdom; a lesson for life. —— is homœopathically cured of a fever. What cured was, however, by no means accordant with *homœopathic* peculiarities; it was cold shower-bath, when the fever was hottest : this looks like reason; but it is not "similia similibus curantur," the great maxim of Hahnemann. —— is getting well of a fever, on the old plan. A bachelor presents me Hutter's New Testament in twelve languages, (1699.) I am at 1 Thess. ii. 9 in exposition. Look at the untranslated force of εαυτης 1 Thess. ii. 7, and at the exquisite tenderness of the whole verse. Jacobus is coming out with notes on Matthew. I know not what to say about the flocks of candidates who fre-quent every even the smallest vacancy. Strangers come to me every week, as if I kept a " vacancy intelligence office." Want of missionary zeal seems to be the cause, not want of room. Cheever's church [Union Square] opens on Sabbath first. Henry Beecher is the Brooklyn star; —— being the comet. Our synod did nothing about the war. The details of Chapultepec are equal to any thing military I remember.

NEW YORK, *November* 16, 1847.

I owe you for yours of the 4th. How time flies! I should have said it was not a week old. Perhaps this is the way the market women make such anachronisms about their eggs. I heartily rejoice in Governor Haines's election, not only because he is my classmate, but because I think he fears God. Good Mr. F. seemed to join in my expression of the same opinion. How the last-named good man is embushel-ed in this our university! Had he abode in Jersey, his light would have been like that of Sandy Hook. He tells me he has been to see old Chancellor Kent, at Chatham; who is sinking. All our young men are ravening for good places; and erring as to what constitutes a good place. There is a congestion of candidates about our cities, while at the extremities and frontiers, all is chill and suffering. Unless we all get awakened, in some extraordinary degree, I don't see how we are to fail sinking into Moderatism. Some people absurdly ascribe the diminished zeal of ministers to Seminaries. This is much as if I should ascribe our poor beef to the change of market-house. Those who never saw a college or seminary are as low as we. It lies deeper, and affects the whole church, I verily believe. It means just this, want of zeal for the salvation of souls. Though you mentioned Mr. ——'s "losing his eyesight," I imagined him to be out of town, till I saw he was dead. Oh how my conscience pierces me that, though he was my occasional hearer, I never urged this matter on him in private! How, how shall we meet people at judgment! Addison's popularity in Philadelphia is quite extraordinary.[1] I am pleased to think that it urges him to regard more and more the great end of preaching. Last week I saw a new painting (small) by Leslie, "the Pharisee and the Publican;" it begat a sermon in me. Item, a copy of the first Bible ever printed—the *Mazarin Bible*—of which only nine other copies are known of. It is perfect; two vols. folio; Mentz, 1450–1455; illuminated, incomparably noble for paper, ink, and press-work; printer *Guttenberg*. This was the copy of Mr. Hibbert. Other copies are (so far as I remember) 1, Bodleian; 2, Mazarin lib. Paris; 3, George III.'s lib. British Museum; 4, Advocates' lib. Edinburgh; 5, late Duke of Sussex's lib.; 6, Duke of Devonshire; 7, Estate of late Richard Heber, Esq. On beholding it, my emotion was altogether a religious one; thinking of the effects of the printed Scriptures.

NEW YORK, *December* 14, 1847.

You see [Chancellor] Kent is dead. Mr. F. tells me he lately talked with him, and found him much troubled about the "new birth," &c. He has been a constant defender of religion. H., in his new book, several times has the pleasant adverb "illy," which does not sound altogether "welly." Pope-stock rises. See how most papers take the Jesuit side in regard to Switzerland. See the avatar of romish prelates in England,

---

[1] He was supplying the pulpit of the Tenth Church during the absence of the pastor, Dr. Boardman.

with legal titles.   I wish I had a copy of the last North British, to send you a review of (Arnold's friend) Bunsen's book on the Church.   I have seldom been more moved than by some passages there.   Do try to get hold of it.   It opens a vista into an absolutely new forest of opinions on the great question of the age—the Church.   For high churchism to be rebuked from such a height as the cabinet of the greatest king alive, is like thunder from mid heaven.   And yet Bunsen's is a kind of catholicism: only it makes Puseyism look very mean and toy-shop like; like a snug China mandarin beside a Jupiter tonans.   For the relief of the red appearance on Hale's church,[1]

> "℞. pap. Kirwan, ℥ iij.
> Van Renss. scrupuli xxxiij.
> Fiat haustus."

Unless penance be your object, I see no rational cause of lament at the freezing off of your bath; for all health-purposes indoor water is cold enough.   Did you ever read the story of Diogenes, embracing the brazen statue, in winter?   Stand in a good big tub, with a good big sponge, and give yourself a swashing of water every morning; that is Sir Astley Cooper's recipe.

NEW YORK, *January* 4, 1848.

I am a little belated with my New Year wishes; but they are none the less sincere in behalf of you and your family, and church.   Dr. Spring very truly said yesterday, at our cleric prayer-meeting, that ministers sinned when they did not care about the edification of their neighbours' churches.   He also said this: "I am almost tempted at this late day to prepare myself to preach without notes; the day a man who reads his sermons puts on spectacles, he is shorn of half his strength."   I do not know when I have begun a year with more serious feelings; even the hurly-burly of New Year's day did not remove the impression.   My verse for the year is Heb. xiii. 8 : "Jesus Christ, &c."   It would "convene" me very much (as an agent said to me in a note) if you would come on, and give me a sermon; why not next Sunday evening?   I have, for some time, had three services; though doubtful about my duty as to health. I have no extras to lop off; never having made a platform-harangue here; exhortations are not *extras*.   Your eclaircisse-ment with H.[2] is characteristic.   Nobody ever knows whose

---

[1] When the scaffolding of the new church at Pennington, N. J., was taken down, it was discovered that the workmen had disposed some red slates among the black, so as to form a huge *cross* on each side of the high roof.

[2] A hearer who falsely suspected a political object in a sermon.

face a "double-header" will fly into. It has already taught you
what something like it taught me. Hardly any thing so raises
my pride and indignation, as when ministerial independence is
assaulted in my person; but I continue to have difficulty in
knowing how the line lies between the man and the minister.
In regard to the latter, we are authorized to take high ground.
I am much reflected on by a few in my congregation, for my
expressed opposition to the war. My Henry will feel thankful
for the coins you send, when they shall have arrived; it is, however, not unfrequently the case, in this island, that expected coin
fails to arrive. You do not mention whether sovereigns, rupees,
or louis d'or. If you have the Missionary Chronicle for 1843,
see how near [the Rev. Walter M.] Lowrie was to death by
drowning in 1842, (page 134.) *Then* it was that he was prepared for an event which occurred five years later, [August,
1847.] What a mercy that he leaves no wife. I am beginning
the year with a weight of 145 lbs. Julius Hare (now Archdeacon of Lewes) has a volume of parish sermons I should like
to lend you; they surpass the other [Augustus William] Hare's
(who died abroad) whose you excerpted from, I think, for the
Journal. The Archdeaon's are as plain, but more racy. Which
of us would say as follows : " What, I ask, have you been doing
during the whole of this year 1833 ? Eating and drinking,
sleeping and waking, working for your wages, and receiving your
wages, and spending your wages. Well ! and of all this, what
fruit have ye now ? Nothing. All this has brought you forward
in the journey of life, just as much as a horse gets forward that
keeps going round and round in a mill. How will you ever get
to heaven in the end ? And if you do not get to heaven, where
will you be ? When this world is swept away, there will be
only two places; and he who is not at the gate of heaven, when
he dies, will find himself at one of the gates of hell. For hell has
a thousand gates, yawning around us on every side, and ready to
close upon us and shut us in; whereas heaven has only one
gate, even our Lord Jesus Christ." [1]

[1] With the saddening associations of January, 1860, I find on one of the
pages of the letters of that month in 1848, the following characteristic specimen of the humour of his brother Addison :

"NEW YORK, 7th day, 1st Month 18, 1848.

"ESTEEMED FRIEND,—Not knowing that thy mouth had been opened in
meeting, nor even that thy principles were friendly, I was greatly tendered
to learn that thou has had a concern to review the Life of Elizabeth Fry,
and has had to give up to it. I trust thy piece was written after the necessary preparatory baptisms, and under a very solemn covering; and also
that thou will follow the opening in which thou has been led to stand up.

" Thy friend,   DEBORAH DARBY."

CHAMBERS ST., *March* 1, 1848.

The day that a child says " I will " or " I won't" a second time, is a bad day for parent and child. It is just the point where our American license begins and where parental capacity is tried. Probably several thousand children under fourteen, in this city, own no allegiance whatever, but are *sui juris*.

Mr. G. of the State Department dined with us yesterday; amazing as a talker, a historian, and a polyglott. His memory of places, maps, dates, and facts, is beyond all I ever thought possible. He is at home in all the southern languages. Though he spent some years in Italy, he thinks Mexico a far more interesting country. There lies on my table a letter, dated Puebla, January 1. I will crib a few sentences : " I am still in Puebla, living under the shade of the glorious Popocatapetl ; what a mountain ! The very sight of it would pay for a visit to Mexico. One of the greatest curiosities in this city is the library and picture-gallery of the late Bishop. The library is the finest private one I have ever seen. Among the pictures are some of great value. He was a man of great erudition, cultivated manners, and elegant tastes, and appears to have been beloved by all classes of people. He died on the 11th of October last, at the ancient city of Cholula, æt. 80. This library, the pictures, and various articles of virtu, were bequeathed to the poor." " I have been reading Prescott ; and you may judge of the pleasure of such pages, on the very soil immortalized by the achievements of the ' Conqueror.' " " I am reading Clavigero, one of the best historians of ancient Mexico ; to whom Prescott is much indebted for his elegant work." " The [theatrical] pieces called *pastorellas* are a mixture of the ludicrous and the religious ; the infant Saviour, Joseph, Mary, the manger, the ass, being introduced on the stage, the piece winding up with *la Polka*." Mr. G. says the constant impression made on him, all over Mexico, was, that the people are an Indian race ; the white and the black blood secondary. The new treaty will give us " little but deserts ; " but better we should have these (for the Mexicans) than they ; it will more effectually keep our fellows off their border. O how desirous one feels that the Gospel might pour in through these channels ! What a glorious thing if the ambition of war could only be emulated by any analogous zeal for the introduction of the Gospel ! I do not perceive why these poor, simple, brave, perfidious, paganized people might not be plied by thousands of books and tracts. They are not more hopeless than were the boors of Bohemia and Germany, when the tracts of Wiclif and the Lollards came among them, or than the Swiss mountaineers

when the writings of Zuingle and Calvin roused them.   Further,
I soberly think some daring young ministers (if any such are
left in these days of literary clerical *petit-maitres*) ought to dash
into Vera Cruz, Perote, Puebla, and Mexico, and blow at least a
long loud blast of defiance, where Satan's seat is.   In 1555, men
were found to go to torrid Brazil, from Geneva; and several
died martyrs there.   I have expressed this opinion in my official
capacity; but my brethren think me flighty.   Would God my
boys might preach Christ in that, or any other foreign land; so
only they be faithful!   Amen.

NEW YORK, March 28, 1848.

Gurley, the auctioneer, who has just died of erysipelas, will
be regretted.   He was a wonderful bibliographer, and a man of
remarkable tact and courtesy, as well as honesty.   I never heard
him make an extravagant remark, in selling.   The news by the
"Caledonia" surprises people.   That the [French] Republic
should slip on the rails, as by a mere turning of the switch, with
no friction and loss of life, is wonderful.   The editor of the
"Schnell Post," a German radical, was off in the "Cambria," as
soon as the first news came, to take part in the revolution that
is to be in Germany.   Two of his comrades sang the Marseillaise
to him, from the wharf.   The horrible treachery of Louis
Philippe, in regard to the Protestants, and especially the Spanish
marriages, is now visited on him; as well as the blood of Frenchmen and Arabs shed for nothing in Algeria.   Algeria declared
part of the French Republic!   We have authorized a new mission under the Equator, near J. L. Wilson, and at his instance.
None of the return-missionaries have instructed me more than
he.   History has often made much of less daring than his.
The practice of funeral sermons months *post mortem* is common
in Virginia; I think the more common way in rural places.   I
lament to hear such painful things of your kind old aunt; my
mind reverts to antediluvian banquets, of steaming coffee, cakes
and sausage.   May the world never want a race of affectionate
old-fashioned people, who shall so spread their bounties as to
make them remembered for a whole generation!   I wish her a
safe and gentle descent down the slippery foot of the hill.   By
reason of preaching twice on Sunday, as I ought not, on top of
a sore throat, I have made myself ("war-horse" as a plain man
translated) *hors de combat.*   I believe I make less of [ecclesias-
tical] differences than I did.   Though a reunion with the New
School body, just as it is, would be unedifying, and a signal for
unprecedented squabbles and disciplines, I think there are many
among them with whom we ought to maintain the most brotherly

correspondence. Nevin [Mercersburg] holds unimaginable doctrines; *e. g.* that Christ is now incarnate in the church; (progressively;) that whoso denies this, is an anti-christ; that we
eat Christ's body, and derive our life from it, so that our life is
the very life (theanthropic life) which Christ has; that we are
justified by the transfusion of Christ's righteousness, as head,
to us as members; (the popish doctrine;) that all other Presbyterians in America are a set of Puritans, who have apostatized
from Calvin.

NEW YORK, *May* 11, 1848.

Dr. Neander's Life of Jesus is about as bad a book, for us,
as could be furnished by Germany. It will keep in countenance
those numerous persons who are half ready to give up all inspiration. The book of the day is the Life of Pollok, by Scott.
Take a few sentences: "Scotland gave him birth, and England
donated him a tomb;" p. 350. "His hair dark, and his countenance touched with the olivaster shade;" p. 360. "His thoughts,
imagery, logomachy, style, and plan are his own, and most appropriate for the great psalm which he indited;" p. 362. If you
ever see it in a shop, read the first sentence, which is too big and
rotten to bear transportation. Dr. Schroeder's people have
bought the Eighth Street church. There had been a little squinting towards it among our folks, but they got no countenance from
me.

At no time have things looked duller in my charge. Additions very few, and a general fluctuation, which makes me doubt
whether our church, like so many others, will not be swept away
before the surge of commerce. About twelve families leave us.
Of nine persons dismissed by us since last communion, all but
one were dismissed to us within five years. If my powers were
of the arousing sort, I might hope for more in a mission-church,
but all the little I can attempt is in the way of gradual training;
and this requires people to stay with you. Our Sunday services
are as full as ever, but our other indications are all bad. When
I look at home, I no longer marvel it should be so. There is
some likelihood that I shall take boarding for my family at
Astoria, for about six weeks in summer; it is an hour by coach,
and half an hour by steamboat; and is right on the strait and
violent channel between the East River and the Sound: "Hurl-
gate."

Accept for self and co. our loves, and allow me to subscribe
myself, in the mode which threatens to become the laconism of
American epistles,

"Respectfully, &c."

New York, *May* 30, 1848.

In yours of the 16th, you speak of "chirography" vice "penmanship;" it would be a good exercise in a school or college, or even for ourselves, to make out a list of cases in which the lean kine have thus eaten up the fat: *e. g.* "commence" for "begin," "truthful" for "true," (though it has a meaning of its own;) "indebtedness" for "debt;" "standpoint" for "point of view;" &c. This month is turning into a Pluviose. I see numbers of waistcoats à la Robespierre; white, with high turn-over lappels. The "café des 1,000 colonnes" has come out fresh as "café de la Republique." Mr. Bridel has large congregations in French; on these occasions he confines himself to the simple gospel. Four prayers and two entire chapters in the service; opening prayer read, and apostolical benediction at beginning, as in France. I have just read the Augsburg Confession, for the first time; it is not a dry list of points, but a beautiful and stirring argument and protest. I fear from hints in papers, that the General Assembly are going to apply the knife of frugality to the very life of our Boards; perhaps I mistake. At a moment when the world, in its very selfishness, sees the importance of giving full salaries, &c., in every bank and insurance-office, what a cowardly concession to misers and Nabals, to complain that such a man as ——, gets his $1,500 or $1,800. Mr. Sosnosky (I need not say whence) is colporting here, among French, as Mr. Rauschenbusch among Germans. On the 28th and 29th the emigrants landed at our Quarantine, for the two days,=10,030; mostly Germans, and no disease but small-pox. Are any of us at all awake to what this influx means? I propose D. v. to take my family out of this noise about the middle of June, to some quiet riverside, near enough for me to do duty. After that, I will make an exchange with you, or will go to you without exchange, as circumstances may admit. I see, beyond denial, that my congregation is suffering from its site. Though we have tens of thousands downtown, they are mission folks, and increasingly foreigners, if not papists. The talent they require is not mine. I say truly, when I add, that I have not even a momentary hankering for uptown: my leading members feel otherwise; so should I, were I they. We have sent away about fifteen families this spring, thither and out of town.

Astoria, *June* 22, 1848.

We have six passages a day, from here to town, by steamboat, besides omnibus and railway on crossing the ferry—the

latter every hour. Price sixpence. This is a beautiful cove on
the end of Long Island, formerly called Hallet's Cove, and just
opposite the upper end of Blackwell's Island. From the upper
windows of this house we can see across to the North River.
All the navigation of the Sound passes directly at our feet; for
the house (Mr. Henry Mulligan's) is on a terraced bank, at the
bottom of which, separated only by a road, is the East River.
I think it an unspeakable mercy to be permitted to bring my
family here, as —— cannot bear a longer trip, and we have a down-
stairs room, two piazzas, a fine garden, and a lawn like a nobleman's. To me it is almost like being in town. Next lot is Mr.
George Douglass; next Dr. Alexander Stevens; next Thorburn's
nursery, &c. Mr. Walker (elder) and Mr. Jas. Soutter are out
here. The sea-air is very perceptible. Last night a quite thick
blanket was in order. I saw old Mr. [Albert] Gallatin yesterday; a wonderful, wonderful man! I am always struck with the
fact, that the whole of his conversation is on important topics,
always in choice language, and always novel. He gave me the
best account I ever had of the respective systems of Boodh,
Brahma, and Confucius; of the Chinese language and of the
Polynesian languages. He showed me the latest Genevese
version of the Bible in 3 vols. 8vo, and laughingly said it was
"very orthodox." He showed me a book on Geneva, by
Goliffe, and complained that he was very unfair to Calvin, whom
Mr. G. regards as one of the greatest mortals. On a former
occasion he drew a comparison between Calvin and the Puritans,
on the subject of witchcraft, &c., very unfavourable to the latter.
He has just completed a volume, of some hundreds of pages,
on the Aboriginal languages of America. His ethical and the-
istical feelings are very correct and profound; I cannot find out
what he thinks of Christ. He is minutely acquainted with all
the nice points of Calvinistic controversy.

ALBANY, *July* 28, 1848.

You will hardly believe me when I say that I went to Saratoga reluctantly; nothing but a desire to gratify my good
mother, who needed the water and a companion, took me
thither. We remained just a week. It is a most unagreeable
place to me, unspeakably less agreeable than the seashore. We
left there yesterday, and made the trip to this place in a heavy
rain and thunder-storm. I propose to preach at home on
Sunday.

I am at the Delavan House, which I continue to think, of
taverns, the best house I ever stopped at. When we came up
in the boat last week, we had the Van Burens, father and son,

with us; Martin looks hale, and had a fresh cabbage-leaf inside of his hat; reason unknown. To one who passes up the East River, Dr. Tyng's church is the most conspicuous building in upper New York, and yet it wants the two steeple-towers, which are to be 250—300 feet high. The church is to seat 2,000, and to cost, they say, $200,000. There is a vestry-discussion as to which of the two houses shall be St. George's church, and which St. George's chapel.

After some hot, steaming days, this is one of the pleasantest of the season. I have been giving my mother and sister a drive around the city; and am much surprised to find so many improvements, beautiful buildings, sweet gardens, &c. The upper part is to be very charming.

NEW YORK, *August* 21, 1848.

This is my first literary act, on returning home, after an absence of 58 days. Seldom have I been gladder to get back, for I have scarcely had a week without illness. The Hellgate end of Long Island is almost as much broken into ups and downs, as a mountain-ridge. My second sojourn was with my elder Walker. From his house I could see, not only Astoria, the East River, and the west side of the North River, but Staten Island, and a fine view of New York in the distance. Astoria is a place of villas. The sea-breeze is fresh, but I opine they will have agues. Nearly 100 embark on the little steamers for New York every morning. My first visiter, on return, was Mr. Bridel, a very lovely little man. There has been great prevalence of dysentery on Long Island, and in other country-places about here. New York has also approximated, this year, towards Philadelphia, in respect to cholera infantum. I observe by the bills, however, that febrile disorders decrease, in the ratio that bowel-disorders increase; *e. g.* last week but one, of all fevers, 14; of all bowel-ills, 114; last week, of former 26, of latter 126. Good old Dr. Miller said to me, the other day : " When the semi-centenary of my ministry came round, I was glad to let it pass in silence, as I was ashamed of my ministerial performances." When Dr. Emmons was dying, he said to Dr. Hawes : " I shall soon be on the other side, but O how ashamed I shall feel, to be there ! " I lately saw, in German, a history of the world, in many volumes, all biographical; *i. e.* a chain of individuals, from Adam down, each comprising the age he lived in : it struck me that a Biblical History, on a similar plan, might fill a series of lectures. It is remarkable how much this is the plan of the Bible itself. Addison is here, on his way to orate at East Windsor.

NEW YORK, *September* 7, 1848.

The rumours of yellow-fever die away. The Board of Health ceases to report any at the *Currentine*—such is the current pronunciation—and no cases are believed to exist on this island. Dr. ——, of Glasgow, was in my church on Sunday. Like almost all these Scotsmen, he seems to have a mighty good conceit of himself, and a superciliousness towards every thing American; this incenses me, because there is so little pretence of foundation for it. I could perhaps bear it in an Oxonian or Cantab dignitary; but in a snuffy Sawney, speaking the horriblest dialect that ever came from the mouth of a Briton, I can't stand it. People are beginning to come back to their quarters; and, after all, there is nothing like one's own home.

I do not think the Sunday School Journal can ever occupy that place in public notice which its *redaction* merits; its title is so narrow, and its period of revolution in its orbit so long and irregular: I would as soon calculate the moon's motion, as tell when it is coming. We have again essayed a ministers' prayer-meeting; I don't know how it will go. Text last Sunday afternoon, Ecc. iv. 9, 10. A clergyman, known to me, publicly read in a service, a chapter in the Apocrypha, and never found it out. I have been reperusing Herodotus, in English. Several things strike me: 1. It is a series of grand old stories; as entertaining as the Arabian Nights. 2. The extraordinary advance of the world, since then, in science. What hideous incredibilities! 3. The equal advance (under Christianity) of humanity. You can scarcely read ten pages anywhere in Herodotus, without lighting on some atrocity. 4. A delightful book might be made, by stringing together the best ancient narratives, cutting off superfluities, and taking any liberties with language, and entitling, *Stories from the Old Historians.*[1] In a month, one might from Herodotus, Thucydides, Xenophon, Plutarch, Diogenes Laertius, Livy, Sallust, and Tacitus, make one of the best and most saleable volumes of the day. It should have many maps, titles, notes, and Christian comments, and should be well printed. It would necessarily comprise the most famous events of olden time, such as people are constantly alluding to, without exact knowledge. Plutarch is an inexhaustible magazine himself.

NEW YORK, *October* 11, 1848.

The loss of good Mrs. Rice,[2] gives me many serious feelings.

---

[1] His correspondent had anticipated this hint in a series of "Old Stories" from Herodotus: Sunday School Journal, September and October, 1839.

[2] Of Trenton, see vol. i., 186, 201.

The more I think of it, the more I believe, that such quiet and meekness of well-doing will be more prized in "that day," than many brilliant qualities. How much better than the self-tormenting pride we have known in some families. I am glad your tour in the Pines has caused itinerancy to rise in your estimation; Presbyterianism owes almost its existence to it, in new settlements. Do you see that Nevin sets up the "Mercersburg Review"? I have been with my children to the Fair of the American Institute, in Castle Garden. There were thousands of things, but not much that I coveted, except the pears. They talk of building out the Battery further into the bay. A balloon and man went up to-day. A military band is going by, which reminds me how vastly that branch of art is improved since my boyish days; I am as much pleased with the sound as I ever was. The number of such bands is astonishing; great numbers of them are Germans. Surgeons see a very bloody side of war. I observe that Luther's original Catechism omits the second commandment, and divides the tenth; just as the Papists do. On the first of this month, my father said it was the anniversary of his licensure, fifty-seven years ago; I have his trial-sermon, though he does not know it.

NEW YORK, *October* 29, 1848.

I congratulate in regard to your North Church; it was time, and it will not hurt the "old South." The Repertory Article on Chalmers, is by my father, who seldom contributes now. Paul Delaroche's great painting of Napoleon crossing the Alps, is in the new style—matter-of-fact; nothing ideal. You see the wear and tear of the breeches, and gray surtout; the mule is a common mule. In this respect, one is gratified. You remember David's on the same subject, in the old Academy. I have just received notice that the Board [of Publication] would stereotype my "Family Worship." Looking over Walsh's "United States and England," lately, I find it entirely free from those twists of diction, which characterize his later writings. It would surely be carrying coals to Newcastle, to give you any *ana* of Mr. [James F.] Armstrong, [of Trenton,] close as you are to headquarters. I remember the old gentleman very well; but he was past preaching. You know he had a fine library. Where are all his sermons? what becomes of sermons? He was very much the gentleman; cordial and benignant, even to children; disposed to fun. I have heard that he was very animated and pathetic in his discourses, when in his prime. I suppose Mr. A. would have been called an old-side Presbyterian. He was of the Stanhope Smith school, and they were very intimate. Ask for the exact particulars of an incident, at the old parsonage, between Mr. A. and Dr. Witherspoon, when the Dr. came with coach-and-four, just after his marriage to a young wife. We are in expectation of the cholera soon in New York. I heard Gough the other night, and still think him a master of eloquence in his way. [David] Lord is really a genius. I don't believe in his applications, but his main principles [of interpreting Prophecy] are the true ones, and are almost self-evident. He takes all the symbols which are *explained in* the Scriptures, and from these deduces rules.

NEW YORK, November 16, 1848.

I have ministered at two instalments, within a week, and have taken a very annoying cold. I never was in the Jersey City church till yesterday ;[1] you know it is the old Wall Street do.; it is a model of beauty to my eye. I know of no good models for cheaper edifices. Potts once named to me, as a great invention of a certain architect, a very economical plan, of so building that the church might at any future time be enlarged in either dimension. At Yorkville, where I was installing[2] last week, Mr. Butts has put up a very snug affair for $1,500 ; wood. A MS. history of Virginia has come to light, several years older than Capt. John Smith's. It makes the bragging descendants of the princess Pocahontas flutter, as it shows that her highness had an Indian husband two years before she was married to Rolfe.

My heart is thankful for the result of the election. Whatever Gen. Taylor may do, or not do, the reign of corrupt office-holders is broken for a time. Old Mr. Johnstone showed me a whole sermon written on half such a sheet as this : he says his father, who was a clergyman, taught him it when he was a boy, and he has used it ever since to the saving of much eye and hand, ink, paper, and time. By a home-made scheme of small marks for the most commonly occurring words, (the, and, for, from, Gospel, church, proof, text,) it is surprising to one who has not made the calculation, how much work is abridged. By about fifty such marks, I think fully half would be saved. What a libel on Mary Magdalene, to name —— after her; there is not a breath of proof that she was a profligate person ; or even that she was the sinful woman of Simon's house : there is every presumption that she was a lady of leisure, if not of wealth.

---

[1] When he preached at the ordination and instalment (as assistant pastor) of the Rev. Lewis H. Lee.

[2] The Rev. Joshua Butts.

NEW YORK, *December* 14, 1848.

I can scarce think of a finer subject for a Philadelphian to write on, than " The first hundred years of Philadelphia." The first fifty would be the chief. Men and manners, houses, antiquities, &c. How Watson [Annals] has murdered this in his Higgledy-piggledy ! The gold fever is wondrous ; thirty-one vessels now advertised for California. Mr. O. hired a ship to government; when arrived all hands deserted ; could not get a raft manned ; consequence, United States forfeits to Mr. O. $80 per diem, for every day the ship is detained beyond a certain time.

Dr. Dill [from Ireland] is a superior man ; young, but canny, like Cunningham. He is tall and eloquent. A couple, former Finneyites, whipped their children, to make them submit ; next became perfectionists ; next rejected Old Testament, and now are wondering after Davis, the clairvoyant. I have just been buying my winter butter at 22 cents ; but I reckon you can get it cheaper, as I know you can better. I have never, in a single instance, tasted New York butter equal to Philadelphia. Old Schoolism has no good chance in New York, where the warp is Dutch and the woof Yankee. See how little room between

Naturally enough all immigrant Yankees go to the Congregationalists. The Dutch churches here command my respect for their peacefulness and conservatism. The state of things in Austria and Prussia looks very threatening. It looks like another general war in Europe. Hengstenberg and his class denounce all this liberalism as Anti-christ itself; and these are the king's advisers. *Domestic Missions* seems to be pointed out as our work. A letter of my grandfather Waddel has come to hand, dictated by him, in blindness, to my mother, and addressed to Dr. Hoge. It has one remarkable sentence : " There is a *minimum feci* written on all the actions of my life."

NEW YORK, *December* 22, 1848.

Lately I sent two small articles to the "American Messenger." They circulate 130,000. I suppose the snow which is coming down here is also coming down on you. The new Congregational Journal, the "Independent," has taken in Joshua Leavitt, as the real editor. They lead off with much spirit.

Another death of cholera in town yesterday. All the old disputes about contagion. Every case thus far is traceable to the crew of the "New York." The rate of mortality here is formidable. Yesterday's case was just from Pittsburg, but had communication with above passengers. Dr. Stevens, who, in last cholera, said "No contagion," now talks otherwise. In looking at the history of the Puritans, I find very few of the things which they scrupled to be such as would hurt my conscience; though I might wish them altered. The tendencies of Independency in England have been very latitudinary and disorganizing.

I was at the New York Lying-in-Asylum, yesterday. What a blessed refuge for poor creatures in their extremity! Last year between two and three hundred confinements, and not one death, or unhappy result!

Carter has imported a very large stock of the Bibles printed at Coldstream, by Dr. Adam Thompson, who broke up the monopoly. As imported books, paying ten per cent., their cheapness is remarkable; and they are worth looking at, by one who loves linen-paper, British press-work, and immaculate typography. The small New Testaments are 12½ cents, small Bibles 25, 50, &c. Large 4to Family Bible, with short notes, calf, $5. All have the Scotch Psalms; all are faulty in regard to size of paper.

I once mentioned to you the erroneous and deceptive retention of the *e* in *Urbane*. The same is true of *clothes*, which should be *cloths*, to be intelligible to modern readers. The Scotch Bibles all have " brasen, morter, caterpiller, jubile, throughly;" in this agreeing with the English. It seems odd to me, that —— should praise A. Monod & Co. for sticking to a National church, which is Arian, and which, by synodal act, has refused to make either baptism or moral conduct a condition of church-membership.

To-day I went to see a sick parishioner. All shut. Dead. What solemn reflections should this produce!

A doctor from Bellevue almshouse tells me they have the ship-fever there horribly; it broke out in a room of eighty persons. Conscience, about such matters, is so dispersed, as to amount to nothing. The filth of our streets is absolutely mysterious. In the driest weather I have seen the crossings quite sloppy; this is chiefly from ordure and swill, squeezed up from between the paving-stones, by the heavy loads, &c. The Irish Deputation [Dill and Simpson] have netted more than $6,000 in this city. With all its faults New York is certainly a giving place.

My old chum, Waterbury, preached for me on Sunday. Princeton must have been very rank for doctorizing, not to be able to contain till Commencement; perhaps they were afraid the candidates would die. So Baptist Noel has come out of the Establishment. I doubt the wisdom of the method.

NEW YORK, *January* 8, 1849.

A Happy New Year! In what country but Scotland would 950 [Prize] essays on the Sabbath be sent in by *labouring men?* This even more strikes me than that the best should be written by a woman, ["The Pearl of Days."] I think almost every body undervalues the actual good done by our Missions; say, among the Indians; which is the one I regard most. Just in their infancy, yet they affect the tribes through and through. Mr. Dougherty has twenty native communicants; at two other places there are sixteen; and among the Choctaws, the Presbyterian church (though under the A. B. C. F. M.) has 264 native members. Where is there more success, proportionally? Dickens's Christmas story is paltry; though one of its puns showed me how the English pronounce "*Ma;*" though I might have inferred it from the concurrence of New England and Virginia. Pittsburg is unfortunate in fires, and New Orleans in pestilences. I hear every day of merchants and people of that class having died of the epidemic in New Orleans. The New Haven road is now open; passage in two hours, fine cars; next thing will be Albany. Already we go on rails (Erie Railway) about 200 miles. Our markets show it. Venison is a drug. For the *cuisine recherchée*, nothing will do but prairie-hens from Illinois, $2 a pair, which is as low as canvass-backs; as Juvenal says: "Instruit ergo focum provincia."—Sat. v. I visit old Mr. Gallatin, in his bed. It is a treat to have his reminiscences of our greatest men, all of them. On such topics his powers are unbroken, and he is equal to anybody I ever heard, for never hesitating, and always hitting just the word, with a *curiosa felicitas*. He professes firm belief in Christianity, and I understand him now to admit the divinity of Christ. He thinks Madison the greatest argumentative parliamentarian we ever had; I have heard that Marshall had the same opinion. It just occurs to me, that in his earlier life Madison used to have family-worship. Afterwards his religion assumed a Washingtonian invisibility. My New Year's text, and motto, is: "Hope thou in God." The condition of our vicious poor is very dreadful. When I think of the hunger and nakedness of some, I cannot lie down in my warm bed, without a feeling akin to shame. Contrary to my expectations, a good many of my young men are away in winter, on commercial travels; it is the only season in which they dare traverse the Western States.

NEW YORK, *February* 1, 1849.

I saw an advertisement which says : " A quill-pen begins a letter like a pen, continues it like a pin, and ends it like a shaving-brush." The respectability of the people going to California is very marked. Among those known to me, many are educated, and many are religious. One party of a hundred has included Sabbath observance in their indentures. One ship known to me is to have daily worship. Having long believed colonies to be the best missions, I see in this a most hopeful means for spreading the gospel. California churches can send missions with ease to China, Japan, and Polynesia. The great proportion of northern men going thither, will be favourable to the preserving of our Union. Miss Martineau comes out Pantheist, in her readable book on Palestine. The pull and vexation of these numerous charitable collections upon us is dreadful, and injurious, I feel sure, to the growth of our congregations. No other sect is so harassed, and no other ministers so " serve tables." Look at an able article on Immigration (statistical) in the American Almanac for 1849. The " German Messenger" of the Tract Society is edited by an excellent German, Mr. Rauschenbusch. There is also here a Mr. Ungewitter, a friend of Hengstenberg, and sometime editor of a loyalist journal in Berlin, but driven away by the Republican movement. The German method of singing is the true one, in these respects : 1. The harmony is confined to the organ. 2. The choir, which is small, sings the *air*. 3. They introduce no new tunes. 4. The *chorals*, which they sing, (Old Hundred being one,) are slow and familiar. 5. Consequently the people all sing ; and all sing the *air*, except as individual fancy may vary to suit the voice.

I have read Miss ——s' tale, and think it wonderful ; but I know, by previous trials, that our booksellers would do nothing with it. I was particularly struck with the knowledge of religion evinced, and with the absence of all turgid language. Except " resurrection-morn," in the last sentence, I do not remember a young-ladyism. Would that Bishop Doane could see it, before again he prints a sermon ! I am surprised your Lutheran knows nothing of Old Hundred. I have it before me in two German collections, where it is referred to two other books, of date 1666 and 1772. The ascription of it to Luther is no doubt mythic. The more pious divines (pietists) in Wurtemburg, look on the democratic uproars as "Anti-Christ;" and expect a speedy intervention of God, by χαρισματα and miracle.

INAUGURATION-DAY OF ZACHARY TAYLOR, *March* 5, 1849.

There is something pleasing in the chase of a text through several versions. I have just been looking at that delightful but obscure one, Eph. iv. 16. The phrase διὰ πάσης ἁφῆς τῆς ἐπι-χορηγίας, is thus given: 1. Eng. Auth. Vers., "by that which every joint supplieth." 2. Geneva, "in every joynt, wherwith one ministreth to another." 3. Tyndale, "in every ioynt wherwith one ministreth to another." 4. Cranmer, "joynt wherwith one ministreth to another." 5. Vulgate, "per omnem juncturam subministrationis." 6. Rheims, "by al iuncture of subministration." 7. Wicklif, "bi eche ioynture of undir seruying." (These last are just the Vulgate transferred.) Robinson, in Lexicon, renders, "by all the joints of supply." This is just the force of the (8) Dutch, "door alle vægselen der tœbreuginge," and (9) the old French, "par toutes les jointures du fournissement." Luther (10) has "durch alle Gelenke; dadurch eins dem andern Handreichung thut," (which is very like the English;) and (11) de Wette, "durch allerlei Gelenke der Handreichung," which is very exact, I think, namely, "by every-kind-of joint of (hand-reaching) supply-help." I do not think our version here maintains its usual superiority. Before leaving this matter, I must copy a sample of Wiclif's literal following of the Vulgate, in 2 Cor. i. 17—19:

"Ether the thingis that I thenke, I thenke aftir the fleische, that at me, be it is & it is not, but god is trewe, for our word that was at you is & is not, is not therinne, but is in it, for whi ihesus crist the sone of god, which is prechid among you bi us, by me & siluan and tymothe, ther was not in him is & is not: but is was in him," &c.

All this arises from the singular fact that the Romans had no word for *Yes*, and had to use Est, Ita, Immo, Maxime. This perpetual moving is a plague to a family situated as mine is. The house I occupy has just been sold over my head, and the new landlord raises the rent from $700 to $800. My congregation is going down, by going up (town). We dismiss two for one we receive. Though the house continues full, it is of transient people; no pews are sold, though all are hired for short terms. About nine-tenths of the property-holders want to sell and go up town; they would do so in a moment if I should say the word; and with every probability of a new and full church there: but that word I dare not say, nor have ever given any countenance to the proposal. Two of my elders move up-town in May. If you want a colleague you had better strike while the iron is hot, and call me now. Addison has a Comment on the Psalms going through the press; popular; no strange tongues. I have not lately met with a remark more exactly suiting me than the following of W. S. Landor, respecting Southey : "no prose writer, except Cobbett and Sydney Smith, has written such pure English." No week passes without some one going from our congregation to California, almost all very respectable persons. I am sorry to perceive that the cholera is increasing at New Orleans and on the plantations.

NEW YORK, *March* 19, 1849.

Addison is certainly printing on Psalms : I am glad of it, as no book is more needed. Poor Ebenezer Mason was buried yesterday, in a vault to which his father's remains [Dr. John M. Mason] had been conveyed the day before. Violent sudden rheumatism. Duncan of Baltimore, on his way to the funeral, was paralyzed in a coach from our wharf, and lies ill, but better. My house is sold over my head, and also rented, and I am as yet houseless. The kind of house I need cannot be had, but for such sums as $800, $900, and even $1,000. Atkinson (when a lawyer) was a particular friend of mine; he was an uncommonly amiable man.[1] I do not expect to lose fewer than twenty families from my church by the 1st of May. I went yesterday to see the man from whom my child took the varioloid; he has had the most dreadful form of confluent small-pox. The mask on his face was half-an-inch thick, so that he cut it off with a knife. I am glad to see the Bostonians have printed Macaulay without the "offense," "chimist," "traveler," "highth," and "luster." There is a third impression for twenty-five cents. I continue to see Mr. Gallatin, and talk to him on divine things. Even at his almost hopeless age, he seems to make some progress; disavows deism; disavows Unitarianism; speaks of relying on the merits of Christ alone; on being saved by faith; and on the last occasion used these words, with tears in his eyes, "My love to my redeeming God." But his mind loses its thread instantly if you oppose any thing he is saying. A pleasant boy of my church suffered amputation of the leg, last week, for the second time in six years : in the last instance he was entirely insensible, under chloroform.

NEW YORK *April* 24, 1849.

I thought you would be pleased with [Life of Dr.] Channing; The book did me much good. How refreshing to find a man

[1] The Rev. William M. Atkinson, D.D., died February 24, 1849.

who is in earnest about something. I make great distinction between Channing and his biographer: who knows how far the
suppressio has gone? My taste increases for books which flow
straight on, as from an inner source; little erudition, no quotation, no heads or divisions, growing, swelling, &c.: not the less,
because I am individually of the opposite sort, and tend to mince
things up, and put them into patty-pans, with numbers. I got a
shove for weeks from reading "Foster's Estimate of R. Hall, as
a Preacher." Don't fail to read it, especially what he says about
Hall's faults. John Howe is the only Puritan writer of the sort
I mean. Addison, in one or two of his best sermons, exemplifies
my meaning. The year's pew-letting (how I hate it!) has resulted in the taking of as many seats as at any time before: it is
with peculiar pleasure that I see the galleries filling up. Coquerel has an answer to Strauss, which (Unitarian though he be) contains some fine suggestions about the life of Christ. Mr. Gallatin joins in the prayers, which I offer by his bed-side, with a fervour and tenderness which fill me with wonder: I certainly never
saw a human face more radiant with emotion. I wonder if every
other Presbyterian minister in New York feels (in secret) the
same want of brotherly support and communion that I do.
Four distinct times I have essayed a weekly ministerial meeting,
chiefly for prayer. All other sects but ours, I believe, maintain
such a service here.[1] The Düsseldorf collection of paintings, by
great modern Germans, strikes me as surpassing any _collection_
I ever saw. Ensingmuller (?) has a picture in the Academy,
"Christ and his Church," from Solomon's Song: but oh, the
amatoriousness of it, when painted, is fearful! It is the most
gorgeous, furnace-like piece of colouring I ever beheld, and yet
has originality and merit. I am greatly struck with Ezek. xxxv.
10, as a text: "whereas Jehovah was there:" it had escaped me
till now.

New York, May 8, 1849.

Our new house [10 Beach street] is an oddity. It is bulging
in front, deep in the basement, and high like a tower. I cannot
account for it, but I never was in a house from which you could
look down on so many others. From our attic we can count
most of the city steeples. From my study I behold Trinity, St.
Paul's, St. Gardiner's, St. McLauren's, St. Hardenburg's, the
Hospital; and from every front window St. John's tower and
dial. A tall liberty-pole, both front and rear, with conspicuous
vane. Though not precisely on St. John's Park, we are in view,
and have sight of the jet d'eau. For the sake of having a bath-

[1] A meeting of this kind was afterwards established.

room, with hot and cold, and shower, we have even consented to have plumbers and id genus in our kitchen for a week, and have not yet cooked a dinner at home. My study is in a chaotic state. Our yard is smaller than before. We have two good trees at the door, a wide street, free sweep of winds, no neighbour on the west, and exemption from all objects of nuisant aspect. It has been a soaking time for the anniverse, (qu.: "any-fuss-eries"?) the Board of (Foreign) Missions yesterday and to-day: several hours of debate about appointing a general agent; postponed till June. I was glad to hear from the Rev. Dr. J—— (indirectly) that you are the author of the " Letters to a Young Minister."[1] They do you credit. Go on, my dear brother, to rear the tender youth!

NEW YORK, *May* 21, 1849.

Dr. Spring goes to Assembly after all, by the illness of Greenleaf, (green leaves have generally followed Spring.) What a time of disasters! Crevasse at New Orleans; cholera and conflagration at St. Louis; loss of steamboat Empire; riots and cholera here. There is little disposition among us to turn this to a religious account, as our fathers used to do. The true state of the case as to our mob [Astor-Place Opera House] is, that it was crushed by one timely, though afflictive blow, instead of being left to dribble on year after year: it is the first street-disturbance since I have been here. I saw and heard no sign of it; all my information being from the papers. Rauschenbusch (a rough but devoted and Luther-like man) is going back to the West. He says the revolutions have driven to America great numbers of royalists and religious scholars. The average number of sick Germans in the Staten Island Emigrant Hospital is seven hundred. For these there is no Protestant chaplaincy; while the Popish priests and Sisters of Charity are constantly there. A learned and pious German of Elberfeld, named Fliedener, has a seminary for Protestant deaconesses, to do the same work in hospitals that the *Sœurs* do. He has trained one hundred and fifty, some of wealth and rank. He is to be here in July, and I have the promise of being made acquainted with him. Whether feasible or not, the scheme is beautiful and gospel-like. New potatoes abound, from Charleston, at 37½cts. the half peck. The gold dollar is a pretty plaything; I can't think it will live. I am trustee for three persons in the Savings Bank. One of them, a servant, has $200 deposited to-day. Our chambermaid

---

[1] This was a series of articles written by himself, and published in "The Presbyterian."

has $500 there.   One of the officers says a few days ago a known prostitute deposited $1,600, and that they receive a great deal from strange women.   At my communion last Sunday five on examination; one on certificate.   I know of a few persons inquiring.   Mr. Gallatin grows constantly more right-minded in religion; this is the more remarkable, as it includes points on which I never address him, and no other religious person has access to him.

New York, *May* 31, 1849.

Just at this time, as you may suppose, I am in much heaviness.[1]   Only a day or two had I any warning of what was impending, as it did not spring from my Princeton friends.   At this moment I am absolutely void of all information except the telegraphic vote.   The thing gives me unspeakable pain.   To you I will say, believing you can understand it, that any little unction of flattery in the appointment is instantly more than absorbed by the greatness of the question, and the anguish of a separation from my charge, if I accept.   They (with no syllable from me) seem to give up at once, and think I have no option. *This* I do not think: but, at the same time, the judgment of our highest court is very grave, in a case where all previous plans seemed to fail.   There is no need of saying so to the public, but to *know* that I might remain here would be a joy unspeakable. No dreams of mine respecting the social happiness of the pastoral relation have failed to be realized: in this I compare it to marriage.   I have tried academic and Princeton life, and was less happy.   Every thing makes me feel solemn, and I am (not metaphorically, but literally) sick.   All my ministerial friends, to a man, say *Go.*   Seldom have I more deeply felt my utter insignificance—the blindness of fellow-creatures, who from some view of outside think me of any value in such a matter—and the unimportance of the question, in all but a religious and eternal view.   Life is very short: Dirigat Deus !

I have just purchased for the College a collection of ancient Greek and Roman medals, imitated perfectly in a composition of

[1] In the General Assembly, at Pittsburg, May 21, 1849, the Report of the Directors of the Princeton Seminary was received, in which it was announced that the venerable Professor Miller, on account of bodily infirmities, wished to resign his office.   The Assembly resolved to continue Dr. Miller's connexion with the institution, under the title of Emeritus Professor, with its salary and all other rights during his life, and to elect a new professor for the active duties of instruction.   On the 26th May, the Assembly proceeded to the election, and Dr. Alexander received a majority of the votes.   The professorship was that of Ecclesiastical History and Church Government.   Dr. Miller survived until January 7, 1850.

sulphur, as to colour, detrition, &c. They are chronological-
ly arranged in twenty-two boxes, each having six *cassettes*.
They number 6,089. They were made for Lord Vernon, by
Odelli, of Rome. A few alumni of the College, being called on,
raised the money immediately. You can hardly imagine the
effect produced on the imagination by looking over such a series,
so like reality; seeing the same emperor's face, going through
phases, and the legends in such Roman-looking Roman uncials.
I have several things to tell you about Mr. Gallatin, but *coram*.
I think he is renewed by direct spiritual agency. There is a
something which looks more supernatural than what I ever
observed. I want to propose to you an article, which you have
facilities for preparing, in the State Library : a Digest of the
Laws of the several States concerning Marriage, so far as they
respect the officiating clergyman. It might lead to excellent results, and open way for kindred remarks, &c. In some States
ministers are liable in heavy penalties, without any authority to
take depositions, or any protection by license. In Virginia,
most sensibly, all responsibility is on the county-clerk, who gives
the license, after inquiry, oath, &c.[1]

[1] Within a few weeks after the date of this letter, Dr. Alexander declared his acceptance of the professorship, and removed to Princeton.
Although he entered upon the duties of the office soon after the opening
of the session of the Seminary, his inauguration did not take place until
November 20, 1849.

CHAPTER X.

1849—1851.

PRINCETON, *June* 14, 1849.

My anxious suspense is so far relieved that I have determined to remove hither. The voice of the Assembly seemed to leave me little option, except in points of which they could not be cognizant. The voice of my clerical brethren, in and out of New York, so far as known to me, has been in favour of my translation. Jones informs me that this is the unanimous wish in Philadelphia; and a number of my own people have reluctantly owned that they think it my duty to go. I have been somewhat moved by this singular concurrence; but more by the unexpected Providence which has secured such a result, by the frustration of all preceding plans. As to competency I cannot judge of that. As to the comparative importance of the two posts, I have never had any question, that (to one competent) the teaching-place was equal in importance to any ten of the other.

I have seen clearly that the Duane Street Church could live only by moving up-town, and thither I wished not to move. I have seen as clearly that my powers were tasked to a tension which must soon be fatal; while, in the steadier routine of teaching, I might last a season, with ordinary favour of Providence.

Do not be surprised to see me on Sunday, but do not look for me. My going, if I go, is merely to attend on my father. I have been very much unwell, even in bed for a time. The cause I think was my extreme trouble of mind about removal.

PRINCETON, *June* 30, 1849.

Again our relation is changed, and you are once more the city, and I the country mouse. President Bonaparte seems to be contradicting all previous beliefs of his imbecility : they say he managed the late émeute admirably. You see *Baptist* W. Noel has become an anabaptist. I am in the thick of painting, scouring, mending, whitening, &c., and have not yet got in any of my furniture. I have never read such personality and scurrility in ecclesiastical debate in the United States, as in the two Scotch Assemblies. In the Established Church they debated three hours about the two nominees for Moderator, Bell and Simpson ; with very unbecoming opprobrium on both. Nobody seems to know any thing of Bannerman, who succeeds Dr. Chalmers ; he may be none the worse for that. Addison (pro more) has moved again, and has chambers in the Seminary, lowest floor, front, next to Dr. Hodge's.

PRINCETON, *July* 19, 1849.

Paint, paint ! Hammer, Hammer ! Still in transitu. When a house has had no regular inhabitant for four or five years, it is wonderful how many things get awry ; locks, keys, grates, pothooks, pins, bolts, panes, drawers, knobs, ceilings, floors, steps, spouts, shingles, gates, hinges, coops, well-buckets, volunteer trees, weeds, &c. We have not got in yet; though I write in my quondam study. I will give you two hundred young paper-mulberry trees, now growing in my grounds, on condition you take away the parent dittos. An excellent, pious cook, whom we left in New York, has had the cholera; a girl of whom I made a little purchase of mint lozenges the other day, has since died of the same. Mrs. S. (New York) was taken with formidable symptoms, including marble-coldness, sinking, and nausea, on Sunday night. Dr. Beatty of Ohio, who is here, encountered cases everywhere on the canal. In an upland village near him, the Rev. John K. Cunningham, one of our alumni, has lost his wife, and seven or eight valuable members of his church. —— is a good-natured fellow, and I think may be led into ways of much more usefulness than he has. When I see how he has gained in a year or two, I have hopes he may get over even his desire *digito monstrarier.* In Princeton College, I am certain, a boy will be better taught, more developed, and made a man of, than in a city college. True, he will be more endangered ; but, after all, strength cannot come but by some peril. I have scarcely ever known a studious boy injured in college; never one who added good habits and dutifulness, on entrance. Though I own my parental apprehensions would forbid me to do it, I soberly think our sons would gain most, by going through the entire college-trials, commons and all.

The only critical case among the car-wrecked people,[1] is that
of Walters. Mr. Schenck, Dr. Maclean, and Dr. Hodge have
been daily with the afflicted. Three of them have chiefly fallen
under my notice; one of these is a black woman, a seemingly
pious Baptist. Another, dreadfully hurt in the legs—wounds
a hand's breadth deep, with iron screw in bottom of one—
is a good-looking German tanner, from Magdeburg. He cannot
speak a word of English. This morning it occurred to me to
quote the beginning of the Hymn, " O Haupt voll Blut und
Wunden;" he immediately repeated the whole fourteen stanzas
of eight lines each; it was evidently to him an act of devotion.
He also repeated two other long hymns, highly evangelical, but
new to me. What an instance of the good of hymns got by
heart! Next to him lies a New York Yankee, who perhaps does
not know one, though the more intelligent, and possibly the
more pious of the two. The Company spare no pains: indeed
no pains or price can neutralize the effect of the testimony before
the coroner. Our lives have all been at the mercy of a switch-
tender, who may be miles away. I think it a kindly Providence
that the sufferers are where they can receive so much soothing
and useful truth. I preached to a fine congregation on Fast Day,
at Blawenburg, and to Africans on Sunday. I desire not to be
away for more than a night, till I can get through my heavy
preparations. After I am a week or two warm in the saddle, I
will gladly give you one, two, or three Sundays. Mr. de San-
dran, the French master, died this morning from apoplexy.
Though somewhat settled, our painters have left us with a number of window-shutters off, front-door barricaded, and stairs un-
carpeted. We took in half a hogshead of water, which entered
loft, attic, and guest-chamber. Chancellor, Bishop, and Dr.
Johns have each a son in College. Accession about 50. Prof.
Loomis is recalled to University, New York city. I fear we
none of us feel duly our exemption from the plague, (cholera.)
What a difference between Trenton and Brunswick! By avoiding all aperient fruits and vegetables, I have, since coming here,
enjoyed (what I never had before in July) a perfect regularity of
health. Still I look on the cholera very much as I do on a stroke
of lightning, and have no notion of charging every one who has
it with imprudence. Two deaths of it on Sourland Mountain, in
a high, airy, secluded nook. At Blockley they tried every variety
of approved practice; almost all died. Several very near neighbours of ours in New York have been carried off by it, including
two physicians, and three in the family of one of them.

[1] An accident on the railway near Princeton.

PRINCETON, *August* 28, 1849.

I do not know that I ever applied myself more constantly or closely than for two months past. On the 30th our duties begin. The next two Sabbaths I expect to preach in Duane street. For some time past Mr. Gallatin was unable to see me, or even hear my name. Just before his death his exercises were as follows: "He has been at the point of death, and his situation is still very critical. During his extremest illness he had the most blessed assurance of acceptance and salvation through Christ, repeatedly praising and thanking God for his mercies and goodness, in that *he* should have been made a partaker of this salvation, as he expressed himself continually. The God-Man still a mystery to him, but (no longer doubted) fully believed and received. For one hour heaven was opened unto him, and he appeared on the threshold of Eternity; but it pleased God to bring him again to earth, with shattered frame and intellect, &c."

I own no copy of Doddridge but the one volume one. By-the-bye, I have got more good from that book than from any commentator. There ought to be a new edition with modernized references; nobody knows the numerous dissenting authors whom he cites in the notes. Addison has saddled himself with a tremendous job in his book on Psalms, but his working-power exceeds any thing I ever dreamt of. I hope you see Copperfield, [Dickens' Tale;] it is delightful and useful. I wish you had been here to meet the Rev. Theodore Fliedner, of Prussia, who has been at Dr. Hodge's. For thirteen years, besides being a pastor, he has been training Christian nurses, (sœurs de charité,) or, "Evangelical deaconesses," of whom he and his wife have trained a hundred and fifty. He has been making a flying visit to the United States, to set up four of his deaconesses at Pittsburg. They are under no vows, but engage to serve five years. I have his reports. Among his subscribers are all the royal and princely names of Prussia, and all the ecclesiastical authorities. He is a most earnest, one-idead man, full of the tenderness gendered by such pursuits. Some of his remarks in conversation abridged: "You Americans far surpass us in some things, especially in practical tact; but O, what a want of tenderness and heart! O, what singing in the churches; not half singing; and some schools where no singing is taught! Your American church is a good *father*, but it is not a *mother;* it lacks the mother-love to the poor, and sick, and prisoner. This you leave to Free Masons, Odd Fellows, and Sons of Temperance. Your young ministers are not trained at bedsides, and in gaols; the best training. Are the difficulties greater for you than for Papists? Surely, there are maiden ladies in America who would love to nurse Christ in his sick members." He publishes a Magazine for the *Poor and Sick*, and for those who attend them. I have it. They have been especially useful in the Magdalen cause, (as it is calumniously called.) I don't think I shall ever lose the impression of his gentleness and energy. If I hear of his coming here, in time, I will send for you, and you must come, if only for an hour.

PRINCETON, *September* 13, 1849.

Since I wrote last, I have passed through a thicket of thoughts and cares, though I have been blessed with unusual health. My new business involves more pressing study than I had thought; and in a new habitation there are daily wants emergent which take time and money. Then the pleasing-painful care of other peoples' cares has been daily. I am glad you have escaped the model of the Pántheon, as all un-hellenistic people call it, even in verse. See Pope to the contrary. My inauguration is to be on the 20th of November: at which time you will appear at bed and board. Phillips and Plumer induct, by charge and sermon. " O Mother dear Jerusalem," is a famous Scotch hymn or ballad, by Dickson of the 17th century. I cannot lay my hands on it: it is very long, and is the mother dear of " Jerusalem my Happy Home." The least of my doubts concerning Fliedner is on the point you mention: I think it clear that there were deaconesses of old. Look at 1 Tim. iii. 11, of which the whole force is lost in our version: γυναῖκας does not mean *their wives* (why should the qualifications of wives of *deacons* and of no other officers be named?) but *the females*, i. e. the *deaconesses*. Just look at this in the whole connexion. I am afraid you will find the chronology of our Lord's doctrines second in perplexity only to the precession of the equinoxes. My poor congregation in New York is in a bad way. The two or three old-hunkers, who can't see that the earth has gone round any since Dr. Romeyn's day, would never believe (what is undeniable) that the Church cannot be maintained where it is, except as a free church. This I perceived two years ago, and discovered six months ago that five-sixths of the people were ready to move. But the plan was quashed by the conservatives, and I fear they will be left alone, unless they in stanter remove. The house is almost embedded in sugar-refineries and other stews. Its real supporters live far above it. Drs. Spring and McElroy will soon go up, and the sense of being a preacher to a fluent crowd was what chiefly discouraged me, and hindered my labours. I say these things to them freely now, because they cannot charge me with any worldly lust of a better *locale*, which they constructively did while I was with them. I have said to Mr. Auchincloss that two years hence there cannot by possibility be a Presbyterian church at that corner. They must choose between scattering (already repeated till the identity is gone) and removal. The greater the man they get, the sooner will he translate the Church. Lower New York is in no proper sense other than as a *warehouse*, compared with a *dwelling*.

Our Directors being done with, do come on and bring your family. I have beans and spinach, and a bushel of sour grapes; and though beef is rare, we have a great diversity of agnine parts, such as neck, breast, loin, kidneys, &c. My dear old father is a little unwell again. He will preach when asked, and people will ask him. Two sermons and a lecture in three days!

PRINCETON, *September* 19, *pridie Æquinoct.*, 1849.

In the sore loss of my parochial comforts, which were always delightful to me, in the net result, and which are to a sincere man a sort of expansion of his fireside pleasures, I try to comfort myself by looking with new eyes on my pupils. We have matriculated fifty-three, and "still they come." I am struck with the amount of good healthy flesh and bone. Nothing is so pleasing to me as the Sunday *conference.*[1] It is a genuine primitive "prophesying." My dear old father, whose feebleness reaches my heart, is nowhere so felicitous. About half the young men are off at schools and meetings. The subjects are always practical or experimental. When you exchange with me, be sure to arrange for attending this meeting. Of Scots and Hibernians we have about a dozen, several being Glasgow graduates; also a Baptist preacher, and wife, from Charleston. Last year there were five or six Baptists, all most promising men. Dr. Miller is really too weak to go about with safety. John Miller, after the tour of Europe, and after being a prisoner for half a day in Rome, seeing the Pope's house at Gaeta, and lying ill in Holland, is on the return, viâ Edinburgh. —— is a good preacher, a pious man, a most affable, unpretending companion, but overladen with extraordinary knowledge of books, beyond proportion to his mental powers. That is a splendid oration of Victor Hugo at the Peace Congress. You have, through ——, an opportunity to get a national thanksgiving on account of the diminution of the pestilence. Poor Blythe is still silenced, by sequelæ of dysentery. The Second Church is nearly ready; a snug little place. Washington Irving, in his "Goldsmith," has *illy*, and several other illiterate expressions.

[1] A meeting for devotion and remarks on topics of experimental religion, held by the professors with the students of the Seminary, every Lord's-day afternoon.

PRINCETON, *October* 4, 1849

I have for you a copy of " O Mother Dear," singularly thrown in my way, how or whence I know not: I picked it up in the mire of the road. The Mons. Perrin you name is an extraordinary violinist; except the miraculous Oles and Sivoris, he beats any thing I remember. As to stoves, I anticipated your despair. The diversification is ridiculous, like Horace's

Qui variare cupit rem prodigialiter unam.

I have stuck an old second-hand franklin in my study-hearth, for wood: it does well enough for moderate weather. I shall miss nothing of New York so much as English coal; for I can't afford to burn it here.

I should like to lend you Milman's History of Christianity, volume by volume, for though it is written with an almost infidel coolness, it is the only English work that gives the distilled essence of the Germanic researches into out-of-the-way antiquities of early mother church. If I live, I must be some years familiarizing myself with the original documents of the former ages.

It would be chimerical to expect the same watch over hundreds of young men as a father has over half-a-dozen; and there must also be a period of transition from home to the world, but this period should be (O how carefully!) guarded. I should like to have the following queries discussed in some journal, concerning any college, or all colleges: How often does the President appear in private chambers? How many times in a year does he avail himself of the prayer-assembly, to make any fatherly remarks? What assurance have you that lads are in their chambers from 11—12 P. M.? Suppose twenty are at a grog-hole all night, what means of assuring yourselves of this? What limit to walking all over the city or village on Sunday? What superintendence at feeding-time, in those houses where ten to twelve fellows take their grub separate from the family?

Great evils arise in the United States from the ease with which new congregations, churches, and even sects are formed. Ex. gr.: suppose a minority in Smithville choose to do wrong. Presbytery animadverts. Minority turns on heel; " who cares!" Presbytery more stringent. Minority turns on heel; new church; two steeples; two miserable handfuls; two starving preachers; perhaps one independent society. There is no disgrace, and little difficulty, in rearing a new sect. Hence an ecclesiastical censure is *brutum fulmen;* and hence church courts shrink from uttering their thunders. Our practice is a century or more below our book of discipline, in all courts but the highest; and nobody abides by acts of General Assembly, whether anent sitting in prayer, or reading in preaching.   A vermilion edict.

PRINCETON, *October* 12, 1849.

There is a remarkable amount of indisposition in the Seminary, though nobody very ill, nor prevalence of any one disease. At least ten are on the sick-list.   One young man of college, native of Scotland, lies very low with dysentery.   I have preached as much as usual ever since I left New York, besides the tough work of getting ready for classes.[1]

On reaching Princeton, I had hard work to get ready for my lecture at 11 o'clock.   Just as we were sitting down to dinner we perceived the house of our neighbour, Mrs. Armstrong, to be on fire.   Our gardens join, though she fronts on Stockton street. The wind was towards us, and at that moment very high. Providence ordered several things most happily : the wind was from the house ; it was mid-day ; Edward Armstrong was in his mother's house ; and a new fire-engine had just been procured to be handselled on this occasion.   Commodore Stockton was soon on the roof, with the face of a coal-man.   Armstrong thinks he saved the house.   Every thing was removed from it.   The chief damage is the kitchen part, which is pretty much unroofed. It came of the country practice of burning a chimney during the heavy rain of the morning.

PRINCETON, *October* 15, 1849.

I wish I had begun early to mark places in the New Testament, in which the play of the sound is lost in English.   I note these in my morning lesson : 2 Cor. iii. 5, 6, " Not that we are ἱκανοι of ourselves, to think any thing . . . . but the ἱκανότης is of God, who also ἱκάνωσεν *us ministers* of the New Testament. O that we could English that glorious passage, 2 Cor. iv. 8, seq. ! The jingle is lost, and in our version what a bathos, from change of usage in a word, is here : " We are troubled on every side, yet not *distressed !*"   Tyndale says, " without shyft."   Try your hand on the whole passage, in translation ; it will at least breed a sermon.   The ἐν παντί seems to qualify all the series.   " In this whole life of ours, we are pressed, but not oppressed," (pressed to death ;) clause out : " ἀπορούμενοι, desponding, but not ἐξαπορούμειοι, despairing ;"   Wiclif renders νέκρωσιν, " sleying," and the Rhemists, " mortification," both actively.   I believe this is the only classical sense.   I had just been reading with wonder

---

[1] The number of his sermons in 1844 was 97 ; 1845, 117 ; 1846, 120 ; 1847, 107 ; 1848, 109 ; 1849, 80.   His farewell sermon was preached in Duane Street, June 10, 1849, from 1 Cor. iii. 21–23.

Prof. Guyot's (Agassiz's friend) "Earth and Man," when I this morning fell in with him at Dr. Hodge's. Guyot and Prof. Henry are busy at the making some thousands of barometers at New York, for government. He is a tenderly pious man; you would be delighted to hear such childlike *French* Christianity from such a philosopher; he is brother-in-law of Grandpierre. "The revolution of 1848, unlike that of 1830, declares war against learning and science; these are aristocratical. Down with all aristocracy!—of mind—yes, even of *morals.*" This avowed by a very distinguished leader, of genius, in the Canton de Vaud: "Down with all mentalism, ideology!" "The next generation growing up in this sensualism." He thinks the secession of F. Monod, Bridel, &c., very wrong. "Result of breaking connexion with state, would be to leave at least half the Protestant churches without service; and this in an unchristian population. Dare we take the responsibility of such a crisis?" He thinks we have no notion of the prevalence of atheism among the mass in Germany and Switzerland.

I feel the week's *ideology* does not fit me bodily for Sunday-ism: I came flagged to the "desk:" yesterday two sermons: this morning nervous. I did not leave pastoral life willingly; I foresaw the very evils I begin to feel; but they distress me more than I reckoned for. I miss my old women; and especially my weekly catechumens,[1] my sick-rooms, my rapid walks, and my nights of right-down fatigue. Prof. Henry is lecturing a rapid course, to the unspeakable delight of the collegians; his studies were always pleasing to them, though he was such a driller.

PRINCETON, *November*, 8, 1849.

Bill concerning Old Correspondents.

"*Sec.* 10. And be it enacted, that in case any citizens shall cause it to appear that they have communicated, conferred, or corresponded, by letter or epistle, for the term of thirty years, the said citizens shall have the franking privilege for the remainder of their natural lives, etc."

Craven has just got back from South Hampton (one of four Hamptons, of) Long Island. Strange place! Puritan settlement: scarce altered in two hundred years: insulated: antique fashions: 1,700 parishioners: no church but Presbyterian in all the district: wealthy farmers: surface of ground covered with

---

[1] He contributed to the Repertory this year a paper on "The History of Catechizing." His other articles in the volume of 1849 were on the Baptist Controversy, on the Family of Arnauld, (as connected with Jansenism and Port Royal,) and on the Autobiography of the Rev. Dr. Ashbel Green.

rotting sea-fish, their only manure. Every serious wound leads to tetanus ; same in adjacent parishes. Five times as many at church in afternoon as in morning. Farmers do not live on their farms, but in hamlets : thirteen elders, one or more in each hamlet. In the village of S—— not one male communicant, but many in the church. All these have joined in revivals. Among their ministers have been Jonathan Edwards, Dr. Buel, and Dr. Beecher. Imperturbable in old habits. Vacant, but won't accept one as candidate till he has preached for them three months. All their produce goes to Sag Harbour. These gleanings from my father. Dr. Hare's sermon, showing that baptized children are church members. Once it was our doctrine, but New England has conquered. Every now and then I hear a new word added to the college lingo : e. g. "Half the Junior class are taking *privates*, (*q. d.* private lessons, with a tutor, so as to keep up with Prof. Alexander's hard mathematics.) Webster's Dictionary, last edition, has all the English University terms, such as Little-go, Tripos-papers, Wrangler, Optimes, Corpus, &c. If you ever need a French dictionary, buy the last and best " French and English, and English and French Dictionary, &c., &c., by A Spiers." 1849. PARIS. 8vo, pp. 1331 : $4 : bound in France. In Boston, Little and Brown. It is under the auspices of Guizot, Villemain, and many savans and litterateurs in England and France. Agréez, Monsieur, &c.

PRINCETON, *November* 14, 1849.

My mind does not easily leave the death-bed scene of our dear young friend Candor,[1] with whom I have spent many hours of the last few days. I went from his speechless countenance to marry ——, and hurried back to find him just gone. He was ill six weeks, and never seemed to me to suffer much more in mind or body than you or I probably this moment. It was a most natural death-bed, if I may say so of what was so gracious. Perhaps a dozen hymns were sung around him yesterday up to the very cessation of his utterance : there was no loquacity or tendency to talk of his exercises, but an uncontrollable thirst for prayers, hymns, and Scriptures. I preached from 1 Thess. iv. 14, on " sleep in Jesus." His friends admitted with surprise that his fellow-students nursed him with a skill, devotion, and gentleness, that scarcely a father's house could have afforded, for so long an illness. He was one of the first minds of our house, as formerly of the college. This morning Dr. Miller sent for me, and for the first time in his life did not rise

[1] John Montgomery Candor, of Pennsylvania, a student in the Seminary.

when I entered. He then formally made over to me the charge
of the instruction, and said, inter alia : " No, sir, my time is
come. I must go to the grave ; no skill of man can do me any
good." He no longer drives out. Every expression connects
itself with his departure. In all my life I never saw a gentler
decline, or a more serene, collected, looking into eternity. Our
numerous cases of illness in the Seminary have kept me in parochial service, and our pot has been constantly over the fire with
beef-tea, broth, &c. One case remains. God grant that our
chastening may mend us, and be removed. There is far more
to reach the feelings in my Seminary connexion, than I knew of.
A woman who works for us informs my wife (but for which I
should not know it) that a highly respectable student of ours, a
fine, cheerful fellow, boards himself at a widow's house, and that
he has had one piece of meat in three weeks. This of course I
will not suffer ; but many a private Christian might relieve such
a case, by intermitting pies and puddings for a month. Two
young men have had to go off to schools.

I am giving you a very grave letter. Sometimes one reads
that men may be known by their letters, and biographies go upon this postulate. Certainly it fails sometimes as to habitual
moods. *E. g.* In my private hours, nine out of ten, I am grave
even to a fault. In my letters I am apt to seek recreation ; they
are a sort of conversation. I never saw it alluded to, except by
Boz, (frequently by him,) but the funniest things that ever come
to my tongue's end, are in seasons of deep affliction, so that re-
pression is needed, to save appearances. While moralizing, let
me add, there is a great distinction between *grief* and *misery;*
how often are we profoundly sorrowful, without being unhappy.
Our adorable Lord was a " man of sorrows," and (beautiful !)
וִידֻעַ חֹלִי, " a (familiar) *brother of grief ;*" but how remote from
being miserable ! I am half afraid I am under some hallucina-
tion, or morbid judgment, but for several years I have sickened
at the common way of outcry against specific amusements ; sermons and tracts anent them, &c. : in one view all the meetings
of our unconverted hearers are frivolous ; but are they worst
when they are merriest ? This is dangerous ground, and I sus-
pect myself ; but my error is corrigible, and it surely does not
grow out of any disposition to practise on the light fantastic toe.
I believe, however, that sourness, moroseness, censoriousness,
malice, lust, envy, and two or three other things, may eat as
doth a canker in people who never danced. The hours of Inauguration Day are these, as per minutes : " Sermon be preached in
the church at half-past 2 o'clock, and that the inauguration services take place in the church in the evening." 1. Sermon by

Dr. Plumer. 2. Charge by Dr. Phillips. 3. Inaugural Discourse.[1]

PRINCETON, *December*, 1849.

I found a warfare waging between Elders A—— and B——, as to whether of the twain should entertain you, [in New York.] Mr. A—— will, however, take no denial, and Mr. B—— reluctantly yields. You cannot go to a more hospitable roof than that of 40 Barclay street. Prepare to hear of perfections in your humble servant, which your lack of acquaintance has kept you from knowing. Try to see the Panorama of the Nile. Drop into Garrigue's, under Astor House, and see German Annuals, &c. If you name me to G—— or to Evans, (Putnam's salesman, son of an East India Baptist Missionary, and born in Sumatra,) they will probably do me the favour of being extra polite, as metropolites to a cosmopolite Tridentopolite. Look (at G.'s) at Retzsch, Reinecke Fuchs, and Outlines of Thorwaldsen's Statues. G. is a Dane, but speaks every thing. Dr. Raphael is making a noise among the numerous Christians who think everybody who is circumcised authorized to expound the Old Testament. M—— is still bedridden; quere: bed-*riding?* The Scotch say bed-*fast.*

Kinney [of Newark] lectured here last evening; a most ornate, eloquent, and patriotic discourse. I never heard a better of the kind. I received from a nameless person in Duane street $200 for sick students, with a promise to sustain two poor students.

Dr. Miller has declined very gradually even till now. His greeting to my brother Samuel was, "Almost home." Take it altogether I never knew such a euthanasy. All the decorum of his long life kept up " duntaxat ad imum." Never one intrusion of doubt. Heaven has seemed just as much a-jar, as his next-door bedroom. Still in his study, among his life-long things, and still in a sort of chair, not bed. It is not four days since he ceased going to the table. He forbids prayer for recovery; longs to depart : has not seemed to have any anxiety but about the church, for a long time. Often has wept, more than of old, on spiritual matters. Greatly revived at hearing of conversions, &c. Our year's text is, *Looking unto Jesus.*

PRINCETON, *January* 8, 1850.

When I heard last night, Dr. Miller was almost gone; like a

---

[1] The inauguration of Dr. Alexander took place according to this programme November 20, 1849. The three discourses were published together by the Board of Directors. The subject of the Professor's inaugural was, "The value of Church History to the Theologian of our Day."

sleeping child, but knew my father. One of the boys came in as I had penned this, to say that Dr. Miller died last night about 11, a few hours after my father saw him ; without any struggle, oppression, or seeming pain. The funeral is to be from the church, on Thursday, (January 10,) at 2 o'clock. It has been a great comfort to the Doctor to have his medical son with him so many weeks. The Doctor was in his 81st year. Of all the deaths I ever knew, this is the most surrounded by all the things one could desire.

[Rev. David] Trumbull gives me a volume of information about Chili : he has a wonderful eye for observation and power of making you know what he means : accost him. I am glad Valparaiso has a man of so much shrewdness. Some day get David King of our first class to preach for you. He is our Asaph, and is singularly discreet and grave.[1]

PRINCETON, *February* 20, 1850.

I have your full letter from Washington. You must have had a delightful time in the " Federal City," as my father, *more veterum*, still calls it. I can't help thinking the responsibility of the Union lies just now on the North. Garrison, &c., of course must feel bound in conscience to change the Constitution, and abolish slavery ; but other northern parties seem to me to have some place for concession, as they are the people who cry out so against disunion. The impending evil all seems to result from the provision of the Californians, a provision which I can't help thinking was unnecessary. Nobody questions the right of a *State* to abolish slavery. Why throw such an apple of gold into the race of Atalanta ?

All the United States Missionaries in India break down, but not the Britons. The Allahabad College teaches as high branches as ours. Bishop Wilson says our men there are the most learned body in India.

Schaff says a number of spicy things in his January number, [Mercersburg Review.] Among others, of " the sad and humbling experiences" of the Episcopalians " with some of their highest functionaries," in New Jersey, North Carolina, New York, Pennsylvania, and Constantinople.   " All these disturbing

[1] Mr. King was a native of Scotland, and remarkable for the melody of his voice in speaking. In another letter he is called " the sweet singer of our Israel David King." He declined a call from the Duane Street congregation in the spring of 1850, and accepted one from Jersey City, where he was installed. His health soon failed, and he was about to take charge of a smaller congregation at Stillwater, in the Presbytery of Troy ; but before his installation he was removed by death, May 15, 1853.

phenomena, besides their personal aspect, have a general signifi-
cancy ; they are not only symptoms of a diseased church, which
is pulled asunder two opposite ways, never having been able to
find as a basis that wholesome mean between Rome and Geneva,
which once she vaunted, but they are also a judgment concerning
all overhasty and impatient attempts to buttress up Protestant
ism from without in a mechanical way. It is true, Protestantism
is making uneasy efforts beyond itself, and struggling also in
other sections, and other ways, besides that of Puseyism, towards
a churchly remodelling ; but its rent garment will not allow
patching with a few rags from the old-clothes-room of antiquity.
New wine must not be put into old bottles, else the bottles are
rent, and the wine lost."

PRINCETON, *March* 5, 1850.

I don't know on whose side the shuttlecock has fallen, but I
have had my hands very full of writing, having worked along to
the Reformation-period, as good Mr. Pollock might say. Renewed studies of Luther have made me admire and love him
more than ever. You will have heard that Mr. Schenck is
having daily meetings. I fail to perceive a very deep stirring
of the people's mind, or special tenderness under the Word ;
but thirty to forty have been to talk with the pastor, and a number are reported to be in a state of hope. It is certainly something to get large numbers willing to be approached, and anxious
to hear truth ; and I believe this is so. My brother William is
about to set up " the Princeton Magazine ;" pp. 48, monthly.
Of course we shall all help. It will not exclude scientific, classical, erudite, sportive, or Jersey articles. Probably a number
out three weeks hence. "Princeton in 1801," will open it, a reminiscence of my father.[1] The oldest graduate, S. Baldwin of
Newark, is dead ; class of 1770. Alexander Hamilton was his

---

[1] Twelve numbers of this magazine appeared in 1850, after which it was
discontinued. The brothers James and Addison made it the repository of
many of their desultory effusions. The hand of the former is seen in such
subjects as "Education among Merchants," "The Prospects of the Me-
chanic," "The Working Man's Aim," "Wordsworth," "Le Pays Latin,"
"Books and Business," "Æsthetics," "Minor Works of Dr. Johnson,"
"Machinery and Labour," "The Physiognomy of Houses," "Letters on the
Early Latin Writers," "Roadside Architecture." The sportive and ironical
wit of the other brother is detected in most of the humorous pieces with
which the magazine abounds. Among these is the satirical poem which
soon attracted extensive notice—"The Reconstruction of Society." In a
letter to the editor of these Letters, from the late Mr. Walsh, (Paris, Nov.
12, 1850,) that eminent scholar wrote—"The promise of the youth of the
brothers Alexander seems to have been fulfilled. The Magazine abounds
with matter which I read with keen relish."

scholar. He was here when Witherspoon came. I have fallen
into a hymn-book-correspondence with Dr. Demme.

I have only within a few weeks authentically traced up my
mother's mother to my g. g. g. g. grandfather Benjamin Harrison, born in Surry, in 1645; ob. 1713. A copy of his will is extant. It delights me to find that I have been erroneously claiming descent from Butcher Harrison, one of King Charles's judges.

PRINCETON, *March* 19, 1850.

I went to bed the night after I saw you, and have not been
out of doors since. Dieting has reduced me very much. Meanwhile I have lost all but the report of the awakening here;
which is very remarkable in the college. Forsyth says: "There
is not a student in the whole 200+, who does not invite or
expect religious conversation." The best scholars, and the very
ringleaders in vice, have been prostrated. Two of the managers
of the Commencement Ball, (for next June,) Virginia bloods,
have proposed to do away the ball; a nuisance which the Trustees have feared to abate, and which for twenty years has drawn
in even several of our less spiritual professing Christians, or
their children. The whole college may be said to be temporarily seeking God. Many of these young men are the only
known members of large connexions, who care about religion.
In this view, when I admit some mistakes and some excitement,
a great point is gained; a great amount of truth is thrown into
minds of ductile youth; vice is silenced; truth is owned; discipline is re-established; even if all who seem to be converted
are not so. But of all these things I have seen nothing. Thirty-
nine joined the Communion; thirty reported converts are yet
behind, in the village. Schenck [the pastor of the First Church]
says most of the awakened say their impressions have been on
them for months; this is usual. In 1844, Dr. Rice admitted
thirty-eight at one time. These show as well, so far as I know,
as other professors. Two Romish republican priests, a Neapolitan and a Genoese, are coming here to study, &c. I hope
they will do better than previous refugees. Duncan Kennedy
has a unanimous call to Duane. Coming doubtful. He is by
birth a Scot. I am slowly and feebly working on a tract, long
on hand, for incoming German emigrants. I desire to have
it published in German, say by the American Tract Society. I
have tried in vain to get something of the kind. It contemplates
temporals as well as spirituals. The Eclectic Review has
fallen into infidel hands; Dr. Price having yielded the rédaction
in favour of a young colleague of W. J. Fox, M. P., the Socinian or Straussian preacher of London.

PRINCETON, *March* 22, 1850.

Monod's extracts (in the Presbyterian) from De Wette's preface is very instructive; I had seen the preface before. It touches your question about Antichrist.[1] Though in difficulty about the Man of Sin, I can't feel satisfied with any thing that reaches through so many ages. " Pantheistic Infidelity " comes near it. Schérer, of Geneva, gives up inspiration. We have an original exposée from him to Merle. He is just a Quaker, as to these things. He calls our old doctrine of inspiration a *gastro-mythic cabbalistique;* rejects 2 Peter, Jude, Revelation, (which is full of lies ;) and makes, of course, nothing of the Old Testament. About sixteen out of twenty students (Geneva) go with Schérer. The " numbering of the people " gives following results :

Blacks converted (it began with them ; say)	15
Presbyterian Congregations . . .	60
College	40
Methodists report	80
	195

There is no abatement of the stir. About thirty-seven additional in college are serious. I observe that our butchers, bakers, and id genus, flock to meetings, and talk of little else.

A black girl (æt 13, but smart) came to me under deep and intelligent conviction ; caused by [Episcopal] Rector Paterson's sermon last Sunday ; she sits in his gallery. About 15—20 of the impressed in college are his hearers. Some of the most resisting and opposing persons in college, are sons of good men, and ministers. Snodgrass has admitted 100 at his new Goshen. The whole east end of Long Island is in a blaze, especially East Hampton, where there is no pastor. It was there that Dr. Buel and Dr. Beecher were settled. Everything in that isolated region remains as 200 years ago.

PRINCETON, *May* 6, 1850.

My father's Reminiscences of Patrick Henry, in the May [Princeton] Magazine, will be worth copying in newspapers. Enter Mr. M. from Baden. " Sare ! You speak ze Fransh or ze German ?" Mr. M. desires to study theology ; has been a

---

[1] The question of his correspondent was—" Is not the ' Man of Sin ' a bigger man than the Pope ? Is he not the αποστασις of all heresy, crime, backsliding in the Church from Paul's day downwards, and appearing to the Apostle in the revelation to him of the future history of the Church, like the one great image of Nebuchadnezzar, foreshadowing many eras and heterogeneous powers ? There were ' many Anti-Christs' in John's day."

functionary in the treasury of the grand-duke of Baden. Our two Italians differ. B. has a plebeian and *patrickian* look; speaks beastly Latin, and no English; says he was Captain in the Revolution, and (I fear me) is some day to be a burden and plague to his patrons.[1] T. (whatever he is in heart) is eminently a scholar and a gentleman; in either capacity fit to be presented anywhere. His chagrin under the other's contiguity, is admirable. They never met till here. The ordination occurs on the very day our Examen begins; I can do no more than run down to the evening diet.[2] Dr. Wayland is proposing a radical reform in Colleges; just what Jefferson set on foot in his University: abolition of four-year course, mock diplomas, honorary degrees, &c. I agree in every point; and did before I left the college. A letter of Dr. W. Shippen, *penes me*, speaks of President Edwards as a " pretty gentleman," and of President Finley as " our stiff, stammering Dr. Finley."

Yesterday, five churches here had Communion. I was with the second (Presbyterian) where fifteen were added on examination. At the first, thirty-four on examination. All disappointed, misanthropic fellows seem of necessity to doubt about church efforts, seminaries, and whatever has grown up within thirty years.

The Anniversaries in New York have got to be scarcely an attraction. It is remarkable how great the proportion of New Englanders is in the crowd. They doubtless tend to keep up very strongly a certain type of religious activity. The only one in which I ever felt any religious advantage, was the A. B. C. F. Missions, which is always managed with wisdom; speakers not snatched up by accident.

PRINCETON, *May* 21, 1850.

On Saturday I went to New York as an escort to my honoured parents, and returned in the evening to New Brunswick. Coming homeward from New York, I fell in with M., who talked abundance of smart things, and some very good, against Agassiz and the many-race hypothesis. I tabernacled with P., where, as before, I was both humbled and edified at his extraordinary ways of making the Sabbath a delight, and teaching good things to his children. I have never been in a family in which so

---

[1] This was fulfilled. B. succeeded in obtaining a Presbyterial license as probationer, but it was afterwards revoked. T. afterwards set up an Italian paper, *Il Esule Italiano*, in New York.

[2] The ordination of Messrs. Horatio W. Shaw and Lawrence G. Hay, missionaries to India, which took place at Trenton, May 8th, at which service Dr. J. W. Alexander preached.

much is made of the Bible, with so little fuss. One of his boys, about fourteen, repeated a large part of a chapter in the Gospel of John, in Greek, evidently understanding it well. A boarder-boy, on Saturday evening, repeated the whole of the third chapter of Colossians.

PRINCETON, June 3, 1850.

You are too severe in your stricture on seminary teaching. I never heard the methods complained of as failing to make ministerial practice the daily end. Whole portions of the course have no other ingredient; as Dr. Miller's lectures on Sermons and Discipline, and the long series of teachings in pastoral theology. Other portions daily include the same, at proper places. The separate teaching of experimental religion, would be finely illustrated by our Presbyterial examinations thereanent.

West Point is as near perfect (for its ends) as any thing I ever saw. What an incomparable locality! esplanade, water, mountains, verdure, ruins, decorations! I had a pleasant day there. The music delightful; the appearance of the cadets, and the separate drill of the regulars, were up to all my imagination of that sort of beauty. The new railway along the Hudson is a convenience; forty miles an hour, sometimes.

6*th.*—Backwardness in Repertory copy, has driven me from epistolary to journalistic elaboration; (there's a fine modern sentence for you.)[1] From Duane St. people I have received, since I left them, (and all but $100 unsolicited,) $1,500 for Seminary wants. The panorama of Italy is the next thing to travel there. Barnum is delivering temperance lectures; will he not one day compete with —— for presidentship? A seemingly crazed minister called this morning, in forma pauperis. B. is on the text "I go a-fishing." He is to settle in a new church in Brooklyn. Lanneau [Missionary to Palestine] tells me he preached eight years in Arabic. C. is going or gone to California with Spieker, the inventor.[2] Dr. T. declares the method new and infallible; but this does not ensure the profit of it. No other preparation, known to chemists, will solve the gold without solving the other things. A pound of black sand was given to the usual operators in New York, and a pound of the same to T. Cost of extracting by former$=2.+$; cost by latter less than one cent. Much of the secret is in the incredible diluteness of the liquid, which pre-

---

[1] His papers in the Repertory for 1850 were on Dr. Foote's History of Virginia, German Church History, The Reformation in Spain, Close Communion, and German Hymnology.

[2] Of a process for disengaging gold from the quartz, &c., which came to nothing.

vents its taking up any thing but the gold. You see diamonds are at length made in Paris.

While R. J. Walker was Secretary of Treasury, the New York collector informed him of an entry of magnificently illustrated books from France, value $3—5,000; but obscene. W. ordered them to be instantly burnt. Importers threatened vengeance in a suit. Walker defied them. Of course they never prosecuted. —— is here: "Give, give!" A certain kind of eloquence he undoubtedly has, but his stock is small. Sundry whole paragraphs repeated bodily. N. B. You will be more likely to be observed, if you do this with the *purpureus pannus;* *e. g.* " We have run up our flag, and we mean to nail it . . . want more nails;" (three times.) Payson's dying words (twice.) " On the borders of the man of sin . . . crevasse into Mexico " (three times.) " My Master never tells lies " (once . . . too many.) After all, I think he probably makes impression on some, even here.

I have just sent seventy-seven vols., big and little, to the embryo college of Austin, Texas. Dr. Torrey has been delivering a course of lectures on the structure, &c., of plants, all which I have attended with great delight. He used drawings, borrowed from Agassiz. You may judge of size by this: pollen-grains were in some cases represented (highly coloured) as big as large musk-melons. T. is an admirable lecturer. Neanmoins, our young collegians treated it (being non-compulsory) with contempt, the number of undergraduates towards the last being 7 . . . 15.

The article on Hymnology is clever, but absurd. Some young Oxonian, fresh from his metres. So little is he at home in his own field, that he speaks of the Reformers as having made *one* version from the old church-hymns; *Veni Creator Spiritus.* I have counted of Luther's alone, from this source, twelve; and in a hasty review of reformation-hymns, in German alone, from old Latin, 134. This is exclusive of Psalms. Of course, my gleaning is but a handful. Few people know how little originality the world possesses. Twenty-four hymns in the Methodist Hymn-book (Wesleyan) are from the German. Of some single Latin hymns, I think I can produce twenty Protestant versions.

Warn Tom [on entering College] against early acquaintanceship. I have seen it make study impossible, by the everlasting run on one's room; and there is no possible preventive, but waiting long, and choosing one's own friends, not being chosen by them. I never saw a perfectly punctual scholar go astray. Get him to go always to the Thursday evening lecture. Encourage him to write you a weekly account of the studies, however repetitious. I think there will prove to be more in this than appears. I hope he will not neglect the French; almost all do. Wistar Hodge is talked of for Greek Tutor; he is the best Grecian I ever saw of his age. Henry has learnt more in a few months with him, than I could have thought possible. Dr. Duff is making a great impression in Edinburgh. I'll try to send you one of his speeches. Though I nauseate a little at their mutual be-praising, how much better it is, in its spirit, than our American sullenness, as to one another's good deeds, in our public bodies! How surprising, if A should laud B, or C descant on D's eloquence, or E glorify F, or G magnify H! Even if sham, this overt pulling-together gives strength to the esprit de corps, and explains the $10,000,000 which the Free Church has raised. American preachers are getting to stand towards one another as do the doctors. Ross, the Cherokee, says they are trying for a Cherokee college. Foreman, once of the Seminary, (a native,) is very useful, preaching in both tongues, publishing Almanacs, &c.[1]

PRINCETON, *July* 2, 1850.

Some people say the temple of Janus is shut. Connecticut Association affirm unanimously (Bushnell and all) resolutions made in terms of catechism, imputation included. Our village is empty. You now have the new experience of the doctorate, and can agree that the half has not been told you. Indeed, the sentiments engendered by this addition to one's title are such as beggar description.[2] Finney is on a high horse in London. Dr. Campbell, of the Banner, puts him as high as the greatest preachers ever heard in the Tabernacle. Inquiry-meetings number 700. Lectures edited anew by J. A. James. Do not you find the grandeur of things English, as such, decreasing in your apprehension? In theology and religion, I really think we get hardly any thing from them as good as our own; while they republish all our books. What can they show alongside of Stuart, Barnes, Robinson, Nordheimer, et al.? I had a protracted meeting with V., in respect to the expected Advent; learn from him that —— has demolished the Repertory, and proved N. an Atheist; that each of us ought to teach his children a manual trade; that all but Millenarians make little of Bible; that

---

[1] Rev. Stephen Foreman, now at Tahlequah, Arkansas.

[2] Another correspondent on this occasion communicated the following admonitory anecdote: "When Mr. C., a good Irish minister, late of the Reformed Presbytery, received his degree, and was admonished by one of his good members not to be exalted above measure, he replied, 'dear madam, I feel that I need a great deal of grace.'"

other books are pretty much superfluous; that Melchizedek is Christ, (so I understood;) and that D. had settled the Advent question when he was in the Seminary. P.'s last, anent H.'s fury against old school : " A man said, 'My wife is mighty zealous, but she haint got no religion.'" Richard Rush graduated here in '97. He tells me he saw Witherspoon's corpse.[1] I am in heart a Quaker as to mourning; I see no harm in a simple badge, but abominate modern "mourning," above all that of females—crape, (the smell is charnelly.)

You will read Duff's speeches[2] with wonder at the chilliness of our Assembly. How few people get the floor in the Scotch Assembly! How little work for the chair! How few points of order! How great the power of Cunningham and Candlish! How warm and good the Moderator's closing speech!

PRINCETON, *July* 18, 1850.

Anna J., a Sunday School child and catechumen of mine, [in New York,] was put into the Rutgers Institute on a scholarship among four hundred. She has just graduated, and I see comes out prima; gold medal for best composition; ditto last year for French; high in Mathematics. I see by Knox's history, that he provided liturgic forms for ordination, &c., with prayers, in full, which are extant.[3]

I was struck with Brougham's saying, that one may buy a newspaper on Sunday, but not a Bible. How hard to legislate about points of conscience, and impossible to enforce! Our dead-letter laws anent Sunday-travel, profaneness, &c., ought to be overhauled, before we add to their number.

The progress of Christianity among the Nestorians is wonderful. The imagination is struck with a missionary at Nineveh, [Mosul.] Gurley's speech gives me new impressions about Liberia. Some day Australia and New Zealand will break on the world with a surprise like that which the United States is causing to Europe. A German writer, long resident in Russia, says : " The Russian life, moving rapidly eastward, will it not one day join with the Anglo-American life, moving westward, on a stage for the last act of the world's drama? When the old-world vitality shall be worn out; when Oregon and California shall play the part that England and France do now; when the American nation, in which the best blood of Western

[1] The Hon. Richard Rush died at Philadelphia in 1859.
[2] In the Free Church General Assembly of Scotland.
[3] In 1857 Mr. Scribner published " A Book of Public Prayer, compiled from the authorized formularies of worship of the Presbyterian Churches, as prepared by the Reformers Calvin, Knox, Bucer, and others."

Europeans mingled, shall have asserted the power of science and art over physical nature; when sail and steam-vessels sweep through the isthmian canal, and railways connect the oceans; and when the people of America by fleets and commerce touch the ancient inhabiters of Asia; then the circle of the globe will be complete, and the last leaf of history turned; and then, perhaps, will the battle be joined between the political and religious despotism of Russia and the principles of freedom and equality. When the command 'be fruitful, and multiply, and *replenish* the earth' is fulfilled, then the creation is at an end. When the command 'Go ye into all the world,' &c., is accomplished, then the work of redemption is perfect, and the Lord comes to judgment."

The negotiations between Lancaster and Mercersburg will be realized, if the German Reformers can raise $15,000 to buy out the Lutheran share in Franklin College, and the people of Lancaster raise $25,000 for buildings. There seems to me to be great wisdom in the German way of having no University buildings, except for libraries. The reasons for it, in a fluctuating or new country, are greater still. True, this would fix colleges pretty much in large towns. I have often thought we could not do a better thing, than to sell out our pinched seven acres in Princeton, and buy a hundred for the same money. The whole method of college "rooming" and "commons," dissatisfies me. In a village, however, it is unavoidable. Demme declines his Gettysburg chair, and they will send a committee to Germany for a man. Three Germans are to decide, viz., Tholuck, Hoffman, (the Hebraistic successor of Gesenius,) and Harless of Dresden, an old-Lutheran of the invariata school, and a pious, eloquent man. It is an attempt to win back the alienated German-Lutherans to the American-Lutheran School at Gettysburg.[1]

Assure "each and every" (law forms and prayers in church are my authority) of my, &c., &c.

PRINCETON, *July* 26, 1850.

[2] It would be odd, indeed, if any court should set aside as invalid an ordination ratified by our General Assembly, sitting not only as our highest judicature, but as our highest legis-

---

[1] The Rev. Dr. Schaffer, of Pennsylvania, was elected to the German Theological Professorship at Gettysburg. Lancaster remained the seat of the College Department.

[2] In the General Assembly of 1850 an attempt was made to obtain the disapprobation of that Court of an act of a Presbytery, in ordaining a licentiate, when but two ministers were present—the third (requisite for a quorum) having approved of all the preliminary proceedings, but being

lature, and competent even in the latter capacity to solve any informalities in declarative acts. As to the ordination by commission, it is a question simply of fact. Nobody holds such ordinations allowable under our constitution. But as to what *has been done* by Presbyterians, in all the Reformed Churches, the fact of ordination by committee is as undeniable as the fact that any one was ever ordained. The Westminster Directory says : " The Presbytery shall come to the place, or at least three or four ministers of the word shall be sent thither *from the Presbytery*," &c., &c. The Repertory has not recommended nor endorsed this well known Presbyterian precedent. The laying on of hands is only a part of ordination. The other and greater parts took place in an acknowledged quorum. If the moderator had, in pursuance of direction, laid on his hands, it would have been, to all intents and purposes, the laying on of the hands of the Presbytery. Or may not some one take exceptions, if (as often) one of a Presbytery of twenty-five is crowded out from the circle, and fails to impose his hands? You refer to Webster, and so will I. In his last speech on the compromise, he says admirably, that Congress has, by its sanction, covered and supplied all informalities in the admission of Texas. So in this case. *Quod non debet fieri, valet factum.* The Assembly censures the irregularity, and constructively forbids it. What more can any large-minded Presbyterian ask ? Reordination ? This would produce endless misapprehension.

Imposition of hands is so far from being the main thing to secure *valid* orders, that Presbyterians have from the very Reformation, separated from papists and prelatists, on this very point. Surely we need not be stiffer than John Knox. See the " Buke of Discipline," confirmed by General Assembly and by Parliament, 1560 : " Other ceremonie than the publict approbatioun of the peple, and declaration of the chiefe minister, that the persone thair presented is appoyntit to serve that Kirk, we can nott approve ; for albeitt the Apostillis used the *impositioun of handis,* yet seeing the mirakle is ceasit, the using of the ceremonie we juge is nott necessarie." This, indeed, proves nothing as to our municipal provisions; which, when censurably neglected, may, by the supreme judicatory, be declared valid, though ir-

absent at the act of ordination. The Assembly refused to disturb the ordination in this case, on account of a formal irregularity, when there could be no doubt of the validity. The remarks of the letter were called forth by some questions as to the admissibility of the decision in a court of common law, and as to lawfulness of ordaining by commission. The reference to the Repertory is to a review of the proceedings of the Assembly in the number for July, 1850.

regular ; but it is very significant as to what the Presbyterian spirit is respecting this declarative formality ; which formality is, after all, present in the act as now presented.

The minister was ordained by the laying on of the hands of the Presbytery, though some of the Presbytery were away, and though some present did not lay on both "hands." The men ordained in Knox's days were not presbyterially ordained at all, according to the narrower construction of Presbyterianism.

It is remarkable that the objections to the Assembly's decision have not proceeded in any case known to me from the older and more rigid ministers, who seem all satisfied. And it should not be forgotten that the Assembly utters no declaration, but simply admits the given acts of Synod and Presbytery, without censure. I hold the Repertory's reasons to be unanswerable.

If the preceding parts of the ordination had been by less than a quorum, the question would have been raised, which was touched in the debate, as to whether *three* or a mere *plurality* is necessary to valid ordination. Of this I might have opinions of my own, but it was not properly before the body. Strict construction can make no whit more out of Form Gov. Cap. xv. § 14. Every Lutheran or Episcopalian minister, who comes to us, is presumed to have a valid, though an irregular ordination ; here the distinction taken by Repertory is fundamental. I think there are sound reasons why acts performed but once, such as marriage, ordination, baptism, &c., should admit of being ratified, in spite of informality, even though some other acts, such as erecting a Presbytery, &c., should be annulled, with orders to repeat them in due form. This is clearly accordant with the views of the canonists, even as to Baptism.

PRINCETON, *August* 2, 1850.

Torrey shows me some mirabilia of infusorial shells, invisible without high microscopes ; their beauty, in form and colour, is inexpressibly sui generis. Yet they have passed through the intestines of Pacific fowl, being abstracted from washings of the guano. A man named Spencer, in an out of the way place in New York, has beat all the world in microscopes. The English ones cannot, like his, resolve lines 56,000 in an inch. I am sorry for the loss of the Compromise, [repeal of the Missouri act.] I hoped Clay and Webster would have carried it over the free-soilers and nullifiers. It seems as if One " higher than the highest " would keep the awful slavery-question among matters for his own hand.

As to the question of legal ordination, I will only observe, that " ordained minister " has been held by some of our ablest lawyers (Ch. J. Ewing especially) to import in the acceptation of the law any accredited minister, particularly (in the case when he was consulted) a probationer. I know a case in Virginia, in which the same was held; and though hundreds of marriages have been solemnized by licentiates, none of them have ever been questioned in law, though often forbidden by church-courts. I have never talked with my father about the late case, but I know his testimony as to the facts above stated. Princeton census = —2,000. I am slowly writing "Sermons to Boys."

PRINCETON, *August* 26, 1850.

I have the letters of twenty years, exceptis excipiendis, filed and labelled: I cannot remember to have ever looked at them ten times. In no one instance has any thing of importance depended on the search. My father and Addison burn their letters. I was at the sea for a week, with less enjoyment than common. I preached in Fifth Avenue.[1] Mr. Donaldson drove me out to Greenwood; my first visit. The locality is unsurpassed, but $\frac{99}{100}$ of the tombs are burlesques or blunders. Cemeteries do not arride me. The last London Yearly Meeting agreed to have plain memorial slabs, like those of the Moravians. Somewhat suddenly I have entered Henry of the Freshman class. They say the Sophomore class is a fine one. The signs of thorough drilling by the tutors are very pleasing to me; short lessons and long inquisition on them.

I am told the Boston and Andover folks regard P. with a sort of adoration. His last great discourse gives them a recipe for holding any doctrine, however repulsive. You have only to declare its strong expressions " the language of emotion." Since capital punishment is so nearly extinct in Philadelphia, it is a wonder they have so many murders. A very promising Sunday School and preaching have been started in the very focus of the Five Points. Children from 8—10 years old come to school drunk. Drunken people appear at the meetings. Mr. Hall, a worthy Methodist, owner of the Commercial Advertiser, is one of the leaders in the enterprise.

PRINCETON, *September* 5, 1850.

We had large numbers of the Black Sons of Temperance here to-day, from Trenton and elsewhere, with bands and paraphernalia; also what seemed to be the Daughters and Grandsons, in considerable force. Thus far, our accession to the Seminary is about 46. They are still coming in. I was unable to go to Dr. Cuyler's burial,[2] as my first exercise with the new

[1] First Church, New York, August 18.
[2] The Rev. Dr. C. C. Cuyler died at Philadelphia, August 31, 1850.

class, and my only one for the week, occurred at the hour. Our situation in this respect is more confining than that of pastors, unless where we have good long notice. We hear of the death of a valuable student, Culbertson, brother of the missionary. He left us, somewhat ailing, for a tour to the Rocky Mountains, and came back perfectly restored, as it seemed, but died of a dysentery, at his father's house in Chambersburg. He was very assiduous by the bedside of Candor, [p. 108.] We have, as usual, [in the Seminary,] several Baptists, and expect a Methodist and an Episcopalian. One of our students has been a year under Cunningham, at Edinburgh. They pretend that Castle Garden will hold 8,000 hearers of [Jenny] Lind. What an organ hers must be! The furore in New York is quite ridiculous; crowds besieging the hotel, and gaping at the windows. The boys tell me there is much excitement about North and South in college. The Whigs have elected Venable as their June orator. We have a student who will not sing any human compositions; Rouse's being perhaps inhuman. I am gratified to hear of a case of marked seriousness in college; I fear, however, this is far from being indicative of the general tone. The London papers give flaming accounts of Finney's sermons and audiences. There is no allusion to his later doctrines of perfectionism. I wonder if a day will not come, when the immense increase of printed matter will cause a reaction in favour of old-time methods, oral learning, discoursing sub dio, like that of the Athenians and the New Testament. Even in Plato's day, he was led to fear the ill consequences to human powers from overmuch reading. News is a very different affair, in daily papers and in word of mouth. We at length have a priest here; I believe they have mass in their unfinished house. The extract you give, respecting our fathers, so many years ago, is very interesting.[1] My good old father has not been less than 60 years a preacher; but I have never heard him preach any autobiography, self-statistics, or census of successes. If fruit was unwholesome, our collegians would all be on their backs, but they seem blessed with uncommon health. The prevalence of dysentery in some parts does not seem to have had the slightest connexion with diet.

Lisco, on the Parables, is a remarkably sensible book to have come from Germany, and very full of sermonizing suggestions, the more valuable because it avoids all straining of the parables. What a delightful negligence in Hume's style; it is the least wearying I ever read; but what nefarious perversion, and what meagerness of research!

[1] It has since been printed in Dr. Sprague's "Annals of the Pulpit," vol. iii., p. 610.

PRINCETON, *October* 7, 1850.

Your note was a little delayed, as the letter lay unopened till my return from New York, which capital I found much in the same state as you left it. I preached once for Dr. Potts, in compliance with a Parthian request of his. He was last heard of at St. Petersburg. Some expect him to-day in the Atlantic. He has a noble congregation. Erskine Mason is still very ill.[1] A Norwegian Methodist missionary, Brother Willerup, called on me on his way to Wisconsin. I heard Dr. Tyng in New York, with much pleasure. The chanting was excellent. Sermon of the most extempore sort.

I have flattering offers to write for the North British Review. I have no present thought of compliance, though I should like the £10 a sheet. Thompson, of the Tabernacle, is preaching against the Fugitive Slave Bill, (when did Bill run away?) This, and the play of Hamlet, excite much attention among the people. Old Mr. Johnstone, of Jersey City, has gone to Britain, (as the Scotch love to call it.) Five Baptist preachers attended at the baptism of my daughter. Spencer has published a volume of pastoral anecdotes and conversations.[2]

Washington Irving's Mahomet is a whitewashing of his hero; "jejune and elegant." Variety in sermons might be helped by an occasional history, with free bursts of remark, whenever suggested; it is remarkable how much of the Bible is history. I think Elijah and Elisha a good topic. The argument of the book of Job would make a good sermon. In general, the argument of a Sunday School book might be occasionally preached with advantage. I have been acquainting myself with Luther's sermons. Nothing can be more natural, simple, earnest, downright, practical, pungent, or affectionate. They are models of the plainest, liveliest sort; the very opposite of modern German sermons, which are as constrained in their elegant partition as a sonnet or an acrostic. I have had to look into some of these professionally; and I declare I am unable to find one, which is worthy of reperusal, except some of Tholuck's, which are beautiful warm rhapsodies. The oldest person found in our three townships by the censor, is a pauper drunkard in East Windsor, a graduate of Princeton College, æt. 96. The number of coloured people in Princeton is about 500; perhaps as large a proportion of free blacks as anywhere, being one-fourth. How little noise is made by the death of the greatest monarch of our day! [Louis Philippe.]

The Repertory's review of Park has led me to look at

---

[1] Dr. Mason died May 14, 1851.

[2] "A Pastor's Sketches," by Rev. Dr. Spencer, of Brooklyn.

Morell.[1] His doctrine is much the same as Schérer's, and is very formidably presented. I have nowhere seen so artful an assault on the common doctrine of Inspiration. It involves the denial not merely of Inspiration but of truth, in many parts of Scripture, and leaves us to sever the errors from the truth by some kind of divination or intuition. Such a belief would make me long for the popish assurances. My poor Duane Street folks make no progress. I look confidently for the stronger portion of them to go up-town, at whatever loss of property in the present building.

Addison's present duties keep him reading the text of the Bible, with versions, &c., from morning till night. The applications for ministers, from Texas alone, would absorb all the young men we are about to send out. The openings in Wisconsin are also surprisingly great.

PRINCETON, *November* 11, 1850.

I was sorry to cross you on Saturday, but I was on my way to New York, where I had not preached for a long time. I found my late charge much dwindled, though communions are seasons in which they try to make a rally. They have authorized their trustees to sell, but I know not who will buy. When old Grant Thorburn (Laurie Todd) came over to this country, it was in a vessel in which was a poor Scotch woman with a child. Grant helped to nurse the baby; who now, after sixty years, as Collector of the Port of New York, gives him a place in the Bonded Warehouse. Hereupon Grant quotes, "Cast thy bread, &c." I did not hear Miss Lind, though she sang on Saturday night. Kirkwood, the mathematician, whose newly-discovered law respecting the planetary distances, makes so much noise among the astronomers, as ranking with Kepler's and Newton's, is an humble, pious, Presbyterian elder. Stephen Alexander supposes himself to have demonstrated mathematically that all the comets, whose periods are known, were once one comet.

PRINCETON, *December* 13, 1850.

I did not mean to steal a march on you, but I was really so overwhelmed with odds and ends of business, before getting off for Virginia, that I went away almost imperceptibly, and *collo obtorto*.[2] Now that I have returned, safe and sound, I ought to

[1] " Philosophy of Religion."
[2] The purpose of this journey was to fulfil an appointment to preach one of the series of lectures on the Evidences of Christianity, in the University

feel thankful for exemption from all delays and all accidents. I
left home on the 2d, and returned on the 12th. I never made so
abrupt a plunge into Old Virginia, and the contrasts struck me
mightily. Albemarle is justly reputed the best specimen of
rural Virginianism. The University is flourishing; nearly four
hundred students. The professors (each) have houses, but
$3,000 is the maximum of their emolument. Staying as I did
within the precincts, I was pleased to observe that there was
not the least rowdyism or unmannerly noise; and I was told
perfect quiet prevails in their lecture-rooms. The audiences at
the lectures on the Evidences are large. A voluntary meeting
for prayers, by morning candle-light, is attended by about fifty.
As you might suppose, much was said in Virginia about the
slavery business. With one remarkable exception, I found,
among a great number with whom I conversed, no man desiring
disunion. All they ask is the carrying out of the Constitution,
by enforcing the late law. Such is unquestionably the temper
of the masses. Yet there are some terrible " fire-eaters" at
Richmond, and these are making great use of the Vermont nulli-
fication. Combinations to use no northern goods, &c., are more
rife than I had thought. From numbers, however, I heard the
remark, that slavery could not abide safely in Virginia as a
frontier State—that its doom was fixed, &c. I fell in with South
Carolina people, and (at Richmond) with B——, on return from
South Carolina. There the state of things is very different, for
they not merely look on secession as a possible evil, but
pray for it as a real good. Northern mechanics, agents, and
operatives are rapidly leaving the State. The fear in Virginia
among sober people, is, that South Carolina will do some rash
act which will draw forth a large number of Southern States to
sustain or shield her. I am convinced, from numerous conversations with leading men, that the repeal of the Territorial Law
would throw Eastern Virginia into the arms of the South, and
furthermore divide the State. After all I had read in the papers
I was unprepared for the solemn views taken by good men of the
crisis. All seem to regard bloodshed as the inevitable result.
I stopped, going and coming, at Richmond, where I found Judge
Cabell on his death-bed, as I fear; he is an old friend of my
father, and one year his junior. At this season the flow of old
Virginia good-fellowship was peculiarly delightful to me. I was
almost surfeited with good things, and almost choked with end-

of Virginia, during the session of 1850–51. Dr. Alexander's Discourse was
delivered December 8. Its subject was " The Character of Christ," and is
printed in the volume embracing the whole course, published by Carters,
New York, 1852.

less parlance. There is soon to be a railway from Alexandria to Gordonsville, by which I should be able to reach Charlottesville in two days. Other roads are in construction. The travelling on those I used is greatly better than formerly. From Fredericksburg to Richmond decidedly more comfortable than between Baltimore and Philadelphia. The scuffles for luggage are lessened, and the ease of sitting increased.

I find all as well as usual. I am struck all of a heap by the news from New York.[1] What Providence means I am at a loss to say. Surely I have done nothing I know of, to invite a re-call to Duane Street. What moves me somewhat is, (1,) I do not feel a special quality for teaching: (2,) I greatly miss pulpit and pastoral work. Yet when I think of tearing up again—it seems next to impossible. I am much concerned, and in real trouble of mind, and shall profit by any unprejudiced thoughts you have.

PRINCETON, December 25, 1850.

I wish you as many Christmases and as happy, for you and yours, as the Divine Disposer shall give in token of love; for as I grow older, I trust I sometimes look forward to something better than the years of this world. The *number* of persons subscribing for the new church is rather favourable. The place talked of is Fifth Avenue and Nineteenth street. I am puzzled and darkened by conflicting opinions. There are some who will charge me with great fickleness, if I leave Princeton so soon. The Philadelphia men will generally think it a wild and wrong move. My father and family think I had better go, on the score of health; and it is especially my father's opinion, that the measure of talent I have is for preaching. It would not be exactly like a new experiment. The people calling know me, and are known by me. The recent move reveals an amount of influence on the New York mind, which (however unmerited) deserves to be considered. I was very happy in my work, and (if I may presume to say so) was improving in it, more than I feel myself to be doing in my teaching-function. These are things I cannot say abroad, but they affect my mind not a little. *Per contra*, I have the New York hum and interruption; New York summers; leaving a delightful home and rural quietude, and academic regularity, and above all my dear old father and mother, whose decline I should covet to wait upon. These, however, are, for the

---

[1] A proposal from the Duane Street congregation to build a new church on a better site, provided Dr. Alexander would accept a call to be the pastor. Subscriptions to the amount of $38,000 were already made, and $32,000 offered for the Duane Street premises.

most part, *worldly* considerations ; while I am impressed by the thought, that many of the reasons for return are *spiritual* in their nature. People say, "You can preach every Sunday in Princeton." So I can—but what a different thing it is ! I feel lifeless in comparison. I make no new sermons. Indeed, I hardly can take my present preaching into the account.[1] The true comparison must be between *teaching* here, and *preaching* there. Looking as modestly and honestly at it as I can, I feel (comparatively) some aptitude for preaching ; at least, I have a most undeserved acceptance—and that particularly in New York : I feel no special aptitude for teaching. In the city I drew young men around me : here, all my efforts have failed with the students, privately and socially : the difference I cannot express to you ; nor is it a matter I can discuss with people generally. I know the matter of health is very uncertain, and the causes of health and disease are obscure : but I think the four to five years in New York were of as much health, certainly they were of as much working-strength, as any similar portion of my life. As you might suppose, the matter is constantly in my thoughts, and I earnestly seek Divine leading ; for I know that my decision must be reviewed in the Judgment, and that if I determine on worldly and selfish grounds, I must expect a blight if not a curse. I wish to settle this question before many days.

My brother Samuel has accepted the call to Freehold. What a happy knack at speech-making Sir H. Bulwer has ! Young Mr. Beers sent me some water from the Dead Sea, and some olive-wood from Jerusalem ; I previously had some olive-leaves from Gethsemane, and some salts from Marah. This is almost enough to fill a *reliquarium.*

PRINCETON, *January* 6, 1851.

We are mercifully preserved ; yet I am scarcely ever without cough this winter. Exposed as I was during my journey, [to Virginia in December,] I had a respite then. They talk of sending me to Europe.[2] From my imo pectore, I say, I have no wish to go. Perhaps it might be good for my health. The impulse to write sermons has come over me very strong, and I have two half done. There is no employment I ever found so uniformly agreeable. It looks as if we never should have a cisalpine Assembly again.[3] How different from the days when we used

---

[1] In 1849 he preached 80 times ; in 1850, 49 times.

[2] He had signified his willingness to accede to the New York call, and resigned his professorship in the following February, but continued to act until April 30. It was also determined that he should take a voyage before entering upon his new duties.

[3] The Assembly of 1851 met in St. Louis, that of 1852 in Charleston.

to see the leaders of the church in the long pulpit of old "Market Street."[1] If they set up a cheap paper, they will doubtless centre it somewhere in the West. Dr. Lindsly is about removing to New Albany. I have peculiar pleasure in A. A. Hodge's unanimous call to Kirkwood, [Maryland.] [Rev. William H.] Rüffner preached yesterday at Penn Square.[2] Gough is less talked of than formerly; I should like to hear him again; it is a great treat. I should have had no scruple about hearing [Jenny] Lind, though I suffer no regrets, and my appetency was not strong; I was in New York one night that she sang, also at Jones's Hotel, Philadelphia, with her, and again in Baltimore. I believe all our cloth went in New York. A happy New Year to you all from us all.

PRINCETON, *January* 23, 1851.

I hardly know how to speak of ——'s death. It came on us like a thunderbolt. The agonizing thought, when such an event occurs, is, *Perhaps I might have saved a soul from death!* What plainness, labour, and earnestness it ought to give us in preaching!

PRINCETON, *March* 7, 1851.

I think if I am favoured with a safe arrival at Paris, I shall prefer Walsh to ——, with or without the fasces.[3] My present hope is to go by steamer, about May 15. You have fair notice to have your trunk packed, your supply engaged, your French overhauled, &c. The architects begin to visit me, and I feel my utter impotency, in judging of plans and styles. I wish a lot could be used to settle it. You express just my views of biography. How much of the Bible is history; and how much of the history is biography. No other reading so much shows me to myself, or so much stimulates me. As we grow older, do we not find a pleasure in the lesser lines of character? seeing differences which formerly did not strike us; just as we learn to detect handwritings, which to children are all alike, and to *idiotæ* are unmeaning. If a botanist loves to collate flowers, how much more, &c., &c. I will borrow for you the Life of good old Bengel, which will much please you. N. B. To introduce into our sermons more biography; I mean detailed pictures of characters; not for ornament, but for searching—to hold the mirror up to nature. Models in Bible, Prov. xxxi. The Hireling. Several sketchy

---

[1] The First Church of Philadelphia.
[2] The Seventh Church, Philadelphia, of which he was afterwards the pastor.
[3] Mr. Walsh had been superseded in the American Consulate.

portraits in the Psalter. Some nice volumes might be made for our Board, by collecting a number of Christian biographies. Proudfit is on a History of the Huguenots; also is about to edit some specimens of St. Basil in Greek. Some of our students take down all the lectures in short-hand. I tried a man to-day, by reading aloud from a book to him; he succeeded well. What an ignoble business this stopping of the House of Refuge is, which is attempted in our [New Jersey] Assembly. Dr. H. brings excellent accounts of Ripley's doings in Burlington. The Quaker body there seems to be breaking to pieces. Burt is doing admirably well in Springfield, Ohio; he has a Bible-class of sixty-five. At Williams College the President preaches one evening each week, and Prof. Hopkins another. The whole Senior class learns the Shorter Catechism, which Dr. Hopkins expounds; and it is a regular part of examination for degrees. I wish I could see a school in which the Bible should be taught every day.

Apropos: since Watts's Catechisms went out, we have had no syllabus of Bible history to give children and young people. My father made some attempts, but the way is still open. Such a book, going over the *whole* narrative, without much remark, would sell by thousands. The demand for such a book would continue. If this snow comes, which I feel in the air, perhaps we may have some sleighing yet.

PRINCETON, *March* 28, 1851.

If you hear any thing about Walsh, let me know. I am trying to brush up my French, on which I shall have to rely, upon the Continent. [Rev. John] Lord begins a lecturing here on Monday. [Mr. David] Lord proposes $1,000 in three prizes, to be raffled for, by essays, pro and con, upon the great apocalyptic question. He makes the rider of the white horse to be the early preachers; and of the red to be prelacy. He is very severe on Brown's late anti-millenarian book. Bethune's new church [Brooklyn] is to have no windows in the sides. The "Union Committee" of New York is doing a harm to the public conscience, by circulating sermons and addresses, denying all right of private judgment, on matters adjudicated by Cæsar. Dr. L. maintains that in matters properly civil we have nothing for it but to submit passively. Illinois is about making all contracts with negroes void, besides forbidding them the State. Gov. Young told me, last week, that they are migrating in vast numbers to Canada, for fear of the late law. It is a wonder more are not urged to Liberia. I will try to send you "London Poor and London Labour," [by Mayhew.] It is rich.

The modern German writers agree that the James of Jerusalem was not the surviving apostle, but a third of the name. Look at the places; you will find it an interesting question. Schaff thinks he was the son of Mary, one of Christ's "brethren," who did not believe; who continued unbelieving till Christ's resurrection; so explaining what is certainly a strange specification, 1 Cor. xv. 7, "after that he was seen of *James*." He gets over Gal. i. 19, by a grammatical turn, analogous to John xvii. 12, "*but* the son of perdition." Nevin seems to incline to the opinion, that God would have been incarnate, independently of the entrance of sin. I have seen circulars, &c., showing that the project of bringing the Great Exhibition, palace and all, to Governor's Island, in 1852, is in actual preparation. Some hotel-men in New York have subscribed $5,000 each; and the railroad companies are invoked. The palace and its freight will cost $300,000.

PRINCETON, *April* 15, 1851.

A telegraphic despatch carried me, on ten minutes' warning, to New York on Saturday, to see a sick and bereaved lady. I heard a Methodist sermon on Sunday morning. I was also at Trinity Church. Dr. Hodges, on the organ, and their choir of boys, I found transcendent. The *Benedicite* was chanted so as to meet every demand of my feelings. The service was read by a drone. It seems to be their plan to make it as hum-drum as possible. After having submitted a number of plans to me, my subscribers have chosen one (Draper's) which I have never seen. It is said to be handsome. Dr. George Maclean is to be my steamer-companion. He goes abroad for health, and to see his Scotch cousins. Schaff has given me a round-robin to about twenty of the German great ones. I am like to have plenty more letters than I can deliver. Ruskin's new book upon "Sheepfolds" is really an attack upon Puseyism. It is well worth reading. Schaff has published the first volume of his Church History in German. It is an enormous book, and will make ten volumes, 8vo, at the rate he has begun. It is learned and moderate.

PRINCETON, *April* 30, 1851.

I this day heard my last recitation. There is something sad in these "Last Things." The African items in the last Missionary Herald are very exciting. The head of the Nile seems to be in sight. A number of young blacks here are thinking of Liberia. A hint towards sermons: make a sermon, one for each, on the different states and stages of mind and character among people not converted, yet not altogether hardened. *E. g.* 1. The occasionally awakened. 2. Those who are already somewhat thoughtful. 3. Those who have gone back. 4. Those who are deeply concerned. 5. Those who are so for the first time. 6. Those who see obstacles to coming to Christ. 7. Those who occasionally hope. 8. Those who are overwhelmed with a sense of sin, &c., &c. I see by Samuel Davies's Journal that his return voyage from England took him three months. Get hold of a paper, and read Sir Henry Bulwer's speech at the St. George's dinner in New York. It is full of sparkle. Hamilton is said to be the writer of the article on Doddridge in the North British Review. I wish this new invention about spinning flax by steam could come true; it would be a death-blow to cotton-slavery. Our anomalous political state, as to this question, seems to offer no light in the future. I pity the poor free negroes from my heart; and wish we had taken a more generous course in regard to their church accommodation.

PRINCETON, *May* 16, 1851.

The time is fast approaching, when I must again cease to begin my letters with the formula at the top of this page. For some days I shall be a good deal occupied, and not much in writing-humour. With a blessing on my ways, I will write as often as I can from the other side. Yesterday I went on board, and surveyed my quarters. The affair is colossal. I do not mean the state-room, which, nevertheless, is more roomy than I had imagined. I shall probably leave this place on Friday morning. Dr. George Maclean, my chum, has arrived. Dr. Potts (who is a judge) says he never knew the power and richness of the human voice, till he heard the Greek priests chant at Moscow. I am recalling my "twenty pence is one and eightpence," and trying to compare pounds and guineas, &c. After lucubrating awhile over my French, I resolved to go on the "crescit eundo" plan. When speaking on the Paris platform, I must endeavour not, like a great preacher, to eulogize *eau de vie* instead of *l'eau de la vie.* Fearful prognostications have I of sea-sickness, which I almost had, by way of rehearsal, on descending into "the sides of the ship," and sniffing the schoolhouse smell of the snuggeries. It seems a sardonic mockery to have such spacious, sumptuous saloons, all plush, gold, panel, paintings, mirror, damask, &c. Let your thoughts be sometimes on me and mine, and mine will on you and yours. I get more and more repugnant to my voyage as the time approaches. We are likely to have 300 passengers.

CHAPTER XI.

1851.

Off Cape Clear, *June* 3, 1851.[1]

Through God's mercy I am here on the Irish coast, in our eleventh day. It has been a perpetual delight, without accident, hinderance, or " evil occurrent ; " without pain, alarm, sea-sickness, languor, low spirits, or weariness ; with as delightful a company as ever was thrown together, with sumptuous entertainment in a floating palace. Will you believe it—our 141 passengers have been like a loving family. Since the 25th we have had solemn and delightful worship every night, and services both Sabbaths. On each I preached once. I suppose we sang forty complete hymns on Sunday night. Mr. Tupper and Dr. Mütter[2] have won my everlasting thanks and regard for the bold and noble manner in which they came out for religion. Tupper sets the tune at worship.

All my anticipations of the Atlantic have thus far been more than realized. I have seen a whale and a paper-nautilus, and several icebergs. The ship-people=140, of whom seventy are connected with the steam. We burn seventy tons of coal a day, and sixteen men are employed feeding our fourteen furnaces.

[1] Dr. Alexander embarked in the steamer Arctic, Captain Luce, at New York, on the 24th May, 1851. In filling up this chapter I have not been limited to the letters addressed to myself, but have also had the use of those addressed to different members of his family. It was indeed the plan of his correspondence, that what he wrote to one of his friends should be circulated among the rest, and then collected as the journal of his tour. Several other letters were addressed by him, during his journey, to the editors of "The Presbyterian," Philadelphia. I should add that what is given in this chapter is but a meagre selection from the materials.

[2] Mr. Martin F. Tupper, author of "Proverbial Philosophy," and the late Professor Mütter, of the Jefferson Medical School of Philadelphia.

Think of its being daylight here at 2 A. M.! On the banks of Newfoundland we had fire, and slept under full winter covering. Mr. Tupper is the most merry, open-hearted creature in the world, and fraught with classical learning. I have his autograph of his own proverb: "A babe in the house is a wellspring of happiness."

June 4.—I just now had the first glimpse of Britain; it is Bardsey Island, in Caernarvon. Beautiful clearness of atmosphere. The blue sea has become green in soundings, but we have the gray heaven of England and not an American azure.

I have had frequent opportunities of religious exhortation, and was never more blessed, than on this voyage, with willing ears. I am sorry to say my health was publicly drunk at the closing dinner on board, "for his services as chaplain." Tupper made a speech, and various poems were recited.

LIVERPOOL, *June* 4, 1851.

My first step in England! We were half a day getting through the customs. They even dutied my sermons. The weather is smoky, muggy, and cold, about like our March, without any keenness. For the first time I see beautiful hawthorn blooms, both white and red. Liverpool buildings are high, solid, massive, every thing on a scale of majestic strength, without beauty.

On the 6th we go up to London with Dr. Mütter, who has been several times abroad, and is acquainted with several of the chief nobility and clergy. Mr. Tupper has given me some valuable letters, and offers to present me to the Presbyterian Duke of Argyll. The beauty of the rural environs surpasses all my imagination. Every charm of verdure, birds, flowers, and luxurious landscape-gardening, appears in this spring-like weather. Americans meet us, almost literally, at every corner. I suppose we have fifty in this house, (Adelphi.)

LONDON, *June* 6, 1851.

The season is transcendent. How can I ever describe the fairy-land we have come through this day! I had fancied much, but it is nothing to the reality. Green, green, green! Such green as I never thought of, bathed in an atmosphere of delicious moisture, a playful mixture of tiny rains and sunshine. Castles, parks, hedgerows, rivers, Trent and Avon, Cowper's birthplace and scenes, cottages, rookeries, larks. Some parts of Warwick, Herts, and Nottingham, with the approaches by Harrow, are like one's dreams of Eden. We were ten in party, all friends, Americans; and all day no foot entered our (railway) carriage but our own. The order, the ease, the respectfulness are marvellous. I have not in several days seen a moment of hurry.

The climate is wet but lovely. You can walk all day. The sun seems to be under a fender. I have walked miles to-day in my great coat, and been in half a dozen rains; but the rain seems to be playing, and sometimes stops before you raise an umbrella.

LONDON, June 8, 1851.

Where should a man go on Whitsunday but to St. Paul's? I fancy half the auditory was American. The nave is boxed up for approaching fête of charity children. Service in the choir. Every thing chanted. I place it clearly at the top of all music I ever heard. The voice of the bassos and of the trained boys, the organ, the modulation, and the universal enunciation, surpass my highest dream of church-music. Milman preached. Large parts of antiphonal song from invisibles in loft. I could not, by search, see one man or boy among the surplices who listened to one word of the sermon. After singing like angels (I never heard such voices) the dogs would sit in their high oaken stalls, and play all manner of pranks.

For an omnibus had to go down to Bank. My heart went pit-a-pat at the corner-names: Bread street, Poultry, Cornhill, St. Swithin's, Eastcheap. Chat with six policemen, seventeen yesterday; all the same—polite, even benignant; 4,000 now in London. I have never failed to say I was American. Effect all the same—overflowing kindness, with abject ignorance of the United States. Birds sing by hundreds in these parks. One is always near a friendly guide in the police. They never tire, and especially aid foreigners. The placards show a great prevalence of religious affairs. Sermons advertised in all languages. Old London rises before me, where I see the Tower, Billingsgate, Lambeth, Old Jewry, and Upper Thames street. I love to lose myself in the culs-de-sac and inn-yards opening in Cheapside and Aldersgate street.

Our hotel (Euston) is at the terminus of the North-Western Railway. There are indeed two of them, quite alike, with a place between them. No bar. Large coffee-rooms, columns, curtains, head-waiter like a clergyman, speaks French and Spanish; no loud syllable spoken; tables far apart. Sparrows numerous in our court, which is clean as a parlour. I heard Dr. Hamilton at 6½ P. M. Mean, large church. Like every minister here, he has trimmed whiskers. Gown and band.

Subject: Eternity of hell-torments. Able, faithful, tender, original, and not flowing. Voice gentle, but intonation positively shocking. No gesture but with head and body. Voice dropped on every cadence, several notes lower than the expected one, with an effect that is horrible. Deep solemnity in people, as much as in any revival. Precentor. All sing, but hideously. People all sit down a minute after blessing, which is delightful. Alms at the door.

Nothing so amazes me as the order of the streets. Even by the river-stairs and in Southwark, no fuss, no groups of b'hoys, nothing like loud laughter. Indeed the policemen, with their handsome uniform, are everywhere; as grave as clergymen, and constantly helping some one. Around the Crystal Palace for some squares, no one is allowed to stop and chat, but the notice is given thus: " Excuse me, Sir; I have indulged you as long as my orders allow; you will find it agreeable to walk on." Common people all say *cowld* for *cold*. Everybody says *'ouse*, *believin*, and *'bus*. If you want a cabman you hollow *keb!* In Liverpool I had my watch, once my father's, set to English time at the shop where it was made, as the number (6,900) showed, in 1804; they now number 59,000 and odd. Everybody expresses assent by " quite so," and no sentence seems complete without " you know," (*naow.*) All words like " member," " waiter " are almost spondees, " waitarr." " Hear " and " year " are " hyurr " and " yurr." The favourite drink is 'alf-and-'alf, or ale and porter. The bell is always answered by a chambermaid, a comely person in a cap.

On the 7th I was in Westminster, and surveyed the courts of law. In Chancery, Lord Truro, sniffing camphor or the like, as if sick. In Vice Chancellor's court, Sir J. Knight Bruce sitting. In Queen's Bench, Lord Campbell, Sir J. T. Coleridge, &c. Lawyers crowded in pews, like people in church. The wigs looked like making fun. The gown and band were becoming. The queues of the barristers' wigs like floured rat-tails.

London, 142 Strand; June 10, 1851.

This is in Old London, the only London that I care for. I have had a couple of good days, one at Greenwich Fair and hospital, and one at Windsor and Eton. My whole day-light I spend, rain or shine, (mostly rain,) on the tops of omnibuses. In my opinion a lady might journey all over rail-road-England, with as much safety as she could go from Trenton to Princeton. In the carriages all is exactly as if you were in your private coach. No passing through. No outcry; the whole mien that of genteel, deferential servants.

I attended the Crystal Palace Exhibition for the first time to-
day. I was chiefly attracted by the Fine Art department. The
sculptures are innumerable. The only ones which greatly impressed me, were Italian, but placed, alas! under the sign of
"Austria." A number of fine ladies, perhaps noble, were trying to lift a little boy up to see the great diamond. I gave my
place and offered to hold him. The lady looked surprised—such
things are not done here—but when I said "I have such another
3,000 miles from here," she complied and thanked me with much
grace. No respect is shown to sex. No one gives place to a
lady as such. There is great respect, however, to every one in
public, for they do not know but the man in plain dress is a lord.
The beautiful skin and teeth of all classes, except artisans, keeps
me admiring. The gray hair, even of quite young ladies, is
universally exposed. It strikes you, when you see it repeated
among ten thousand. Whitsun holidays have brought the provincials in by shoals. You would laugh to see *vans*, or long and
wide cars, crammed full of rosy lads and lasses, perhaps thirty
in one, riding twenty and thirty miles for sixpence. My Virginia friends agree that they never saw such horses as came up
to London. They are like elephants in the brewers' drays. I
understand better now what Dickens and the Earl of Carlisle
mean by calling the Americans a *grave* people. At these fêtes
of Whitsun-week the whole *bourgeoisie* seem to be pleasuring,
all on a broad grin, all gratified, and without strong drink or any
rowdyism. Nurses and young mothers, with little children, go
seven miles by water, and stay all day amidst thousands. Every
time I lift my eyes from this paper, I see St. Paul's. I blame
myself for contemning St. Paul's. How gloriously it predominates over every part of the city! Temple Bar and Char-
ing Cross are pleasantly near. I have seen the paintings at
Hampton. You know my peculiarity as to portraits; but these
are the men themselves, as they lived and moved. Corregio's
enchanted me more than any before I knew they were his. The
very clocks and furniture of 1536 are at Hampton. The horse
guards passed me to barracks, in Hyde Park, in the rain, cloaked,
and each leading a second horse. There are always two regi-
ments on duty, picked men, six feet high. They are just as
polite as the police. Every common man I have talked with,
wishes to go to America. The last cad that took my sixpence
asked me "is not New York in Philadelphia?" Another, when
I said I was a foreigner, said: "Ay! you must be talkin' hyper-
bolical. I suppose you know the meaning of the word; you
may be a furriner to *London*, but you're an Englishman born."
Windsor Castle covers thirty-two acres. The park (see

Midsummer Night's Dream) looks endless. Green, green, green, velvet, emerald, no break in the verdure—a prairie covered with trees, such as you have often heard described. One broad avenue of oaks and elms reaches three miles. My first rapture in a Gothic edifice was in St. George's Chapel. All words must fail to express its awful beauty ; no gloom, no sombre colours, all bright from the cream-coloured stone columns and arches, rising into vaults of fearful grace. In the church is the group of statu- ary forming a monument to the Princess Charlotte. The grief expressed by the veiled, prostrate, dishevelled creatures, makes me shudder when I recall it.

I next went across to Eton. These little old towns are in- describable. High street is a place to dream of. Nobody ever told me how pure and clear and wide the streets were, nor how low were the houses, nor how nice, quaint, cheerful, and roguish- looking. Some breathe the very spirit of Chaucer. Then the College ! I cannot express how my musings went back, in those cloisters. The trees, the pavements, the Master's (Hawtrey's) house, with comical gables peeping out of the deep green ; the boats in great numbers on the sweet narrow Thames, rowed by the boys, the cricketers with gowns and coats thrown off.

England is a more flowery country than I thought. The roadsides are besprinkled with endless bloom, often as much so as any garden walk. The green is so dense that girls at work in fields sometimes seem as if in waves of a river. Ancient footpaths wind far away where there is no high road, gravelled and even paved.

LONDON, *June* 13, 1851.

Last night I went to the House of Commons, and heard Cobden, Hume, Baring, Admiral Berkeley, &c. All spoke alike : all had a stammer, save Cobden ; all colloquial, rapid and sometimes funny. The noise was tremendous. I had no notion before of the ironical cheers, which are a yaw-yawing you would hardly distinguish from dogs. I am not desirous to go again.

After all my study of the localities, I can hardly believe my eyes. Such dark, dim, tall, narrow, winding ways—plainly just so for ages. Here is Watling street, part of an old Celtic road all across Britain. The places are redolent of Saxon times. Buy Cock Robin at Newberry's Corner. Newberry has been dead sixty years. Peep into yards of old inns. Heavy carts of country carriers and broad dialect. I pushed into Doctors' Commons, and had a dozen touching their hats and offering to find a proctor for me, to show me the cells of the wills, &c.

Serjeant's Inn is another close. But the most awakening is the Temple, Middle and Inner, which surprises me by its insulation, retirement, and sweetness. Templars here in 1184 !

June 14.—[After visiting Covent Garden market, St. James' Park, hearing the Queen's band, and seeing the Queen and Prince Albert pass, he spent the rest of the day at the Crystal Palace.] I was about to retire at 4, when I saw the Duke of Wellington. Exceedingly trim in dress, new hat, white stock with broad silver buckle. No greatcoat. A handsome woman was on his arm—wife of one of the Commissioners. The crowd stood off with peculiar delicacy. The Duke turned into the American department, and stood half an hour, within six feet of me, listening to a detailed description of Day and Newell's (New York) lock. He gave fixed attention, and asked some questions. He is evidently the idol of the people.[1]

I have three tickets to a Conversazione on the 16th, signed by the archdeacon of Middlesex, "to afford foreign pastors, and other religious foreigners, opportunity to become acquainted with the clergy and such lay members of the Church of England, as take a special interest in its affairs."

I had my shoes blacked in the Park for one penny, by a boy in a blouse, marked "Ragged School Society of Shoeblacks, No. 35."

You cannot think how deeply I was affected, when looking over the exhibition in the French department, to see at a type-founder's platform the Chinese types of the "Presbyterian Board of Missions," especially as four of the Executive Committee are here this moment.[2]

June 16.—I found Dr. Hamilton at his house in Gower street, who received me with indescribable cordiality. I am pained to think how few there are whom I have ever received with as much. He is a tall, thin, American-looking man, with the gentlest, sweetest, most innocent manners. He gave me the latest "Presbyterian," which completes my news anent the Professorship, [in Princeton Seminary.] He gave me two books for ——, with his autograph. Then he took me into the next room, and introduced me to Dr. Sandberg, Professor of Church History at the University of Lund, in Sweden.

I then proceeded through a maze of streets to Carlton Terrace. I found No. 9, and saw the arms of Prussia on the house of the Chevalier Bunsen, and entering found a number of persons waiting in the ante-chamber. The big-legged footman, in

---

[1] The Duke died on that day fifteen months.

[2] Dr. Jacobus, Mr. Lenox, Mr. Soutter,—I do not know who was the fourth.

blue and gold, took my card and instantly came back, taking me
in precedence of all the rest. He received me in a long, lofty
library-office, looking out on the corner of St. James' Park. He
is a noble-looking man, somewhat corpulent, with a blue eye,
temperate but ruddy skin, and fine teeth. He took me as un-
ceremoniously by the hand as you would have done, and led me
rather gaily towards a sofa, seating himelf at one end. He
began at once with great fluency, elegance, and heart, in excellent
English. He had read a letter which I had placed in the hands
of Mr. Kennedy, respecting German emigration. After hearing
me on this topic, he entered on religious subjects, spoke of the
iron extremes of Anglicanism, and of hymnology, and presented
me with a copy of his own book of hymns and prayers, with
this inscription, " To Rev. Dr. James W. Alexander, as a token
of Christian regard. J. Bunsen. Carlton Terrace, 16 June,
1851." He offered me letters to Germany, which I declined,
begged me to come again, and kept me there till a German, apparently of rank, came in. I observed open at his standing desk
a Greek copy of Origen.[1] There is no trace of stiffness in his
manner, and his reception of me was not only affable but loving.
Tears stood in his eyes several times during our interview. I
suppose he felt that he could entirely unbend with a foreign
Christian.

Going at random into Westminster Abbey, I found the
Bishop of London preaching before the famous old Society for
Propagating the Gospel. Among the first words I heard were,
" the United States of America." It has been so everywhere.
Our republic seems to be perpetually in the mind of England.
I went a second time to Westminster Hall. The speeches are
eminently condensed, scholarly, and colloquial ; more of a dia-
logue than any thing known among us. The barrister or solicitor
is not allowed to deviate an instant. All the English speak
alike, and almost all affect a stammer which gives an odd emphasis. On my return I looked in at the old Savoy church, with
respectful remembrance.

I am now convinced that I must leave this most noble of
cities, not only unlearnt, but unvisited in a score of most important places. I could this minute name thirty which it would
take a week barely to *go to*.

[1] It was about this time that Mr. Bunsen was preparing his Letters to
Archdeacon Hare on Hippolytus, author of the recently discovered book
ascribed to Origen. The first volume of his large work on Hippolytus did
not appear till 1853.

PARIS, *June* 19, 1851.

We left London at $9\frac{1}{2}$ this morning, and here we are (at midnight) in Paris, after a journey of 345 miles. Feel the climate to be like that of America; it is from winter to summer. The delightfulness of seeing the sun and feeling the warmth is indescribable. The ride through Picardy is flat and monotonous, but verdant, cultivated, and delightful. Sometimes thirty windmills at once. No fences, few hedges, many ditches. All roads and ditches lined with pollard trees. Almost always in sight of a Norman church predominating over the flat but cosy hamlet. I never saw any thing more lovely than the groups of villagers in the summer evening. Immense herds of cattle and flocks of sheep. Our way was through forty-six towns and villages.

21st.—Hotel Meurice. Right across is the Garden of the Tuileries. The shade is beyond all I ever dreamt of: it is almost like night. There is not a blade of grass, but the ground is baked and trodden hard. Children in any quantity in the garden, with their *bonnes ;* not so chubby and cherubic as the English, of whom also there are many. I saw 30,000 men reviewed by the President [now Emperor] in the Champ de Mars. I was in an open calèche, with Mr. R. L. Stuart. Louis is not great-looking, but modest and soldierly, and "un bon cavalier," as our driver said again and again. Jerome was on his left. The troops of Paris are 100,000. There were 180 drums. The soldiers singly look mean, but in mass are incomparably fine. We drove back along the quays, and so across by the Elysées and Place de la Concorde. This is probably unequalled on earth. On one side the Madeleine, on the other the Chamber of Deputies. There is no longer any aristocratic wealth in France. One-quarter of an hour in Hyde Park reveals more grandeur than all France can show. The women of Paris are the ugliest and the prettiest I ever saw. The general impression on me is, that England is the cleanest and France the dirtiest nation in the world.

June 22.—Lord's Day, but no Sabbath in Paris. They were painting this very house, and tearing down buildings not far off. All the shops are open. It is a great Romish feast, the *Fête-Dieu.* As time allowed, I went into the church of St. Mary of Loretto before Protestant service. It was full, each paying two sous for a chair. High mass. Various bands of singers, boys and men. Processions round and round with the host. Perhaps fifty priests, arrayed in purple and gold. Two beautiful young priests, in graceful white robes, with pink sashes, carried the censers. Four little children, in same apparel, scattered rose-leaves. Twenty-four novices, girls, all in white, veiled, carried candles six feet high. An orchestra of perhaps fifty instruments on the north side of the choir, the leader making all the motions, just as in a theatre. The pyramidal band of priests at the high-altar, moved and changed and turned and parted with all the complication, but with all the regularity of a cotillon. The Gregorian chant by voices like Russell's, [deep bass,] all like one voice. I never in all my life felt such grief and indignation at the "man of sin." Architecture, painting, and music, here combine in their highest point to make Christ's cross nothing but a stupendous plaything. The hundreds of tapers, and the indescribable gorgeousness of the chasubles, &c., and the wailing, soul-entrancing music, all belong to the wine of incantation of the scarlet woman. May God destroy this Babylon with the brightness of his coming!

Thence to the Oratoire. I hoped to hear Mr. Adolphe Monod, but found Mr. Coquerel in the pulpit. He is an eloquent Socinian, and a fine-looking man. Text: "Who gave himself for us." Doctrine: Unity of belief is impossible; unity of morals is what Christ died for. He is a consummate orator. No notes. Large, respectable assembly. They sang the old Beza-Marot psalms to the old tunes. People all stood most reverently during prayer.

June 23.—To the National Assembly. Saw Lamartine, Cavaignac, Coquerel, Leroux, Berryer, Odillon Barrat, Girardin, Lamennais, and some others. I never heard such a noise. A hundred would be talking as loud as the orator. Coming away I joined company with a priest. Told him I was a Protestant. He said, "N'importe, monsieur, vous etes Chrétien." He was polite, as every one is. No one enters a café or an omnibus without salutation.

June 24.—One month from home. It seems a year, but a year of delight. For the first time I can say my cold is better. Soldiers have now become as familiar as flies. Paris is more like an American city than London. It is filthy and has abominable stenches. But there are thousands of flowers and birds here, which cannot be said of any American city. O what a meeting, Sunday evening, in the little chapel Oratoire! Adolphe Monod—"God is Love." Huguenot women in caps. Old Psalm (103d)—old tunes. It was an hour to be remembered for life.

Mr. Rives gave me a distinguished reception, called in person, and has written me two notes, and given me entrance to the diplomatic box at the National Assembly. Tea at Dr. Monod's, with Bridel, and several others. Good Christian evening. I conducted prayers and expounded. I had previously spent an hour with Adolphe Monod. We ran together like two drops. I am to be at his soirée on 26th, where perhaps I meet Lady Trotter, sister of the Marchioness Normanby. All ranks of evangelical people meet here like brothers. All ranks are equally polite. I never hear or see any thing in the streets which would be rude in our parlour. The persuasive, deferential, affectionate tone of their voices, especially the women, is surprising. But every one dreads an outbreak, and then they become tigers. Such flowers and fruits I never beheld. The flower-market near Madeleine, beats Covent Garden hollow. The poorest, meanest things in Paris, are arranged with taste. A fruit-window is a perfect still-life picture. A half sous stick of cherries is pretty enough to take home. You must imagine what it must be when they lay themselves out to be ornamental.

June 27.—My days are spent in rambling, : for the things I want to see differ from the common sights. I have been in the principal churches, have heard masses enough to keep my soul in repose (if they have any such virtue) a thousand years, have seen paintings till l weary of them, have sought out the burial-places of some great men, some Protestant antiquities not commonly visited, and have learned to hate Popery more intensely than ever. At two soirées I have good opportunity to scan the customs of Parisian Christians. I have never seen any thing more simply elegant or affectionate. In both instances we had prayers before tea. Last evening a company of about thirty united in singing a hymn, hearing chapter, and offering a prayer —all in French. I have passed much time in the *Pays Latin*, or region of the old colleges and convents, and in rummaging the antiquities of Paris. When I plunge into the oldest, narrowest streets, &c., of the Seine, I have most that attracts me. My uniform method is to hire a coupé and sit with the driver. This teaches me more French than a week of solitary walking. Then I make an excuse to sit half an hour in some cool shop and chat in my bad French with the smooth-tongued Parisians. I have to-day visited with great curiosity the markets which had escaped me. Strawberries as large as English walnuts are abundant for money. Both in England and Paris the most beautiful butter is universally set before us in pats about as large as two dollars laid together. No spot has attracted me so much as the Louvre. If it were Christian so to do I could spend hours there daily for a year. Yet I do not enjoy Paris as much as London. One I admire, the other I love. Except their poor, ignorant nonsense about slavery, I saw hardly any thing in England which I did not like.

Paris, *June* 30, 1851.

Yesterday was the Lord's day, the octave of Fête Dieu, (Corpus Christi,) a day specially devoted to the idolatry of the wafer. I felt it my duty to go to the Madeleine before worship. How can I make you conceive the worldly grandeur and beauty! It is the greatest of modern churches. It is more beautiful outside than St. Peter's. Conceive of a Greek temple of massy marble: images on images by the greatest sculptors, many times as large as life, all outside. Hangings of velvet, purple, and gold between the columns. Ancient tapestries hung outside the walls, within the vast pillars. Inside, the smell of millions of flowers. It is called the *fête des fleurs*. If I saw one bouquet I saw ten thousand. You cannot imagine the art in their disposition. The high altar was so backed by a forest of flowers, that the singers were perfectly concealed. Scores of priests, deacons, boys in graceful albs with pink girdles; scores of girls all veiled, all white for their first communion, as they went in procession, and carried a rich bouquet. The nuns and girls had bouquets wholly of lilies and other white buds of flowers. The music was such as I am sure I shall never hear the like of in this world. The vast area within was filled with people.

From this I went to the poor little English Wesleyan chapel. About one hundred and fifty: about seventeen men: generally servants and governesses of English residents and visiters. Sermon by Dr. Ritchie, a Wesleyan of Canada. Good sermon on "Behold the Lamb." The application of it was such gospel, gospel, gospel, that I laid my head down and almost dissolved. These things which are daily bread in blessed America, are here like God's manna. The beauty, the grace, the extent, the glory of these illuminated forests, these spacious *places*, these statues, buildings, orderly crowds, this music—a hundred orchestras and concerts every night in open air—these things pass description, and steal the soul of the people from God. Since the cities of the plain, vice has never had such blandishment. Most, even of religious Americans, forget all restraint. Not that I have seen drunkenness or heard one profane word. All is courtesy and *bienseance*. The common people have a grace which reproves me every instant. Around a puppet-show or dancing dogs, the folk in blouses are so polite and still; they do not even rub against you without a "Pardon, monsieur," the tone of which is more than the words. But they are Godless, and at one rap of the drum (especially just now) are ready to become *simiotigres*.

Mr. Walsh has gone out to St. Germain-en-Laze. He sent me a most warm and characteristic letter, mistaking me for Addison, and went to the Director of the National (once Royal)

Library, and requested that I might be introduced to the principal Orientalists of Paris.

All the time I write I hear from the large courts a perpetual sound of French chat among the servants, with that Parisian *tune* to the words which no foreigner can ever obtain, but which is so cunning and musical and insinuating, as to reconcile me to the sound of French.

Mr. A. Monod is the most remarkable mixture of sweetness with intense solemnity I ever saw. Three months ago his mother died leaving twelve living sons. All the connexion seem to be in the fear of the Lord.

PARIS, *July* 3, 1851.

My first opening of the lips was last evening at the Wesleyan Chapel. Though it rained I suppose a hundred and fifty were out. Spies of this free government are always there. One of the most interesting of all my hours abroad I had yesterday morning with l'Abbé de Moligny. Mr. Walsh gave me a note to the Abbé evidently as a specimen of the most cultivated French clergyman. Every thing in his apartments was in the highest bachelor taste, like a boudoir. He was all attention and cleverness; showed me specimens of binding; offered to take me to his bookseller and buy for me, which he could do to advantage. He alluded several times to my being a Protestant with much gracefulness and sobriety. We talked of German emigration and of politics.

I greatly wished to see a religious house, and the greatest Romish theological seminary of France; both coincide in St. Sulpice. Mr. Walsh gave me a note to Dr. L. R. Delual at the Seminary, and sent me a kind letter inviting me to-day. The Seminary has about three hundred religious, of whom a hundred and fifty are students. I was conducted to the room of Father Delual in the third story. He began to talk rapidly in English, and did so for three hours. He soon told me he had lived thirty-two years in Baltimore, and was twenty years President of St. Mary's College. He knew much about Princeton, Dr. Miller, my father, and Addison. He had a vivid recollection of meeting Dr. Hodge on the Delaware when he was accompanying the archbishop of Baltimore to embark for Rome. There are nearly twenty other Sulpitian seminaries in France, all affiliated under this. I was placed in *rapport* with a number of students in different parts of the cloisters, and of a beautiful and spacious terraced garden within the wall. I visited the small lecture-rooms, which are plain but full of pictures. There is a series in oil of all the Popes, as he said, "from St. Peter to Pio Nono."

I saw numerous younger students carrying light desks on their
heads to the recitations. They study in their cells. They look
unhealthy and meager. The refectory is divided into two parts;
to the right go the valid ones, to the left the invalid. The
covers for the latter must have been thirty. Each, as he enters
the dividing passage, takes from a great pannier as much bread,
wheat, or rye as he needs. Each has his half bottle of *vin ordi-
naire* at each meal. The fragments are dispersed to the poor at
a side-gate. The garden is full of trees, gravelled and beautiful,
with covered sheds. The old man joked paternally with those
he met. He pointed out two who had been " Presbyterian ministers in Scotland." He encircled us in his arms, saying, " All
three Presbyterians." I replied, " My reception here is too
courteous for me to engage in controversy." One of the two
said to me, " We must pray for you at *Notre Dame des Victoires.*"
I have no belief that either of the two was ever a minister. We
went into the chapel. It is a beautiful building, the whole area
being clear. Oaken stalls in two rows along the walls accommo-
date the worshippers. They never fairly sit except during the epistle; the rest of the time they either kneel, or (turning the thick
oaken seat up by a hinge) rest on a ledge which is called a
misericorde. There are seven large paintings, some very fine,
by Lebrun. One of the Scots had a little Latin Testament in
his hand, and was going to the " Scripture lesson." They are
mostly young, with much appearance of austerity. Their courses
of studies seem low, puerile, and generally memoriter. Dialec-
tics and casuistry form the chief part. The surveillance and
separation are perfect. All the youth have tonsure. Dr. Delual
answered all my questions with great promptness, and constantly
presented me as a Protestant and a Presbyterian. He talked
much about revolutionary atheism, and said the days of Marat
would return if the red-republicans gained power. He added,
what I believe, that there is a great revival of ceremony and mass-
going, even among *men.* He is a very venerable and even
elegant man, with a fresh complexion, and chirping merriment.
He often quoted Latin, but never said any thing against Protestantism.

Yesterday I was at the College of France, and had several
hours with the celebrated mathematician Biot, who intrusted me
with several things for America. He is in his 80th year: yet I
have some of his writing, done without spectacles, smaller and
firmer than mine. He spoke of Peirce, Henry, Gould, Wilkes,
and Bache.[1]

[1] On the 10th July Dr. Alexander left Paris and reached Dijon that evening. On the 12th to Geneva.

GENEVA, *July* 12, 1851.

All this day we have been in mountain-raptures; but when suddenly, through a near gap, the Alps burst on us, it was so different from any forethought of mine that I was relieved from swooning only by tears. I am thankful to say all my thought at the moment was of God, of Christ, and of heaven. Though a hundred miles off in many parts, they were clear as diamond. I was absolutely speechless. I had dreamed of vast dimensions, and of big mountains and chains, but this was mother-of-pearl, azure, agate, all colours, more solid than granite, and looking among the clouds, heavenly. We all sank under the religious impressions. The impression of death, heaven, and eternity is unavoidable. It has been a means of grace on the blessed, quiet Sabbath in the city of Bernard, Calvin, Farel, Vinet, Knox, Beza, and the Turretines. Yet around this lake lived Voltaire, Rousseau, and Gibbon. "The entrance of *thy words* giveth light."

July 15.—On Sunday I went to the cool retreat of Dr. Malan's chapel. Neat but plain: oaken pulpit and unpainted galleries. About thirty-five present. The Doctor preached; very short and affectionate. Two members, perhaps elders, were called on to pray. Afterwards I went to his house, and had a hearty, loving welcome.

This is the greatest day I could have in Geneva. The national shooting-match, the *Tir Fédéral*, has been going on for ten days, and people from all the cantons, to the number of 30,000, have been here. The prizes = $37,000. The targets are by hundreds in a row. Every man who makes a good shot carries a card in his hat, and I have seen some with more than fifty. I never saw a more healthy, brave, honest, orderly people. But they are becoming corrupted by French infidel democracy.

We went to the St. Antoine quarter, where there are seats and walks, near the wire bridge, by the ramparts. We visited the Cathedral; a very old church, like St. Denis in some points. Here the Byzantine arch is seen growing into the early Gothic. The old stalls from before the Reformation remain, with figures of apostles and prophets in wood, and blazonry indicating the alliance between Geneva and Florence, as republics. The pulpit is modern, but the sounding-board is the same as when Calvin preached here; this was his favourite place.

The flora of the Alpine valleys is prodigious. The emerald hill-sides are a mosaic of hues more brilliant than any greenhouse. The air, or some luxuriance of growth, makes the grass and flowers appear brilliant beyond telling. Every great rock, on its warmer side, has a perfect garden of plants and flowers. The people are very loving. Every heifer and every goat is petted like a cat.

From the very point of leaving Geneva, there was one panorama of gardens and beauty ; but as we came up and up nearer
to the " monarch of mountains," the views became so amazing
and so unlike all ever seen before, that I felt almost in a new
planet. You are sufficiently familiar with the description of
such valleys as those through which we came. You have seen
models of Swiss houses, but oh ! you must magnify and roughen
them ; you must make them dark and smoky and filthy ; you
must turn stable and dwelling into one ; you must people them
with the most homely, rude, bundled creatures ; you must cause
to issue from them disfigured idiots, maimed and livid beggars,
and objects with goitres from the size of an apple to the size of
their own heads. I never beheld such an appearance of ill
health, as in the lower valley of the Arne. When we began to
rise yet higher at St. Martin, the people looked better, but still
our carriage was beset with horrible lazars. Occasionally a fat
priest might be seen. The women work like oxen, and have no
trace of comeliness. The men are sometimes well-looking.
Crosses and roadside chapels abound in the passes of the Alps.
But " only man is vile." These very objects, seen in a landscape
a little way off, are picturesque in a high degree. To describe
the valleys, heights, precipices, grottos, perpendicular rocks, and
passages along edges or shelves, where heaven was darkened by
the barrier of awful rock on one side, and the pit yawned on the
other, is more than I dare attempt. In one place a cannon was
fired (by a woman) and its echoes were undistinguishable from
severe thunder. Nothing more surprised me than the luxuriance
of vegetation. You never saw, even in a favoured meadow, such
green as clothes these depths and heights, from bottom to top,
wherever any soil can stick. Even here, where I seem almost
to touch Mt. Blanc, where its tremendous slope comes down to
the very Arne, which sounds in my ears, as it rushes from
masses of ice ; where the weather demands greatcoats and fires ;
and where I see two glaciers and a world of snow above me on
the South, and overhanging as if in reach, glistening in the sun,
even here the pastures are indescribably rich. The velvet green
goes up to the very fields of snow, and beyond it. This moment
the echoes of bells on the home-coming cattle, are in my ears.
The flowers are more numerous, beautiful, and fragrant than I
ever saw at home. We have abundance of strawberries, cream
which is almost too rich, and honey which is famous all over
Europe. The Alp-horn was sounded for us and we listened to
its echoes. I did not properly understand a glacier, before I
came here. It is most like a mighty river, tossed into fury, and

then turned to ice. Glaciers have a constant, though imperceptible motion. They look like frozen cataracts, coming down the hollows of the mountain-sides. They give origin to rivers. The air is very rare, cool, and clear, so that objects seem greatly nearer than the reality. The clouds, and fogs, and snows, which play fantastically about the mountains, keep the great peaks most of the time concealed ; but enough is visible to make us adore Him " who setteth fast the mountains."

COLOGNE, *August* 2, 1851.[1]

The revolutionary spirit [through Germany] connects itself with a hideous levelling jacobinism. I bless God, from my soul, that I am an American, and that America is a quiet land. The evils of over-population and iron prescription look incurable. Yet such labour, such lands, and such plenty, I never dreamed of. The amount of soil in vineyards shocks me. They could exist without wine. Yet I have never seen any one drinking mere water at table. Add coffee and tobacco, (now largely raised in Baden,) and the waste of soil and labour is alarming. Even yet every plough has a wheel, and very little horse or mule power is used. Indeed, women and children take their place. To-day I counted seven baskets on one woman's head, and eight on another. At Heidelberg I saw two fine girls remove a load of cut wood on their heads, carrying almost a small wheel-barrow-full each time. Every inch of soil and every odd chance of labour are subsidized. Hedges, and even paths, are unknown in many parts, to save room ; and along the crags of the Rhine some of the most famous vines are set in baskets, and dressed from suspended boards or ladders. You will often see a patch of wheat no larger than a bed-quilt ; and, wherever the reapers have removed the sheaves, plowers and harrowers tread on their heels. Fields of poppies for oil. Fruits go from hereabouts to London, especially cherries. The great staple, however, is wine. The tip-top sorts reach none but princes. The common wines are in my humble opinion little better than raspberry-vinegar, and far below their own beer. The Rhine-wines, which everybody drinks, are acid though lively, and require a training to endure. I confess, the peasantry look happy, dwell cosily, and enjoy a merriment unknown with us. The instances of personal and table filthiness, common in German inns, would nauseate you if described. At Basel, a German gentleman, at the table d'hôte, dinner going on, cleaned his teeth with his

---

[1] The places since Chamonix were Vevay, Lausanne, Lucerne, Zurich, (where he "could not find a man who had ever heard of Zuingle, till I met an American,") Basel, Baden, Freiburg, Strasburg, Carlsruhe, Heidelberg.

brush, and spat into a glass. The female sex, generally, tends to a masculine coarseness. I have learned to prize an American woman. Of Cathedrals, I have now seen the greatest, Freiburg, Strasburg, and Cologne. Next to God's works, no work has ever so amazed me. In the gorgeous temple, amidst painted windows and music that made me tremble and sink, my soul was oppressed at the heathenism to which Christianity is here reduced. And then to think what the Protestantism is, which is to oppose it! I deeply fear some judicial dealing with this whole continent. Unless Christ work some pentecostal miracle, where is the hope?

The scenery of the Rhine was very beautiful, yet I felt how inferior in mere natural points it is to the Hudson. The vineyards, harvests, towns, and ruins, however, give it a character all its own.

STEAMBOAT "RUBENS," ON THE RHINE, BETWEEN
COLOGNE AND ARNHEM, *August* 4, 1851.

There is nothing more curious here than the rapid change of languages. An hour ago, it was all German. Now, having got on a boat for Holland, it is all Dutch. When I came aboard, I really thought everybody was talking English, the sound is so different from the jaw-breaking German. The *look* is American. I write on deck at a mahogany table. A little forward is a company of six, three men and three young women. They have just had their lunch. So gentle, so home-like, so Protestant-looking, I am soothed and comforted after filthy, wicked Cologne. The river is just like the Delaware about Tacony. We are just passing Dusseldorf, which I am sorry to leave unseen. How glad I am I did not stop! Dr. E. Robinson just got on at D. You cannot understand my thankfulness: how my pent-up English rolled out in a flood! He is from Halle and Berlin, and goes with me to Holland.

The Rhine-wine is cheap here. The true Johannisberger is produced by one vineyard only, which belongs to Metternich, and which I saw. The people all drink wine, and always dilute it. Undiluted it is weaker than cider, and just the colour.

Utrecht, 9½ P. M.—In Holland my first landing was at Arnhem, then hither by rails. I longed for English cleanliness, but Dutch is more marvellous. It seems as if dirt could not stick. Entered this Venice-like city by moonlight. It is the poetry of niceness. The canals are shadowy with trees. The best idea I can give, is to refer to *old* Philadelphia half a century ago. Nothing in England so resembles it. The squat houses, gables, glazed brick, trim doorways, shade, absence of glare, in a word a wealth too proud to be fine. Every house, door, chair, and tea-cup, is new to me. Surely this is the China of Europe. Population 50,000 ; 30,000 are Protestants. The University is the aristocratic one ; between 400 and 500 students. The Jansenists are here in force—nowhere else. I am surprised that I see nothing as yet that strikes me as funny. I am so overcome with the purity and peacefulness. The Germans and French are ten times droller. The Dutch children are just little Philadelphians, only with a cunning rig of their own. I have just been shaved. No brush, box, &c., own soap and towel. This is German also. The hydraulic power between the Dollart and Scheldt is estimated at $1,500,000,000 ; the value of windmills is $3,600,000.

I observed signs of strong drink in Holland. Schiedam has 300 gin distilleries. The house in which Erasmus was born, is a gin-place. I observed, for the first time in Europe, pallor among the children ; yet the people look healthy. The working-women are as neat at their work, as ours on Sundays. The churches are full. My general conclusion is, that the impulse of the Reformation, and its traditionary customs, abide very strong, and that, while they are on the descent towards German rationalism, they are not so far down as we think in America. They are dead and formal, but not universally erroneous. In the country places, I am assured, people read the old books and cling to the old doctrine. Catechizing and pastoral visiting are kept up. Country pastors are " orthodox," but I failed to learn precisely what that term imports in Holland. Two educated and sensible men agreed in declaring that Utrecht is still orthodox, and that the body of the churches hold the divinity of our Lord and the atonement.

LONDON, *August* 12, 1851.[1]

I dare say you think I am in Belgrave Square. Not a bit of it. I am at the George Inn, Aldermanbury, opening into Milk street, and so, southwardly, into Cheapside. You need not fear my lavishing all my admiration on England. I have been admiring all the way. If my geese are all swans—" at mihi plaudo." It is so much in my pocket. But I have not failed to go, perhaps too largely, into the Mayhew-places.[2] I continue to think the English of Englishmen, the ugliest language I ever heard. It is a tin-pan throat with the nose held. Every Englishman I have heard (and it has been many every day) says knōwledge, nīther, wroth, vaws, (vase,) 'ow, sovereign,

---

[1] The intervening dates are Amsterdam, Leyden, Hague, Rotterdam.

[2] Mayhew's articles, first in the *Times*, describing the condition of the London poor.

(a word of every minute.)   But they are by odds the best people to meet with I have seen.

August 14.—This morning I surveyed Billingsgate, the oyster-sloops, Coal Exchange, Old and New Corn Exchange, Leaden-hall Market, and the India House.   At the last I inquired of the doorkeeper about Charles Lamb.   He said "I have been here since I was sixteen years old, but I never heard of any Mr. Lamb." [1]   But the door-keeper of the Museum remembered him well : " Oh yes, Sir ; he was a very little man, with such small legs, and wore knee-breeches."   He directed me to a private stair, which would take me down to the Accounts.   I went into a place below, like a bank, and was shown to a principal person, Mr. W.   It was the room in which Lamb wrote many years, but had been altered.   Mr. W. showed me his window and where his desk was.   I looked out at the high blank wall, not five feet beyond, and understood Lamb's " India House."   Mr. W. showed me a 4to volume of *Interest* Tables, with such re-marks as these, in Lamb's fine round hand, on the fly-leaf :   " A book of much interest.—*Ed. Review.*"   "A work in which the interest never flags.—*Quar. Review.*"   " We may say of this volume that the interest increases from the beginning to the end.—*Monthly Review.*"   Mr. W. knew Lamb well.   " He was a small man—smaller than you, and always wore shorts and black gaiters.   Sometimes his puns were poor.   He often came late, and then he would say, " Well, I'll make up for it, by going away early."

As I was prowling about, I saw over a dark entrance " *Little Britain.*"   It was not in human nature to overpass Little Britain, and glad am I that I did not.   A great monastic walled court with quadrangle after quadrangle, cloisters along the sides, and lofty ancient piles of the Elizabethan style, surrounding the paved areas—black, dingy, and quiet, with statues, pumps, and double iron fences in parts.   It was Christ-Church Hospital !   There are the dear little fellows, in the ancient dress.   No hat, black velvet small clothes, yellow worsted hose, a long coat or frock of blue, a girdle of red leather, and bands like a preacher. There are about a thousand, but only eighty are here in vacation. The great Hall is modern and cost £30,000 ; all in one room. Here they eat, at tables which seem two centuries old.   I went into the Mathematical school.   The forms are very long and narrow, with the merest strip of a desk.   The little scholar, who was my cicerone, said he was learning Greek and French. Wherever they go, in the remotest part of England, they have

_____

[1] " Elia " died in 1834.

to wear this garb. Coleridge and Lamb were blue-coat boys. All round the cloisters, or covered walks, marbles are set into the wall commemorative of teachers, benefactors, &c. One runs thus:

" HERE LYETH

A BENEFACTOR,

MOVE NOT HIS BONES."

I wondered at this antique silence in the heart of London, and came away with regret. I find myself to be an undeniable antiquary. My portrait ought to be taken, as Savigny is caricatured in Germany, with eyes at the back of the head. I have been such a miserable book-worm for forty years, that I live almost in the past.

When I say I like the English hugely, more by far than any people I have seen, I certainly do not mean that I like the fire and fury of the movement party. Religion is with them made up of politics and aggression, just as in some parts of America, of abstinence and abolition. There is less known of us in England than on the continent. Here the papers cull chiefly what is laughable, discreditable, or capable of turning to their own account. You cannot get through an Englishman's hair the first notion of our confederation. They all have the grossest views of our slavery, and lose temper when spoken to. The people here press me to stay to the Evangelical Alliance, which has a great demonstration beginning on the 19th; but their programme contains some phrases which move my American spunk, and show they still have the same spirit they had last year.

I think the British Museum worth my whole voyage, and journey, and expense. It is just by my lodging. At last, after years of wishing, my highest desires are accomplished, by sight of the greatest MSS. and antiques. To-day, on a third visit, I came away, worn out, after superficially seeing about the hundredth part. If anybody asks you whether I have been to the cemetery of Père la Chaise, at Paris, say No: but I have been to Bunhill Fields, where are the ashes of Isaac Watts and John Bunyan.

LONDON, *August* 20, 1851.

I spent last evening in company of Dr. Dacosta and Dr. Capadose, of Holland, both celebrated as converted Jews, and promoters of evangelical piety. Capadose is full of Christian warmth and love, but he speaks English very judaically. Dacosta cannot open his lips without your perceiving that he is an original. It has been said that he is the greatest mind in the Low Countries.

At the Evangelical Alliance I heard Noel speak. His pronunciation is precisely that of an educated South Carolinian, except a few words. Mr. James presided, with great *empressement* of manner, and great voice and rhetoric. The great house (Freemason's Hall) was thronged, and they sit from ten till six. I must admire the temper of the Assembly. They are full of heartiness, and every one speaks to his neighbour. They receive the poorest, stammering speakers, with perfect forbearance. Indeed, it is all free and easy as a dinner. I have had an explanation with Dr. Hamilton about the Alliance, and declared to him that I would not submit to any queries about my opinions on slavery.

When I saw the sculptures from Italy, on my first visit to the Crystal Palace, I had never seen any thing so lovely in art. But when I visited it lately the charm was gone, for I had seen hundreds of ancient works in the Louvre. Yet, nothing equals the Elgin marbles.

Seeing Gothic churches has gone far to make me a convert to the Greek, in regard to exterior. As to interior, the Greek temple had none, for the *cella* cannot be so named. Inside I admit the sublimity of the structure. Henry the VIIth's chapel is marvellous. Yet sitting there in one of the antique stalls, I owned in the very place that Gothic architecture is not the highest ideal of *Bildkunst*. So much is grotesque, so much is reducible to no canon, so much excites wonder, like over-learned music for its seeming impracticability, that I go back to the perfect beauty of Pæstum and the Parthenon for repose.

CAMBRIDGE, *August* 24, 1851.[1]

Yesterday we left London, and got here in two hours. In our railway carriage was Mr. R. H. Wilkinson, a Senior Fellow of King's College, and Bursar, (which is only fifth in rank, and in certain things only second,) who insisted we should put ourselves under his care. His elegant apartments are the same which good Mr. Simeon occupied. We (Dr. Robinson and I) dined one day in the Hall. The service was solid silver, with the College arms. All the china had the same. Rising, we went across the passage to the combination room, really a very sumptuous parlour, opening into one larger still. Here they sit at wine. Great reverence to "Mr. Vice Provost," who is always so addressed. Here we had six added, only one

---

[1] On the 23d of August Dr. Alexander's youngest child, and only daughter, died at Princeton. Her age was about fourteen months. The afflictive tidings reached him at Glasgow.

clergyman. The conversation was perfectly easy, without a word about learning.

On Sunday attended service in the famous chapel of King's College. Service chanted; all in surplices. Wilkinson looked grand in his white robes and master's hood. I admired the manners of these learned Sybarites, especially the absence of all interrogations about America. I heard Scholefield, the Greek Professor, preach in St. Michael's an admirable extempore sermon. We saw every thing, visited all the Colleges. It was as if we had been old chums come back on a visit. The kingdom rings with the victory of the American yacht. They are very open and manly, in expressing their chagrin. I have never seen or dreamed of any persons so full of real, though peculiar kindness, as the educated English. I like America best, though lost in admiration of England.[1]

EDINBURGH, *August* 27, 1851.

This is the ninety-seventh day of my absence, yet the first in which I expect to lie down in a private house. You cannot imagine how I felt to get into a sweet, happy, elegant Christian house, [Mr. Wm. Dickson's, an Elder of the Free Church,] and have family-worship and sing the old psalms. Then, oh how delightful to be among Presbyterians! To-day for the first time have I seen the hills covered with heather, and beautiful it is. We visited Melrose Abbey and Abbotsford, and saw Dryburgh Abbey, where Scott lies.

August 29.—I saw the Queen come in yesterday afternoon, and stood so near as to have a perfect view of her Majesty and Prince Albert, the Prince of Wales, and the Princess Royal.

September 1.—I preached yesterday for the Rev. C. J. Brown, in the Free New North Church. I will only say I was never so *helped* by a congregation. Imagine me in the Geneva cloak; five hundred Bibles rustling at once; such deep, penetrative, animated looks from whole rows of people, all seeming fired with zeal, and all singing without an exception that I could note. I thought it far better than the Madeleine or Cologne. Mr. Dickson edits a youth's paper. He teaches two Bible classes. I preached to one of them. It contains 70—80 girls. An hour was spent studying rather than saying the lesson. I should have thought the examination a good one for the first [the youngest] class in the Seminary. They answered the questions with a

---

[1] On the 26th left Cambridge, and to Ely, Peterborough, Lincoln, York, Alnwick, Berwick-upon-Tweed.

pertinence, knowledge of Scripture, and exactness which amazed me.[1]

GLASGOW, September 9, 1851.

That my journeying has done any good to my body, I am not sure. I am sure it has been good for my soul. And especially these few days in Scotland have shown me a permanent revival of religion, such as proves to me that God has a favour to his covenanting people. The preciousness of it is, that religion is founded on chapter and verse; free from outcry and sanctimony, and even talk about personal feelings, but is so courageous, active, and tender, that I am as certain as that I am writing these lines, that I am among the best people on earth. A thousand times have I said to myself, "O if my father could just for one hour hear these prayers, and observe these fruits of unadulterated Calvinistic seed!" Here is the fruit of prayers sent up by Rutherfords and Bostons. Don't think all are such, or that these people are faultless. Their faults are as prominent as their good qualities. They have the bad points belonging to strong, sanguineous, choleric, fearless, outspoken people. Their quarrels about hairsbreadths (for they are all agreed about doctrine and order) are inexplicable.

In Glasgow there are more hideous, half-naked people, than I ever saw anywhere on the continent. I own they generally look hearty, but the public charities are kept in full operation. Thousands of Irish are here. While a low, radical infidelity is doing its work, and whisky is slaying its thousands, there are tokens that Presbyterian institutions are acting vigorously. Our system is more than a theory. Church power makes itself felt. Elders are more numerous than with us; sometimes twenty and even thirty. The Kirk has no Deacons, but some Free Churches have twenty each, who do every thing that is done among us by voluntary collections. The sums raised are almost incredible. Indeed, religious arrangements take the place in public conversation which politics do with us; and I scarcely meet two men without hearing them talk about some scheme of church-operation. All the piety is not in the Free Church.

Dr. Robinson left me on the 4th, to go to Southampton. We have been just a month together, and have had many mercies in common. I have cause to be thankful for the lessons I

---

[1] I have to omit the details of the visits to the institutions, libraries, historical localities, churches, eminent ministers, &c., of Edinburgh. He said, "I find it utterly vain to try to journalize here." "Particulars would fill fifty sheets." On the 1st September he left the hospitable city—to Stirling—by the lakes—to Dunbarton, where he took steamer for Glasgow.

have learned from him. Truly he has been " eyes " to me all the way, by reason of his stupendous topical penetration.

I spent some days at Helensburgh opposite Greenock on the Clyde, at Mr. Mitchell's. On the Sabbath I preached once for Mr. McEwen. The Edinburgh and Glasgow ministers spend more time in summering and in excursions, than those of the United States, while their climate gives less reason for it. The colleges and theological halls have a vacation of at least six entire months. But the places of worship are never shut up.

It is altogether impossible for me to describe the kindness I received at Glasgow. The M.'s are a generation even beyond their own countrymen.

BELFAST, *September* 17, 1851.

I arrived here on the 12th. There are seventeen Presbyterian churches in Belfast. I heard Dr. Cook at his church, on fellowship with God; I regard him as the nearest perfection as an elegant orator, of all I have met with. His hospitalities were Irish and Christian. We mounted a jaunting-car, and rode by Carrickfergus, Ballygelly, and Ballycastle to the Giant's Causeway. All along the incomparable coast of Glenarm Bay, people were bathing. The world can scarcely offer a more delightful place, and the day was mildly warm, with a golden haze. Fair Head is a lofty sea-mark, a promontory of majestic loveliness. Bengore Head is second only to this; and the intervening long sweep of bay, shut in by the isle of Rathlin, with its blue pearly heights, almost sickened me with its fairy-like softness. We reached the excellent inn at the Giant's Causeway about the end of the long northern twilight. In all my journeyings, there is no day I would more gladly repeat. The people interest me more than any thing else. How sharp and how merry! The mixture of Scots and Irish here, is very obvious. In the oatsfield they show finely. Here only among their own scenes can Irish beauty be seen. I have seen many faces, which had the beauty of expression, among the poor women and girls. Tuesday was given to the Causeway and accessories. Description is unnecessary. From the Causeway in a jaunting-car through the county Antrim. There are no barns. The grain is stacked, and hereabouts in beautiful English-looking ricks. The land is very fertile, and wherever an owner has it in hand presents a noble appearance; but in the poor, little patches of the cotters, even here in Antrim, it is a chance agriculture, like the slovenly patches about a negro-quarter. They live from hand to mouth. You pass single cottages, and groups of cottages, all in ruins, as after a fire. These are of people who, ruined by the rot, have

beeu swept into the fine spacious poor-houses. The cottages are
all of rough stone and thatched. Their general average look
is thus : [Here is a pen and ink sketch of a hovel.] Out of
such houses I have again and again seen handsome and joyous
families pouring, with here and there a pallid, fever-looking
creature. So open and welcoming a smile I never saw prevail
in any human faces. Calves walk in and out of many cottages
as freely as the yellow-haired children. About Antrim and
especially the Moravian settlement, Grace Hill, we see what care
and taste may do. Such vales, such hills, such gateways, bleach-
ing grounds like fields of snow, such hedges, and such green and
gold, as even Devonshire might own. Such might all Ireland
be, if the priests had chosen to instruct their slaves.

DUBLIN, *September* 17, 1851.

From Belfast we crossed the county Armagh to Castle
Blayney and Dublin. Thus far, there is no part of my travels
which I would so readily repeat, as my Irish trip. The mode
of travelling, the roads, the access to the people, the awakening
of human sympathies, the physical geography, the rapid comparison of races, must make me ever mindful of it. I have
seen grander scenes, and a few more beautiful, but none more
lovely than all Ulster and a part of Leinster. True I see much
misery, but compassion is a healthful feeling ; and while I admire
some nations, I can truly add I love the Irish. For *surface* I
believe there is no such country in the world. I have seen no
part, out of towns, where there is any level. The roads are as
smooth as this table. You have no idea of the demigods the
priests have become. They might this day make Ireland happy,
by teaching their wretched worshippers to read, to build, to till,
and to keep clean. The Protestant regions are like Scotland ;
you can instantly tell the difference by rags, stench, and merry
ignorance.

Dublin shows extremes of magnificence and squalid woe,
such as seldom meet. The better sort of people strike me as
the handsomest I ever saw. There is one type of face which
predominates and is peculiarly Irish—black hair and eye-lashes,
large clear blue eyes, red and white skin of unusual delicacy, and
a joyous, arch expression playing through all. Happy Dublin,
if it were not the capital of a ruined land.[1]

----

[1] Leaving Dublin the 19th September, the traveller passed through Kildare, Thurles, Inch, Limerick. Thence by Ennis, (County Clare), Gort,
(County Galway,) to Galway, the fifth city of Ireland, but "far, far beyond
all I ever dreamed of for squalor, filth, and poverty." On the 22d left Gal-

OXFORD, *September* 26, 1851.

I came here to dinner yesterday from Liverpool, 176 miles. We touched Rugby village, about a mile from the school. It is vacation here, which is bad; but the claustral silence, and venerable solitude, and regal-ecclesiastical state of this monastic city of palaces is surely unique. The impression is that of an awful dream. You have read so long and so much about Oxford that I should think it idle to repeat what is in a score of books. I will set down some incoherencies not in print.

Oxford is larger, greater, and lordlier than Cambridge. It has more colleges, more large colleges, and an aggregate of architectural glories beyond Cambridge ; but Oxford has nothing like King's College, Cambridge, and little like Trinity, and no grounds like those of the last named. There is a family-likeness in the two towns, but Oxford is more antique, civic, mediæval, and proud. Cambridge has incomparably the more beautiful site. There is no chapel in Oxford, or the world, like King's at Cambridge. There is no Hall at Cambridge like Christ Church here. The turf is close-shaven, cut every few days, rolled and swept, and is unlike any thing known among us, the moist climate favouring grass. Flowers abound, not only in the landscape-gardening of the immense college-greens, but in the windows of fellows. Some of the quadrangles here are not green, but gravelled. Christ Church meadow is surrounded by a walk of a mile, and elms three centuries old. You may lose yourself in the groves and thickets of some of these river-gardens. I learn that the " men " seldom prefer them to the streets. The halls or refectories, are, as a whole, less regal than at Cambridge, except only Christ Church, where they daily provide for three hundred in term. Around these are portraits, generally full-length, of great members. The painted glass windows in the chapels are by far the best I have met with, especially five Flemish windows in New college chapel, (William of Wyckham's.) The feeling in these cloisters, " quods," and parks, (where deer come to your hand,) is that of absolute sequestration from the world. Pusey's house, in one of the inner corners of Christ Church, is just the spot to generate such fancies as his.

The system here, though inexpressibly fascinating, is out of harmony with the age. In every buttery-entrance, where you look to espy a monk under the black honey-combed arches, you see the placards of " Time Tables of N. W. Railway." The present Warden of All-Souls (where there are none but

way and crossed the country by Athlone and Maynooth to Dublin. On the 23d to Holyhead and Liverpool.

fellows,) is the first married warden. The pressure of the age will certainly bring collapse on these outworn cenobitic shells. I feel it every moment in a country where steam affects every inch, and trains thunder by some places twenty in a day. The agitation about exclusive privileges and overgrown foundations every year shakes down part of the old pile, as in regard to the income of Bishops, by the late Act. A clergyman here is regarded everywhere with a deference unknown anywhere else. But as a class they evidently feel very fully that they are on their good behaviour, and that public opinion cannot be disregarded. Some, I believe many, are labouring to gain good will to the church, in the best of all ways.

It would consume pages, and emulate guide-books, to tell of college after college, chapel after chapel, halls, gardens, portraits, statues, libraries, and cloisters. Books of great size are taken up with this. Dr. Routh, author of the Reliquiæ Sacræ, Master of Magdalen College, has his portrait in the Bodleian, æt. 96. He is the oldest living Oxonian.[1]

The general effect produced by Oxford is soothing to my mind in a high degree. Such self-contained wealth of learning, such seclusion from the stir of life, such yielding of every thing to learned honours, such architectural glory, such libraries, such lawns, such trees, such prizes held out to studious ambition, such histories of past genius, such mighty and beloved names, such costly display of taste, such approaches to what Rome was and would fain be, exist here only and at Cambridge, and more here than there. But it all strikes me as a tree whose root is dead in the earth, vast, green, and lovely, but destined to die presently. I doubt whether the glory has not already passed away. The true Oxonian spirit is that of Newman and Pusey ; but it is not of the age. Such a chapel as Christ College, which has lately been repaired at an expense of $90,000, is fitted to absorb a young man in reveries, but they are of an age which cannot live again. My hopes rise beyond what I am able to report during this rapid tour, that God is working by new agencies, and a new *zeitgeist*, and our new world, to bring in a new kingdom. So far from letting my intense and scarce excusable fondness for the relics of darker ages tempt me to wish them back again, or try to imitate them, I am even more filled with a sense of the gigantic progress of the modern arts and civilization. One day at the Exhibition, one day at Birmingham and Manchester, or one day on any one trunk of English railways, is worth volumes to awaken expectation.[2] I have meditated, I trust not unusefully,

[1] Dr. Routh nearly completed his century, dying December 22, 1854.
[2] Dr. Alexander left Oxford September 26th, arrived the same day at

amidst objects which have the odour of past ages. My reigning sentiment, after hurrying and exciting travel among the thousands of this unspeakably teeming population of Europe, is an impression that men and generations pass away like the herb of the field, but the Word of the Lord abideth forever ; his kingdom is coming ; his house is going up ; his plan is unfolding ; old traditionary things which vain man calls eternal, are crumbling ; new things predicted, but not expected, are rolling in like a flood ; our life and that of our children, is but a link in the great chain. I trust I can sometimes add, " Thy kingdom come : Thy will be done."

Birmingham—on the 27th passed on to Liverpool.   Here he heard Mr. Mc-Neile, whom he places with Dr. Cook, of Belfast, as "by a long way the most eloquent men I have heard in these climates."   On the first of October he embarked on the steamer Atlantic, Captain West.   On the 12th (Sunday) he and Bishop Otey preached in the saloon.   After a stormy run, the steamer reached New York October 15th, and the same evening Dr. Alexander joined his family at Princeton.

CHAPTER XII.

LETTERS WHILE PASTOR OF FIFTH AVENUE CHURCH, NEW YORK.

1851—1857.

PRINCETON, *October* 18, 1851.

I WRITE more to stay my mind during hours of waiting than to communicate much. My father seems to grow weaker. He believes himself to be on his death-bed, and this more than any symptoms of a grave character makes us apprehend the same. I think his perception and judgment greater than in any moment of his life. An endless train of minute arrangements have occupied his mind, each of which he has settled in the most summary way. He says his views are what they have always been; that he has never feared to die; that he has never seen so proper a time to die; that all his prayers have been answered; that he has no ecstasy but assured belief; and that no one should pray for his recovery. He says his views of God's goodness are expressed by "How MARVELLOUS is thy loving-kindness, &c." Every one of us, even my dear mother, feels most calm when nearest to the scene of suffering. The affairs of the Church employ far more of my father's words than any family concerns. He talked an hour with me on the prospects of the truth in Scotland. The whole tone of his discourse is free from what John Livingston calls " shows," being precisely what it always was—passing with childlike ease from the settling of a bill to the grace and glory of the gospel. He said, " I have this morning been reviewing the plan of salvation, and assuring myself of my acceptance of it. I am in peace. The transition from this world to another, so utterly unknown, is certainly awful, and would be destructive, were it not guarded by Christ; I know he will do all well."

My father, with an authority which no one could parley with, forbade the calling in of any city physician, declaring his view of his case, and his perfect satisfaction at what was done. In every sentence, there is a surprising conciseness, clearness, and weight of command, unlike his manner in latter years; and when he has given orders, he adds, "Enough for that point; let me speak of another." And then, "I have done; you must leave me." There is not a trifle respecting coal, supplies, &c., which he has not settled. He yesterday ordered a ten-dollar library to be sent to a minister in the West. My father's last publication, we suppose, is " A Disciple " in the *November* American Messenger. I am naturally led to think of unseen things, and am strangely beset with mercies, chastenings, and lessons.[1]

NEW YORK, *November* 26, 1851.

We have got into our new house, (22 West Nineteenth street,) but are not yet in any order. What they will do at Princeton I know not. Whatever changes may supervene, I earnestly hope there will be none to lower the general standard of our theological training. There is a view of it in which one minister might teach every thing; but if we would maintain that high ground which I solemnly believe American ministers now have in comparison with those of other countries, we must have at least one well-sustained Seminary. This was my father's great desire, which gained strength in his more sober hours, and formed part of his dying conversations with me. I am troubled in my mind at the sort of church I am coming to. I certainly should never have accepted the call if I had dreamt of such outlay. I fear the total exclusion of the poor, and the insufficiency of my voice. As I had no hand in it, and know myself to be crossed rather than gratified by it, I hope God will turn it to some good. On Sun day I urged the destitutions of New York, and proposed the erection of a free church down town. On Monday a man whom I never knew before came and offered me $1,000 towards it. We cannot hope to get even into our lecture-room before May.[2]

Even since I went over the water the changes here are surprising. Sabbath-traffic and grog-drinking have increased. The whole talk now is about Kossuth. The newpaper, the " Times," is going full sail. It already has 16,000 subscribers in two months. Greeley [" Tribune"] writes powerfully, when he lays himself out. His late articles on Hughes are

[1] Dr. A. Alexander lingered until the 22d day of the month.

[2] While the church was building at the corner of Fifth Avenue and Nineteenth Street, the congregation worshipped in the chapel of the University. The first sermon of the pastor, after his return from Europe, was preached there on the 26th October.

tremendous batteries. But he goes full-length with the Chapman-Foxton-Westminster Review party. His book on Europe is worth reading, though sour. P—— sends me the proofs of an embryo book on Charity.[1] It is —— raised to the nth power; abuse of clergy; abuse of churches; abuse of theology; everybody wrong but *moi;* sneers at societies, creeds, catechisms, &c., &c.; yet, after all, a book that no one can read without deep and anxious reflection. The mixture of truth is great and suggestive, and the style is tip-top, sometimes as keen as Pascal.

Note any thing you can remember or hear, about my father's Philadelphia labours. Do try to see any old people who know. Could not you find old Mr. Nassau? Addison and I, or one of us, will, Deo adjuvante, write a life. The MS. autobiography is voluminous, but only for material. How strangely we misjudge often. Dr. Miller left not one line of diary!

New York, *December* 2, 1851.

Surely there are divine uses of pain which we cannot fully understand. Nor can we reason much about the rules of its mission to individuals. The amount of suffering such persons as —— and —— have endured often amazes and puzzles me. Yet in ——'s case the spiritual joy resulting is almost as specific as of a medicine. I have thought much of this as a point in divinity. The Papists have missed the right doctrine of pain; but have we made enough of it? Some day we shall see what it was sent on good people for. I have known moments when it has seemed to me a great boon to have the will broken, and self-pleasing mortified.

We are among a good many open lots and much rubbish; and to feeling, as far from the New York I knew, as if in another city. I find a good smart walk from here to Trinity Church quite tonical. My mind works incessantly on such themes as these:—the abounding misery; the unreached masses; the waste of church energy on the rich; its small operation on the poor; emigrant wretchedness; our boy-population; our hopeless prostitutes; our 4,000 grog-shops; the absence of poor from Presbyterian churches; the farce of our church-alms; confinement of our church-efforts to pew-holders; the do-nothing life of our Christian professors, in regard to the masses; our copying the Priest and Levite in the parable; our need of a Christian Lord Bacon, to produce a Novum Organon of philanthropy; our dread of innovation; our luxury and pride. I

---

[1] "New Themes for the Protestant Clergy." Philadelphia: Lippincott & Co.

preached twice on some of these things ; but I work at the lever very feebly. Since I saw the drinking-customs of Britain, I am almost a tee-totaller, and half-disposed to go for a Maine law against venders of drink.

After settling a little from the shocks of late events, and looking back on my tour, I find my judgment of differences among Christians somewhat modified. Surely our battle is too momentous, to leave much time or zeal to spend on niceties of old school and new. Ah! how I daily feel "I have lost my adviser!" How often, "I must tell this to my father," and then I awake to the reality. But there is no bitterness in the reflection. If it please God to touch our sons, our work will seem more clearly less needed here.

New York, *December* 20, 1851.

This morning, being on an errand, I saw a black-garbed whitenecked procession going into the Irving House. It was the "Evangelical Clergy." I followed, and saw Kossuth again. He looked commoner and worn. Spencer sermonized him, with specs and MS. The following is a correct report of the Governor's speech, as I heard it : "m—m—m—(sh—sh—sh—) 'country' (sh—sh) 'the most free country,'—(sh,) 'Gentlemen,'—(sh) m—m—m—."

I heard every word of Spencer's. I believe K. was saying he could not make a harangue, but would answer in writing. He declares himself a Lutheran. I greatly admire his frankness. He loses no chance of showing it. He is getting to think himself a messenger of God. Some of his expressions smack of the Hegel doctrine of God's voice being the voice of humanity. Colwell, in his episcopo-mastix, ["New Themes,"] seems to be in favour of a plan which shall dissolve all churches, charities, and associations, and solve the great social problem by this formula, "Let every man be perfectly good." This is the avowed conclusion of his strange book. The reason why people go to Cardinal Hughes is, I think, to be found in one character of the Church of Rome, its matchless *organization*. Me judice, we shall as little counteract it by the dissolving plan, as we should benefit warfare by disbanding troops, and setting each warrior on his own hook. B—— comes out quite a war-man ; so suddenly do the movement-people change to any tune which will make the mob dance. Furnaces, gas, and Croton pipes have almost literally employed every day since our "flitting," with amendments. Pipes frozen, gasometer ditto. My rent is $900, in a very narrow, tawdry, shelly, ambitious, half-done house. The neighbourhood, however, is as quiet as a country village.

NEW YORK, *December* 31, 1851.

Christmas Day saw me in nine churches, St. Francis Xavier's, St. Patrick's Cathedral, St. Joseph's, St. Vincent de Paul, St. somebody's, (German,) Bellows's, Grace Church, Calvary, and Muhlenberg's little Gothic free-seat chapel, where there was at 7 and 8 communion, and at 9 a baptism. I never heard a Unitarian sermon before in English. B—— said the Unitarians were endeavouring to resume the " feasts and fasts." He is a scholarly writer, and a theatrical though Yankee speaker. Progress, no matter what Jesus held; theology rising; let every man believe as much as he can; inspiration untenable; all men are Christians; Jesus the Head of the Church, *i. e.* of humanity; the great matter is the *truth*, which is not dogma, but being conscientious, kind, fond of freedom. All Christians in three classes, *church*-men, *creeds*-men, and *life*-men. All through he essayed a sort of mysticism, and wrought himself into a factitious peroration-heat about coming days, fight of freedom, martyr spirit, &c. It was fearful to see genteel and moneyed sons of New England trying to take in his Emersonian rhetoric and ultra-liberality. There was nothing redeeming but the style, which was elegant, novel, startling, and a little affected. Voice very rich in low notes; but he plays with it, and lapses when earnest into a Yankee tune. I feel a great admiration of Kossuth, especially since reading Madame Pulsky's Memoirs, and History of the War. But the tide already ebbs here. Stocks would fall if the Hungarian tricolour should rise; and our canny capitalists go by that. Young men and workies take on the natural enthusiasm. The ministers who preached against the slave-law, preach for Kossuth. As you will see by my " Travels," I was quite prepared to hear of the *coup d'etat.* The great quality which it needs is yet to be revealed—military genius; this made Cæsar, Cromwell, and " mon oncle." I do not believe any true news gets to us yet by newspapers. The Canada brings three days later, but no change.

NEW YORK, *January* 19, 1852.

My young men are about to employ a man who speaks the Irish, and has laboured twenty years in Connaught, to look up the " strangers scattered abroad " in this city. My late church is occupied by several hundred emigrant families. What a pathos there is in every thing connected with Mr. Clay's last days! There seems to be some good reason to view him as a converted man. At no time have we had a greater concurrence of good news from our Foreign Missions : accessions of converts in almost all. The China men are an extraordinary corps, and their work is going on with great energy. We to-day appropriated $1,000 for another chapel at Ningpo; and had notice of an equal gift from an individual for the same purpose. After years of defeat our Foreign Board is at length incorporated, under the recent law of this State. Broadway is a carnival of sleighs. The noise, glee, turn-outs, and throngs are quite a Russian spectacle. Schaff has a vehement and very able article against Kossuth's notions. Dr. Spring told me he lately sat at his sermon-desk from 9 A. M. to 7 P. M. without dinner; but felt worse for it. His morning services are over-crowded, which can be said of no other Presbyterian assembly here. One can't help feeling an admiration for Louis Napoleon's quiet force in his coup d'état. Several priests said to me in Paris, that the only hope for religion was the putting down of the *rouges*, (sc. rogues.) They talked of this much as we should have done, but I dare say with an eye to their own power. Father Delual, once principal of St. Mary's College, Baltimore, but now retired at the great College de St. Sulpice, [page 146,] spoke to me in his nice little chamber with high admiration of Sibour, the archbishop of Paris, who was also a Sulpician, and his coeval. The adhesion of Louis Napoleon to a church very much in the ascendant in France gives a basis to his power which was wanting to " mon oncle" at the eighteenth Brumaire. M—— reports the Popish churches as unfrequented. I spent much of my days in them at Paris, and saw a very different sight. Not women only, but men in great numbers. I was particularly struck with the great numbers of children and youth under drill, often hundreds together, preparing the motions, &c., for processions. At Dijon, I was present at a catechizing, in an ancient church; the curé sat, and was lecturing a host of boys on a point of Christian morals. I spent my time on the pictures, but Maj. Preston heard it for some time and pronounced it very sound. When we consider that France was all but atheistic, we must regard even the acquisitions of Popery as conversions to a sort of Christianity. I find it very hard to swallow the tenet, that the existing church of Rome is incapable of being improved, and is to be looked at only as for hell-fire. My prophetic specs are very dim. When Louis XVIII. was restored, Bernadotte said to him at a dinner of the sovereigns : " Faites-vous craindre, Sire, et ils vous aimeront: sauvez seulement avec eux l'honneur et les apparences : *ayez un gant de velours sur une main de fer.*" He knew the French, and Louis Napoleon seems to adopt his maxim.[1]

---

[1] While this is in the printer's hands, "the eldest son of the Church" is giving a new exemplification of the velvet glove on the iron hand, in his policy with the Pope.

I am pleased that our collections are increased, notwithstanding church-building. I never had so many volunteer offerings for poor. One man has offered $1,000 now, and $500 a year towards a Ragged School, and another $1,000 towards a free church. Another promises to keep me in books for the poor as long as I live. The Irvingite Prayer Book is very good, being compiled with much taste from the ancient liturgies. They have "seven churches in London," as headquarters, with their respective angels. But there are angels in other churches. The twelve "apostles" are for great countries. Ours is Woodhouse, who is not here at present. We are served by F—— and M——, probably prophet and angel. It is a consistent Puseyism. The Advent is not made so prominent as unity, real presence, prayer for dead and extraordinary χαρισματα. They profess great peaceableness, and ask no one to their meetings. Daily prayers at 6 and 5. Several University men are among their speakers. They have ample vestments, and no metrical psalmody. Their Psalter has some odd things, e. g. :

> " He that *doeth these things*
> Sha . . . *ll never be moved.*"
> — " My *li . . . ps shall praise thee.*"   Et sic passim.

NEW YORK, *February* 13, 1852.

I don't know whether it is so elsewhere, but here the Valentines have become a plague. As the day approaches, whole rows of shops of every sort fill their windows with valentines, from a penny up, which from having been amatory have become cynical and opprobrious, affording boobies and snobs an opportunity of venting cheap gall on a neighbour. For the first I find some tending to irreligion. You have seen the account of the perfectionism and promiscuous abomination.[1] How few cards after all the devil has in his pack ; this is only the " Brethren and Sisters of the Free Spirit " over again. It more than fulfils predictions made by Nettleton, which at the time I thought absurd.

A youth died the other day, at 19, who said he had used every day for eleven years a prayer I gave him on a card, when my catechumen.

I am getting to think professing religion much less presumptive of grace, than once I did. Nor do I see that any strictness at the door helps the matter. Have we not added to the New Testament notion of communicating in the Lord's Supper ? The anabaptist essays at a church of pure regenerate

---

[1] Public assemblies held in Broadway of the advocates of " Free Love "— eventually suppressed by the police.

believers have not worked well. I used the word " catechumen "
in the vulgar sense ; but the κατηχουμενος was as such unbap-
tized—under schooling—long watched—slowly indoctrinated.
The Church *as a school* has declined ; hence the Sunday School
has been built up alongside.

NEW YORK, *February* 25, 1852.

The meeting for prayer this morning at St. George's [Epis
copal church] is one of the most hopeful things I have seen for
a long time. Dr. Spring made an address and a prayer such as
few but he can utter. Dr. Potts was in a tender melting frame,
and prayed so as to carry a large assembly up with him. I had
not heard of Mrs. L.'s death. Brooklyn is, as to any visits,
about as far as Trenton. I was this very day meditating a journey
thither to see her ; but daily visits of three to four hours have by
no means allowed me to " overtake " my pressing parochialia. I
agree anent Webster, and was going to write so. Moreover, his
estimates of Livy, &c., are equal to the Sophomore class. His
comparison of Sallust to Dr. Johnson is absurd.[1] I don't yet
believe in the Maine law. The radical principles of the whole
scheme are rotten. 1. The Bible speaks well of wine, even
as *exhilarant.* 2. Christ chose, for a sempiternal ordinance,
that thing, which of all others is (according to Maine) what ought
to be everlastingly absent. 3. Islam (according to Maine)
is ahead of Christianity. 4. The Decalogue is defective,
for the first command ought to be, " Thou shalt not drink." 5.
If what they say is true, *pledging* is not the way ; else, why not
pledge never to touch *that,* the love of which is a root of all
evil ? or never to lie ? 6. It is questionable whether the true
ethical principle is to remove all *material* of sin. 7. We have
too many laws already which can't be enforced.

I can't help seeing that the apostolic preaching could never
have been conformable to prophecies in John xiv.–xvii., unless
greatly different from our Lord's. Progress and development
mark all the teachings through his and theirs to the end. I look
on a system as a mere *report of progress* in understanding Scripture, at a given point in history. Our *preached* system differs
from the Confession of Faith, both by addition and subtraction.

I have heard [R. W.] Emerson. There is a singular fascination in his delivery of his sentences. These end in a surprise,
almost always, and he artfully stammers and halts, so as to
make expectation extreme. No gesture. No outlay of voice.
Yet he keeps you intensely anxious to hear his soft, hesitating

---

[1] The allusion is to Mr. Webster's unfortunate selection of a classical
subject for a discourse before the New York Historical Society.

tones. A disjointed series of "good things." Audiences not large; apparently New England residents, ladies, uppish clerks, &c.

Carlyle's Life of Sterling is a dreadful book, to popularize Pantheism, warm up the swelling germs of doubt in young minds, and prepare the soil for every extreme. I nowhere find in English, except in Th. Parker, such dark menaces. It is evident C. converted S. from a mere nominal Christian into a black despairing skeptic. The Irvingites have a great proportion of persons out of the most indoctrinated circles; most of their prophets, &c., having Episcopal orders, and several privates known to me being Presbyterian, and even Seceder-bred. Six scribes take down the dicta of the prophets. Judge Story was a great man; but as to enthusiasm in professional studies, I have no doubt a hundred American clergymen have as much. In this one point I do not see him to surpass Stuart, Robinson, Hodge, or Barnes. In extra-professional literature he seems to me inferior to any one of these. I admit that our period is singularly barren of great divines and great preachers. Yet the average working talent, I apprehend, was never greater. As to what is called pulpit eloquence, I grow in disbelief of its importance. The gaping multitudes who fill churches are little reached, as to the main matter. *Worship* is certainly overshadowed by our sermons. How few quoters of our Directory ever quote p. 497, where the sermon is compared with " the *more important* duties of prayer and praise."—Quere: Whether we do not err in ciphering so much about the time, men, and money it will take to convert the world? Whether God's plan is not to work upon, in, and by a peculiar people, elect and called; ἐκλεκτοί? Whether his plan may not be doing well, even though in a "little flock"? Whether the other world is not the great collection of saints? Whether God is not taking out of this world a constant select addition to that? And whether, consequently, both hopes and fears do not mislead us, as to the extensiveness of visible success?

Absurd as it sounds, the spiritual-knocking business is like to be really alarming. If Satan ever interferes, one might think it would be in such mesmeric and analogous delusions. I am told there are scores of distinct and stated meetings in town, for these spiritual investigations. Miss Martineau, in her late book, avows high-mesmerism and utter atheism.

NEW YORK, *April* 3, 1852.

I attended the funeral of M. R., on the 1st inst., æt. 13. She had been of my catechizing class, and was, I trust, a renewed child. I am expecting soon to go to the grave of M. S., who is sinking fast, but with the loveliest aspect I ever saw death put on. Her sayings are as worthy of record, as those of any woman I have read of. Her mother and sister, who both died of consumption, had just such blessings in their decline. Mr. Lowrie is going to visit our Western Indians. The death of Dr. Wm. S. Potts, of St. Louis, is truly a solemn event. He had attained great eminence and influence, without the employment of any arts, or the perpetration of oddities.[1]

Grote's Greece is a wonderful book. He is a hot radical, but a great scholar and historian. His style is true English; no balance, rhythm, or expected cadence; his mind is John Bull-ish, as much as Gifford's, (they say *Jifford* in England,) and there is no flummery or fog of any sort. You read his account of debates at Athens, with the same matter-o'-fact feeling, as when you read about a debate in Parliament. All is made to uphold democracy.

New Orleans seems to be the small end of Kossuth's horn. What a pity, to see the noblest fellow living kill himself by " power of slack-jaw," as Yellowplush has it. What extremity of asinine folly, to prefer a Parisian education! Except for the name of it, French is of no more use to women than Cherokee.

I think with all its airiness and sweetness the up-town is less agreeable to me than the old parts. I feel more at home among the noise and kennels. A wealthy, zealous Norwegian, is here; he lent the American Bible Society $50,000, unasked, without security, for their new edifice. We are near the moving season. A number of my people are coming up. I think not five families of my old charge are below.

We have not the least stir in our congregation; but at no time have I known so many persons under a deep religious concern. I have perceived something unusual in the manner of hearers, for some weeks. The proportion of non-professors in our assembly is small. In every place where I have been, I have observed that I never have marked increase of hearers, but always a striking adhesiveness in those who come. We are suffering greatly for want of a good place for meeting; it is most obvious in our weekly lecture. A lady came to me under great convictions, produced by the funeral services of E. B.

Think of 3,000 Chinese in California! One of our Canton missionaries writes, that there were forty vessels in that port preparing for California. I am looking to the printing of a few hymns in Hungarian, for a little congregation of Mr. Acs, (pronounced something like our old school-phrase *Ouch!*) More

---

[1] There is a memoir of Dr. Potts in Dr. Sprague's Annals, vol. 4.

than $20,000 have been raised here within a few weeks, towards the endowment of the still unendowed chair at Princeton.

My health has not been improving lately. Constant pastoral visits and anxieties, and mental work without relaxation, have run me down exceedingly, so that I am sleepless in a good many nights, and quite nervous by day.

I have my father's little book on Moral Philosophy very near publication. I suppose I shall have to throw in a Preface. It will rank with his Evidences, but will awaken more opposition. He wrote nothing more simple, clear, or convincing. It is the only work which he left ready. Among his papers, the only diaries are a few, (chiefly in cipher,) of which the earliest goes back to æt. 17.

Does any one properly estimate the approaching certain influence of the Germans, as a power in our country? I often hear as much German as English in my day's walk. Of all the Protestant portion, nine-tenths are infidel. All I meet with are radical. Most of the German newspapers are infidel, and some blasphemous. A friend of mine heard some talking yesterday; one said, "Our grand error in Germany was not using the guillotine; let them employ it freely, and let them begin with the *Pietisten.*" The second Psalm comes to my mind as affording the only hope.

NEW YORK, May 4, 1852.

I almost envy you your chance of going to Charleston.[1] I have always wanted to see that proudest specimen of sumptuous slaveholding hospitality. Try to see Dr. Smyth's library.[2] Perhaps I will enclose a letter to my classmate, W. P. Finley, President of the Charleston College.

When elected Moderator, the properest speech may be from these heads: "Unexpected—seldom in the chair—most will depend on members—good intention will atone for inexperience—will know no section or party," &c.

I wish I could see my way clear to promise you pulpit aid. But I am so sure to have to flee myself, when it grows hot, that appearances demand pretty full labor from me as long as I can. Something may indeed turn up to make the thing practicable; and it would be very pleasant to me. Yesterday it was a French minister seeking a place, to-day it is an Irish one. These Irish think "vacancies" are gaping for them as soon as they disembark. They have no drawings towards the bush. I ob-

---

[1] Where the General Assembly was to hold its meeting.

[2] Now the property of the Theological Seminary at Columbia, South Carolina.

serve an absence of all "onction" in all Irish Presbyterian preachers. It is very different with the modern Scotch school. Guthrie of Edinburgh talks of coming hither for a jaunt. Guthrie draws more crowds than anybody since Chalmers. He has both poetry and wit, with plenty of fire. I hope to receive next Sunday about twenty on certificate, and seven on examination. I hope you mean to go by sea. The change is so entire, and so breaks the home-thread, that I know nothing like it. Don't forget summer clothes. Verify the rumour, that the common Charlestonians say *wen* for *when, wail* for *whale, peer* for *pear, fare* for *fear,* and *steers* for *stairs.* Find out whether South Carolina extempore preaching is the best a-going. I wish for you that protection and happiness, which were vouchsafed to me so largely by sea and land.[1]

---

[1] I throw into the margin a piece of playful satire on style and sentiment which he addressed to me at this time.

HARD SHELL BOTTOM, S. C., *May* 3, 1852.

REV. DEAR BROTHER,—On yesterday I was first aware of your being a commissioner to the General Assembly. Sentimentally accordant with you, though differing perhaps in my verbage, I would have defined my position in regard to true blue Presbyterianism, if I hadn't have gotten an impression that you were tinctured with Princetonism. I didn't have any test, till going to dinner yesterday evening, I received a statement tantamount to a denial of the above. No unreliableness of my informant will prevent my approbating his sentiments on the issue about to be made, since a crisis has arrived in the affairs of our beloved Church. Talented men in our Southern country think I would have done better if I would have consented to have given you my views on Boards. If we do not return to the basis of Scotch testimony, we will go to the gulf of Erastianism, and we will become a byeword in the camp of the Philistines. It is mighty easy to talk of the Boards of the Church as doing a great work. Unless arrested in their nefarious derelictions, they will stultify us, by bringing in a class of ministers who are merely literary men, ready to fall a prey to the demons of choirs and organs. It is high time to testify against carpets in churches ; a rag of the scarlet woman which has been privily brought in. As I lately said to brother Mc-Rouse, "show me the pattern of the carpet which Paul and Silas were on, at Philippi, and I will use it in the Hard Shell Church." Note-books are against the second commandment, and also the fourth. They were unknown to the primitive age. *Sol, fa, me,* &c., are clearly from the man of sin, and are nearly as bad as cruciform churches, being taken by a rank massmonger, Guido Aretini, from an idolatrous hymn,

" *Ut* queant *l*axis *r*esonare fibris," &c.

The practice of tokens and of lining hymns went out when reading supplanted preaching. Who knows but our sons may see the day when the paternoster may be used in public prayer!

Rev. dear Brother, contend for the faith against all new light and Northern innovations. I am yours in bonds, &c.

DUNCAN McKILLIKRANKIE.

NEW YORK, *May* 24, 1852.

Ask President Finley, with my regards, after any of our college friends. I have my father's little "Outlines of Moral Philosophy" in press, as well as an 8vo of my own, intituled "Consolation," &c. ; a rifaccimento of about eighteen sermons. Do any thing you deem discreet, even by placard or advertisement, to get *letters* of my father; this is like to be the desideratum; especially letters before 1812. "Use a little (port) wine for thy stomach's sake" while in the tropics, and follow the instinct of all hot countries, by increasing your spicery. A rumbling betokens new troubles with Mexico. Have we not whipped them enough? Wicked as it is, I believe the manifest destiny will annex Cuba, and, as Punch says, promote free trade to Japan by opening our ports on the Japanese. God reigns, even in wars, and truth has made its way very often through the breaches opened by conquest. M.'s new book is very little talked about, while 50,000 copies of Uncle Tom's Cabin are sold, and 100,000 will be. Yet the nigger-talk of the book is often pure Yankee. Dogwoods and lilacs are the blossoms which denote our time of year. This day last year I embarked. Time was when I would have attempted to give you some public news, but newspapers and telegraphing have taken this pleasure clean away from us poor epistlers. M.'s case is not yet decided in court, though it can go only in his favours (as the Scots say ;) they also say *severals.* Not one descendant of Scotchmen in a hundred ever gets his *shoulds* right. Dr. C. would be sure to say, "I would think he ought to accept," or even, "if the mail would come," &c. No Englishman or New Englandman ever goes wrong here. Hence the prevalence of the *woulds* among southern Presbyterians. S. is one of the few who *more Anglicano* writes, "The Assembly, *it should seem,* has a moderator." Here endeth the first lesson in subjunctives. American lawyers are much honoured in Westminster Hall. I see what I said as my hearing confirmed by an English paper, which speaks of My *luds* and my *lud* as universal at the bar. I heard Earl Derby say so repeatedly in the House of Lords. And every Englishmen I heard said cort for court, and morning for mourning, &c. The only Walkerian pronunciation I heard was from Irishmen, *gyard, kyarnal, skyie, kyined,* &c.

The Directors in Princeton joined Polemic to Didactic Theology again, but did nothing anent the vacant chair. They rescinded their former recommendation about a fifth chair.

You are now in the focus of light and heat, while I have nothing to say. I am glad you like Charleston; the city and people, I am led to think, have as much a character of their own, as Philadelphia and Boston once had, and as New York never will have.

If any one's thoughts turn toward the Germans in America, do give it a serious consideration. 1. The immigration thence is enormous. 2. Famine, &c., will increase it. 3. They will soon be "a power" in State and Church. 4. The Protestant part (a full moiety) is largely infidel. 5. The existing German *Christians* in the United States are either poor, or devoid of missionary zeal and tact. Nothing is to be hoped from them. 6. The German Reformed Church is mad after a delusive transcendentalism, and has endorsed it. 7. The call on us is greater than that of any *white* portion of the world.

A common man said to-day down-town: "The New School Men do not discover that the secret of Old School efficiency and increase lies in *tenacity of doctrine, and liberality of sentiment.*"

NEW YORK, *June* 21, 1852.

I am in a very false position as to my edifice, [its costliness;] while I never saw a *congregation* so suited to me. They are all drawn around me, by partiality for my explanatory and uncoloured ministrations. For years I have seen people who want to hear oratory, &c., come once or twice, and then depart. Elderly and afflicted persons, of the plainer sort, are chiefly those who drop in. Once I scuffled to be other than I am; now I see a providence in it, and even rejoice. I look back, and see that I have often erred by trying to be (1) more original than I am, (2) more animated; especially No. 2. No man can be anybody else. Don't you, as you go on, feel increasing complacency in variety of gifts? We could not miss a ——, or a ——, little as you or I fancy them. I was pleased, when a friend of McNeile's said: "He is a *teacher*." That we can all be. If tears break out—well; but the teaching is effective, sans halloo and spasm. I have lately had unusual comfort in my lectures, by omitting my little notes of one or two pages; and, after hard study of the context and more of the words, going on without any sort of MS. The briefest notes ripple and detain the current. This method I seldom venture on, on Sundays; for in the morning I read every word—usually. The past winter has been one of too unremitted labour; I am conscious of having had a pride which made me do double duty, to prepare for the incapacities of summer. The consequence is, that my nervous system is very much shattered. I do not feel it inter loquendum, but afterwards and in any excitement which unmans me. God rules—but I have serious apprehensions about being able to bear up. I find my four-mile heat, walking to the University, quite disabling.

The German singing-bands from all parts, are to be here in tremendous force. They do the thing German-fashion, for several days, with garlands, torch-processions, picnics, choruses, and wine. I was at a German (Presbyterian) meeting t'other night, where about 150 made as much hymn-noise, as any ten of our assemblies. I think to go to Newport about the 2d.

NEWPORT, *July* 31, 1852.

After four weeks at the Bellevue, I came to lodging in Broad street, where we have a good table and good rooms. Nothing delights me more in Newport than the oldness of its old parts. I know nothing so English; the narrow streets and trottoirs, street-gables, overhanging eaves and even stories, square casements, vines, &c., every thing but the material of the houses. Generally the temperature has been such, that any more coolness would have been unpleasant. I was out fifteen hours in a sail boat; having two calms and a small gale. These waters are singularly varied and beautiful. The healthiness of Newport is vouched by the extraordinary number of very old people. The boys and girls play in the streets of the old parts, almost as freely as in France. The talk among squads at the corners is not horse-talk, as with us, but always sea-talk. I have not developed any taste for fishing, of the kind here practised. I should almost as soon think of taking a day at butchering. Neither do I admire the sea-fish as food. My boys have, however, made up in both ways for any delinquencies of mine. What a charming writer Hawthorne is! I greatly prefer him to Irving. His sea-side descriptions (in " Twice told Tales ") smack of the very beach and surf. I have been to Bristol, which is just a smaller Newport; on a very beautiful bay, not far from Mt. Hope, the home of King Philip. I have read two lives of Roger Williams, here among his haunts, with great admiration of that eccentric old hero. In respect to mere bathing, I do not consider Newport namable along side of Cape May or even Long Branch. Unless you walk, every dip costs $37\frac{1}{2}$ cents. The times for bathing without dress, are much restricted; and every thing goes by hours, not by tides. But the air is incomparable; indeed I should wax extravagant, if I said all I think of it. This is the Shiloh of New England quakerism. The orthodox preponderate. In our part of town one sees the sweet young plain quakeresses, passim, *more antiquo.* The Maine law works no visible change in hotels, but produces a dreadful exasperation. I think the moral influence plainly deleterious.

NEWPORT, *August* 26, 1852.

I do not find my health much benefited, except by the repose. Within a fortnight I have had a bad turn of disabling rheumatism. Fishing is said to be the favourite clerical sport. I am an exception. The sailing is delightful. I can imagine the delicate play of fly-fishing to have a charm; but this dead pulling up of sea-fish is merely a nasty trade. Yesterday I caught a shark, about four feet long, having pulled to the surface two others, one apparently seven feet long. But it is a useless and horrid butchery, and I would as soon stick a hog or a calf. I have been twice out sailing with Dr. Boardman. The Newport men say he ventures beyond his sea-knowledge. Their boats have a peculiar rig, and great alacrity in sinking. [Rev. Mr.] Thayer is a Triton; I have seen him row across Bristol harbour in quite a gale, and he often rows himself out to vessels, during pretty rough winter weather, to visit their crews. M. has a gay sloop of eight or ten tons, which has luxurious accommodations; I have tried it twice. You may judge of his zeal, when I add he keeps a man, whose sole employment is to gather crabs for bait. I have seen a letter of Berkeley, wherein he says, in 1730, that Newport has 6,000 inhabitants, and is the chief place for trade in America. The house which he built, (Whitehall,) two or three miles off, is much visited. I found in it a family that goes to no church, with a young man dying of consumption.

Revolutionary memorandums and reminiscences are sufficiently frequent here, but it is mortifying to see how little has been preserved of their earlier archæology. The earliest grave-mark I have actually seen is 1648, and this is a late stone. More Indian traditions and names remain, than is usual. For example many of the names of fish are plainly Indian, as *Squid, Squeteek, Scup* or *Scuppang* [porgy], *Choxy, Menhaden* [mossbunker], *Totang* [blackfish]. The more I see of Narraganset Bay, the more I admire it. Among its numerous islands, there are spots where the views of coves, villages, and remote uplands, are equal to any thing of the flat sort.

I hope to resume labours on the first Sunday of September.

NEW YORK, *September* 23, 1852.

I have this day brought home my little flock from Newport; thanking God that we have been kept in life, and that some of the number have derived such benefit.[1] Our church still lingers.

---

[1] The intermission of his *preaching* in New York was only from July 18 to August 29.

The pews are in, but not the pulpit. I am less and less elated
with the magnificence of this pile. I feel, however, a growing
desire to spend what is left of me, in plainer, simpler, more
instructive preaching. I am in low spirits about the condition
of the New England churches. The whole feeling, in their
assemblies, is different from that of ours—bad as we are. The
choirs carry matters clear away from the congregation, who in
very numerous instances stand during singing, gazing up into
the singers' gallery. The sermons are never expository ; and
those which are reputed the best are extensively on general
topics of national law, ethics, and philanthropy. A sort of cold
revival is superinduced in many of them, which adds communicants, but does not help the matter much. An ordinary laying
open of a large context, especially with any stress laid on particular pregnant expressions, would, I am sure, be received
with surprise in most places. They admit themselves, that the
new generation of preachers is giving all its zeal to the construction of rhetorical specimens.

I am glad you are willing to do the service in Princeton.[1]
Young men need and desire the very plainest directions how to
go about their work. Religious biographies will furnish many
suggestions. Dr. Waugh's life contains some grand things about
city work. I have not, for many years, seen a little volume by
Innes, a Baptist of Edinburgh or Glasgow, which struck me as
containing some of the best results of pastoral observation I
ever read ; the title escapes me. My father used to go largely
into ministerial life and ways, marriage, economy, choice of a
field, principles about settlement and removal, and a great deal
concerning preaching, that is commonly left to Homiletics, or,
more properly speaking, omitted. I mean all that considers
preaching in regard to the private religion, &c., of the minister.
I know he also lectured fully and frankly on revivals ; on missions ; on call to foreign work. Be advised not to withhold
facts and deductions from your own ministry.

I am prepared to pronounce Newport the most delightful
climate (to the feelings) in America. It is singularly like what
I found Ireland to be, at the same season.

NEW YORK, *October* 25, 1852.

Our Synod sat from Monday till Tuesday night. Our
judicatories here are more churchly than religious ; too formal
and perfunctory. We have no very great men left now, and
seem not to need them.[2] John Bell [of Tennessee] seems to

---

[1] A temporary supply of the chair of Pastoral Theology.
[2] Mr. Webster died October 24.

me one of our soundest trunks of the old forest. I begin to
think military skill is more of a trade than I once thought, and
involves less mental greatness. As to France, I am heretic
enough to think it has made a happy escape from infidelity and
socialism. Walsh's letters, in the Journal of Commerce, promote this judgment, I dare say.

I have not had a marriage for six months. So they have a
professor of Mohammedan literature in Amherst College. I am
out of heart about the delay of our church. There is no reasonable
prospect of entrance before December. And if the acoustics should
prove bad, as my fears predict, from the immense vaulting and
needless recess, I suppose I shall have to look for another house.

The Moral Science sells well, and is much lauded by some
sound judges. It is indeed the only work which enters largely
into elementary morals. W.'s piety has loomed up wonderfully
since his demise. Our preachers find it a fruitful theme. A
French wine-house has this sign:

| *Rendezvous*
des
Bons Amis. | FRIENDS'
MEETING. |

Commend it to your Quaker neighbours. A famous mourning-
store in Broadway, has for its sign : *Maison de Deuil*, which imperfect scholars may interpret variously. I have a book in
hand, partly new and partly sermons, addressed to " the suffering people of God," [" Consolation."] Dr. Rice (æt. 70) looks
as firm as ever ; not gray ; indeed not changed. He is a truly
affectionate old man. He is now at Addison's. Mr. Talbot
Olyphant of my church is going to China for the fourth time.
His brothers have also been several times, and his father spent
ten years in China. They are all deeply interested in our missions. They speak confidently of the railway to San Francisco,
as a thing that must be, and that speedily. The present route
to China is shortened to sixty days. Accessions at last communion eighteen on certificate, six on examination. Collections:
for Church Extension $1,106 ; for Bible Society $990. My eyesight is failing me very rapidly.

NEW YORK, EVE OF THANKSGIVING, }
November 24, 1852. }

You make believe I owe you a sheet, so here goes. On your
overhasty departure, I perceived that you had left a book, &c.,
on my table. I have not spoken of these little lapses of memory, they are to be expected. Do you not find the events of
your middle life more easily remembered than the occurrences

of yesterday ? A spectacle-case is also lying on my table—did you leave that also ? So Napoleon III. is at length enthroned. Strange that both he and Louis Philippe should have had such adventures in America. Add Joseph Bonaparte and the Murats. What a pity saints' days and anniversary festivals should be so dangerous ! Governor's appointments lack the prestige and the legends and the traditions and the games and the flowers in season. I saw in Europe some things to show that thousands on thousands may keep a fête without the least disorder. The modicum of religious association tends to prevent this. We get over boyish hilarity too soon. Far up in the Alps of Savoy, I came upon a group of men, in the highway in a circle, hand in hand, singing Swiss songs, with every coloured ribbons in their broad hats. With us, they would have been stupefying themselves with adulterate brandy at some hogsty of a corner gross-ery. In Paris, on Corpus-Christi Day, which they call the Fête de fleurs, I reckoned that there were in the Madeleine not less than 5,000 bouquets, of which the great ones would have sold at our florists for $10 a piece. I happened to be at Cologne on St. Martin's day. The whole parish of St. Martin's, *pro more*, turned out in procession on a great *place* around the church. There were hundreds of girls and women, and thousands of men, all very orderly. The natural tendency to anniversaries breaks out among us in such holidays as New Year's, Thanksgiving, Forefathers' Day, Evacuation Day, &c. The degree of excess and abuse which occur on set days, will be in proportion to the decay of religious feeling among a people ; but I am by no means sure that these are greatly increased by set days. Yet as a good son of Mother Church, I subside into the tenet, that all such feasts are against the second commandment. I wonder the homœopathists have not taken Elijah as their patron saint, who was the first ὁμοιοπαθής ; James v. 17. The nexus between one credulity and another is seen in the fact, that ——, our prime homœopath, is prominent in the convention of spiritual rappers and mediums. I wish you a happy family meeting. My text is, Psalm ii. 11, last words.

NEW YORK, *December* 24, 1852.

I wish you and yours a merry Christmas. The week has been an exciting one, in regard to our new church. Our treasurer has just been in, and says (though he has not had time to foot up the items) that the debt is cancelled—the sale of pews equalling the entire cost of ground and building. All the very high-priced pews are taken. About ninety-five remain unsold. It is my wish that sales should now stop, and that the remaining pews should be rented, at low rates. Now that the immense cost is met, the future annual expenses on pews need not be greater than if the house had been built for a small sum. The assessment on pews is eight per cent. Since Monday the treasurer has actually collected $85,000. We had a very full house on Sunday; benches and chairs brought in till all was crammed. Drs. Potts and Plumer preached. I have been again reading Erasmus's Colloquies, in the old full edition, with great delight. Old Cass gains on me, by his magnanimity towards opponents. Old Benton in the House will be almost as racy as J. R. of Roanoke. Peter Cooper is building an Institution just below the new Bible House, for which he has appropriated $300,000.[1] These two buildings will beautify and improve a very ugly part of town. That neighbourhood already has St. Mark's, St. Anne's, the Baptist Tabernacle, Opera House, and Astor Library; and very near are Lafayette St. Church and St. Bartholomew's. A Mr. Milne has been here about two months, begging for a church at Cannobie. I am unable to see the propriety of such a course. Churches are probably thick-set all around the place, where they demand a Free Kirk. In 2 Cor. xi. 28, ἐπισύστασις has a force not commonly observed, i. e. " the being run down by so many people." In 2 Cor. iii. 6, our version fails. The free version would be, (to keep up the play of words,) "But our *ability* is of God, who has given us whatever *ability* we possess as ministers." I wish you and yours facile digestion of the mince-pies, and kindly resignation to the drums, accordeons, &c., of the season.

NEW YORK, *December* 27, 1852.

Thinking you might be pleased to learn something authentically about our church, I proceed to report progress. We had $13,000 from the old building. Last week we sold pews enough, added to the above, to clear us of all debt, that is, to equal the whole cost of the ground and edifice; which we reckon at $105,000. This left us seventy-seven pews on hand, which we determined to *rent*. To-day all these have been rented, except seven below, and three in the gallery. The whole number, I think I told you, is 204. My concern is now of a very novel kind; viz., where there is to be room for any increase. Indeed, I fear some of our worthy slow people will have found themselves without seats.

So poor old Mr. Steel is gone.[2] He was a good friend of my childhood. Often have I partaken of good buttered bread spread

---

[1] The cost reached to more than twice this sum, and was wholly a gift.

[2] Mr. John Steel, of Philadelphia, a member of the Third (Pine Street) Church.

thickly with sugar, from the hand of Betty, in that little dark back parlour no longer to be found, unless in England. John was perhaps happiest, when he was a linen draper bold, in the New Market. He could read the "Aurora," and go out to the Republican meetings, with little risk. I remember Betty's mother, old Mrs. Blair, and how helpless she was with rheumatism. Did I mention to you, that the assessments on our pews are less than in Duane Street? They have to-day been reduced to 7½ per cent. I wish I could turn out about twenty pews of rich folks and fill them with poor. But this is one of those dreams not to be realized. I never was stronger in my opinion, that all church-sittings ought to be free. Yet we can't reach this without establishments, endowment, and all that. Even in the popish churches in Paris, I calculated that at one *sous* a chair, the common price, people of regular attendance would pay $2 a year, which is just the price of a cheap sitting in our church.

NEW YORK, *December* 31, 1852.

Here is my last letter of the old year, with my best wishes for you and yours, for the new. This has been a period of events and mercies for me. Some of the things, which I dare say people think tend to elate me, have a quite contrary effect; especially the worldly increase of my cure. Seldom, if ever, have I had any private exercise more solemn, than in the whole progress of this matter. And I never more felt the necessity of dealing plainly with my people. My congregation is fearfully large. Every pew which was not sold, is rented, except about two and a half. One of my responsibilities is that of begging and dispensing large alms. Yesterday I had to raise some money for poor members of a German congregation. I went nowhere for this purpose, but mentioned it in calls, and received $68. On the first Sunday we collect for our Foreign Missions, and I hope we shall do better than ever.[1]

The question of riding in our street cars on Sunday, is agitating our community. I have not been able to decide it. The poor go in cars; the rich in coaches. The number of horses and men employed is less than if there were no cars. It is a query whether as many cars as these would not be demanded by those (among half a million) who have lawful occasion to journey. If so, the question of duty would be reduced to one of individual vocation to this amount of locomotion. The whole matter of the Christian Sabbath is a little perplexed in my mind. 1. All that

---

[1] The collection proved to be more than $3,300. In the next month, for Domestic Missions, $3,750.

our Lord says on it, is *prima facie* on the side of relaxation. 2. The apostles, who enforce, and as it were re-enact every other command of the ten, never advert to this. 3. Even to Gentile converts, they lay no stress on this, which might be expected to come first, among externals. 4. According to the letter, Paul teaches the Colossians (ii. 16) not to be scrupulous about Sabbaths. I am not therefore surprised, that Calvin had doubts on this subject. The very strict views of the Sabbath have prevailed in no part of Christendom unconnected with the British Isles. I must wait for more light. I admit the fact, that spiritual religion has most flourished where the strict opinions have prevailed. My good father used to say : " Be very strict yourself; be very lenient in judging your neighbour." I have always taken milk, without scruple; which is an offence to hundreds of good people among us. Some began to have qualms about Sunday gas; but on inquiry they found that the labour which produced it fell on Thursday or Friday. As I always give my people a motto for the year, and preach on it, I have chosen " My Grace is sufficient for thee."

Cakes are imported by our confectioners from Paris. Our restaurateurs advertise daily beef, mutton, partridges, and hares, from England.

NEW YORK, *March* 9, 1853.

With more than two hundred pew-holders, I find my circuit wide enough. In regard to visiting, I am forced to seek how to please God and not man. Cases of illness, &c., break in very much on what I have heard called a " routine of rounds." The pleasure of having our big boys at home must soon end; a forewarning of partings yet more serious. O that grace might " apprehend " them ! Bickersteth's life [by Birks] is a plain book, but O how full of healthy, ardent piety ! I think him one of the loveliest ministerial models.

Mr. Beers's death is a loss indeed.[1] He was every thing I could ask, as to prompt and willing help. Mr. Auchincloss [another Elder] is sinking apace. I shall try for a considerable enlargement of the session, but fear I shall not be successful.

Chalmers's " Life " [by Hanna] contains an extraordinary amount of trifling matter. The plan seems to have been to publish all that could be raked and scraped. It is, however, a wonderful monument to his frankness of nature. Amos Lawrence, though called a Unitarian, delighted in such books as McCheyne, Haldane's Life, &c., and bought them largely for dis-

---

[1] Mr. Beers, one of his elders and most esteemed friends, died in February.

tribution. There is a somewhat singular case of activity in my congregation. A young man, who took first honour at Prince-ton, and then studied law, devotes his whole time to the distribution of the Bible. He has boarded every foreign vessel in this port, for four or five years. He argues, exhorts, battles, and generally succeeds. Our congregations are full to a degree which oppresses me. I believe only half a pew is unlet. Our collection for Education Board, on Sunday, was $3,510. Our weekly lecture is crowded. With much external attention there is little proportionable coming out by profession. Next Sunday we shall admit about twenty on certificate, and six on examination. Of the whole twenty-six, about twenty are made up of husband and wife. I am very soberly apprehensive of failing under my burden, and that before long. I generally lose my rest on Sunday night, and on the last had the addition of a vomiting. In no winter have I had more of nervous tremor. But I try to disregard these symptoms, as I see no way out of my present duties. The translation of a French book " the Preacher and the King," which is really a treatise on homi-letics, is a capital book. I have Bunsen's " Hippolytus," a book about every thing, (4 vols.,) but of which the real intent is to give an exact portraiture of Christianity about A. D. 225, as to the creed, liturgy, and manners ; and for this portraiture the material afforded by the chevalier is very rich. It includes a complete series of the very earliest liturgies, in the original. Antipuseyite, anticalvinist, antipedobaptist, antirationalist, tran-scendental, mystical, poetical, erudite, interesting, bold, with occa-sionally pickings of a very suggestive kind. His facts and quota-tions are a great basis for thought. His central point is the *Eucharist,* in the view expressed by that word. He proves very clearly that the ancient church made this the great thing, and that all the liturgies grew out of a simple communion service. It is to him the Christian sacrifice, not in the popish sense, but as expressing in common what he regards as the great central feeling of religion, viz., the unselfish offering-up of the whole man, thankfully to God, as Christ once offered up himself. He thinks this idea pretty much lost in the modern church. He is as little of a Trinitarian as Neander Schleiermacher, or Bushnell.

NEW YORK, *April* 8, 1853.

Mr. C., a Scot, gives striking accounts of the surplus of labour in Scotland. There are about 400 probationers, and about thirty annual vacancies. Twenty missionaries are wanted for Australia, and they can drum up only six. He is familiar with labour among the poor in Edinburgh. Spoke of their district methods. Two or three ladies have about twenty houses allotted to them, for visits, &c. But these small cantons are sometimes visited by three different sets, one Free Church, one Establishment, &c. He is *en route* for Cincinnati, but I almost wished to detain him here. There is such a spirit of work about these real working Scotchmen. Mr. C. has lately traversed those parts of Ireland where the conversions from Popery have taken place, and confirms the most favourable accounts. Thousands have become intelligent Protestants. The beginning has always been by schools. He represents the Bible knowledge obtained in these as wonderful. There are about forty Presbyterian schools. Dr. Duff has taken this matter in hand with great zeal. In our city-work, the great lack is not of money, but of men. I am astonished when I consider the supineness of our young ministers. There are half a dozen licentiates hanging about here, waiting for vacancies, who might instantly have their hands full of work. Any man of the least energy could, in a school-room or loft, soon gather a houseful of hearers. I even think our young laymen are not backward in their part. But we want a revival of zeal among preachers. I am increasing my eldership, and minded to increase it more: Joseph Hyde, James M. Halsted, Thomas U. Smith, and Jeremiah J. Greenough.[1] It does not often happen to me to discover four new cases of religious inquiry in two days; but such is the event of this week.

The only error I see in the Brick Church movement is, that they did not move fifteen years ago, when they might have made a better bargain. The supporters of the church have long been up town. Free churches must be established for the class remaining below. The position of that church has long been intolerable, from the noise of cars and newspaper steam-presses, next door. The year has added to our church 109, of whom only twenty on examination. We are just about opening a mission Sunday School, in 20th Street near 7th Avenue. We have plenty of teachers, and a room capacious of 250, in a neighbourhood filled with poor; the streets toward the North River being thronged. I have completed that part of the memoir [of his father] which precedes Princeton, and in that whole period have not one letter. When I think of the new generation in Princeton, I feel quite old—Dod, Green, Cattells, Hope, Duffield. C.'s case reminds me of a frequent saying of my father, that he never knew a poor man go crazy for fear of starvation.

For some months I have been studying Galatians, with a

---

[1] They were ordained April 10, 1853.

feeling of increased understanding. Poor Byers's wife embarked at Shanghae the day after lying-in, and so came five months with a newborn child, and a dying husband. A week ago we attended his funeral, in the same church where he was ordained a year since. Coulter, our missionary printer, is just reported dead at Ning Po. The Hippodrome is rising near us, like magic; they say to contain 8,000. The Crystal Palace is not merely less than the original, but is ill placed, and diminished to the eye, by the contiguity of the great massive Reservoir. One of the prettiest little electrical experiments I know, has been repeatedly performed in my parlour by James and his comrades. If new to you, it will be surprising. It is the lighting of gas by the finger. One person, in old slippers or the like, shuffles about on a thick rug for five minutes, until the body collects a sufficiency of the electric fluid. He then suddenly applies his finger to the vent, (held open a moment before, by another person,) and the flame instantly breaks forth. I can at any time produce a spark, but have not succeeded in kindling the gas. I am not a believer in Gavazzi. I heard him in Glasgow, and thought him eloquent; but there was no religious ingredient, and little but a Mazzini-like damnation of the pope. Dr. De Witt lately preached a sermon for me, extempore, more like my father's best, than I have heard.

Having exchanged with Krebs on Sunday, I walked home through Avenue A. My way lay for above a mile through the German quarter—all the signs in German—children talking German. It was not only not like Sunday, but was like a 4th of July, or exactly like a Sunday in Cologne or Heidelberg. Every fourth house was a drinking-place. Some of these were large, with numerous tables, and filled with as many women as men. There are half a dozen Romish chapels within a few hundred yards of Tompkins Square; one of these, (Holy Redeemer,) a tawdry thing, is said to be larger and higher than Trinity church. I think there is more stir among our good people than I ever knew, about the condition of the poor, ragged boys, &c. I cannot get any other churches to agree with me in a favourite scheme, to have a great and inviting building erected, far down town, with a striking preacher, seats free, and no proximate regard to what is called a church-organization. Our folks are nearly ripe for a mission church; but I do not mean it shall be down town. The churches left in that quarter are nearly empty, as for example the spacious North Dutch. Soon every thing below will be warehouses, &c. The teeming population of the upper wards are falling a prey to the Catholics. O that our sect-divisions did not make territorial operation impracti-

cable! How much more we could do, if we could only mark off
nine squares, as our own field—for schools, church, charity,
care of poor, &c. I sometimes scruple whether a uniformity,
like Sweden, properly worked, would not overbalance the
advantages of our ultra free inquiry and individual judgment.

NEW YORK, *April* 28, 1853.

Yours is " to hand," a beautiful Americanism, which electrifies
one at every telegraph. Another is, Howel's " *Print;* " which
I observe on the imprint of a sermon. Addison will sail in the
" Asia," 18th prox. We spent hours in Presybtery, upon city
destitution and church extension. I came away with a heavy
heart, persuaded that as a Presbytery we shall do nothing.
Whatever is effected must be done congregationally. Just think
—our great and wealthy Presbytery has not one preaching-
station for the poor and wicked. As it is, the only work that is
doing, is by the irresponsible City Tract Society, under A. R.
Wetmore. The plea of some is, that the only mode is to set off
colonies from large churches. But how can we get our members
to leave us? And the worst necessities are just where self-
supporting churches can never exist. I would rejoice from the
bottom of my heart if the twenty best families in my charge
would leave me to found a new church. But this would by no
means reach the layer of population that I have in view. We
opened a mission-school last Sunday; five in the morning,
twenty-two in the afternoon. Gavazzi continues to draw enormous houses. His histrionic powers are unequalled. The purlieus of the Palace are growing up into a young San Francisco,
of tawdry shells, saloons, grog and oyster holes, mountebank
stalls, &c.; very unlike the boundless lawns and groves of Hyde
Park, which begirt the English one. The building itself is beginning to look well. Dr. Muhlenberg's church, which is a free-
seat one, has parsonage on one side and school on the other, and
employs a doctor and an apothecary, to serve all attendants
gratis. I suppose none but the poor apply. We go to Sharon
springs on Wednesday.[1]

SHARON SPRINGS, N. Y., *June* 24, 1853.

Ink-privileges are scanty here, though brimstone and water
abound.[2] The season has not fairly begun. There are about a
hundred here in all. We are the only visiters at a farm-house
about a mile from the springs: real country; a sweet, quiet,

---

[1] By medical advice for the benefit of one of his children.
[2] The letter was written in pencil.

pastoral farm of a hundred and forty acres. The fare is abundant and wholesome, and the sights and sounds very composing after being " in populous city pent." I sit out of doors all hours that the heat will permit. Yesterday the boys caught a ground-squirrel, here called by its Indian name, *chipmunk*. Innumerable birds are in the trees ; the young just taking wing. Ten quarts of strawberries at the last picking. We churned twice yesterday. Mrs. Swift gets about fourteen pails of milk daily. To vary the routine, the bees swarmed just now, and you will be pleased to learn that the outgoing hive was saved.

The water is of two kinds, in one of which magnesia prevails. It is surprisingly crystalline, and deliciously cool, but the taste is that of hard-boiled eggs raised to the nth power. It does not tell its story with the promptness of the Saratoga, but is very potent on the system, and in rheumatic cases works wonders. There is a settlement of Canadian Indians (Abenaqui) here, who make the most beautiful and various basket-work I ever saw. There is no church here. About a mile off there is a building which is occupied in turn by Lutherans and Methodists every Sunday morning, and by Universalists in the afternoon. It would be difficult to find a more beautiful country. The surface rolls perpetually : there are some high hills ; no end to streams, often running through dark ravines, tumbling water-falls, and mountain springs. There is an appearance of great fertility. The county is Scoharie, and is about seven miles from Cherry Valley. I feel refreshed and rested by being here, but not well. I shall try to get away on the 28th. I have not found the least diminution of heat, though the sweetness of June air in the country is very refreshing. I had no idea of the thousands of emigrants filling the trains westward, until my late trips. Thirteen hundred left Albany in one day. Two of them died in the cars from excessive heat. The tract distributors are active among them. The chief house here is the Pavilion, on an eminence which commands a truly mountain view. The farm on which we are is in the lap or valley just below it, at the foot of a green, smooth, rounded descent.

NEWPORT, *July* 26, 1853.

I received with much emotion your intelligence of the death of your brother Charles. Every thing is gained when the soul is safe ; and I am not surprised to hear good tidings in this respect, knowing how lively an interest he always took in the means of grace. Yet it seems strange to think of him as carried away by disease. He was always a favourite of mine, from very childhood, for his cheerfulness, frankness, and cordiality. May

Heaven protect and bless his bereaved little family! How rapidly the associations of our youth are growing dim! Perhaps the most wonderful thing of all is, that we ourselves survive; unless it be this, that we still cling so closely to the earth.

I received your previous letter while I was yet in New York; where I passed a dull and solitary time, my family being in Sharon. I then resorted thither, and spent some days with them. It is a delightful resort. The scenery is romantic, and the air dry and elastic. We had no feeling of oppressive heat, but a sort of mountain freshness. The waters seem very efficacious in a large class of diseases. We were on a large farm, less than a mile from the spring, with an unbounded range for the children. I was almost sorry to come away, though the air of Newport is, after another fashion, very refreshing. We came in two days, by way of Albany, Springfield, Worcester, and Providence, a very pleasing route. Springfield is a charming town, and the trip from Worcester to Providence is through a very novel series of grazing valleys, meandering streams, and beautiful factory-villages. On the Sunday of our arrival Henry came in from hunting and fishing in Sullivan County, up the Delaware. He took lots of trout, and slept two nights out of doors. I shall give him as much boating and sea-fishing as his vacation allows. I was very poorly, with choleroid affections, in New York, but have rallied. My church is kept open. When last heard of, Addison was stepping from Dover to Calais. In the face of much foregoing prejudice, he thinks Candlish immeasurably above any preacher he ever heard. He had heard McNeile, Hamilton, Cumming, Melvill, and Blomfield.

NEW YORK, *September* 17, 1853.

I am under a very strong impression that I answered your penult letter from Newport. Though I returned to my own pulpit on the 1st of this month, I did not bring back my familiars till to-day. Willy, who had been very ill, has been mercifully recovered. James has gained a good deal of strength, by maritime pursuits, winding up by falling into Narraganset Bay on Wednesday. We spent the night in a small and over-crowded boat, and got here about ten. Both going and coming I had agreeable chat with Dr., once Captain V—— of U. S. A., and Grace Church, Brooklyn. He is a great fisherman. He and a party this summer killed fifty sharks in thirty-six hours; one which Dr. V—— hooked measured eleven feet. I spent some days on Cape Cod, among a primitive and homogeneous people, as much like the old Puritans, I suppose, as any living. The chief places were Sandwich, Yarmouth, South Yarmouth, Barnstable,

South Dennis, North Dennis, and Harwich. There are no
negroes, no Irishmen, and no foreigners. In the houses I visited
I saw nothing like domestic servants; yet surprising comfort,
great improvement of mind, and apparent religion. The men
are all seafarers, and generally captains. Our congregation were
in a very fair way of raising $18,000, to buy an old church in
which we already have a mission-school; when the matter was
quashed by a reclamation of another people building in that
quarter, who thought that our setting up a chapel would affect
them. So we are looking round for a new scheme. Few of my
flock have returned. Church pretty full all summer, but mainly
from other congregations. I have gained nothing during the summer.

NEW YORK, November 11, 1853.

We are in an odd state as to music. Lowell Mason is our
leader; but since his return from Europe he is so bent on
severe, plain tunes, and congregational singing, that while I am
tickled amazingly, the people are disappointed. His success in
making the people sing has been marvellous. I enter no house
where so many join. But I fear we cannot hold it against such
odds.[1] We are planning to build or buy a house for our Mission Sunday School.

My father's eldest sister, Mrs. Graham, is dead. She was a
woman of strong mind and solid piety, with whom my father
kept up a correspondence for sixty years. The interruptions of
a city pastor are sometimes the occasions of his chief usefulness.
I have had three to-day, all beyond my church pale. I preached
[November 6] at overture of Dr. Parker's lecture-room. A
Presbyterian church in Rochester, known from the patron as
"Mr. Ward's Church," [St. Peter's,] has the commandments and
creed, &c., on tablets, and is to have responses, &c. The article

[1] In a note to the editor of this correspondence Mr. Mason says: "During
the four years or more that I had the privilege of leading the singing exercises in Dr. Alexander's church, he often spoke to me on the subject. Indeed, I did not often meet him when this was not a leading topic of remark.
He always spoke with great decision, and once certainly he told me, when
it was suggested that there might be danger of a return to choir-singing,
that he would not remain pastor of a church where the singing was exclusively in the hands of a choir. He often spoke to me after the public service, of the gratification he experienced from the psalmody, and I well remember on one occasion he told me he had never before enjoyed so much
the exercise of song in the house of the Lord. He spoke to me also of the
growing importance of the singing service in his own estimation. He used
to attend our little preparatory meetings, often making remarks, suggesting
topics, &c., and always closing with prayer."

in the October Edinburgh, on Church Parties, gives the most readable account I have ever seen of the peculiarities and relative force of the great divisions of Anglicans, with many important facts and explanations entirely new to me. The "Christian Remembrancer" (Puseyite) notices Fanny Fern's book, and says, "What a language in America, where a young lady can call trousers 'pants!'" I observed the word pantaloons was not used by London tailors, [always trousers.]

What a change the sculptures of the Exhibition [Crystal Palace in New York] will make in our popular estimate of nudities. Shop-windows and parlours show the revolution. Paris can scarcely equal some of our Broadway solicitations. Such an autumn as we have had I suppose no one remembers. People love to predict a hard winter. Coal is high, and the "stringency" will throw thousands of operatives out of work. There is but one point in which I ever feel drawn toward the millenarians; their belief, namely, that Christ will visit and renew his church *ex abrupto*, by a sudden burst. This often seems likely to me. Our whole system of modern means works slowly, and seems often to work backward. And yet, as to the influence on the world at large, it has not been ever greater, in my opinion, since the Reformation, than at this moment. I do not see that Christianity was ever more enlarging itself. By-the-bye, I think the talk about supporting the ministry is good and indispensable; I can say so as suffering no personal need. Nothing seems more prominent or more plain to me in the New Testament; I often wonder, indeed, that it is alluded to so much, as it is plain that primitive Christians did not neglect that duty. I do not, however, agree with those who ascribe the fewness of candidates to this. Having lived much among such, I never knew a youth who seemed to me to be held back by this reason; and he who should be so had better stay out.

I find this great change in my pastoral experience: I am more concerned about the *quality* of religion in my flock, than when I was young. Sometimes I am almost as glad to observe a ripening, as once to observe a conversion. A few instances, very striking, have come under my knowledge. Doubtless from some grand defect in my preaching its influence has been most on professors; this beyond any hopes of mine. Awakenings are rare with me. My father long ago pointed out this evil in my sermons, and it has caused me many a pang. The invitatory part, I am always free to hold forth; but in every instance when I have tried the alarming and more pungent, I have been like David in Saul's harness. I am often depressed beyond expression at the apparent waste of my exertions. Private addresses and expository lectures have done most of the little good that appears. Sad, sad, to think how nearly the glass is run out!

NEW YORK, *December* 4, 1853.

The modern German rule, of sticking firmly to grammar-laws, helps some passages. *E. g.* Acts xix. 3: ἠκούσαμεν can mean only, " We *did* not hear of any Holy Ghost;" *i. e.* we were not baptized with the formula, including that name: v. 5, " When they heard this, they were baptized in the name of the Lord Jesus;" so their previous baptism had not been in his name either. Dr. C—— is here, as accompanying a minister from Wisconsin, who solicits for a college. This fungus of col-lege-building on our Education Board is like to eat out all the vitals thereof. I have had a tea-visit from Rev. R. Steel and Dr. Gray. Steel has been thirty-four years at Abingdon. Addison preached a grand sermon for me yesterday; he is very unequal. I have arrived at the last Feast of Tabernacles, in lecturing on the Life of Christ. It has been by far the most delightful homi-letical exercise I ever tried. Holmes is delighting audiences with his brilliant and witty lectures. Our City Tract Society has twenty-six missionaries and eleven hundred distributors.

NEW YORK, *January* 4, 1854.

I wish you and yours a happy New Year. The last has been to us a year of mercies. As years roll on, the most despondent thought I have is a fear of never being much better in this world; I am glad there is another. I used to make resolutions at the new year; but now I am disheartened. The same habits, the same tendencies, the same selfishness, the same " old man," and warring σαρξ. My people lately agitated the question of raising my salary to $5,000. When they met, a letter of mine was read, earnestly requesting that it might not be done. They nevertheless voted it unanimously, in such a way as not to raise the pew-tax. After deliberating a few days, and in opposition to every adviser, I wrote positively declining. To this, after a week, I have no reply.[1] Our church-collection for Foreign Mis-sions on Sunday was $5,189 63. Add $1,000 for China Mission about a month ago. Our Mission-school goes on well; we have more than two hundred of the ragged sort. I expect to go to press this week. No one knows the anxiety I have had in pre-paring this work, chiefly from the absence of diaries and letters for the last forty years. I think I have been benefited, however,

---

[1] Upon his declining the additional salary, the congregation made an equivalent provision, which enured to his family at his decease.

by conversing with so many of my father's best thoughts. I have been reading a Unitarian book, intituled "Regeneration," by Sears. It is wonderful how he uses all our evangelical language, and tries to gain all the spirit and warmth of gospel grace. Hollow as it is, I consider it sincere, and in the light of a confession of the nakedness of their own system. Osgood, of this city, preaches in the same strain; a sort of revulsion from Parker and young Channing. Poor old Mr. Comfort [of Kingston, N. J.] had an easy end; the clock quietly ran down. Of what are called anecdotes, my memoir will be singularly destitute; also of smart sayings. I wish I had even two or three. Gavazzi still holds forth. Achilli is claimed by Bush as a New-churchman. My New Year's text was ἐνδὲ, Philip. iii. 13.

I humbly thank God for his mercy to H———; though now I am almost as anxious that he should be the right sort of Christian as I was that he should be converted.

Daily do I grow more opposed to pews. I honour Popery and Puseyism for this point. Free churches are unanimously voted a nuisance by New York Christians; but my mind is unchanged. They have, with us, always been undertaken by poor preachers. If such Chrysostoms as you and I wot of were to open a free church, it would tell another story; and I am persuaded the only way to effect it will be for individual preachers to lead the way. I have not the spirit of a reformer, or I know what I would do. My Tuesday lecture is the only service in which I feel at all apostolical. Addison preached here once on Sunday for McAuley's young men. A new school of Evangelicals in Germany has broached a doctrine about the church which would solve some enigmas about the broken condition of visible Christianity. It is this: 1. God founded and organized a Jewish church. 2. This was the only organization. 3. It is in suspension and abeyance since the Advent. 4. There is no explicit founding of a Christian church. 5. The Israelitish church will be restored, with a spiritualizing of its forms, &c. The Irvingites agree with this in part. At our communion we had twelve on certificate, and five on examination. Almost all the catechumens I personally taught in 1844, have come in. One of such revealed his case to me this evening after lecture. I should feel the mysteries multiplied by supposing Christ not to have been God before his baptism. It would then be "The flesh became Word," and not "The Word became flesh." Nor do I see any gain as to the "body prepared," which is equally true of the moment of conception, and which does not necessarily imply a pre-paration. On every point respecting the Trinity and Incarnation the Catholic (I may say Tridentine) doctrines seem to me most fully to meet all objection; having been gradually worn into shape by the collision of short-lived heresies.

Prince Albert seems to be threatened with evil days. The queen must come in for her share. There seems to be something very vacillating in the recent policy of England. No hand at the helm bears strong. Who knows but Providence means Constantinople to fall again as in 1453? There is a long account to settle with the Turk. In some unknown way the Greek church, not near so corrupt as many think, may be made to countervail Rome, and perhaps to be herself reformed. I lately got a Greek prayer-book, and among much rubbish find an extraordinary amount of long, beautiful, pathetic, evangelical confession and prayer. Two of the Chinese insurrectionists, leading men, lately visited Shang-hae incog., and talked with Culbertson. Though they had never seen a New Testament, they seemed to be Christian and converted men. Happer's letters in the Presbyterian are evidently on the unfavourable extreme. It has not been mentioned that the dynasties now threatened in both wars, Chinese and Turkish, are both Tartarian. The Gog and Magogish aspect of this ought to be nuts for our prophet-mongers.

NEW YORK, *March* 14, 1854.

A Scotch Presbyterian of my acquaintance lately gave his son $300 for reading through Pool's Annotations on the Old and New Testament. My sermon on the prayers of the unconverted was not so pleasing to one hearer, who sent me eight pages of confutations—said she uttered the "voice of God," that she hardly refrained "from rising in the church and uttering the true doctrine," &c. More young persons are serious among us than I have known before. Our Mission-school does well. We have set up another down town, in which is a class of adult Germans. I think the "Household Words" contains some of Dickens's best writing. Now and then there is a sneaking dab at evangelical religion. The Astor Library is a-going; but no library I have ever seen, not even the Bodleian, has left such traces on my imagination as the Old Philadelphia, which I want to see again. I hardly ever buy a book, and latterly have read few. I have almost to say, " Quand je veux des livres, j'en fais." Yesterday I put the last sentence to the Memoir. Without my planning so, this fell on the day of my completing my half-century. The occasion was celebrated as much as my modesty would allow. The President of your Senate [his brother, W. C. A.] appeared at breakfast, and accompanied me out of the house. The steamship Knoxville conveyed me out to Sandy Hook and back, with about five hundred invited guests. It was really beyond my

wish that the Asia, which we spoke, should have fired two guns.
In the evening about one hundred gentlemen, chiefly of the cloth,
attended at the house of Mr. Stuart. I was handsomely received.
The speech was much applauded ; it was by Dr. Duff of Calcutta. The band of music, nearly opposite, played till the conclusion of the 13th: I have every reason to be satisfied.[1]

It is really delightful to hear Duff, and to see him. His awk-
wardness and lobstering defy description. He seems to have a
bet that he will get the collar of his coat above his left ear once in
every sentence. His accent is the pleasantest Scotch. There is
to me great music in his intonations. What commands me is
his wonderful sense. His humour is native, and bursts out
everywhere. At times he is sharply sarcastic. I feel that he is
eminently a spiritual man. I hope they will not kill him. He
spoke two hours and twenty minutes at the Tabernacle. From
his schools at Calcutta there have come 20,000 Hindoo pupils.
A plain but pious man of our church lately made a suggestion to
me, which indicates Christian labour in a right direction. He is
a clothier, employing five hundred hands. He is impressed with
the fact that in our efforts to do good the relation of *employer
and employed* is ignored. He proposes that every Christian employer should seek the benefit of his employés. He points out
methods. He suggests associations of employers for mutual
illumination and incitement, and to accomplish jointly through
visiters, Bible-readers, &c., what cannot be done so well singly.
He has a number warmly engaged with him. The scheme contemplates the Germans chiefly. He astonished me by saying
that the calculated number of hands engaged by wholesale
clothiers in New York is 25,000, of whom two-thirds are Germans. There is so much real working-spirit among these pious
clothiers, that I can't help hoping it is of God. At our sacrament six on examination, and two on certificate. About seven
are ready in my judgment. One of my Sunday School women
sees almost every one of her pupils brought into the church. I
hope our Mission-school and chapel-edifice will go up after all.
Within three weeks we have collected for it $15,500.

NEW YORK, *May*, 1854.

At no time in my ministry have so many been coming to me
to talk of their souls. These are not known to one another.
One interesting case is of a young lady from Central America,
who did not know a word of English four years ago, but now
seems to be an instructed and converted person. A refugee

---

[1] This mock celebration of his birth-day is made up of a trial trip of a
new vessel, and of a soirée in honor of Dr. Duff.

Italian painter is a constant attendant, and professes to have embraced Protestantism.

The noblest Gothic church of modern London is that of the Irvingites. The millenarian pamphlet entitled "The Coming Struggle," which has had so prodigious a run, on account of several happy prophetic hits, has already falsified itself; as it boldly declares that England is to stand aloof, and have no part in the contest with Russia.

I had no proper idea of Dr. Duff's eloquence until I heard him before the Bible Society. His personal religion shone out very much in his later speeches. He has a marvellous command of a sort of long-winded but most expressive diction, and his adjectives are generally substantives, and not epithets.

Dr. Proudfit has, in his new Review,[1] fully demonstrated against Schaff, that none of the Fathers made Peter to be the Rock; nor any one else before the Middle Ages. I never had any doubt about Christ's naming himself by *petra*, any more than himself by [Destroy] "this temple;" but I did not suppose that all the Fathers held so too, against all their doctrinal prepossessions. There continues to be much quiet seriousness among my hearers. Yesterday I heard of five cases unknown to me before; but this concurrence is very extraordinary. My lecture is very full and very serious. I have arrived, in the Life of Christ, at the last passover. The Nebraska bill has passed. I have never opposed it, but feel very sad at the prospect of increased slavery. As to what would be the fact, I suppose this rests on causes which will not be affected one way or the other by this bill. The marshalling of South against North is more open and violent than I remember. My "Consolation" is out in 12mo.[2] I see great defects in my "Memoir;" but this plan of stereotyping every thing is very unfavourable to the perfectionating of one's works. My quondam chum, Waterbury, has gone to Europe, his eyesight being threatened; he is one of the best and kindest of men. I have just sold a tract of land in Virginia; the names of the creeks amused me: Little Pedler, Sinking Swamp, Enchanted, and Love-lady. The avails are $111 05. L—— M—— said to me t'other day: "I have been an organist all my life; yet if a congregation should say to me, 'Shall we have an organ?' I should scarcely dare to reply 'Yes.'" Old Mr. Scott said in 1849, "We fare well in our church; last Sabbath we had *Kittle and Potts*; to-day *Krebs* (pronounced by him *crabs*) and *Eells*." Such was literally the fact.

I have often tended to your opinion on the fugitive business; but these things make me pause, viz.: if the slaves are not

[1] "The New Brunswick Review."   [2] The first edition was in octavo.

sent back, the peril of their escape and their other sufferings will
be much increased : again, we shall be flooded with runaways,
and our free negroes are burden enough already : lastly, I don't
see how such a state of things can continue long, without war *ad
internecionem* upon the borders.   Yet I believe that the Fugitive
Slave Law will be repealed, and that the Union will be dissolved
on this question, sooner or later.   The second Psalm is my chief
comfort in politics.

Though not quite a millenarian, I was struck with these
words of Chalmers to Bickersteth : " But without slacking in the
least our obligation to keep forward this great (missionary)
cause, I look for its conclusive establishment through a widening
passage of desolating judgments, with the utter demolition of
our present civil and ecclesiastical structures."   I find no meeting
so hard to conduct as the Monthly Concert, so called.   Now and
then I have some keen chagrins at finding, from imperfect lists,
&c., that I have neglected some worthy family for several years.
Such things plague me more than greater trials, and not always
in a warrantable way.   Houses about here are so near together
as to be almost a Fourierite phalanstery, and now that windows
are up we have sometimes two or three sets of piano-twangle
and opera-squalls at once.   A hundred Chinese have been found
in New York ; of whom thirty-five last week attended instruction
in Chinese from a missionary, Mr. Syle.

New York, July 4, 1854.

Thermometer 85° in my study at 11 A. M.   I went to
Albany yesterday, and returned the same day, having six hours
in Albany.   In going there was no oppression of heat, but the
return was distress equal to any thing of the torrid sort I ever
felt, and this is *par excellence* my weak point.   I took a warm
bath and two cups of tea, and was quite restored ; but the
pandemoniacal squibs and crackers prevented the sleep I hoped
for.   Some good chat with Sprague.   Says his correspondence
is from five to ten letters per diem, and that he despatches these
before breakfast—that he regularly goes round his flock in visits
twice every year—that he writes two sermons every week—that
he has not preached an old sermon for seven years.   His communicants are more than 700.   He visits each family of his
charge twice a year, spending on this the hours from 11 to 2.
My congregation is thin indeed—though more than half present
are strangers.   We shall again keep open this year ; but I expect to take my family to Newport on the 11th.   Our church
was entered last week, and the pulpit Bible abstracted.   A fire
was also made under the stairs, with a bundle of combustibles,

but it burned out, leaving a pile of cinders and ashes on the floor. I have had donations of port-wine from two quarters, during the heats; showing a remarkable discrimination in my worthy parishioners. One of the parcels purports to be real Old London Dock, imported to order.

Scribner is gone to England. My book on Consolation is about to be put out by Nelson of Edinburgh. Cholera is plainly increasing among us, but without that feeling of panic which commonly accompanies pestilences. The papers pretend that rain-water keeps off cholera; but it has never been worse than at such islands as St. Thomas, where they drink no other.

NEWPORT, *July* 31, 1854.

Ink runs in these latitudes. Thayer is as agreeable and instructive a preacher as ever. He is much beloved by his people, and does good among all classes. Stanhope Prevost, a grandson of President Smith, and an old playmate of mine, is here, from Lima. His Spanish wife and children speak no English. The current is setting in New England so much in favour of congregational singing, that at the commencement at Andover, next week, they are to disuse their choir-display, and sing old-fashioned psalmody. Prof. Stowe has been preaching some weeks to the students on the Millennium. I have been studying Maurice's book, [the Boyle Lectures.] He is all fog; belonging to that class of minds who are great at starting objections, and taking the side of adversaries, but impotent in the work of upbuilding. I am now upon Candlish's answer; a work of some strength, and sufficiently confutative of M., (no great task,) but hasty and often obscure. Maurice really surrenders the Trinity, Atonement, Inspiration, Resurrection, and Future Punishment.

NEWPORT, *August* 21, 1854.

Your letter, in its closing part, so entirely removed all expectation of our seeing K., that I was really surprised when she called on us to-day. She is looking exceedingly well, and is full of that happiness among new scenes, which sits so well on youth, and which it is one of the peculiar pleasures of old folks to contemplate without envy. I am glad to see how thoroughly she has escaped all affectations, even those conventional ones which one looks for in young ladies; it is a negative charm worth a thousand et ceteras. There have been some cases of cholera here, but it is said they are abating; and there is no evacuation of the hotels. I hope there is no harm in going to a boat-race, as I did on the 12th. I was in a yacht, and went out some miles to sea. The sight was beautiful. Besides the racers, the harbour and outer bays were covered with hundreds of beautiful craft. Last week, John Auchincloss took a shark twelve feet long. The drought is oppressive here, but the air is temperate and agreeable. I took my twenty-fifth bath to-day. I am the only clerical loafer here; last year there were many. My intercourse with T. continues to be very pleasant; he strangely unites the philosophical preacher with the laborious and affable pastor, and is uncommonly zealous in looking after the lower classes. Mary Williams's "comfortable boarding-house" is still fraught with goodly broadbrims. Congregational singing is unknown here. At Dr. Choules's, psalmody is the act of staring at the gallery, with all backs to the pulpit. We have here Bancroft, Sumner, Archer of Virginia, Curtis, and Gen. Almonte with coach and four. B. has purchased, or will purchase, a house here; he is a candidate for our little Rhode Island mitre. He has the proper size, and preaches evangelically. The orthodox Quakers have an immense barn here, in which the New England yearly meeting assembles; but they talk of taking it to Lynn. There is a secession of " Wilburites," led by John W. of this State, whom I suppose to be like the Hicksites. The Baptists are very strong; they dip in the salt-water. Several churches are open-communion. The early (Roger Williams) Baptists disused singing at worship, as having no Scripture precedent. The traditions of the slave-trade of New-port and Bristol are curious. I know no town which has such a proportion of blacks and yellows, as this. With no disposition to judge harshly, but all the reverse, I am led to think that what we regard as experimental piety is at a low ebb in New England. The revival day has gone by. I hear of no savoury old-time Christians. Of Unitarians, I find many more than I expect-ed. The absence of a spirit of worship, in assemblies, is very striking. Communion-seasons are brief and perfunctory, and the ordinance is just an addition, as when we baptize a child. The New England clergy seem to me a highly cultivated class; but the elegant or ingenious essay-style gains ground in sermons. Expository preaching is absolutely unknown, so far as I can learn. I have seen a number of young —— preachers. They are scholarly, but somehow impress me as totally devoid of ministerial zeal. The intellectual and tasteful in —— appears to have a forming influence on all the new race of preachers. I own my survey has been somewhat narrow, but I should have expected an exception here and there.

New York, *September* 21, 1854.

Yours of the 5th was backwarded to me from Newport to-day. I have read Gurney[1] with much pleasure and some admiration. As in the case of Mrs. Fry and William Allen, I was deeply impressed with the truth, that whatsoever in him is good, is independent of Quakerism. One is ready to blush, to read the petty arguments of such a mind, for the hat and the plain language. He was a good man; but I am unable to see wherein he even approaches, either in spirituality or self-denial, most of the good missionaries and ministers whose biography is written. I read Judson's Life about the same time; and while I differ as much from J. as from G., I see in him a hundred-fold more Christian greatness. Who can imagine that the travelling sermons of Gurney did much good? whereas Judson was instrumental in giving a noble version of the Scriptures to a great empire, and of converting thousands of Burmese. I heard two of Gurney's sermons; they were good for a Quaker, but no whit above the average of our plain preachers. I ran up to Newton, Sussex. Though I had been there once, many years ago, I really had forgotten how lovely a country it is. Without being Alpine, it is most picturesquely mountainous, and the air is as good at Newton, as at Schooley's Mountain. Their railway will soon complete the remaining twelve miles; and then you could get there via Newark, in a few hours. Never have I passed a summer with so little gastric trouble. The only death in my charge has been a consumptive, æt. 80. Mr. H. has been talked of, in reference to a new (or revived) " enterprise " at the beautiful village of Oyster Bay, L. I., which is fast becoming a summer resort. On your authority, I spoke well of him to one of the chief men. I hope he would not object to be ostracized.[2]

New York, *October* 21, 1854.

This is the fourteenth day of my illness, and I am still in my room, though dressed and sitting up a good deal. My disease has been obscure. It has given me more severe pain than all my previous sicknesses put together; but it has been *clean* pain, without nausea or depletory processes. It has been a series of dreadful paroxysms, averaging about eight hours each; of these

[1] Memoirs of Joseph John Gurney. Edited by Joseph B. Braithwaite.

[2] In the early part of October of this year Dr. Alexander was prostrated by an excruciating and alarming disease, the progress of which will appear in the letters. On the 14th October he informed me by an amanuensis that he had been laid up for seven days. He was not able to preach after October 8 until November 10.

I have had about five. In their acme, the pain was all but intolerable. One night I took what would equal 480 drops of laudanum, without effect. My doctor (Delafield) is a very Napoleon in decision; but his methods are mild, and he exactly resembles Dr. Belleville [vol. i., 125] in his expectant practice. I have from the beginning supposed that the root of the evil was calculus. Spasmodic colic co-exists. In the intervals I am wonderfully smart. I ought to say that Divine considerations have been of great support to me, especially when I was almost gone with pain.

NEW YORK, *October* 29, 1854.

Since the 20th I have been free from the peculiar pain, the very remembrance of which makes me shudder. At present I am suffering chiefly from the impression on my nervous system of so much severe pain. I have appetite, take a glass of port and gentian bitters, drive out for an hour, and walk fifteen to twenty minutes. You may imagine I have a great feeling of worthlessness. I ought ever to be thankful, that in my most painful moments, the great truths, which I trust I have believed, were not less clear or less precious than usual, but unspeakably more so. I wish to make record of this. I did not find that intense and wasting pain took away the power of thinking, but all the other way. While it is fresh I wish to write down, that in, with, and under all the very poignant distress, there was an under-current of peace and religious satisfaction, which now comes up associated with the pain—but more abiding in my mind than the pain. These are new experiences for me. In former illnesses, my head was always cloudy; in this, I had pure, unadulterate pain.

Dreadful, dreadful war! [Crimea.] Bootless carnage, and for what? I have been skimming Alison's new series of volumes, and have not had my love of the Turk or his allies increased, by reading of the Greek revolution, Scio, Navarino, the former campaigns of the Pruth and Balkan, Diebitsch, &c. While an uncontrolled sway of the Czar over all the east of Europe would seem bad, I own I am struck with three considerations: 1. The Turk is antichristian, fanatical, faithless, bloody, and doomed. 2. The Czar is the natural counterpoise of the Pope; and it is significant that most of the Romish powers are against Russia. 3. Russia is the only European power from whom America could hope for much, in case these same allies should direct their forces against the United States. Well, " He that is higher than the highest regardeth; and there be higher than they."

Did you know that the Free Church people publish a handsome quarterly at Edinburgh, almost entirely made up of articles from American reviews ? [1]

NEW YORK, November 3, 1854.

I learn that the late diplomatic congress at Ostend has settled that Cuba is immediately to be ours—I suppose bloodlessly. [A prominent politician] said the other night : " If I were President, I would declare war against England in two days ; so as to be beforehand with them." I did not hear the *casus belli*. It does not seem to me that the Bible House is a bit larger or grander than it ought to be ; especially as it has been a source of revenue, and was built by special subscription of friends. The moral impression of such a structure gives me pleasure every time I pass.[2] It is said that one of the passengers became perfectly gray during the night of the Arctic.[3] I have a sermon which I preached on board that vessel, [May 25, 1851,] on the text, " And the sea gave up the dead," &c. ; in which is a description of just such a mode of death. It was much censured at the time, as alarming and unseasonable. The crimes of our city are horrid, but they are committed chiefly by foreigners. Of the 1,500 who daily land here from Europe, the worst, for various reasons, never get beyond New York, except to go to the State's Prison. Balloons go up every few days in our neighbourhood ; one to-day with four inmates. I have a little handbook for young communicants in the press.[4]

I have expressly consigned to Adams & Co. the parcel of books. If you have not been familiar with Bengel, [Gnomon,] you will be struck with his pith, and the unexpectedness of his remarks. I was so delighted with Dacosta as a man, that I read his volume with great pleasure.[5] You will, amidst his enthusiasm, find some new remarks on the comparison of the gospels. Being now near the end of a long course on the Life of Christ, I

---

[1] " The British and Foreign Evangelical Review." In the successive volumes of this work many of Dr. Alexander's articles in the Repertory were reprinted.

[2] This was said in reply to an opinion his correspondent had expressed the other way.

[3] This steamship was wrecked on her trip to America, September 27, 1854.

[4] " Plain Words to a Young Communicant : " published by Randolph, 1854. Pp. 113. His only contributions to the Repertory of 1854 were—1. " Curiosities of German University Life." 2. " Sketches of the Pulpit in Ancient and in Modern Times."

[5] His meeting with Dr. Isaac Dacosta, of Amsterdam, is mentioned in Chap. IX. of this volume. The work alluded to is " The Four Witnesses : a Harmony of the Gospels on a new principle."

am more averse than ever to the method of a Diatessaron, except when used as a mere tabular help for collation. One could endure no other history, made up thus. I agree with you about Jay. It is servile and does him injustice.[1] Never put off your reminiscences till you are past 80. I remember how different his " Life of Winter," which ought to be reprinted. The new edition of Bickersteth's Works, 16 vols. 18mo, $10, is a cheap book. Even when I cannot see with him as to the prophecies, I always feel that I am conversing with an eminently holy man. This impression is made on me especially by the " Signs of the Times," one of his last works. The little prize-essay of Winthrop is not to be despised.[2] It really seems to me that Lord starts right.[3] His way of finding what a symbol means, must be the true one. It is some merit, where all was ἀνομία, to digest some laws. But his results are often odd enough, and sometimes bathetic. His conception about the seven kine and seven ears, is funny enough. I like an expression of Trench, in his book on Bible synonymes : " to awaken in our scholars an enthusiasm for the grammar and lexicon." This has been my great " Help to Preaching," and more and more so. Nothing has so suggested not only meanings, but parallels, illustrations, divisions, and inferences. As I twice declined the augmentation of stipend, our trustees have insured my life ; payable to relict. It is indeed a Godsend, to one who never would lay up, if his salary were $20,000. As we are cutting ourselves off more and more from the old world, and likely to carry out the Monroe doctrine, it seems to me that Christians in the United States are proportionally more bound to devise means of sending the gospel to Spanish America. Brazil is quite open, and New Grenada nearly so. It seems to me that this, along with the black and red men, falls more justly to our share, than Hindoos, Nestorians, Druzes, Arabs, or Turks. If I could have one sufficient ex tempore prayer in each diet, I should be glad to have a prescribed form for those things which we ought *always* to pray for : e. g. government, general thanksgiving, &c. I would have the Lord's Prayer, Creed, Te Deum, Gloria in Excelsis, and a few more ancient portions. Our church singing is of the very plainest sort, and the people join pretty generally. This has been the result of (1) a limited list

[1] The Autobiography of the Rev. William Jay, edited by Dr. Redford and Rev. J. A. James.

[2] " The Premium Essay on the Characteristics and Laws of Prophetic Symbols. By the Rev. Edward Winthrop." New York : F. Knight, 1854.

[3] Editor of the Theological and Literary Journal, who offered the premium.

of tunes, and (2) these very easy, with no repeats, and scarcely any slurs or dividing of syllables. But the protest of our young people has been formidable.

NEW YORK, *January* 23, 1855.

The trembling of my hand, which I inherit from mother and grandfather, makes me try first one hand-(writing) and then another—as I can go steadiest. I answer two of yours in one; and accept your apology for poor paper, as valid for the whole ream. I wish I knew Mrs. Gurney. I once saw her at David Clark's before her marriage; it was in J. J. G.'s company that I went there. I wish she would put the life of Anna Backhouse into the shops. Just before opening your letter, I opened one from a young lady, in deep affliction, thanking me for the copy of A. B.'s life, (which I received from Mrs. G.,) lent her by me. Anna is one of my saints.[1]

Most that doctors do with success seems to be opening an alley for nature to have fair play, and elbow room, to carry the disorder out of doors. This accounts for the seeming success of homœopathics. I doubt not that poor S.'s case was greatly aggravated by doctoring; I talked much with him while the medication was proceeding. Our communion was a week earlier than yours; nine on examination, and three on certificate. Several of the cases were very interesting. I think *if I could support myself*, I would leave my charge any day, and begin down town; I ought to add—if I had any prospect of life. This is not a new " spirit;" I never, in all our correspondence, said any thing more seriously. I perfectly *long* to preach daily in our now finished new chapel.

I have read Muhlenberg's pamphlet with great delight, and rank it very high as a literary production.[2] It has led me to fall in his way, with increase of satisfaction. He tells me his Sisters of Mercy, four in number, have relieved 1,200 cases of distress since New Year's. R. has been amongst us.[3] To save

[1] The widow of Joseph John Gurney, the eminent preacher and author of the Society of Friends, was of New Jersey. Her Memoir of his daughter was printed at Burlington, in 1852, for the use of the family and friends.

[2] " An Exposition of the Memorial of Sundry Presbyters of the Protestant Episcopal Church, presented to the House of Bishops during the General Convention of said Church, 1853. By one of the Memorialists." The object of the Memorial was to obtain some modifications of the " modes of public worship, and traditional customs and usages " in the Episcopal Church.

[3] The reputed author of a volume (" Charity and the Clergy ") sustaining the strictures of " New Themes " on the want of active charity in the Christian Church.

my credit, he attended one meeting at which our people pledged $400 a year for our down town mission-school, and another at which he learned that we had just raised $600 for poor of this ward. In reference to this last matter, I attended two meetings of clergy of the Eighteenth Ward, last week, at which remarks were made by Tyng, Adams, Cheever, Hawks, Muhlenberg, Bellows, Van Nest, and Alexander.

The gratuitousness of the preaching, to which I alluded, [page 205,] would presuppose a fund or collection for a Free Church. If I were ten years younger, I would have a building erected to hold 2,000, and would preach to free seats; not that I think the existing plan ought to be abandoned, but because I think we ought to have several, yea many plans, yea many sorts of preachers, " unlearned deacons " and all.

I find no girls decently educated except at home, or in the country. I have lately examined several eminent scholars of the highest establishment. Except French and drawing, they have nothing accurately, though pretending to have ever so much German, Latin—ologies, &c. I have a Spanish book from a Cuban ex-professor, and very fine old man, inscribed thus: " Al Sen' D' Don J. W. Alexander, D. D., en memoria del Editor." My good friend and excellent sexton Peter Tarlsen is dead. We buried him from the church. The captain who first brought him to America was there. Our landlord has raised our rent from $900 to $1,200 ; we shall therefore move again.

NEW YORK, *March* 14, 1855.

I am truly glad that the old college bell is not lost; its sound is sweet in my ears.[1] The Palmerston ministry seems hard to fix. Sebastopol is taken less easily than was at first supposed. The Irvingites number 30,000. They now have an Evangelist here, preaching ; only on these occasions do they invite any hearers. We are about to lower our organ loft, and get an organ, and perhaps change the pulpit : we shall expect you after the high places are removed. I visited a bon vivant very ill, whose only tie to church or religion seems to be the memory of a little boy who was several years in our Sunday school. The father repeated whole hymns which his boy used to say at night; the child's portrait hanging all the while in sight by the bed. The intensity of paternal affection led me to dwell on that particular view of God's love in Scripture. Only two join our church on examination ; one a boy of fifteen, the

---

[1] The main edifice of Nassau Hall was burnt March 10.

other a man of fifty. On Sunday I preached twice and spoke something at three other meetings. Secretary [J. L.] Wilson gave us a truly awakening account of the India missions the other night.

The life of the Rev. Andrew Broaddus has interested me highly. In my young days he was the star of the Baptist pulpit in Virginia. He was a great and good man, and a preacher of singular fascination. Dr. Jeter's "Campbellism Examined" is a most able book on that subject. I accord with you in missing the society of sons, but this is not so grieving as to suffer the same in regard of daughters. All these things tell us that the σχῆμα passeth away.

April 3.—The dealings of God with Ahab make me believe that the great outward piety of Nicholas will not go unrewarded. His death was not an unchristian one.[1]

I expect to leave here for Virginia on the 9th inst., and to go first to Charlottesville, and then to Charlotte. We open our chapel for preaching next Sunday. Dr. A. D. Smith has more than 1,400 Sunday scholars.

Give profound salvos to all inquiriturient and amicable vicinities, from your observant orator, who will ever pray, &c.

INGLESIDE, VIRGINIA, *April* 20, 1855.

The spring no longer coquets, but embraces with oriental voluptuousness. Yesterday would have done for Florida. In a north porch, in shade, the glass stood at 95° all the afternoon. This morning it is less burning, but still hot. When 1 arrived in Virginia, the spring was still behind, but for two days we have almost seen it growing. All the ten million blossomings of this wide plantation are out together—peach, apricot, cherry, plum, crab, and apple, the last being sweetest; also lilach, strawberry, almond, corcoras, hyacinth, pyrus japonica, &c. The wheatfields, often of a hundred acres each, are suddenly green. Before breakfast I counted fourteen species of birds known to me, and two unknown. There are about fifty mocking-birds in and about this lawn, and forty robins were counted on the grass at once. Herds and flocks on a large scale variegate the prospect. This estate joins Retirement, where I lived, and which is more in sight than once, from cutting of woods away. The house or houses are ruinous, but the noble oaks stand. The place is to be at once improved by Henry A. Carrington, to whom his father has given it. It was twenty-nine years on Monday, since I preached my first sermon at Charlotte C. H.

[1] The Czar died March 2, 1855.

There is now a plank-road of about six miles from the C. H.
to Drake's Branch; a line which is about bisected by a planta-
tion-road of one mile, striking it from this spot. This place has
very much improved by the growth of trees, and the horticultu-
ral improvements. In all this country there is no sign or suspicion of any suffering. I have renewed my acquaintance with a
large number of the old blacks, and have been struck with the
ease of their life. The old coachman of Mrs. Le Grand, Uncle
Billy, now aged 84, is really a handsome old man. I have earnestly laboured with him among the flowers, which he is gently
tilling; and have read and preached to him—for he is still an
unbelieving old creature. I have felt bound to seize every occasion to exhort these servants, in consequence of the weight which
the words derive from my former residence here. Some of
them seem to me as good and as experienced Christians as any
white people of the labouring class. There is plainly an important increase everywhere in labours for their instruction and
conversion. The political rage about Know Nothingism is such
as could hardly be "realized" in the North. The high prices
of wheat give great internal prosperity to planters. I found at
the University of Virginia a signal change. Almost all the professors pious: large voluntary assemblies of students; one hundred attending Sunday prayer-meeting, and a goodly number daily
morning ditto. Cabell is most instructive and striking on all the
questions of ethnology, races of men, &c. He dissents totally
from Agassiz, and agrees with Maury, Hewes, and Bache.[1] He
showed me some stupendous microscopic things concerning the
circulation of the blood, &c.

217 FIFTH AVENUE, NEW YORK, *June* 13, 1855.[2]

Our organ is to be put behind the pulpit, and the choir reduced to one or more male voices beside the pulpit, thus giving
us seventy-five sittings aloft. Nothing tends to reconcile me any
more to pew-property. If Papists did not falsify their theory by
their practice, their method of free churches would be noble.
Then one could be complacent in a costly church, if thereby "the
brother of low degree" (James i.) "is exalted." The sustentation
of the preacher is as clear as the gospel-message itself, but the
rich should pay so as to lighten the burden of the poor. I have
long been an admirer of some things in Madame Guyon. Up-

---

[1] In 1859 was published the first edition of Dr. Cabell's "Testimony of
Modern Science to the Unity of Mankind;" with an Introductory Notice
by Dr. Alexander.
[2] In the absence of his family in Virginia he was dwelling with Mr.
Thomas U. Smith, one of the elders of his church.

ham[1] makes her far better than she was, and has left out a thou
sand of her gross blandishments and nursery endearments. I
think the best thing in the book is the annihilation of her theory
by Bossuet. Fenelon, though her pupil, has wonderfully exalted
and spiritualized her system, in the " Maximes," and " Lettres
Spirituelles." But it is all given better in Kempis. I have not
read (since Gil Blas) a merrier narrative than Mons. Huc's
Travels through China. *Quere.* Suppose every Popish priest
now extant were a true spiritual Christian, how far would the
existing machine of hierarchy (influence and all) be compatible
with true churchship? *Item.* In such case, might not certain
conceivable reforms be expected, such as should place the Catholic body short of damnation? A ship-load of immigrant Mormons, seven hundred souls. Hardly any were Papists; most
from England. If the Eutaxian Liturgy[2] come into actuality, the
only result will be to train people for the " Common Prayer."
If I must pray other people's prayers, I prefer the venerable
grace of Anglicanism to any thing A, B, and C will concoct.

Adams's steeple is going to be the great ornament of up-town
New York; I see it while I write, slowly growing, day by day,
above the houses in Twenty-sixth street, over which I look
southward. The church will stand them in not less than
$160,000. Even St. John's Church, as Dr. Berrian tells me, is
nearly deserted of worshippers; though, when he was at its con-
secration, it was thought in the suburbs. Mrs. C—— and my
brood will make for the Red Sweet Springs,[3] near the Sweet
Springs, Alleghany County, about 16th prox. The Boardman
and Thornwell debate [on Church Extension] was of that dignified sort, that we have latterly missed in our Assembly; I wished
for a fuller report. I am now about five or six lectures deep in
the Acts. I also have a Bible-class on Romans. Strawberries,
though slow, are as fine as I ever saw. This year will be
memorable among cits for its incomparable weather in May and
early June. I had made all preparations for a reduced $1 25
edition of the Life of my father, leaving out nothing material,
when Trow's printing-house was burnt. Though I am thankful
to say our plates in the vault escaped, all the paper for this new

[1] " Life, Religious Opinions, and Experience of Madame de la Mothe
Guyon. By Thomas C. Upham." 1847.
[2] " Eutaxia; or, the Presbyterian Liturgies: Historical Sketches. By a
Minister of the Presbyterian Church." New York: 1855. This was followed in 1859 by " A Book of Public Prayer, compiled from the authorized
formularies of worship of the Presbyterian Church, as prepared by the Reformers Calvin, Knox, Bucer, and others. With supplementary forms."
[3] The first mention of the spot in Virginia, where the writer closed
his earthly course.

impression was consumed.[1] It has been a great disappointment to us that Mr. E. T. Williams, who had come on as preacher in our Mission-chapel, was forced to go instantly away, on account of his wife's ill-health. Father Otterson is preaching temporarily, but there is no flock as yet; our chief hope is from the school.

RED SWEET SPRINGS, ALLEGHANY }
Co., VIRGINIA, *July* 28, 1855. }

The drive to the Warm Springs, though short by measure-ment, was, I think, the severest I ever took. We got in about half-past nine. The place is delightful. A former tasteful own-er has done much landscape gardening. The view from top of the Warm Spring Mountain is worth going a hundred miles to see. The servants are the best I know, having that oriental deference and tact which belong to old family menials. We rested a day. Twelve passengers on the coach on Thursday. The squeeze was annoying, but the road pleasant. In crossing the Alleghany we encountered two thunder-storms, and rode four hours in heavy rain. I omitted that we found no chance direct to this place, and so had to come viâ White Sulphur. At Cal-laghan's, where we dined, two deer had been brought in; man says sometimes five in a day : six cents a pound. At a water-ing-house, two rattlesnakes had been slain during the day. I recognized the import of the moment, when, after an easy ascent, I found the waters tending towards the Gulf of Mexico. Lodged wretchedly at the noblest place I ever saw, the White Sulphur Springs. No reporter had prepared me for such Eden-like varie-ty of lawn and landscape, within the proper bounds, such ex-panse, and such a town of rural cots, &c. Next morning up at four. Course south-east. Except about four miles of the six-teen, the drive was transcendently beautiful. We recrossed the Alleghany. I think our whole road was along the bedside of two foaming, tumbling, roaring little rivers, *up* one, and *down* the other, with a slight hiatus on the water-shed. The second was Dunlap's Creek. Compared with the country around the Rock Alum, [Rockbridge County,] this region is noted for immense timber, cascades, and torrents, rapid changes of hill and vale, and exuberant productive power in every vegetable way. We broke fast ten miles from the Warm Spring, at Col. Crow's, on the side of Dunlap's Creek, which we crossed many times; and just under the broad shadow of the Sweet Spring Mountain. Good breakfast and fine venison. The colonel is a jovial Boniface, full of hunting-stories; and this is a famous place for deer-shooting.

[1] The smaller copy was afterwards published.

Here about nine. The place = 1,700 acres. The capabilities for landscape improvement are unlimited. I look straight over a broad green lawn ten times as big as yours,[1] and up a hillside to a knoll beautifully crested by trees and grazed over by both herd and flock. The Springs are in a dark glen, with rustic seats, two fine natural cascades, and a grove of irregular ancient trees; a spot for nymphs. The bath is (say) 40 × 20 feet, and deep enough for swimming. At the Warm Spring the bath is 98°, and 38 feet diameter. The "Sweet Springs" are a mile from us. The Cabell party are here, and the calm retirement is very taking.

About sixty here, and about seventy at the Sweet. They have four hundred and fifty at the White Sulphur.

RED SWEET, *August* 6, 1855.

Our company is yet small, but we shall be overflowed when the "White" is empty. Our number about seventy-five. Table good, though not sumptuous as at the Old Sweet. We have printed bill of fare, entrées of French cookery, always soup, &c. Absence of drinks striking. We have a Polish count, two Episcopal ministers, and one Methodist. The walks and drives around here in every direction are delightful. We go almost daily to the Sweet. Can walk to a cascade of forty to sixty feet. Frequently ascend neighbouring mountains. Dr. Cabell is daily pushing his microscopical observations which brings me some entertainment. The swimming here is worth all the journey. The tepid chalybeate is mawkish enough.

RED SWEET, *August* 11, 1855.

The disheartening dampness continues. Our number is two hundred, and many are daily rejected. Rooms for some fifty to eighty are finishing. I just saw a deer brought in of a hundred and nineteen pounds; yesterday one of one hundred and twenty-six pounds. The Sweet Springs have one hundred and fifty. The fashion chiefly there. Here we have a hop every night. Rev. Castleman was upset near Bell's, on way here. Next day he drove from three A. M. till daylight, because the driver could not keep awake five minutes at a time. I weary of the mode of life.

RED SWEET SPRINGS, *August* 14, 1855.

If this crosses yours, please make all right by considering yourself as the debtor. Though we have rain daily, there is

[1] The Rockbridge Alum Springs, where the two correspondents had met the week before. We continued at different Springs during the time indicated by the Virginia dates.

more dry air. I am thankful to say that our indispositions abate. Mrs. T. of Baltimore, the R. K. of my youthful days, is here with her husband. I last spoke with her in 1826; she is now a grandmother. Judge Potts [of Trenton] is at the Sweet. He is thin as ever, but seems very fresh, alert, and well, and is an addition to our society. We have Edward Ruffin, the celebrated agricultural philosopher of Virginia. I preached here and also at the Sweet Springs on Sunday; here I had a large assembly. Our small evangelical library of books and tracts is in free circulation; and religious talk is easier here than with us; while religious people allow themselves more liberties. The over-dressing and over-jewelling of the women are indescribable. Have they not mistaken the caricatures in Harper for the fashion-plates? Great numbers here from the lower Mississippi. One Methodist, who sustains "a supernumerary relation," and one Episcopal schoolmaster in orders, constitute, with thy servant, the chaplaincy. John Van Buren is at the White. Dysentery of a fatal type prevails among the mountaineers. In one house, a mile off, three deaths have occurred. Henry saw five deer on the 12th. The Red Sweet water is doing wonders with some cases of chronic diarrhœa. A. A. Hodge goes to Fredericksburg vice McPhaill.

RED SWEET, *August* 21, 1855.

Yours of 15th is " to hand ; " I was not " to home " when it came, but no further off than the Old Sweet, where I go daily and sometimes twice. This morning I called on Wm. Collins, of Baltimore, a classmate in college, now a lawyer in Maryland, and son-in-law of Gov. Jas. Barbour. Kirk, another classmate, is there. He preached a powerful sermon here last Sunday. The most interesting converser here, is ———. His knowledge and diction are extraordinary. Ultra States-rightsman. He says of Dr. Adams, (" South Side " :) " After reasoning from certain exceptional cases, to show that slave-holders live for nothing but to make their slaves happy—an absurd assertion —and after making slavery to be a most happy condition, he avows his wish gradually to put an end to this state of felicity." Cabell perseveres in regular morning lectures on Natural Philosophy and Natural History. We have about 400 at each Spring.

Thompson, of the Independent, writing from Maine, says, (in substance,) " Though Southerners hate the Yankees, yet they will every year come among them, so long as the North has the monopoly of mountains, *springs*, &c." Mulattoes decrease in Virginia. The air is now dry, but cold; almost every one has fires. I have at no moment been so well as my average in New York; rheumatism and headache pursue me.

RED SWEET SPRINGS, *August* 24, 1855.

Yours of 18th to-day, *simul* with one from Princeton, of 20th. When the mails do so, it is best not to delay exchange of notes for the usual diplomatic period. Littell's Nos. 586 and 587, [" Living Age "] are great; but why does our old friend grudge the price of all proof-reading? Your proximity to the Hot and Warm will make the Lukewarm [" Healing Springs "] very much livelier than the Cold, [Alum.] Our number is about 280. The weather, for a few days, has been warm and agreeable. Several cases of illness in the neighbourhood. It is a copious hemorrhage of the bowels, and intractable. The indigenous women and children in these wet valleys, look tallowy and anemic. The fewness of Northerners is remarkable. My reading has from necessity been in Cabell's books; so I have learnt some Comparative Anatomy, and Zoology.

Mrs. A. feels very " pōly," (such is the expression,) and William is still " delicate." You have probably learnt that " trifling " means " worthless." We have a very " respectable crowd " at these Springs. Mrs. C. is " mighty weak," but is " fattening." Willy talks of a sig-yàh (segar) and of " waw-tah." If it comes at all in your way to visit Lexington, do not hesitate an instant to go with your folks to R.'s, and stay as long as you choose. The truth is, " comfort," in Virginia, is not at public, but private houses; the case being reversed in Northern cities.

RED SWEET SPRINGS, *September* 1, 1855.

What you say is certainly just; your path of duty is very clearly marked out, and you are left in the best hands; 2 Sam. xxiv. 14. Whatever thoughts may supervene about your congregation, you are obviously in your right place; and if any censorious saints should class you among absentee " city-ministers," you will feel inwardly right before God, 1 Cor. iv. 3, 4.

Your Jews are probably negro-traders. That business in Virginia has fallen almost entirely into the hands of the Circumcision, and Mr. G. tells me they have greatly humanized it; so that where negroes have to be sold, they prefer it should be to the Hebrews.

We are very full—the running over of the White Sulphur. No Philadelphians, or New Yorkers, and but half a dozen Northerners. I shall wait till the 11th, when we can fill a coach for

Lexington, making stops. I am advised we cannot possibly have entry to our church before October 1, as the carpenters have us on the hip. Our house, 30 West 18th Street, is pretty much (or Yankicé "about") done. Peaches in New York are late and unpromising; in lower Virginia fine and abundant; here none. Delightful Indian plums of three varieties, are in our woods here, and probably in yours, [Bath County.] I occasionally overhear some hellish cursing and swearing, horribly sticking in my memory from its perverse ingenuity; it is from certain sporting gentry.

NEW YORK, *October* 2, 1855.

We arrived at Princeton on Thursday. Our journey was without "evil occurrent." On return, I find my flock still ungathered, and church still incomplete. For the twelve new pews, for 60 persons, we have twice that number of applicants. We preached in our Chapel of Ease, which was full, but mostly of strangers. No death, but of an infant, has taken place in my proper flock.

The renewed bustle of moving awaits us; but we are thankful for a new, convenient, and clean house. We cannot have full delivery of the same much before the 15th.

To-day Mr. Smith took us to our new house, No. 30 West 18th St.; where we had the surprise of finding the chief trouble of removing removed, by the downputting of new carpets, and the inputting of furniture and books. Yesterday we entered again our remodelled church. My feelings are complex in regard to it. Some things are beyond my hopes: 1, the acoustical trouble seems thoroughly cured: I could not wish it better for speaking and hearing; 2, the lowering of the west gallery is altogether pleasing; 3, the singing led by a precentor, and no consolidated choir or band, pleases me; the people joined heartily. On the other hand, my pride suffers at being made, with my pulpit, sermon, &c., a mere appendage to a great big organ. A savage, on entering, would certainly take the instrument for the divinity of the shrine. My head spins with the numerous conflicting businesses now competing for notice. I have an edition of Memoir (abridged) to oversee, a book to finish, a preface to write, a Presbytery to attend, two sermons to prepare, a house to fit and inhabit, a boy to school, "help" to hire, &c.

NEW YORK, *October* 26, 1855.

I am expecting, besides my own service, to preach for Dr. T.'s folks, after their communion. He is a much more earnest man than most of us, breathing some of the good Free

Church spirit, as I observed it in Scotland. He tells me that a number of families of his charge have it for a custom, before leaving home for church, to unite in prayer for a blessing on the Word which they expect to hear.

Bible instances show us that God is concerned in our private sorrows. The Psalms especially appear more divine to me every day. What a body of experience! How they have formed the character and devotions of the Church! How remarkable, to have issued from such a land and age!

In regard to the future state, continual, earnest, and I believe reverent reading of God's Word, has produced in me some persuasions and hopes, which I should not like to be called on to prove in mood and figure. It is my belief, that many things are made true to us, and from Scripture too, for which we cannot cite a particular proof-text. The general result is, that I look on the world of disembodied saints as nearer to us than is usually held, and on the future glory as less unlike the good things of the militant church, than many teach. Holiness here is found not in abstractions, but in the concrete feelings, words, and acts of human creatures. Some good people talk of holiness in heaven, as if they must secure it from carnality by making it vague, dreamy, and metaphysical. Though "equal to angels," Luke xx. 36, the blessed are not dehumanized. All New Testament allusions show them as *ours* still.

The anxiety I feel for my children, oppresses me at times very much. It is hardly at all about their temporal advancement—even their learning; but I am deeply solicitous that they should be truly religious, and more painfully alive to their perils in this respect than once I was.

We are hardly yet arranged in our habitation. It is eminently commodious, clean, and spacious. Church continues surprisingly full; with very little token of awakening. I fear I entertain rather than impress my hearers; this has long been a sore place within me. Yet when sometimes I have for a little attempted the pungent method, it has been Saul's armour to me, and I have been fain to come back to my natural way.

NEW YORK, *November* 12, 1855.

Yesterday was Communion. One on examination, and twelve on certificate. Dr. Duff's speech, [Scotch General Assembly,] though abundantly self-exhibitory, has some daring flights of old-fashioned eloquence, such as our fastidious, carping age and people do not willingly hear. Th. Dwight translated a book on New Grenada, by Gen. Mosquera, late President thereof, who now lives with his son Gen. Heran, just back of us. It is instructive, and gives one a new view of the capabilities of that wonderful country of mountains and *paramos,* a word which means high, cold, uninhabitable plateaux. The way is perfectly open at Carthagena for the gospel. I know no experience which has grown on me more, within a few years, than the impression of nearness of the other world. I have not a corresponding temper; but I certainly *realize* this as never before. Concerning the future, I do not see things so distinctly and definitely as some; for example, Baxter, in the "Saints' Rest." Howe's "Blessedness of the Righteous," comes nearer my views. But my persuasions of this seem natural, rather than religious. They do often, however, furnish me a motive. Poor unlettered saints (I am now caring for one on his death-bed) unquestionably have more comfort of their faith than we. Books, disquisition, analysis, habits of objection, looking at difficulties, hearkening to latitudinary talk, all tend to break the charm of childlike faith. Would we were more like children!

NEW YORK, November 14, 1855.

If univocality were all, we have, I think, fully attained the end of making our people sing. I have never heard a louder chorus out of a German church. As to melody and harmony, your deponent saith not.

How gravely things look in our families, when we project our thoughts into the future! My yearnings about my household are sometimes very affecting. "The fondness of a creature's love," &c. To have these affections sanctified is greatly desirable, but how little realized! Some parents seem to be cheered with a continual confidence in regard to the salvation of their offspring; and I own this comes over me too, in my best hours. Happy, happy are they who are safely landed on Canaan's shore. Some of the most serious reflections I ever have, are connected with the lapse of time and nearness of eternity, as viewed along with my small attainments hitherto; especially with the thought that these are not likely to be greater. I am deeply sensible that these and the like thoughts give a sombre cast to my manner, of late, which is by no means fitted to make religion attractive. The normal or ideal sort of Christianity would be beautifully cheerful. Mr. Williams, our mission-chaplain, returns to Africa in the spring. Poor Dr. Hare's lecture had a craziness beyond what the reporters give, in the perfectly bedlam character of the costly apparatus which he exhibited.[1] I have been part of the day with a dying woman, who has neglected religion, and is in

---

[1] The late Dr. Robert Hare, of Philadelphia, had lectured on "Spiritualism," with mechanical illustrations.

terror of death. Such cases (I mean the terror) are less common than I expected to meet when I began my ministry.

The military were out in force to-day; a beautiful sight. But all the trappings do not hide the bloodiness of War. How loose and perfunctory are the notices of books in the religious papers! I have often remarked it. *E. g.* Whately is commended, without a hint of his rationalism about Inspiration, Future Punishment, &c.; while a breath against limited Atonement or Imputation would bring down their wrath. I heard Milburn, the blind preacher, at a Bible Society to-night. His voice and manner are very lovely, and sometimes Summerfieldian. He is also a genius; but like all the crack —— of the Young America, is over-learned—full of Bacon, Des Cartes, Frederick Strauss, Auguste Comte, æsthetics, &c., &c. A. also made a fine address in his way. More than any man but Todd, and in a better way, his mind strings innumerable fine stories, phrases, allusions, and verses altogether; and he sacrifices every thing to the entertainment and arrest of the hearer's mind. His manner, too, is good, and he has much pathos. But you carry away no *one* deep impression, as from Chalmers, Edwards, or Nettleton. Love to all yours, whom we remember in prayers.

NEW YORK, *December* 25, 1855.

We dined to-day on a white-fish from Michilimacinac. Dr. Muhlenberg always has a Christmas-tree for his charity-children at his church. We had, notwithstanding the rain, 350 urchins and urchinesses at our cake-and-candy fête at the Mission Chapel. Our two Industrial schools promise well. The lower one, at Duane Street, (where we also have mission-preaching,) already numbers 200. We talk of going in largely toward the purchase of a building for a coloured congregation.

Every day sickens me more and more with Congress. Just consider what sort of work they carry on under the pretence of voting for Speaker; the debates running on matters of mere party-name, such as did not use to be mentioned.[1] I am fully persuaded, that if all parties would be patient, would drop the naked question of slavery, and would bend all powers towards abating the *abuses* of slavery, it would result in the speedy emancipation of all who should be fit to enjoy freedom. In this way history shows us that slavery has heretofore ceased and determined. Hush the angry quarrels, and appease the natural pride of slave-holders, and thousands among them would

---

[1] This scene was re-exhibited in the House of Representatives of 1859-'60.

go even for legislative reform, in the matters of marriage, property, separation of households, reading the Bible, and so forth. This, I think, will take place anyhow; but in a less favourable way, so long as Northern violence retards the meas ures. Huidekoper, of Meadville, sent me his treatise on the *Underworld*, or Hades of the Fathers. He proves pretty con-clusively that the " descended into hell " of the Creed originated after the unscriptural fiction of an underworld arose in the church. He impugns the candour of Christians who now try to swallow it, with other meanings.

For the coming year I have fixed on the year-word, " God with us." This method of year-motto I have pursued now for about fifteen years, with much comfort to my own heart, and I believe to others; especially as I have preached on the text whenever I had a congregation.

NEW YORK, *January* 14, 1856.

The Repertory makes me say " apostacy," [1] which I wrote not; and sundry other things. Another article has " forceably." I was ea*gre* to find out your article in which you write " meagre " for " meager." A divine writes to me about " schollar-ships," several times thus spelt. Unless Providence interpose frequent frosts our formidable force of snow-banks will furnish a fresh. Torrents entered our Church yesterday. It was our Communion. Dr. Carrington, just from Charlotte, says the snow is deeper there. The lowest mark by my thermometer was —5°. Dr. Ewing's plan is an excellent one, I wish he would carry it out; the technical name for such a word-book is a " glossary." [2] You probably had Hall forbears in the Siege of Derry, as I had Alexanders and Reids; so you will read third Macaulay with peculiar zest. In parts, the new portion is almost a Church his-tory. I am deeply convinced that a majority of the South will one day come to the point of mitigating slavery so far as to make it a sort of feudal apprenticeship; and that it will be abolished. Every year—even in the face of Northern rebuke—hundreds of new voices are raised in behalf of marriage, integrity of families, and license to read. To a practical mind it is striking that Abolitionism has abolished no slavery. I have been seldom more provoked [than by a newspaper notice laudatory of the

---

[1] A very common misprint. His articles in the Repertory for 1856 were: 1. Quesnel and the Jansenists. 2. Memoir of Dr. John M. Mason. 3. Waldegrave on Millenarianism.

[2] The suggestion of our friend, which he did not live to undertake him-self, was a vocabulary of the English Bible, giving the changes of meaning that have taken place since the translation.

singing in his church.] Earnest endeavour on my part to make *worship* supersede *music* is disturbed by these newsmakers. Amidst much that is mortifying at Washington, there is something favourable to observance of rule, in the substantial quiet of so many weeks, on the eve of a great national quarrel. From the same number of the " Clerical Journal " come the following paragraphs :

" *Religious Libels.*"

"After many other remarks, the speaker says, as reported in the *British Banner :* " *If I were a Churchman, furthermore, I might go into my pulpit every Sunday and read a homily, and by so doing should discharge all the obligations which I took upon me by my ordination vows.* But you, young men, who go forth from this college, must not take homilies into the pulpit nor other people's sermons, but you must take your own." Now here is a serious charge, conveyed in the presence of a miscellaneous audience and of young men about to be trained for the ministry among Dissenters."

MS. SERMONS, &c.

FIFTY MS. SERMONS, Original, Compiled, and Selected ; preached during 1854-5 to a Country Congregation. Price 5*l.* Address " OXONIENSIS," Post-office, Worcester.

MANUSCRIPT SERMONS, either for purchase or temporary use, supplied by an M.A. in Priest's Orders, of St. John's College, Oxford. Apply to " E. O.," 4, Brudenel-place, New North-road, Hoxton.

PAROCHIAL SERIES, Four Original Sermons for November, 8*s.* Quarterly Sets as usual. Also Curates' Aid, Propagation of Gospel, Church Building, &c., 2*s.* 6*d.* each. Prospectus List and Specimen, 2*s.* free.
HENRY F. GAYWOOD, C. MOODY, 257, High Holborn.

IMPORTANT SERMONS.—Church Building, Clergy Orphan, National Society, &c., &c., 2*s.* 6*d.* each. Six Sermons preparing for Advent, Quarterly Series as usual, Plain Practical Sermons. Prospectus and Specimen, 1*s.*
GEORGE ROSE, 93, Amiens-street, Dublin.

EDITED AND PUBLISHED BY A CLERGYMAN.
Fcap 4to., 9*d.* each, free by post,
PAROCHIAL (MS.) SERMONS, based on Discourses by BISHOP BEVERIDGE, and suitable for any Congregation, are published every THURSDAY. First Twenty-one Sermons now ready. Prospectus gratis.
Address, "MSS.," Bath.

Guthrie (" The Gospel in Ezekiel ") is more florid than Hamilton, but also more evangelical. His figures glow as much as W.'s, but he has some sense. Macaulay does justice to George Fox and the Quaker Sham. If there was any thing left to attack, his paragraphs might be published as a tract.

We are about to lose Mr. Williams from our missionchapel, (thus Macaulay prints all such compounds,) as he returns to

Africa. He has done us good service. I preached there on a late Sunday evening. Juvenile hearers are far the most numerous. Other families increasing, but only where they have been visited. Besides the missionary, we have an Irish Reader drumming up hearers. I wish I could find such a Scotch—or Irishman, as I have occasionally met, for this work. There are men to whom it would be delightful, and it is very promising.

NEW YORK, *February* 7, 1856.

I write with a thumb which is wounded in the very place where the pen goes. The 40th day of sleighing has increase of slipping by reason of rain that freezes as it falls. The sufferings of in-coming ships have been very great. One known to me, has been off our Atlantic coast for a month. Henry B. Pratt, of the Seminary, from Georgia, is here preparing to go to New Granada. I hope the Gospel will go into Central America, at the hole made by the filibusteros. The outlay on furs this winter, is enough to remind one of the Roman luxury in Gibbon and Montesquieu—$2,000 for a sable cape is frequently given. The white-and-yellow furs from the neck of sables, for carriages and sleighs, though less valuable are of monstrous price from their size. The prevalence of cold at the South is unexampled. The marked decrease of emigration to our port has been evident in the less pressing necessities of the poor this month, as compared with the corresponding portion of last year. The arrivals are about one-fourth for the last reported week. The stream of German emigration is showing a disposition to seek Spanish America; this is true especially of the Catholic part. I see both Peru and Mexico are holding out special inducements to Catholic German settlers ; and as in both countries this is synchronous with renewed struggles of the clergy for political power, it looks somewhat like a concerted scheme to forestall the protestantizing of the South. Lieut. Gilliss, of the U. S. Astronomical Survey, after several years in Chile, (so he writes it,) gives the worst account of popish misrule I ever saw. The *peons* (which by an Americanism means *hirelings*) are very far below Southern slaves. He declares flatly, that most of the births are illegitimate and a frightful proportion incestuous.

In your life of Washington Irving, mention that he is a homœopathist, and that he still rides young horses. He is very smart and kidglovish, but with a sunken manner and anile voice. I have never known any one who came to the truth so *regularly* as old Mr. C., just deceased. He was a highly educated man, both in America and Europe, and Jefferson's *ami prochain*. He said : " I was a victim of Mr. Jefferson's infidelity." Many years ago, he attacked the subject by regular approaches—reading all the works which are famous on the Evidences. It was his method in other things. He would talk with every one on these points, just as on the Tariff, &c. He satisfied himself of the authenticity of the books. He went as deliberately about the question of Inspiration, with like results. He cautiously went through all the doctrines, and settled on what we maintain as evangelical. Thus far was headwork. But Grace was carrying on heartwork also ; and on his dying-bed he recounted all this, and much more, as the process of years, and partook of the sacrament with clear avowal, good confession, and a most edifying joy.

About 1824, there was hardly a more irreligious family-connexion anywhere than ——. Now the religious members amount to scores. And every day we hear of the work going on. Of a truth, we make too little of such silent ramification of the true Vine.

I am now at Acts ix. It is really my Bible-class, though I have another, so called, of young men. My heart sickens at the prospect of war,[1] and for what? For ill-minded party-men. I have no fears of any one's dwelling unduly on Christ as a Saviour, and know none who have the fault you seem to apprehend.[2] The other extreme, viz., propounding him chiefly as a Master and Lawgiver, is that of all the Ecks, the Blairs and Robertsons, and Channings. Every orthodox preacher I ever heard, gives prominence to Christ as Prophet and King.

NEW YORK, *March* 4, 1856.

Yesterday was twenty-nine years since my dear affectionate uncle Rice preached my ordination sermon from Col. iv. 17, an admirable text.[3] The only articulate words after he was carried away were, " I should like to preach again—but the will of the Lord be done ! "

Yesterday Dr. Nott, æt. 85, married a couple in our church. His father died of disease at 62 ; his brother, a sedentary minister of Connecticut, died of an accident, in his hundredth year. Everett's oration is the great event. The immense assembly fondled the orator, and almost chaired as well as cheered

---

[1] The Central American question between the United States and Great Britain.

[2] The suggestion referred to was that in preaching, Christ is not held forth in his Divine authority as Lord, in due proportion with his gracious office as Saviour.

[3] Dr. Benjamin H. Rice was attacked with paralysis in his pulpit, (Hampden Sydney, Virginia,) January 17, 1856, and died on the 24th of February.

W. Irving. The argument was that Washington was great, because he was good.

The streets of New York have now reached a degree of flood, ferment, feculence, filth, and fragrancy, at which they become curious and almost sublime. There is a wall of block ice-muck in the middle of Broadway, from three to six feet high, for a mile; and this after more than $40,000 spent on that single object.

I agree with you in the importance of varying one's position. Dr. —— had decided symptoms of stone from a constant use of one posture, and this in a rocking-chair. *Et sic de similibus.* As a specimen of what the transcendentalists call the Philosophy of History, one of them lately said to me: "Judaism is the divinest fact which God could make out of the materials he then had." Addison is printing on Acts. Wiley frequently imports English copies of his large Isaiah, which cannot be "gotten" here, as the Southerners still say. So many around me are mad with Cumming, that I have lately been examining his prophetical volumes, four or five in number. He has a great charm of clear, beautiful, picturesque language; beyond this, he is a cross of —— on ——;[1] superior to either, but as conceited, as shallow, as uncharitable, and as one-sided. Of real original proof—nothing. As to prophecy, he merely hashes up Elliott. His interspersed pious addresses are good.

NEW YORK, *March* 26, 1856.

I forgot to say that I am falling into the very same *tremolo* which you detected in S., and find my voice materially altered in preaching. The religious romance of early Methodism interests me more than Macaulay, and I think John Wesley's English better than Swift's or Cobbett's. I remember going to Dr. Mayer's to an Easter Communion, with my father, forty odd years ago.[2] On Maundy Thursday I assisted at mass at St. Ann's, and on Good Friday was at the doors of three chapels; not however *in forma pauperis;* numbers attended to that function. The proceedings of the priest with his acolytes profanely reminded me of a juggler and his aids.

There is something distressing in the uniform decay and transitoriness of the free blacks. The few exceptions are like feeble exotics reared at great cost. W. himself is a good man, but even he is far below the smallest sort of village minister.

---

[1] Popular Anti-Romanists.

[2] Dr. Philip F. Mayer, Pastor of St. John's Lutheran Church, Philadelphia, commemorated the fiftieth anniversary of his pastorate, October 5, 1856. He died in 1858.

I am unfeignedly humbled, though not a whit surprised, that people are not converted under my teaching ; and it is always far from me to lay the blame on " the church," and scold my communicants for the default. I should wonder if any good number should ever be awakened by me ; and as a personal matter, own with abasement that I accept unfruitful ministry as an intelligible chastening for sin. Let me add—none of these things give me any freedom to press measures. I have no doubt, either you or I could get up a stir in one week, which would fill a column of tabulated statistics. Ah me ! I am sadly and increasingly unfit to work in the conventional traces. I utterly reject the entire pew-system—I speak of cities—as against the spirit of Christianity. But all my opinions are held too tremblingly for me ever to be a reformer. So I quietly and sorrowfully go on expounding those things I am sure about.

NEW YORK, *April* 17, 1856.

I shall not be surprised if you hear there is some awakening among my people. And so there unquestionably is—but only in one corner. The " Church," to use the Yankee phrase, is not awakened at all. There are, all since I last wrote to you, appearances of converting influence in about seventeen persons. These have all been gradually led on for months, and some for years. Except where they are in the same households, they are almost all unknown to one another. I have not had any inquiry-meeting. Once I have met " those willing to be guided about seeking their salvation," (writing down this form of notice, and reading it,) and thus have drawn to my house yesterday more than forty. With these I had no private talk, *then,* but expounded a Chapter. I am troubled as to whether I shall repeat even this. I have no additional meeting, as yet, and have not departed from my routine of lectures on Acts. It is a remarkable coincidence, that the meeting of Presbytery was almost a Bochim, and from beginning to end exhibited tenderness, humility, and affection on the part of ministers. I am dreading, beyond expression, the rise of a fanatical breeze among my church-members, and shall humbly endeavour to suppress rather than arouse human passions. You will understand me, better than anybody, when I say, I will, as at present advised, continue private address, but use no precipitating means. I even deprecate them. And so I feel about the whole affair. The way I am taking would be deemed a quenching of the spirit by sundry of my brethren. But I distrust every thing in revivalism, which is not common to it with the stated, continued, persistent presentation of the gospel.

NEW YORK, *April* 23, 1856.

I have nothing to change my opinion, that the inquiry among our people is lately discovered, but not lately produced. It was not an inquiry-meeting I held—but an exposition, and I had no private talk. I never met with the misapprehension you surmise.[1] On that ground, we should never have a Bible Class, or a Young Men's Meeting. Above all, the objection would lie against your taking a child into your study for advice and prayer, which would yet more suggest the esoteric scruple. Though I have no "inquiry-meeting," I should make the having one a simple question of degree. If a pastor cannot conveniently see them apart, I think it would be prudery not to see them together. As an instrument of excitement I have always feared them. I add but a few to the cases first known. But a very large proportion of my flock appears in the very state you mention, "in the place of the bringing forth of children." All this winter I have preached doctrinally—in a disguised series—and chiefly about conviction, conversion, faith, &c. I generally conclude, after interviews, that this reluctancy (in truly serious persons) arises from dim views of doctrine, feeble grasp of the truth, legal notions of the preparation which they must see in themselves. New-measure people undertake to use instruments, and often kill the child. In spiritual as in natural travail, I suppose there must be much waiting. I hope we shall, May 11, add some sixteen.[2]

A Spaniard, a civilian from Madrid, is here, on Bible Society business; a thorough Protestant; says there are many such in Spain; considers the country on the verge of religious freedom; brings a liberal work of his own in sheets; explains the late vote in the Cortes very clearly, &c. I never before saw beauty in the pantomime of feature and hands. He speaks French fluently. We parsons are often and justly rallied for being taken in; but every few days I find the same happening to sharp worldlings. A wealthy merchant told me last night this anecdote: He had a large and costly set of china fraudulently taken from him by a woman. Not long after, this very woman got $100 from him for a charity, since exploded; at the very moment his suit against her was in progress.

[1] "The trouble I have about the private meetings is the apparent admission that all the directions for 'guiding those that are seeking salvation,' are not given in the pulpit, and so countenancing the notion of some that there are esoteric instructions which they must get in some other than the ordinary way. Would it not be well to hold the inquiry-meeting in the church? I mean, to make the regular services take the direction of the simplest colloquial advice."

[2] On that day 17 were admitted on examination; 7 on certificate.

NEW YORK, *May* 29, 1856.

The Assembly was dissolved last night, with exercises of a most touching character. It is the unusual opinion that no G. A. has been so edifying. From beginning to end there was no squabble, nor was one sarcasm uttered. No decision of the Chair was appealed from, and only one was questioned. All this, under God, was owing to the good sense and affectionate piety of Dr. McFarland, [the Moderator,] who has carried away both reverence and love. There was an absence of stars; but the average talent was uncommon. Probably no Assembly has had so many valuable laymen. The men most listened to were Thornwell, Rice, Peck, Marshall, D. Lord, Johns, Judge Leavitt, Judge Allen, Humphrey, Harrison. Welch, in Committees, and once on the floor, made his remarkable powers of mind known, and will be remembered as much as any one.[1] The feeling of satisfaction, as to the way they have been treated, is very warmly and generally expressed. I never felt more complacent as to my church, and am grateful that a meeting for which I entertained such fears has turned out so much to the honour of religion and the satisfaction of all. The ablest speech, and one of the ablest I ever heard, for argument, adroitness, tact, style, elocution, and modest power, was Humphrey's, on the Danville Seminary.

NEW YORK, *June* 10, 1856.

I own our desert of national judgments, and that the signs are alarming. Yet I think the present concussion is a temporary thing. The affair in Kansas I trust has reached its acme. A minister from the heart of the troubles has just left me; he is hopeful. The exaggerations of the journals are horrible. Such questions should never have been left to be settled by a border mob. Whatever Democracy may be in settled States, it is only strong government which can rule frontiers. Dr. Hodge has most admirably stated the slavery doctrine, in his Ephesians. Inter alia: " It is just as great a sin to deprive a slave of the just recompense for his labour, or to keep him in ignorance, or to take from him his wife or child, as it is to act thus towards a free man;" p. 369. How nobly this clear enunciation of a scriptural principle towers above all the extravagancies of both sides!

NEW YORK, *June* 21, 1856.

I made my first acquaintance with Bridgeport (Connecticut) this week, having gone there to preach, and converse, and pray with Mrs. H.[2] I dare not say it is the most beautiful place I

---

[1] Ashbel Welch, Elder of Lambertsville, N. J.

[2] He preached in Bridgeport, June 19; also June 27, July 10, and August 24.

ever saw, but I dare as little say the reverse. The railway passes far away from its surpassing rural villas. Mrs. H. is a wonder of knowledge, wisdom, humility, faith; every thing, in a word, which can glorify religion. I never had what seemed to me a holier sojourn. I propose to take part of my family to Bridgeport on the 27th to board for a week—maybe longer. Cases of awakening still drop in. Two new cases awaited my return yesterday.

No public route gives any idea of the English beauties of New England. The villages grow so into one another, in the south part of Connecticut, that men confidently predict a row of lamps a hundred miles east of our city, as they now are eight miles to Harlem.

NEWPORT, *July* 28, 1856.

I am to be addressed at " Cliff House, care Ch. T. Hazard." There are thirty-six Mrs. Hazards in Newport. We are on the very beach or bank, only a broad field intervening between our yard and the cliffs, at whose base the sea breaks. Looking across a horse-shoe cove, on the left or north of which is the bathing beach, I see three points or capes, between which are two coves with their respective beaches. Beyond all, the village of Little Compton glitters in the sun. The waves are gently swaying without breaking, and the scene is very calm. In the sun it has been pretty warm to-day, but there is a breeze, and whenever we drive out in the evening we need an overcoat. The hot Friday, when New York and Philadelphia thermometers marked 100°, it was 74° all day on the Point, south of us. In the town, however, there is a good deal of glowing heat. The place at which we are is part of a tract, which Hazard has just lost by a decree in Chancery. The house in which I stay, was once rented by Longfellow and his friends. I have news of our Henry to within a week, by Mr. J. Auchincloss, who unexpectedly saw him on board of a propeller in Lake Superior. He and his companion have nearly disposed of the six boxes of Presbyterian books which they took on. The chief buyers have been the Cornishmen in the mines. He is in the land of the Dakotah, of Indian lodges, dog-trains, and snow shoes. Their journeys on foot, with sacks on their backs, have been numerous. The time I spent in Bridgeport was very agreeable. It is a beautiful place, with pleasant drives around it. Stratford, Fairfield, and Greenfield Hill, are very charming. In no part of rural Connecticut do I see any of those marks of a degraded white population, which Southern orators say must appear where there is no servile class. On the contrary, I am more and more struck with the thrift and equalized comfort of the small yeomanry of Puritan New England. In this I do not include Rhode Island.

Several rather extraordinary instances of good done by simple reading of the Bible with inquirers have lately turned up in my ministry. Addison is writing on Acts, in my study, and printing also. A new Presbyterian Church is about to be organized at Deep River, (Saybrook town,) Connecticut, under Mr. Connitt. I have nothing but what the papers will give you, concerning the terrible disaster to the " Empire State" near us on the 26th. Mr. Thayer preached an original and grand sermon yesterday on Self-conceit.

August 4.—The thermometer keeps about 76° on our Cliff, but it is pretty hot in town. People are very proud of thermometers which go higher and lower than their neighbours'. Thayer and Cheever yesterday. The latter strangely and uncouthly original and fascinating. He reached me deeply. Thayer's sermon was great on "take heed how ye hear." On or about August 14th, we go to Bristol, R. I., for a week ; thence, perhaps, by a short detour to Bridgeport. The absence of common piety and religious feeling in society, is much more manifest here [New England] than with us. The spirit as well of hearing as of worship, seems gone. Politics, Abstinence, and Slavery, usurp the " sacred desk."

NEW YORK, *August* 23, 1856.

I came here yesterday from Bridgeport, where I left my wife and child, and write from my own house, where, however, I do not expect my folks till September. I have some preaching yet to do in Connecticut, by which I may contribute somewhat to hold up the hands of the Presbyterian brethren.[1] Through what we call an accident, there met at Henry's table last night in 27th street all our brotherhood, except Archibald, making, with my Henry, six. When are we likely so to meet again ! I trust your mother will rally, but every year brings its painful warnings at such an age. God grant her a blessed evening !

How ridiculously American is the scuffle of the Scientific Association at Albany about Constitution and By-laws !

The German Fremonters make infidelity and drink figure largely on their banners. In New England I found no Democrats, but sundry Fillmore men. There is a feeling that he would conciliate.

I spent some days in Bristol, R. I. ; from which place I think I wrote to your worship. It is a thorough wreck ; grass every-

---

[1] He preached in the Presbyterian Church of Hartford, August 31.

where literally growing in its broad, beautifully shaded Philadelphian streets. Numerous Cubans of wealth summer there. The harbour and surroundings are enchanting. They kept up slaving as late as 1816. A negro *ghetto* of Bristol is still named *Goree*. The aspect of interior New England is pleasing; from the total absence of any patent squalor. Mechanics everywhere live in houses a hundred per cent. above the same class in Pennsylvania or New Jersey. I wish our Calhounites could see that the small farmers of Connecticut have more comforts of civilization than many wealthy planters. The remaining of certain old Puritan habitudes is striking; such as a noon bell and curfew.

NEW YORK, *September* 5, 1856.

I should have gladly kept my wife and boy a little longer in rural air; but we were made uncomfortable at Bridgeport, whither we came from Bristol, by overcrowding in the house, so we returned yesterday. There is no place like home. My pulpit has been very well occupied by the Rev. Mr. Myers, of St. Augustine. Congregations fair—though very few of our own people.

There is no harm in repeating, what I said in my last, how seriously I feel the tidings you give respecting your mother. It brings my own warmly before me. Not only were they mutual friends, but they were lovely persons, long permitted to escape the uncomely accidents of old age, and carrying much of the sweet natural interest of girlhood into later years. Where shall we ever find such sympathy with us—especially in the minor trials of life? Who will ever so understand the little weaknesses of our character? If I go on much in this strain, I shall lose my composure; especially if I touch on other associations, more equal, and as strong. Let us bless God for such relations and affections. From what you say, I am prepared to hear something grave concerning your mother's case. If it should ever be proper to do so, assure her of my love and prayers.

It is wonderful that the yellow-fever has moved so slowly. The ravages at Fort Hamilton and Governor's Island have been great, in proportion to the subjects. At the former, two men fell yesterday at battalion-drill. Maj. Morris, the Commandant, married a Ritchie (née Alexander) of the Delaware Fairfield family. He and his were in the midst of it before, at Tampico. It is too much to expect that it should not alight and spread in our Water-streets.[1] If reports are true, there have been some

----

[1] Water-street—a narrow, confined street, on the Delaware front of Philadelphia.

cases to-day. What a remarkable respite from cholera this year, all over the country!

My "heft," as the Yankees say, has increased to 164 lbs. At Hartford I visited with pleasure the only original portraits of Pres. Edwards and his saintly wife. They are in the Edwards family. I also saw the Charter-Oak lying in massive glory on the earth : "The Charter Oak, it was the tree, that balked his sacred majesty." I have never seen so much of the country and every-day life of New England, as this summer, and it has been with increased respect. The average of domestic comfort and even refinement I believe to be unequalled in the world. We talk of Scotland, and justly ; but Scotland has thousands of squalid peat-smoky hovels, where the best fare is oatmeal-porridge. There is nothing of this in Yankee-land, but by importation.

NEW YORK, *September* 17, 1856.

I am less surprised than pained by the tidings you give me. *Requiescit in pace.* My recollections go back with a sad pleasure to the old Sixth St. house. What friendly, long-continued, unvarying kindness to us and ours ! What shadows flit along the back-ground—some friends and some only acquaintances—and how many gone !

It is a trial to me not to be able to go to the funeral of one of the truest friends I ever had. I have notice of an invalid passing through town, who makes an appointment with me for that very day ; and the circumstances are important and delicate. You will now comprehend a feeling of family-headship, which comes heavily over one, upon the departure of a last surviving parent.

[I subjoin a letter written on the same afflicting event to a sister of my mother.]

NEW YORK, *September* 25, 1856.

It was impossible for me to hear of the departure of your beloved sister, without thinking very much of you. Few persons, even of the connexion, have been with her so constantly during her decline. Perhaps none on earth knew her better. Naturally, therefore, your sorrow must be great.

Among the consolatoins which you have so richly, one is the knowledge that our dear and valued friend was esteemed by so large a circle. No one of my whole acquaintance was ever more spared the deformities and disagreeable points of old age ; in this resembling your father, whom I well remember, as the sweetest looking old gentleman I ever saw. Then you have the pleasing reflection for life, that it was placed in your power to minister with sisterly affection, in the dwelling and at the couch of one whom you loved. But, above all, we must be consoled by the bright hope which we entertain, concerning the present and future happiness of our deceased sister. Though a silent and humble, she was a sincere and a consistent Christian. Her trust was in the Divine Saviour of sinners, to the rejection of all self-righteous merits. This faith diffused serenity over her closing hours. Little as is revealed to us concerning the details of the eternal blessedness, we know that the souls of the righteous are with the Lord, and that those who are absent from the body are present with the Lord.

It is a source of great comfort to those of us who survive, that your sister was not content to cherish religious sentiments in her private thoughts, but spontaneously added herself to the Lord's witnesses, by becoming a communicant in his Church.

How natural it is for our minds to go back to those who are gone! Where are our parents, and the religious teachers of our youth? Where are our own companions? Well do I remember Mr. Hall, with that spare, and dignified, and gentle form which belonged to him. My dear friend, "The fashion of this world passeth away." May we find grace to appear clad in the righteousness of Christ at his coming!

NEW YORK, *September* 30, 1856.

A letter of my father (1809) has turned up, in which he states that I had been at school a week. I remember it well; it was to "Madam Thomson," in Lombard street, [Philadelphia.] A sort of self-pity always comes over me when I think of my days of childhood; I do not detect it so much in others. It seems to me I had more unuttered distresses than most children. How long a poor child will harbour an afflictive scruple about religion, which would have been instantly dissipated by disclosure!

Bush writes to me. He expatiates on the excellencies of Howe, Owen, and Burroughs, in precisely the terms which he would have used thirty years ago. My folks are coming in pretty fast, but many are yet absent. Mauch Chunk is looking for a pastor—not too young—man of experience; schedule of gifts—not this, not that. Webster lived and died on a stipend of $400. If it had not rained, a thousand carters were to have turned out last night for Fillmore. Within a few weeks, I hear many more voices in this state (it is very hard to say "*our* state") for Fillmore. Numerous private accounts speak well of Mr. Monsalvatge's preaching and labours at Carthagena. He has a great body of young Granadans on his side. He has sent me several sermons, openly printed in the city newspapers. Mr.

Pratt, late of Princeton, writes encouragingly from Bogotá. I forgot whether I wrote from Bristol about Mr. G., an accomplished Cuban gentleman, one of several persons of wealth who summer in Rhode Island. He was bred in Spain, and is an author. What is pleasing is, that he is a pious and courageous Protestant. Lecturing on Acts xv. 1—35, I find it very tough to make that Council at Jerusalem a college of Bishops, or a General Assembly, or a Synod, or a Presbytery, or a Kirk-session, or an independent congregation. The common fiction of the Church having been organized on the plan of the Synagogue is " revolting " to me ; incredulus odi. While the Apostles lived, they clearly had supreme authority, and they as clearly had no successors. Where they were not, Elders ordained by them had local and temporary rule. I have searched in vain for a single instance of *one* pastor tied to *one* congregation, or of the call of *one* congregation as necessary to orders. All the ministry, for what appears, was *ministerium vagum*, which the impugners of ordaining *sine titulo* do so eschew. My love to your environs. What a barbaric pomp about the crowning of the Czar !

P. S. *October* 2.—I retain the preceding in order to say that I will preserve the letters for you, and thank you for them.[1] All these things carry one back—back ! I like the allusion to the house in 6th street. The *old* Philadelphia carries a great charm in my recollections. I have the only severe cold I have had in three years, and do not see how I can do duty on Sunday. At my prompting Randolph gets out a book for Business Men. I chose the subject of *Clerks*, and what I have written on it will probably appear also as a little tractate.[2] Your libretto and tract were received, and would have been reviewed by me but for the heavy pressure of the above, and of completing my MS. on Sunday Schools, which went to Philadelphia yesterday.[3]

[1] Letters of his father.

[2] " The Man of Business, considered in his various relations." The contributors to this volume were Drs. Alexander, Sprague, Todd, Tyng, Ferris, and Stearns. Dr. Alexander's subject is, " The Merchant's Clerk Cheered and Counselled." This chapter was afterwards reprinted by itself, and one person sold more than a thousand copies in the stores of New York, in about four weeks. In April, 1856, Randolph published McLaren's Sermons on " Glorying in the Cross of Christ," for which Dr. A. wrote an introduction.

[3] " The American Sunday-School and its adjuncts. By James W. Alexander, D. D. ;" published by the American Sunday-School Union, 1856, 342 pages. In the preface he says: " More than forty years ago it was my lot to sit on an humble form in one of the earliest Sunday-Schools set up in America. In process of time I became a teacher in similar institutions ; and ever since my entrance upon the Gospel ministry I have counted it an honor to work collaterally in the same cause. In attempting to promote the same ends, I have constructed and launched from the presses which now

NEW YORK, *November* 19, 1856.

The young woman gives very good satisfaction, and appears to like her place. She went away for one day and night without my leave. She appears to be steady and industrious; good at mending and at washing up tea-things. My wife has said nothing about baking or ironing. It is our wish to keep her during the winter.[1]

My sprained foot is not much better, though I go about. Thanksgiving sermon adds a somewhat to the week's writing. I intend to touch on the importance of our being united in peace with all English-speaking people. My text is Deut. xxxii. 8, to word "Adam" inclusive. Sprague's book[2] is both valuable and entertaining. I like it all the better for the number and brevity of the articles. Some of them are quite in the manner of the late Joseph Miller, Esq. If you have not read Trench's "English Past and Present," it will give you a pleasant half-hour. What a wonderful fall we have had, for fine weather! Greatly do I feel the deprivation of walking freely, and more than ever do I sympathize with those who halt alway. Strange talk this in the papers, as if the Southern fire-eaters would not vote for Buchanan, unless after some ultra pledges on his part. I hope and pray he may give none. Dr. McCartee has come into our Presbytery, and taken the Westminster Church in 22d street. Some sermons, which I have on hand, (having preached about eight,) will perhaps grow into a book on Faith. Robinson's [Palestine] new impression puts the former three into two volumes, and adds a new third. Stewart's Brazil is not very lively, but full of information. Brazil must be a horrible country, as Portuguese is a horrible lingo. The Hungarian officer, who formerly appeared in Trenton, awakens my pity; he is now in abject mendicity—a handsome soldierly fellow too. It is a dreadful thing to be an exile in poverty. The thought is good for Thanksgiving Day.

NEW YORK, *January* 2, 1857.

January 1st is a *dies non* with us, except in regard of calls,

produce the present work, more than thirty trifles, which, 'for better for worse,' have gone sailing out upon the ocean of print, some to be high and dry on the strand of oblivion, and some to be still floating on the wave, protected, like the paper-nautilus, by their very frailty." The object of this work is to prove the necessity and duty of providing for general religious education, and to show how this end is promoted by Sunday-Schools and religious reading.

[1] This pleasantry refers to a visit from one of his correspondent's children.

[2] "Annals of the American Pulpit," vols. 1 and 2.

so I now wish for you and yours a happy New Year. We had 175 calls. I am told Dr. Spring sometimes has 300. Holten's New Granada is a very entertaining book, in some places a little free. He lets you well into Granadan manners and customs. I do not see that —— differs materially from Wright and Garrison, save in decorum of language, when in his late book on Slavery he says : " Unless the Bible teaches my doctrine about slavery, it is not of God." A member of my church has been spending a year in North Wales. He hired a furnished house, library, &c., of ample size, with about twenty acres of pleasure-ground, for £200. The whole stood within a walled park of 400 acres, as good as his, and well-kept. He had half-a-mile of wall, ten feet high, for wall-fruit, and had every sort of fruit in plenty. In consequence of the low rent, wages, &c., he calculates that he did not add a penny to his year's expenses, though he includes the transportation, to and fro, of ten persons.

A soliciting missionary from Port Natal in South Africa, is here ; a fairspoken Scot, named Campbell. Prof. Owen of this city is about to come out with a commentary on the Gospels. He is of the Free Academy.

I lately attended high mass for the soul of Father Andrade, and saw about ten priests officiating. The incense is scarcely more than nominal. In my day, we used to get a very tolerable sniff ; and in Paris, I think, I saw a dozen censers going all in a row, with a dexterous perpendicular hoist, which it must take some time to learn. Our motto for 1857 is : " Rejoice evermore." [1]

I have arrived at the 16th chapter of Acts in my exposition. Sometimes I wish no other sort of preaching had been invented. I wish I knew more about the Doverites, Derbyites, or Plymouth brethren. They seem to have made much progress among the French Protestants. An odd fish has applied to me for my life towards his " Eloquent Divines," about to appear. I have refused and derided, but experiences teach that this is no protection. This is the seventh letter at this sitting, and some of them more lengthy ; this, therefore, can only be strengthy, as is the regard of, Sir, your friend and subscriber.

[1] His sermon on the year-text was usually preached at the afternoon service of the first Sunday in the year. The morning service of that day had usually a reference to the annual collection made at that time for Foreign Missions. The collection on Jan. 2, 1857, amounted to $7,600. In the preceding month, the collection for Domestic Missions had been nearly $4,000. In February, 1857, the collection for the Board of Education was $4,600 ; in May, for Sunday-Schools, $1,300 ; in November, for the Bible Society, $2,600.

NEW YORK, *March* 9, 1857.

Louis Napoleon has introduced a new kind of state-paper, racy as a vaudeville; it is too witty.[1]   Addison calls my attention to the remarkable revolution, which, under the Palmerston rule, is going on in the English sees, in favour of Evangelicalism.   Both archbishops and the three leading bishops are now on that side. I find "grand-daughter" in Webster and Worcester; the only authorities I have.[2]   Mr. B., of Leavenworth, Kansas, writes to me that the new houses building there, are "hundreds."   He also says, if things go on so for two years, that the region 200 miles west of the east border will be the most thickly peopled portion of the Western States.   Mr. M. bought $500 worth of land on the site of Milwaukee, thirteen years ago.   Its sworn value now is $400,000.   The Ferguson who wrote "America by Rail and Steam," is a banker and a deacon of Dr. Hamilton's. He has been here on a second visit.

There is something very striking in the prayer, with which St. Augustine commonly closed his sermons : "Conversi ad Dominum, Deum, Patrem omnipotentem, puro corde, Ei, quantum potest parvitas nostra, maximas atque uberes gratias agamus : precantes toto animo singularem mansuetudinem ejus, ut preces nostras in beneplacito suo exaudire dignetur ; inimicum quoque a nostris actibus et cogitationibus sua virtute expellat, nobis multiplicet fidem, mentem gubernet, spirituales cogitationes concedat, et ad beatitudinem suam perducat : per Jesum Christum Filium suum, Dominum nostrum, qui cum eo vivit et regnat in unitate Spiritus sancti Deus, per omnia sæcula sæculorum. Amen."   It is beautiful Latin, and much more full of matter than "a Prayer of St. Chrysostom."[3]   Its first words, with an " &c.," so often close the "Conciones," that I presume he always used it. Augustine is the only father of whom I read much; and the more I read, the more I perceive that if you leave out predestination and justification by faith, his scheme, and that of the Catholic Church of his day, was just that which Pusey would restore.   Nothing can be more garbled and misleading, than the centos given by Milner.[4]

[1] I suppose the allusion is to the Emperor's speech, at the opening of the Chambers in 1857.   The "wit" must be in the sentence where, in reference to the inundations, it is said: "I make it a point of honor, that in France rivers, like revolutions, must return to their beds, or that they must not leave them."
[2] I had insisted that such a purist as he should follow the old standard dictionaries, which give but one *d* in this word.
[3] In the "Book of Common Prayer."
[4] In the New York "Journal of Commerce," of March 10, there is a free translation, with comments, from Horace, Ode 24, Book 3, in application to the vices of the age, which I think I cannot be mistaken in attributing to Dr. Alexander.

NEW YORK, *April* 27, 1857.

Addison preached for me yesterday, though I think I could have preached once myself. My chief annoyance is a difficulty of breathing, oppression, or strangling sensation, which comes on at times, and especially at night.[1] While Hugh Miller's new book[2] contains lots of things which I do not believe, it has some —many—of the sublimest views respecting creation and redemption, that I ever met with. Some of his sweeps of high description are inimitable. Yet he always says *ere* for *before*, and *mayhap* for *perhaps*. The biographies by Macaulay, in several numbers of Harper, are worth reading ; they are from the last (8th) edition of the Encyclopædia Britannica. In a life of Sir H. Davy, by Rogers, it is said, (1812, &c. :) " A certain change (it must with regret be owned) came over his state of mind, tarnished his serenity, and gradually, though imperceptibly, weakened his scientific zeal. It was to be ascribed solely, we believe, to the severe ordeal of exuberant but heartless popularity, which he underwent in London. The flatteries of fashionable life . . . . . by degrees attached Davy to the fashionable world, and loosened his ties to the laboratory, which had been to him the sole and fit scene of his triumphs." We have a cold easterly drizzle—as yet more wind than rain. Addison visited his native house on his birthday, and ate an ice-cream in what was my father's study. I distinctly remember the day J. A. A. was born.[3]

When Peter Cunningham shall have digested all Walpole's Letters into one chronological series, with the promised notes, it will be the richest collection of gossip in the world. Some one of my congregation visits the Holy Land, every year, at least. Lord Napier is surveying our town.

I have seldom been more pained by a thing of the kind than by your account of S., [lost at sea.] Poor little S. ! We remember him as coming into our sick chamber in 8th street [Philadelphia] to show his little fat leg. Poor mother ! I earnestly hope she will have spiritual indemnity. Mrs. H. was buried yesterday. She was free from extreme suffering towards the last. Mr. J., a good friend of ours, has died of dreadful disease of the heart. How voluminous would be the list of the dead

---

[1] On the 9th April he had written : " I am laboring under a very painful irritation of throat and fauces." He was able to preach but twice in April, and four times in May. His cough had then become so threatening, that a voyage seemed to be the only resort that promised permanent relief.

[2] " The Testimony of the Rocks."

[3] The house was in Lombard street, Philadelphia; the date was April 24, 1809.

whom we have known; and how strangely some of them pass out of mind!

Dr. B. used to read Voltaire as the best Christians read the Bible. Mrs. B. often said to me that the only comfort she had was in going to church, and that she looked forward to this all the week. I have often pondered on this and hoped it might prove to be the case with many whom we overlook in estimating the value of Divine service.

There is a certain point at which a man's mishaps operate against him, much as if they were moral delinquencies.

NEW YORK, *May* 26, 1857.

To-morrow, it may be presumed, will be too busy for writing. I take to-day therefore for farewells to you and all your house.

My address is: *W. A.* and *G. Maxwell & Co., Liverpool.*[1]

Every thing preparative has been ordered very favourably.

There is something serious in such separations, which I feel just now; in better moments we will remember one another.[2]

[1] Dr. Alexander, accompanied by his wife and youngest child, embarked in the steamer Baltic, for Liverpool, May 27th.

[2] The frequent allusions which have occurred in the letters of this and other chapters, to their writer's interest in the American Tract Society, will make acceptable the following notice communicated to me by the Rev. Dr. Hallock, one of its Secretaries:

"The memory of Dr. James W. Alexander is precious to the Executive Committee and officers of the American Tract Society. As his father, Dr. Archibald Alexander, was, from the formation of the Society in 1825 till his death in 1851, an unwavering friend, supporter, and counsellor, making valuable contributions to the list of its publications by his pen, and acting for three years as a member of its Publishing Committee, so the son, in similar relations and by almost all the same means, gave the Society his cordial and efficient co-operation.

"When, in 1842, a public deliberative meeting of the Society's Board and friends was held for three days in the Broadway Tabernacle, Dr. James W. Alexander, who was then at Princeton, communicated an able document on a momentous topic, with the bearing of which his wide range of reading and observation made him familiar, 'THE EVILS OF AN UNSANCTIFIED LITERATURE.' The document was read to the meeting by the Rev. Dr. Potts, and was published in a volume comprising ten other documents presented at that meeting, and a record of its proceedings.

"In 1845, when Dr. Archibald Alexander retired from his labours as a member of the Society's Publishing Committee, Dr. James W. Alexander, who was then pastor in New York, was elected as his successor; and fulfilled the duties of the office for three years, when the pressure of his official duties in the ministry compelled him to retire, and the Rev. Dr. Magie succeeded him in that office.

"Dr. James W. Alexander, soon after the establishment of the American Messenger, in 1842, commenced writing for it valuable but anonymous articles, which were continued, from time to time, to the number of thirty or forty articles, all on great and momentous themes pertaining to the common salvation. In this way alone, addressing each month not far from two hundred thousand families, he conveyed messages of Christian love to millions of men quite beyond the reach of his preaching or other written works.

" The Society published in their series his excellent tract on Revivals of Religion; showing that by true revivals of religion God is glorified, the plan of redemption accomplished, the Church raised to its highest prosperity, and that such an extension of the Church is demanded by the present state of our nation; embodying, with singular discernment, a brief, comprehensive sketch of the history of revivals from Apostolic days.

" The Society also publish his volume of seventeen revival tracts, originally issued under the modest title of " Wayside Books," in successive numbers during the progress of the revival of 1858, when, in his high position as pastor of the church in the Fifth Avenue, he wished not only to benefit his own people, but others, by bearing his testimony in favour of the good work, but to give individual souls in the various stages of awakening or quickening under Divine influence, the needed instruction, counsel, and guidance.

" The very titles of these seventeen tracts (one of them written by an intimate fellow-labourer in the ministry) show their high evangelical character and aim, and the wide range of usefulness to which they are adapted, and in which they will doubtless long continue to give what may be almost regarded as their author's dying testimony to the truth and excellency of the gospel of Christ. They are: The Revival; Seek to Save Souls; Pray for the Spirit; The Unawakened; Harden not your Heart; Varieties in Anxious Inquiry; Looking unto Jesus; God be merciful to me a Sinner; O for more Feeling; Have I come to Christ? My Teacher, my Master; My Brother; Sing Praises; The Harvest of New York; Compel them to Come in; Help the Seaman; To Firemen.

" As counsellors in all questions of doubt and perplexity, Dr. James W. Alexander and his father were uncommon men—single-hearted, far-seeing, calm, practical, judicious—and favoured was the friend, the benevolent institution, the congregation, the church, or the community, who could resort to them and receive their heaven-guided lessons of wisdom. Pleasant were they on earth, and it is a cheering anticipation that we may meet them with all the redeemed in the world above."

CHAPTER XIII.

LETTERS DURING HIS SECOND VISIT TO EUROPE [1]

1857.

LIVERPOOL, June 11, 1857.

THROUGH God's mercy we arrived here in safety on the 7th, after what seamen call a very favourable passage. We found valuable friends on board, and have also found numerous acquaintances of ourselves or our friends, in this town. I had really forgotten how cool the weather is here. We have been under the necessity of having fires every evening, and I shudder with cold most of the time. Though my cough is less, it has not left me. We have just returned from the Exhibition of the "Art Treasures" at Manchester—sixty miles going and returning since morning; so much for English railways. The structure itself is fine, and much resembling the Crystal Palace. The value of the paintings is reckoned by scores of millions of pounds. Every great public and private collection in England has given its gems. Without being a connoisseur I was ravished with the sight of the great works of the greatest masters. Twenty or thirty Raphaels! English aristocracy owns more of Italian art than Italy itself. Among the moderns, I was not prepared to be so delighted as I am with Sir Joshua Reynolds. All his great works are here. You learn to recognize them at once, and their gracefulness is indescribable. The gallery of water-colours opens quite a new field of art to me. Few of the sculptures awaken me much. Canova's all seem to be injured by mannerism. I more admire Chantrey, Marshall, and Gibson. Hogarth's paintings added very little to my pleasure in his engravings. Gainsborough's best pieces are enchanting.

---

[1] In making up this chapter I have followed the same course as in the letters of the visit of 1851, and for the reasons given in the prefatory note of Chapter XI.

LEAMINGTON, *June* 13, 1857.

We left Liverpool at 11, and came by Crewe, Wolverhampton, Birmingham, and Coventry. Haymaking is going on, and we saw and heard a lark ascend, and give his delicious song. Leamington is the cleanest and most brilliant place I ever saw. Every thing has a miniature look. The trim houses, neat shopfronts, white flags, and perfectly pure streets, affect me with a sense of being in a play-place. I can hardly think it real. English neatness here becomes almost Dutch. I forgot to say that the everlasting succession of beauties, in hedgerow, field, and meadow, with unvaried culture and perfect green, produces at length the effect of gazing on a pretty face without expression. One longs for a bare spot, a morsel of rude, brushy land, or a small piece of bad road.

June 14.—We have been to All Saints, the old parish-church, large and full. We were ushered in through the singing-boys to a seat in the choir immediately behind one of the reading-pews. The service was given cathedral-fashion. Mr. Bowen, the curate, preached an evangelical sermon from the Rich Man and Lazarus. Soldiers went home from church to martial music. The rooks were cawing in their nests among the tops of the trees as we came to our inn.

Such has been the popularity of the Springs here, that the place numbers 15,000 inhabitants. There are two Leamington *seasons* in the year; the chief one being in winter, as is true also of Brighton; the other is in the hunting-time. The Cheshire hounds have a famous meet in that county, but all this is a fox-hunting district. Lord Lonsdale (as we guess it was) told us that railways have greatly facilitated hunting by carrying men and even horses to the meets. He said the lands on our way rented for about three pounds an acre, but some in better districts for five pounds.

I have formerly noted the practice of having a little hymn-book for the particular church. The one here was full of our most evangelical hymns, "Just as I am" and the like. In no New England town have I ever remarked a more exact and still observance of the Sabbath. Invalid persons are trundled to church in bath-chairs, as an everyday thing; most worthy of imitation among us. The throngs of people in the street are perfectly well-dressed, and all with brilliant red and white complexions. As with us the complexion runs often into pale and yellow, so here the faulty visages are red, crimson, scratchy, erysipelatic—there are many such. I am inclined to think that the purest English is spoken in these midland counties. I detect very little provincial in the guards or waiters. Nothing like

mendicity or even poverty has met my eye at Leamington Priors.
A little to the north-west is Baxter's Kidderminster, and a short
journey eastward is Doddridge's Northampton. Worcester and
Edgehill are not far off, and if we took the old mail-route, we
should go through the forest of Arden. In this town of so many
thousands, there are doubtless many " brethren," but how shall
I find them out? Every thing in the church-way is set and
petrified. I went into a shop for tracts, but the woman looked
like a nun, and the books all smacked of Oxford.

LONDON, June 15, 1857.

We left Leamington about 10 for London, viâ Rugby. At
R. we saw the church, but could not see the school. The whole
country along our way was full of hay-making and sheep-shear-
ing. As we neared Olney, I sang " Begone unbelief" in memory of John Newton, and much of the scenery on the Ouse was
pleasant as of the very sort which prompted so many passages
of the Task. These impressions were not the less strong, because I own my prevalent mood has been somewhat sombre,
ever since I left America.

It is now 10 P. M., but the boys are in full caper in the
street below, and there is still a lingering blush in the horizon.
People here knock and ring. All servants ring, except the post-
man, who gives two knocks. Coals are brought to the door in a
cart, but in sacks, and each of these is emptied down a hole in the
sidewalk; it is a cleaner and even quicker operation than ours.
The free-and-easy prevails all over England in regard to vehicles,
pony-chaises, phaetons, flies, &c. You see two rosy girls drive
up to a railway-station, and, perhaps, take a relative into their
low-wheeled drag. Numerous cases have been observed by us
of a pony drawing four adults in a sort of buggy, and two looking backwards. But then all the roads are as smooth as this
paper.

4 BERNARD ST., RUSSELL SQUARE,
LONDON, June 18, 1857.

Last evening I attended an anniversary soirée of the Regent
Square and Somerstown Sunday Schools, held in Somerstown, a
neighbourhood much like the Five Points. Lady and gentlemen
teachers present for a tea-drinking. Then up stairs, where a
meeting lasted two and a half hours. Dr. Hamilton in the
chair, who received me with great warmth. Numerous speeches.
Of course, I made an address. Hamilton's gifted vocabulary
flowed in my behalf. The cheers and " hears " were a little
appalling to me; but good nature and a disposition to be pleased

marked every thing. I thought the talent displayed by these teachers very remarkable. The heartiness and almost convivial glee of the meeting were unlike what we have at such times.

In our immediate vicinity is the vast but unfinished cathedral of the Irvingites. London is their Jerusalem, being the seat of their twelve apostles and seven churches. They have two daily services, and I have been to their even-song. The church is a sublime one. About sixty persons were present, of whom part were clergy in rich and varied robes. The chief one, who was forward and apart, near the altar, was wrapped in a heavy dark cloak over his alb, with a stole; he took the lead, and was either angel or bishop. The service was chanted cathedral-wise, and most delightfully. Altogether it was a very solemn affair. Much incense was used.

June 21. *Sunday.*—Very warm. Dr. Hamilton's church. The text was Proverbs viii. 1. It was an admirable sermon. He began it by comparing the choice of Hercules with the choice of Solomon. A shower having come up, I went in the afternoon to the neighbouring church of the Apostles (Irvingite) in Gordon Square. A sermon of an hour was first preached by Mr. John Wells, on the "procession of the Holy Ghost." It was read, was well-delivered, and very theological and orthodox, until near the close he declared that the day of miracles and prophecy had returned. Then followed the regular even-song, which was altogether distinct. The big ones sat in common seats during the sermon with purplish cassocks and small capes—three having lace sleeves; but during the vespers, all were in the choir, which is of immense size. There were twenty, exclusive of the singing-boys in white. The Angel or Bishop (Mr. Heath) had a purple cloak over his alb, and performed his part to admiration. Of the rest, some had yellow and some red stoles, (or scarfs,) and all had albs or white dresses. I heard one pray in the spirit, one prophesy, and three give the word of exhortation. The organ and Gregorian chant were in perfection; all being in good training, and the congregation (about a thousand) generally joining. The sound rolled majestically through the Gothic vaults of the great edifice, which is quite a marvel of modern architecture. The incense, the intoning, and the bowing to the altar, are perfectly popish, but the service and ceremony are very fine and impressive. I do not believe they have better music at St. Paul's.

LONDON, *June* 23, 1857.

The new buildings of Lincoln's Inn are noble. In the fine library I found numbers studying and compiling. A whole alcove and more is devoted to American works, [on Law.] Then to the Middle and Inner Temples. How ancient and beautiful these gardens, walks, and green trees, opening on the river and full of associations from Shakspeare downward! Professor L., of King's College, who accompanied me, greatly admires American jurisprudence, and amidst all his compilations says that American reports are most useful to him. He may be called a disciple of Story's, whose entire works he showed me. In the four Inns there are lectures, Monday on Common Law, Tuesday on Civil Law, Wednesday on Constitutional Law, Thursday on Equity, Friday on Real Estate.

After all this, it was highly proper that I should go to Smithfield. I made my approach by Skinner Street and the Old Bailey, by Snow Hill and Giltspur Street, near St. Sepulchre's and the Compter. This is one of the mustiest and most delicious parts of old London; for here enters Hosier Lane, (Swift speaks of the " veriest cockney of Hosier Lane,") and Cock Lane, famous for Dr. Johnson's and Wesley's visit to the ghost. And here is Pye Corner, where the fire of 1666 stopped. The great area of Smithfield, vast indeed, remains, and the innumerable stalls are left, but the glory is departed. Not only are there no martyrs, like John Rogers, but there are no beasts. I saw a timid flock of sheep looking out of Cock Lane, like intruders, but the principal reminiscence of former days is hay and straw, and the advertisements of butcher-tools, cattle-medicine, &c; besides advertisements of two lost children. I took the pains to count the parish vagrants, posted as having deserted their families, and found the number thirty-one. All this end of town is old, black, and profoundly suggestive. The smell is peculiar, and was doubtless known to Shakspeare and Bunyan.

The strawberries are very plenty and very large, and the English way is to serve them in the hulls, and eat them out of hand, dipping in powdered sugar.

I heard Dean Trench read prayers at Westminster Abbey, and *saw* him preach in a surplice and scarlet hood. He is a robust, hale, good-looking Englishman, with much of that " holytone " which belongs to all readers here.

The funerals are solemn mockery. The hearse is surmounted with immense plumes or bunches, as big as a man, and I have seen a dozen persons in black, perched on the top, driving full tilt to act as mutes. I can't get over the horse-flesh of Hyde Park. I never saw such blood, condition, and grooming. In the streets one sees the biggest and the least horses in the world.

LONDON, *June* 29, 1857.

I have heard the wonderful Spurgeon. I am told the effort

was feeble, for him.   He has none of those captivating intonations
which we remember in Summerfield and others ; neither should
I judge him to have any pathos.   His voice is incomparable, and
perfect for immense power, sweetness, and naturalness.   His
pronunciation is admirable, with the never-failing English eÿther,
knŏwledge, wroth, &c.   Though very like his likenesses, he becomes
almost handsome when animated.   His gesture is sparing and
gentlemanlike.   I detect no affectation.   The tremendous virtue
of his elocution is in outcry, sarcasm, and menace, and his voice
improves as it grows louder.   I seriously think his voice the
great attraction.   His prayers were concise and solemn; a shade
too metaphoric.   His short exposition was so-so in matter, but
well-delivered.   He preceded his sermon by a shot at Lord
Lyndhurst's late remarks on the obscene Print Bill, and said:
" Holywell Street had at length found an advocate in Westminster Palace."   He requested the people in the gallery (there
are three one over another,) not to lean forward.   He said you
could tell a Dissenter in church, by his sitting down before the
hymn was over.   During the sermon he described broken-down
preachers, spitting blood, going to the continent and travelling
at other people's expense.   This did not please me, for

> " Who e'er felt the halter draw,
> With good opinion of the law ? "

He told a very funny story of a minister with a rich wife.
He was very severe on the establishment, and rather intimated
that the gospel was very little preached.   In this part of the
discourse, he preached himself.   Notwithstanding all this and
his dreadful onslaught on written sermons, I think his work
here matter of the greatest thankfulness.   He preaches a pure
gospel, in the most uncompromising manner, with directness,
power, and faithfulness ; and he preaches it to hundreds of
thousands, to beggars and princes.   I am at a loss to say what
they come for.   They seem to be led of God.   All strangers
go.   Some of the nobility are always there.   Church ministers
abound in every assembly.   I ought to have said there is nothing
that savours of the rude or illiterate.   Such a building I would
beg a year to have in New York, for some stentor.   It is the
beau-ideal, being the theatre of Surrey Gardens, where Jullien
has his concerts.   It will hold ten thousand seated.   Every aisle
and corner was filled by a dense mass of standing persons numbering perhaps a thousand.   The attention was unbroken.   What
struck me, was the total absence of the ill-dressed classes.   A
person behind me pointed out actors, Waterloo officers, noble-
men, &c.   Old Hundred by about ten thousand voices was really
congregational singing.   His sermon was fifty minutes, Ezek.

xxxvi. 37—on the connexion of prayer with blessings.   1. Fact.
2. Reasons.   The first head was admirable; as scriptural,
simple, chaste, direct, winning, and full of Christ, as one could
wish.   Only I wondered all the while why it drew the masses
so.   Then he began to suffer with the terrible heat; said so;
and evidently lost his strength of body and mind.   The application was common-place, but his felicitous language and glorious
voice will carry along any thing.   I am persuaded he seeks to
save souls, and believe that he is as much blessed to that end,
as any man of our day.   My childish recollections of Larned,
represent him as much such a speaker.   Spurgeon is a blended
likeness of Prof. Atwater, and Mr. Bartine, the Methodist.   His
eyes are disproportionally small.   In many points of assurance,
dogmatism, conceit, and sarcasm, he reminds one of ——, to
whom he is greatly superior in gentlemanlike bearing and
absence of nasal twang, while he falls far below him in learning,
original illustration, and I think inventive genius.   But Spurgeon preaches the blessed gospel of the grace of God.

You know my passion for London : it is next to impossible
to get away, though the *feeling* of heat is as great as it would
be at New York, while the mercury is about 77°.   Drives into
the environs are very sweet.   All the banks of Thames are lovely.
No words can describe the verdure, the cottages, the roses, the
green lanes, the field-paths, the hay-making, the parks.

The thoughts are very serious which one has amidst the
most favourable circumstances, in a foreign land.   I trust they
are not without spiritual profit.   My friends at home are certainly not less in my mind.   The feeling of being so much a
truant is very oppressive to me at times.   After all, I would a
thousand times rather be at home.

The speakers whom I heard in the House of Commons, were
the Attorney-General, Mr. Henley, (a fine, blunt John Bull,)
Mr. Collier, (a fine orator,) and Mr. Rolt.   As I never heard
Randolph say more than one word, viz., " Palgrave," so all I
ever heard Palmerston say, is : " Because they (the Proctors)
are to be swept from the earth."   I was mightily struck with
the gentlemanly tone of the debate, and the subdued and delicate
manner in which adverse opinion was stated, even when the argument was point-blank in opposition.

This was the day for our visit to the Crystal Palace.   It is
far nobler than the original one, forty-four feet higher, and with
three transepts.   As it takes a volume to describe it, I will bring
that with me, for little can be done in a letter.   The park and
gardens and fountains are on prodigious scale.   Even within the
building every sort of tropical tree and plant is growing, and

there is almost as much vegetable matter as any thing else. Landscape gardening is producing its chef d'œuvre without. In a wild part of the grounds, you have models of life size, and in appropriate surroundings, of all the hideous creatures of the early formations, pterodactylus, hylœosaurus, ichthyosaurus and all. On our way, E. stopped me and said : " O look what a noble little boy ! " We presently found it was Prince Arthur, who, with two sisters, was viewing the palace. We heard two excellent orchestral concerts, stayed all day, and all for a shilling. The pleasantest thing was the great number of the lower class. On reaching lodgings, I found cards of Messrs. Dallas, Senr. and Junr., [the American Minister and son,] and a letter from the Earl of Waldegrave, expressing regret that his son was not in town.[1]

I have seen all the Inns of Court, and of the Inns of Chancery, Clement's Clifford's, Furnival's, Thavie's, and Staple. Strand Inn is pulled down. Barnard's I cannot find. The only remaining ones of the nine, Lyon's and New Inn, I will look for. With Christ's Hospital some of these are my favourite spots. Some say the very first wool-staplers of London lived at what is now Staple Inn. Such an antiquity would not abide a year in New York. Even in London such cool, moist, monastic spaces are preserved only by belonging to guilds or other corporations.

LONDON, *July* 3, 1857.

The House of Lords is superb, but bad for hearing. Lords appear in morning-dress—many with hats on ; some lounging, and one asleep. Law Reform was up. I was glad to hear Brougham at length. He is erect, and agile, though very gray. The manner of a vehement old preacher. Able and emphatic. Lord Chancellor Cranworth spoke, leaving the woolsack. His voice and manner that of the late President Maxwell, [of Virginia.] Lord Fitzwilliam spoke ; tall, thin, quakerish, hat over eyes. I afterwards saw him canter off on a spirited horse, brought by a groom in white livery ; the Earl is 75. Lord Campbell spoke. Without his [Judge's] wig, looks bluff and hearty ; dark hair, baldish ; age 76. Afterwards they went into committee, Redesdale in the chair. I also heard him speak. Then came on

---

[1] The son of the Earl is the Hon. and Rev. Samuel Waldegrave, now canon of Salisbury, and author of several excellent religious works. Of one of these—" New Testament Millenarianism "—Dr. Alexander gave a synopsis in the Repertory, July, 1856. Mr. Waldegrave's book has many acknowledgments of the value of Dr. J. A. Alexander's " Isaiah," and some letters passed between the two authors.

a second reading of Lord Campbell's bill about immoral publications. He spoke with much animation. Lord Lyndhurst made a few remarks. He looks young when sitting, with hat on, having a youthful wig ; but when he walks, his spindling, failing shanks, betray 85 years. I had pointed out to me the Duke of Argyle ; red head, slender, strutting ; fine forehead. Lord Nelson rather foppish. Lord Shaftesbury youngish and graceful. Lord Wensleydale (Park) very burly and strong. I heard some very poor speaking. The general look of the Lords reminded me of Virginia gentlemen ; quite so in manner ; but more neatness of dress, though not more simplicity, in most. The fine hale condition of so many old Lords, speaks well for English climate, dinners, sports, and general habits. The law-lords have no easy times. After a long day on the bench, Campbell comes to the Lords' and makes speeches ; he has no Scotch accent, of which Brougham has much. Shaftesbury is 56. His son, Lord Ashley, is in the House of Commons. S. is the great philanthropist of the aristocracy. I have never been in Parliament, without hearing America mentioned. In connexion with law-reform, it is always honourably. The Lord Chancellor, Lyndhurst, Brougham, Campbell, and Fitzwilliam, all agree in urging simpler forms. They are now hammering at complications of the mortgage. Contrary to the genius of English law, they seek to make the transfer of real estate as easy as the transfer of bank-stock. I saw two bishops, both in and out of rig. Their undress is nobly beautiful ; with their robes and lawn they look like Falstaff in the buck-basket. Lord Ellenborough made a speech of some length on India. He is 66 ; tall and stout, heavy voice, more than the usual stammer, little of the peculiar tin-pan, palatal utterance, which makes Granville resemble the lower classes. It appears to be quite the thing for members to go home on horseback.

We went to Albert Smith's Ascent of Mont Blanc, Piccadilly. It lasted two hours, and was a union of first-rate painting with irresistible humour. Indeed, I never heard any thing so comic as his songs and dialogues " up the Rhine."

Smith is one of the Punch set. The entertainment is modish, the rooms elegant.

LONDON, *July* 6, 1857.

At 6½ yesterday I sought out Baptist W. Noel's chapel in John Street, near Gray's Inn. As I approached I heard a man say it was " ordinance day," a dissenting phrase, which I happened to understand. The chapel is old and old-fashioned ;

showing what the Ranstead Court Tabernacle may have been copied from. Galleries on all four sides, and very wide ; seats under the gallery lengthwise; pulpit high ; vestry-end thrown in by moving a partition ; full house of plain but earnest people. Precéntor gave out hymns and notices. Mr. Noel is a thin-faced pale, refined, American-looking man. I recognize the incompar,- able elocution which I admired so much in '51. I also perceived afresh that the higher you go in society here, the more the talk is like that of educated men at home ; say of Charleston. I don't say Boston, because of the Yankee *bens*, and *dooty*, and *stoodent;* nor yet of Virginia, because of the R—phobia, as Dr. Rush used to call it. Otherwise, it is more like Virginia. He used no notes, and in an hour's preaching never broke into any intonations which would sound wrong if he had been speaking to three people, by his fireside. He was on Matt. xxv. 25—29, the Institution. It was simple and chaste, but scholarly ; deeply interesting and even delicious, but not impassioned ; no fancy, no illustration ; eminently didactic and parenetic. Altogether I must place it among the most pleasing, useful, and holy discourses I ever heard. He made a bold declaration of free-communion.

BRIGHTON, *July* 13, 1857.
Brighton itself is a large place, with much elegance of struc- ture, and all the appliances of sea-bathing. The air is like New- port. Just before our windows (Pier Hotel) is a drive frequented by ceaseless processions of gentry in every kind of vehicle, ladies with grooms, donkeys, goat-carriages, foot-folk, and just beyond, still very near us, the sea-beach, with rows of the machines out of which they bathe. The surf is much less than at Newport. There are innumerable children wading in the low tide. One pleasant thing is the total absence of that glare which prevails on our beach. The streets, moreover, are watered with such English faithfulness, that there is no dust. Remember it is not the " season " at Brighton. That begins in October. Walking and driving on the beach are here in their perfection. The parade is three miles. The high banks are paved and pali- saded, so as to be charming. A pier, highly ornamented, juts out into the sea, on the widened end of which a band of music plays in the evening. So gay and brilliant a spectacle I never saw out of Paris. I no longer wonder at the popularity of Brighton, nor at the fondness of George IV. for it. The stone and brick buildings give a look of permanence, wanting in our

---

[1] A church in Philadelphia, built for Independents, but afterwards the Seventh Presbyterian.

summer-resorts. It is a wonder Brighton is not always full of people, but they go by thousands to the continent. England is over-peopled, and they flee from one another. Watering places at home compromise them. As Albert Smith says of Baden-Baden, "all the English get up from the table at once, because each one is afraid he shall make a blunder, and each one wants to be a greater swell than the others."

The beautiful downs, or wavy hills, which mark all the coast, afford charming eminences, and the perfect roads tempt to drives, especially as villages, plantations, and meadows with ancient hedges, are numerous. The high, solid drive for miles, on the brink, is totally novel and the effect is surprising. Long streets and squares are built up uniformly with the cream-coloured " composition " fronts, which bulge out so as to afford window-views both ways. The beach is divided into inclined planes of perfect smoothness, with low partitions. Here the machines are. The old granny who waits, assists the practitioner, who is under cover till the instant of dashing into deep water. There is nothing of the social bathing and aquatic fracas which makes much of the fun in America. It is a separate, exclusive, Anglican immersion. Brighthelmstone, which is the full Anglo-Saxon name, was a British settlement. Flemish men settled here 800 years ago. It became famous as a resort about 100 years ago. See Madame d'Arblay for later popularity. In Madame's day hoops were worn, as again now. George IV. came here in 1782, and this made Brighton. It is confidently said that the high paved promenade is the finest in the world. So much does uniform building prevail that whole rows look like palaces, and it resembles Swiss or French architecture. The Downs extend fifty or sixty miles. Their exposures show pure chalk, and like all hills of chalk, they are beautifully rounded and covered with fine, close, velvet turf. The great peculiarity of these hills is the graceful serpentine curve formed by their contour, and the plush surface of short grass which precisely resembles a fine rug in its feel.

We took a drive on the 10th to the Devil's Dyke, five miles. The sea was almost always in view as we climbed from one graceful ascent to another. As if by special order, a sky-lark was scarcely ever out of hearing, though often out of sight. We would hear the laughing, ecstatic song, long before we could descry the tiny creature as he looked. Then he would come into view, mounting higher and yet higher, and drifting a little adown the wind, so as to get before us, but often just overhead, in a passion of joy, fainter and fainter to the ear, and dashed to pieces by the wind, till at length with circles lessening every moment he would drop down to the earth. When we reached the summit, where there is an inn, the sudden view was amazing. You are astonished that a few hundred feet should open such an expanse. Before us is the whole Weald of Sussex, a plain 100 miles by 40, like the parterres of a garden. With the naked eye we saw the isle of Wight. They tell us that sixty churches are in sight. I cannot express the thronging suggestions. In some degree of purity, from all these churches has for centuries ascended the song "Thou art the King of glory, O Christ!" It was beauty rather than sublimity, though even the sublime was caused by extent, and by the wide prospect of the Channel from Beachy Head to Portsmouth.

The little hamlet of Stanmer is the prettiest about Brighton. The old houses of the peasants are absolutely hidden with running plants and flowering shrubs. On one we saw currants trained to run even over the roof, and bearing red fruit there. You will judge from the length of my twaddle, that we are engaged in the *dolce far niente*. We have the delightful prospect of Mr. Stewart's[1] company all through Scotland, Germany, and Switzerland. This is matter of great thankfulness.

VENTNOR, ISLE OF WIGHT, *July* 17, 1857.

The resemblance between the Isle of Wight and Staten Island is very striking; but the parts of the isle which we have seen, are beyond any word-picturing. To say that the fields and woods are of a soft green, all moist and pure, and without any mixture of fading or decay, even now in the dog-days, would be only to say that it is England. But Wight has very peculiar features. The north and south parts are unlike; the north being all garden and the south broken and wild. For ten miles from Ryde, southward, every route was as beautiful as any park or pleasure-ground. The roads were, of course, hard and smooth; but they were also hedged, and ever winding, and ever changing level, and ever and anon entering some quaint village or hamlet, or bringing us suddenly in view of the sea. We passed the church and rectory of Legh Richmond. No exaggeration need be feared as to the cottage-life; no fancy of yours, however melodramatic, could make a picture to exceed these one-story, old, thatched dwellings, half hidden in creepers, and parti-coloured with flowers. The romance of hill, dale, copse, glen, cliff, spring, dark shady lane, and look-out to the sea, cannot be carried

---

[1] The Rev. Charles S. Stewart, who had joined our travellers in London, and whose kind attentions and agreeable society are frequently and affectionately referred to in many letters.

further.   The fields, as Emerson says, look as if finished with
the pencil, rather than the plough.   In considering the scenery of
this back part of the island it occurs to me that its exemplifies
the production of great effects by combination of few elements;
as the ancient Greek painter had, they say, but three colours on
his palette.   In this little corner of a little island, effects are produced which are really Alpine; as if the Creator, in his overflowing bounty, had determined to show his child on a small
scale, how he sometimes works on a large one.

We visited the smallest church in England, if not in the
world, called of old St. Lawrence-under-Wuth.   Till a late
enlargement, it was 25×12.

On the 16th Mr. Stewart and I determined to circumnavigate
the island—a sail of about 70 miles.   In order to commence it,
however, we must needs go thirteen miles to Ryde.   At 11 we
went on board a small steamer and proceeded westward.   The
company was genteel.   I soon cottoned to an Anglican clergyman, who cheered our whole voyage by his clever and witty talk.
We had a capital view of Osborne House, Norris Castle, (the seat
of Bell—"Life in London,") Hurst Castle, Lymington, Yarmouth, &c.   Where the island begins to turn southward, the
scene becomes very remarkable.   The chalk cliffs are cut straight
up and down, and assume fantastic contours and colours, like
cornices, like walls, like mantels, like tapestries, like ruled music-
lines for giants.   The streaks of ore, in and near Alum Bay
and the Needles, are of many hues, and the formations unlike any
thing I ever beheld.   The Needles are exactly like monstrous
icebergs, and they, with the rocks, present a spectacle not only
interesting but sublime.   Ventnor showed nobly on the terraced
cliffs of the south point, but it is too fresh and American-looking
to compare with such thatched, hedged, embosomed spots as
Bowchurch or Godshill.   We made our periplus in 4 hours 30
minutes.

Next day we made a pilgrimage to Legh Richmond's place,
Brading.   We saw his church, and the grave of Jane, "the
Young Cottager," and then by a delightful drive over high commanding downs, to Arreton, where we saw another old church,
and the grave of "the Dairyman's Daughter."   We also called
at her cottage, now occupied by her nephew, and saw her Bible,
&c.   After dinner we went to tea at Mrs. Pelham's, by her kind
invitation.   Her grounds join her brother-in-law's, Lord Yar-
borough's, and we strayed over the whole—an earthly Paradise
which only great wealth can produce.   Here she introduced us
to her pastor, the Rev. Charles Livingston, rector of the tiny
church.   Mrs. Pelham is a grand-daughter of the duchess of

Manchester, and cousin of Lord John Russell and of the duchess of Wellington. Mr. Livingston lives in a superb place on an ornamented cliff, commanding the sea. It gave him pleasure to hear of his relatives in America; and he several times related the story of his ancestor of the Kirk of Shotts. He spent a long evening at our lodgings, and awaited our stage-coach at the avenue of his house to pronounce a blessing on us.

Some of the best descriptions of the scenery of the isle are in Richmond's three tracts. For example, in the " Negro Servant " he paints a series of scenes, which we instantly recognize, though he does not name them. They are the Down between Allerton and Newport, the vale of the Medina, the Solert, Southampton, and Alum Bay. I shall never hear the name of the Isle of Wight without a thrill of recollections, nor without gratitude for having been allowed so leisurely and thorough a survey. Moreover, there my cough seemed to be suspended, if not ended.

PARIS, *July* 24, 1857.

I am overwhelmed with the greatness of the changes in Paris, [since 1851.] The mere extension of the rue de Rivoli, with rows of palatial edifices, is but a part. Entire boulevards have been opened, with names gratifying to the Emperor, as B. de Strasbourg, B. de Sebastopol, &c. Two grand objects are plainly in view, the holding Paris as a great walled encampment, and the filling of the people to the brim with amusement. Without a nocturnal drive no one comprehends Paris. The world has no such turn-out of population; no word but *swarming* gives any idea of it. As we approached the Boulevards, where the great cafés seem one complex of glass, mirrors, and light, the rows on the broad pavements were often ten, twenty, perhaps thirty deep. Among these thousands, we heard nothing like outcry, observed no rudeness, and detected no signs of drunkenness. People drive out *after* dinner, and the stream of carriage-lamps continues till midnight.

Mr. Stewart visited the Emperor at Plombières, and was received by him in such a manner as would have been impossible at Paris; dining, walking, and chatting with him for three hours, with every mark of sincere friendship and the absence of all ceremony.[1]

MACON, (SAONE ET LOIRE,) *July* 28, 1857.

Here we are, having come at one stretch (from Paris) 275 miles. This, and the region we have passed lately, is the country

---

[1] The Rev. Mr. Stewart had known and befriended the Emperor during his stay in the United States, in his early career.

of the famed Burgundy wine. "Corn and wine" are given to these plains in abundance. The country wine is weaker than cider, and more refreshing. I never saw a town of uglier houses. In no instance do we see any flowers, or plants, trained over the doors and windows. Apricots and figs are by bushels, and the country wine is without charge.. The people seem quiet, innocuous, and stolid—that is not precisely the word—unambitious and uninquiring. On this blazing day I look everywhere for what we call a shade-tree; I see nothing but the stiff rows of poplars, and these in places where there are no houses. There is a promenade, with shadeless trees and no grass.

Points observable in our rapid tour yesterday: All champaign country for 200 miles. No cottages, no barns, no lanes, or cross roads, no divisions, no groves, and almost no beasts of burden, except the human ones. Women universally the majority of workers in the harvests. Country fertile, thoroughly tilled, and pleasing for a first view, but unutterably monotonous. People seem quiet, like so many sheep. In a few instances I descried little edifices, which I have no doubt were Protestant *temples*, and the sight was affecting. A little bread and a little wine seem to be the fare of the peasantry, who are universally temperate. Chalons-sur-Saone is a fine town, the Cabillonum of Cæsar; it is known to have been visited by Augustus, Constantine, Attila, and the Saracens.

GENEVA, *July* 29—*August* 6, 1857.

Delightful place; one can't help breathing the air of Protestantism and freedom. The lake and environs and mountains are as lovely as Rousseau, Cooper, and Byron have described. I drove to Dr. Malan's, at Vendœuvre, a beautiful hamlet. The venerable man was sitting with his wife and daughter. At the Bergues I found Dr. Tyng, returning from Palestine. What a pity that the very best descriptions of the Leman and its shores are in Rousseau's worst work! There are few places I ever saw in which I could more willingly reside. Shops, libraries, &c., are abundant; there is the best of Protestant society and preaching; schools numerous and good; mild winters and luscious fruits; neighbourhood of Paris, the Rhine, and Italy; a perfect laissez-faire as to the way in which you shall live.

Dr. Malan said: "Most of your countrymen have what I call the American venom—they want to feel before they believe." For a place of its size, Geneva has an air of polite letters and refined art, which reminds one of Athens. Like Athens it is also a resort for many nations. We had a beautiful view of Mont Blanc from Dr. Malan's, and afterwards from Col. Tronchin's beautiful place. On a steamboat excursion around the lake I made the acquaintance of William Turrettini, lineal descendant of the great three; he is an eminent lawyer and legislator, and a pious, orthodox man. The arch-duchess Marie of Russia was on board, with forty-five in party; a handsome woman, with a handsome daughter.

On Sunday I heard Dr. Malan; who is certainly eloquent, though he evidently speaks without the least preparation. The congregation was about eighty. At seven we had a service in our own room, which was very delightful. Dr. Tyng expounded John xxi. The present government of Geneva is radical, Fazy being President. They favour Papists. Protestant and Popish interests are about in equilibrio. At the treaty of Turin, Geneva obtained increase of territory, but with it an accession of Papists. The Sabbath is much profaned here; for an age the elections of the Canton have been held in the cathedral on a Sunday. There is a Greek chapel here, entirely for the convenience of a sister of the late Emperor Nicholas. The princess goes there on Sunday, for some formal cause, and then rapidly drives to one of the French churches.

Geneva is full of old covered alleys or passages, running clear through piles of buildings. They probably have some connexion with the defences of other times. One finds a remarkable number of ancient noble houses degraded into factories and dwellings for the poor. They are too massive to be pulled down, as would be done in the United States. I found one this morning, of grand proportions, with a defaced blazonry over the door. No one could tell me what it was formerly, (it is now an iron warehouse,) but a little street back of it, named *la rue de vieux college*, reveals the story.

I have been at the cathedral, and once more saw the canopy under which Farel, Calvin, and Knox preached. They also have Calvin's professional chair. I suppose no place of its size has half as many book-shops as Geneva, and I have never seen a place so stocked with beautiful prints and engravings. The truffles of all this region of the Rhone are fine, succulent, and savoury. Every variety of fruits in market; mulberries, immense yellow and crimson gages, strawberries, raspberries, pears, plums, apricots, and such potatoes as rival Ireland; sold chiefly by a poor, withered-looking set of brown women, sitting on the ground, many with goitres, and though in this Alpine land, devoid of rosy freshness and all grace. At our breakfast we have honey, black cherries, and very large figs.

Geneva is a sweet home-like place, which I am sorry to think I shall never see again.

BERNE, August 7, 1857.

It is surprising how many persons speak English, and how many Russians we meet. The Bernese are far better looking as a people than the Genevese. Among the latter, even the young women look haggard and withered. Here there is much of the blonde character, which belongs to the better sort of Germans. Berne is a strange, solid, grotesque, middle-age place, built so mountainously that nothing but an earthquake could well alter it. The view of the Oberland Alps is very fine in good weather.

INTERLAKEN, August 9—20, 1857.

Interlaken lies between the lakes Thun and Brienz. Never since Niagara have my descriptive talents been more tasked and baffled. The village combines every thing, both old and new, which the most romantic fancy could demand in Swiss architecture. The streets crooked, the houses tumbled about with all lines but straight ones, in a way to drive a Philadelphian mad, the eaves overhanging, stones on the roofs, every chraracteristic which we see in the stone villages. All this in a little circular basin quite surrounded by irregular mountains, with the Jungfrau in full sight from our windows. This, as the most ravishing spot in Switzerland, has been seized on by the English. In the height of the season, I reckon there are two thousand of them here. I sit and muse with a sort of childish admiration at these great and lovely works of God, now half-veiled with clouds and mists, the fantastic changes of which make a new picture every minute. The thought of my dear and honoured father's pleasure in such sights, often comes to me; he sees better than these—perhaps these also. The hour at which I write, allowing for longitude, is that of morning service in our church, a season which I always remember with a sense of communion. Our Sabbaths abroad have been memorable, and not the less so for the mingling of pages from God's two great records. I have just read the whole of Ezra, hard by the Jungfrau.

For the first time (August 11) I heard a band of Swiss girls sing Alpine songs, with that peculiar falsetto voice which is called *yodling*. It was sweet, wild, and in such surroundings, delightful. I cannot think there is any more lovely place than this on the face of the earth; a vale, a river, two lakes, a wall of mountains, snow Alps beyond, English shops, society and service, clear air and luxurious accommodation. A trip on horseback into the Oberland gave me a thorough acquaintance with snow-peaks, mountain paths, avalanches, alp-horns, singing-girls, ranz-des-vaches, cascades, &c. The cow-bells of the innumerable cattle are large and musical, and every cow has one, so that the sound while they graze is peculiar.

BADEN-BADEN, *August* 23—31, 1857.

I never dreamed of such a Vanity-Fair. The Champs Elysées afford no such *concentration* of trees, lamps, dresses, music, crowds, and fashion as the promenade before the Conversations-Saal here; all in full dress; a ball-room out of doors, and the numbers 1,000 to 3,000; nothing heard but French. The waters are about 160° Fahrenheit.

The Anglicans keep up service here, and in a Roman Catholic church. When I entered the door, I thought I had been misdirected. The epistle and gospel our British brethren must always read at the altar; and here the two parsons had the regular thing, with all its mantel-furniture, candles, and framed papers, more tawdry than usual. While I say this, I must do honour to the English for everywhere keeping up the service of God, and for the frequency and decorum of their attendance. How profound and distressing is my impression of the irreligion of these countries! No Sabbath and apparently no grace! The boors are so ground to the earth, that they look like slaves. Blessed Americans, *sua si bona norint!* I am refreshed by a handful of precious German tracts, (some by Ryle,) which Dr. Marriott, of Basle, sets forth. That hot but sincere man does much good; and among these epicures and Sadducees (Phil. iii. 18, 19) every thing is notable, that tends towards the saving of the soul. Wo is me, if I seek it not more zealously on return. A series of tracts in large print, by old Andrew Read, entitled " Cottage Tracts, or Christ's Welcome to all comers," is very fine.

You must consult Sir Francis Head,[1] or some of the guidebooks, about Baden-Baden. I had no idea of the grand scale on which every thing is conducted. It is a lap of earth among high, near, and round hills, which are cut into innumerable walks and drives. The water is drunk hot as well as used externally. But the great thing is raving, idolatrous, expensive pleasure. The princes of all the continental states are to be seen here during the season. Every moment we look for the king of Flanders, and a cloth is already laid for his feet. People suffer as much with heat as in America.

Our windows are just beside the front door, so we see royalty [king of Belgians] whenever he goes or comes. The king is a good-looking old gentleman; he is well made up with black wig, but no whiskers or moustache; full suit of black, an orange something under his waistcoat. Legs a little shaky. In the

[2] " Bubbles from the Brunnen of Nassau."

afternoon a coach and four postilions, footman and outriding groom, drove up. Two ladies in white muslin got out. The king descends—grand uncovering and bowing. He ascends the coach, leaving one of the ladies. These are the princesses of Prussia, who have a summer-house here. The king travels *incog.*, as Count d'Ardennes; his suite consists of seventeen persons.

The gambling-scene at the Conversation Hall is very stirring. A woman very eager and prominent, booking her profit and loss. Mothers showing boys and girls how to stake. The roulette-table is just such as I have seen in my childhood, with sweat-cloth, &c.

In Switzerland I thought much of Wordsworth's poetry concerning it, and of Scott's Anne of Geierstein. On the Rhine I consider Byron's stanzas descriptive of the same better than any painting. Goethe often occurs to me. People get to be great polyglots here. I often hear the same person speak three languages in as many minutes. The African servant of a Russian prince has just been talking fluently under our window in German, Italian, and French; he says he is from Central Africa. The princess Helena of Russia is here, and the Emperor is to visit a camp at Stuttgart next month. We have had the best instrumental music I ever heard, from the band of the 28th regiment of Austria, now at the neighbouring city of Rastadt.

The more I view Baden, the more I see its walks to be inexhaustible; they wind around all parts of the valley, and creep up the numerous hill-sides, with clumps of trees, gravel-paths, parterres of flowers, and well-placed seats. The Old Castle has a grand site, and is a fine ruin. Every thing Mrs. Radcliffe could desire is afforded by this crumbling, ivy-covered castle. So long has it been vacant that numerous trees of the largest size grow within the walls. On our way home, we went to the New Castle, such only by comparison. It surmounts the acropolis of the town. The old margraves of the Palatinate lived on the high place till 1471, when the modern Schloss was built. It was burnt by the French in 1689, but restored. The dungeons are horrible; subterranean vaults of great extent through which we groped with candles. The contrast to the inhabited parts is striking; here the rooms are brilliant. The young couple now reigning live chiefly at Carlsruhe, but their private apartments here are very comfortable. The Orphan House of Baden was founded by Stultz, the famous London tailor, who was made a nobleman by his prince.

HEIDELBERG, *September* 1, 1857.

The woman who accompanied us as guide through this castle of castles, and who spoke good English, was a most agreeable and accomplished person ; thoroughly versed in history and literature, and quite intimate with Bryant and Longfellow. I heard some capital singing at St. Peter's, and a very legal sermon from a very young divine. The Church is Reformed. Here we have more Germanisms of the table—raw meat, rolled boiled pudding of meat, sourkrout, fish after flesh, sausage and omelette. I went to the University and Library before breakfast.

FRANKFORT ON THE MAIN, *September* 2—4, 1857.

This is a noble city. The *Zeil* is a broad street, resembling Broadway in cheerfulness, brilliancy, business, and crowd ; it is wider, and the trottoirs twice as wide. We are next door to Rothschild's town residence. Statues in honour of Goethe and of the three inventors of printing adorn our neighbourhood. To crown all it is full Frankfort-fair; and the booths, shows, and tantarara, beat all since I saw Greenwich Fair in 1851.

The deep gloom apparent everywhere in the English, about the Indian mutinies, awakens my sincere sympathy. How I wish America could at least speak some words of neighbourly cheer on this great occasion ; it would be profoundly felt by the magnanimous part of the British people.

The Römer is a famous old building. Here the Senatus was sitting, with men in scarlet at the door. I did homage to the magistracy of a great city-commonwealth. I saw the Golden Bull of 1356, the fundamental law of the German empire ; it is in Latin, and perfectly well kept. The banqueting-hall is surrounded by full-lengths of fifty-two emperors, the last filling the last niche. Since Car. V. they are portraits. In this *Kaisersaal* the new emperor was always feasted, while princes waited on him. Some Prescott or Motley is wanting for this subject.

Every available broad street and area is occupied by the (Michaelmas) fair ; miles of shops, booths, and stalls. The Jews predominate in this Feast of Tabernacles. Imagine twenty Bear-markets, all in one, with tents and sheds for the stalls, and twenty different languages. I suppose it is chiefly for exchanges, and for giving and receiving orders ; but it is far more stirring than the got-up World's Fairs, and has antiquarian relations of high interest. I see many Russian advertisements and stores of Russian books. The show and mountebank department is extremely broad. In the presence of many a *miles gloriosus*, order was perfect. Every thing, all over town, came to a dead stop at 9 30'. I went to see the house of Goethe's birth, a truly patrician old pile, seven windows across. The earlier parts of his autobiography and his Wilhelm Meister came very strongly before me. I see hair-dye advertised of " a celebrated American chemist, Dr. Wanylliam." I have seen forged labels for wares in unmistakable German-English. American gum-shoes (Gummijschuhen) grace the fair. I traversed the Jews' Quarter. Formerly this old Jewry was locked up every night. The houses are tall and rickety, mysteriously dark and judaically dirty, and seem squinting and nodding towards one another. There are six thousand Jews in Frankfort. We have suffered much and unexpectedly from heat, but never from musquitoes, bugs, beetles, or those dire-voiced crickets, katydids, and night-frogs, which have been my dread from my infancy ; the dryness and wholesomeness of the night air is likewise creditable. But O how I long for home, and for the glory of all lands !

At the Public Library (200,000 volumes) saw Marchesi's fine statue of Goethe, also Cranach's portrait of Luther and wife, some autographs of Luther, and a pair of his shoes. Then around the former ramparts where now are fine avenues, to the Bethmann Museum, and saw Dannecker's Ariadne. In the even-ing, during a direct interview, a young lady of St. Gall, aged 21, and of very good manners, addressed Mr. Stewart in German and Italian, and conversed with me in French. She is going to Hamburg, and then to England. Her stature is eight feet five inches. She is attending the Fair. The giantess is pretty-behaved, and shook hands at parting.

WIESBADEN, *September* 5—7, 1857.

First impressions of Wiesbaden are favourable. It is natu-rally less picturesque than Baden, and improved in a less pic-turesque manner, but with more elaborate beauty. The strong points are a dozen boiling springs, covered promenades near them, *Kursaal* with cafés, billiards, rouge-et-noir, le roulette, and immense colonnades, the court within shady and with fine jets,— behind is a grand promenade, where thousands take coffee and ices to the almost perpetual sound of music ; an artificial lake with fountain, rustic bridges, innumerable seats in numerous groves, walks winding and climbing up into the eminences, a capital grand ducal residence, extraordinary cheapness of living. The com-pany is evidently two or three carats coarser than that of Baden.

Church in the Ducal Palace, a temporary chapel off the riding school. No sermon, but I enjoyed the service greatly. A large congregation ; among them Sir Frederick Thesiger. At dinner to-day (10th) ten Presbyterians of us sat together. We are commonly waked by a hymn-tune. When I rise I see the *Koch-*

brunnen steaming about fifteen yards off. The procession of all nations, holding tall glass cups of hot water, which many carry half a mile, is amusing. They do it all to music. So perpetually are we amidst English talk, that I must needs, from my imitative ear, pick up some brogues, though I shall not intentionally carry home any English pronunciations. We are now eating the first ripe grapes. The white are like the Chasselas of our hot-houses, but with a more rich raisin flavour. The carp of the hot brooks are fine and healthy, testifying well of the bath; they serve it after the meat. The Germans have no moral scruples connected with gambling. The toy-shops contain little roulette-tables and sweat-cloths, which enter the youth early in the sport. Probably I have had a better glimpse of continental, and especially German life, than I could have had in months at ordinary places. My good opinion of the Germans, in all social relations, is much increased, and I think far more highly of their comforts than I did. As to religion, I have little means of judging. The negative marks are very black. The gambling here is more eager, hot, and vulgar than at Baden. The order of these countries, in things which they choose to order, is marvellous. Every street-noise is prevented, and every inn and café is cleared at the " police-hour." All the gambling regulations are by Ducal authority; not only a *tarif* of cabs is settled by the same power, but every donkey-ride to this or that place is rated, and the very order of dances in the balls at the Kursaal is prescribed in a placard, signed by the Grand Duke's Commissary. Accidents to vehicles are severely punished. Placards prescribe where wheels shall be locked and paces slackened. The Grand Duchy contains about 360,000 souls, half Romanists.

Of *Langenschovalbach* nothing can be added to Sir Francis Head's " Bubbles "—a work full of entertainment, and less exaggerative than I once thought. I refer you to it for this, Schlangenbad, and Wiesbaden, as no one can say as well what he has said. The Springs are powerfully chalybeate, delightfully cool, and sparkling with effervescence. The taste is far more winning than that of the Congress Spring. The baths are celebrated for their tonic character. The L. is much what the Red Sweet [of Virginia] would be, if artificially improved. The surrounding eminences strongly resemble American forests. The bath is incomparable for velvet softness, and the water is exported as a cosmetic.

COBLENZ, *September* 9—11, 1857.

We had a very fine afternoon from Biebrich, down the Rhine, to this place. The four hours were of almost painfully exquisite

interest: the earth has no such shores. Our windows face the
Gibraltar of the Rhine, Ehrenbreitstein. This fortress has cost
five millions of dollars in its reconstruction. It can hold 100,000
men. I arose in the night, and saw the waning moon in the
high heaven, and Orion just ascending obliquely over the grand
fortress. Byron's descriptions of Rhine scenery are to me
beyond any lengthened detail in prose, or even any painting.
What a power of true poetry! I feel it here on the spot.[1] See
his stanzas beginning "On the banks," &c., and "The castled
crag of Drackenfels." We have visited the famous castle of
Stolzenfels, (Rock of Pride,) now a summer residence of the
King of Prussia. Thence to Ems, the most ancient of the aristocratic Brunnen of Nassau. The water is somewhat warmer than
the Red Sweet.

[1] The coincidence of the place and the subject, induces me to insert on
this page the following lines by the late Professor J. Addison Alexander,
which were "literally composed, though certainly not written, on recrossing
the Rhine at Coblenz, after an absence of several months to the eastward."
This was during "a sleepless night in the month of March," 1834.

STAGE-COACH STANZAS.

I hail thee as an ancient friend,
And as I cross thy line,
My democratic knee I bend,
To greet thee, royal Rhine.

The day and hour, when last we met,
Come o'er me like a dream,
And then I saw, I see thee yet,
Unchanging, changeful stream.

The rush of waters o'er thy bed
Distracts my labouring brain—
Forever dying, never dead—
Buried and born again.

What is the secret of thy life?
What holds thy channel fast,
Amidst the elemental strife,
The earthquake and the blast?

Why is it that the swollen tide,
Which ever northward sweeps,
So warily on either side
Its well-marked station keeps?

Why dost thou not, old Rhine, at length
Break thy ignoble chains,
And mustering all thy mighty strength
Submerge the adjacent plains?

Thou art a king among the streams,
Thou river deep and broad,
In regal pomp thy surface gleams—
To man, but not to God.

Thy full deep current bold and proud,
In his almighty view,
Is but the sprinkling of a cloud,
A drop of morning dew.

Though thou shouldst empty every rill,
And drain the neighbouring land,
Thy giant-waters could not fill
The hollow of his hand.

The same almighty hand, that drives
Thy current to the sea,
Can well control it, when it strives,
And struggles to be free.

And if at times that hand grows slack,
And lets thee do thy worst;
He brings thee still at pleasure back,
And rules thee as at first.

So when I bend my stubborn knee,
To greet thee, royal Rhine,
I render homage, not to thee,
But to thy Lord and mine.

COLOGNE, *September* 11, 1857.

On the steamer from Coblenz was Macaulay, (soon to be Baron,) and I fear I studied him more than the Rhine. He greatly resembles Inman's portrait: stout, broad, and stalwart, but pale and slightly flaccid in cheeks; bluish gray eye; gray hair and whisker; blue surtout and cap, plaid waistcoat and gray trousers; about five feet six; gold spectacles near the end of nose. Very arch but subdued smile sometimes. An ugly but *distingué* man with him who read " Cicero de Republica," while the Baron read a vellum-covered Italian book, seemingly a history, interchangeably with Murray, [Guide-book.] They ha-ha'd cheerily over some of Cicero's passages. Only one or two points attracted Macaulay; such as the Seven Mountains, Drackenfels and the Dom. I expected talent in his face, but I was delighted with its moral traits, tranquil content, gentleness, and benignity —the last finely displayed towards an infant. I am sure he would break into tears sooner than into laughter.[1]

Four hundred men are working on the cathedral. The row of windows presented by the late King of Bavaria is superb, but nothing to the ancient glass. Then to St. Ursula's and the osteology of the 11,000 virgins—to St. Peter's to see Rubens's great painting of St. Peter's death. In all these churches, as throughout Prussia, the children (Catholic) are gathered every morning before school hours. I heard a thousand sing German hymns at Coblenz. This tells powerfully on the next generation.

SPA, *September* 12, 1857.

We have to-day passed from Prussia to Belgium. The country is beautiful; unlike all we have recently seen, and very like England in hedgerows and verdure, especially about Aix-la-Chapelle, which lies in a picturesque way beside a charming hill. Spa is very famous in old Chesterfieldian times, and is still visited by kings, dowagers, and *vieux moustaches.* The water is carried all over Europe, as containing the most extraordinary mixture of iron and effervescence. The Germans are great tipplers of mineral waters, and those of other Springs are brought to each and sold in bottles. All agree in giving the palm to the genuine Seltzer-water from Niederselters, in Nassau. It is a most refreshing beverage, greatly useful to pulmonary patients. It is used at tables to correct the acid of the white wines. I have seen no one at table yet who did not drink wine, but I have seen no intoxication. The labouring classes are hard driven. A chambermaid at Frankfort gets $18 *a year.* Women are seen

[1] Lord Macaulay died Dec. 28, 1859.

yoked with cows in the plough.   Nine-tenths of hay and harvest
are carried on women's heads, and a horse is not seen in one field
of a thousand.   Women work at railway excavations in gangs.
These remarks apply less to Belgium, and not at all to Holland.   Belgian agriculture has a noble appearance; a neatness
like the English, but in kind, in extent, in absence of cattle, roads,
and division, altogether French.   No spot is in a state of nature;
weeds and brush quite unknown.   Root-crops are predominant at
this season.   I see a blue clover, not known in America.   A
great deal of tobacco is grown on the Rhine, making good light
cigars.   Indian corn is frequent, but low, straggling, and with
irregular ears.   It is hard to think how large a portion of these
crops goes to the crown.   A crazy bridge, a rutty, rough, or
stony road, or a miry spot, I have not seen, unless in the Alps.
No apprentice or field-hand goes from one hamlet to another,
without falling under the municipal argus.   The creatures seem
ruddy and merry.   As a sort of indemnity, the government offers
numerous public and accessible pleasures; parks, music, bands
of singers, illuminations, Sunday frolics.   The grand instrument,
however, of subjugation is the priesthood.   You will hear it said
that the hold of Popery on the masses is declining; in my opinion
the reverse is probably true, and I see an advance in six years.
The priests are more numerous and obtrusive, the churches are
fuller, and especially the rising race is more under their hand.
Belgium is politically liberal, but religiously priest-ridden.   The
English service is performed at every principal place by a regular
chaplain every Sunday.   At least ten thousand persons hear the
gospel in English, on the Continent, every Lord's day.

ANTWERP, *September* 14—15, 1857.

The country from Spa hither through Louvain and Mechlin,
is flat but garden-like; people contstantly dressing the crops
with spades, hoes, rakes, and the hand.   Our hotel is just over
from the great Notre Dame.   I was in the immediate neighbourhood of the great tower, 405 feet high, when the bells began
to play before the stroke of seven; it was in parts, and several
minutes long.   As I thus stood, in the dreamy twilight, in the
irregular area in front of the majestic pile and surrounded by
quaint old gables, I felt the impression to be deeper than even
at Cologne.   But these architectural emotions with me are not
religious, as are those of Chamonix, the Jungfrau, or the Natural
Bridge, [Virginia.]   This piling of man's hand is Babel-like.   I
am deadly sick of popish ceremonies and of all liturgical aping
of them, and approximations to them.   Read John Owen on
Liturgies; read it; read it!

I went to early mass in the cathedral; there were some hundreds, as it is a jubilee and octave of the something, with plenary indulgence, &c. The music was seraphic. I have always thought men's voices in a vaulted cathedral attained the musical acme. The five aisles came out well in the morning gray. The number of Rubens's *chefs d'œuvre* which are in Antwerp is stunning. Though I had seen many of his works, I really had never conceived of his power till now. The Magdalene in his Crucifixion is, in Reynolds's judgment, the best profile extant. In the "Doctors in the Temple," he has given likenesses of Luther, Calvin, and Erasmus, all fine, and the first admirable. At the superb old church of St. Jacques we saw a funeral and three masses all at once. Different parts were in progress, and while the bell jingled, a beadle was trotting us about and explaining the pictures; but whenever a tired lady took a gentleman's arm, it was arrested—it would have been *promenading*. There are ninety-nine bells in the great tower, one of which it takes sixteen men to ring.

At St. Andrew's we saw the wonderful pulpit of wood-carving, representing the calling of Andrew and Peter from their nets. We had seen many such things and despised them, but this is a noble piece of sculpture. The figures are of life-size; the boat is real; the net and fishes marvellous; the manner in which the pulpit and stairs are concealed in rocks and trees is most ingenious, and the expression of the forms and faces masterly. The whole is about 30×20×15 feet.

Most of the Walloons understand me when I speak German. The great favourite among their writers is Hendrik Conscience, who has ennobled the Flemish tongue as Burns did the Scotch; a genial story-letter for the people; a Goldsmith in ease, a Franklin for adages, and a Scott for nationality: so they pretend. His whole works are publishing here, about 20 volumes, 18mo, being out. He has just been made viceroy of Flanders, and is considered as having given himself to the Catholic, or retrograde party.

BRUGES, *September* 16, 1857.

There is certainly no spot so redolent of grandeur in decay. Once the Tyre or New York of the continent, it stands with its rows of towering, tottering, ghastly palaces and halls, a builded desert. The streets remind me of London before dawn. Greatness and beauty are in these streets. I would have missed any thing rather than this.

The region we have just passed through is acknowledged to be the most highly cultivated in Europe; small properties—700 passed in 18 miles—not metaphorically but literally tilled like a garden—hundreds of women on their knees, weeding with the hand.

BRUSSELS, *September* 17—18, 1857.

We breakfasted at Ghent; saw old churches, old streets, and marks of that wealth which existed in *Gand*, when its great native Charles V. said he could put all Paris in his *gand*, (glove.) To-morrow we part with Mr. Stewart.

LONDON, *September* 19—23, 1857.

To get back to green, clean, cool, Christian England, is just like enchantment. The verdure seemed an illusion, and "we were like them that dream," (with words following.[1]) At the "Old Slip" in Dover, we resumed our familiarity with tea, toast, sole, big basins, thick towels, soap and *joogs* of 'ot water. When we last saw the green meads of Kent, we undervalued them, being just from the Isle of Wight; but coming now from rich but russet Flanders and Normandy, where are no grazing herds and flocks, and no detached cottages, we were in amaze.

On Sunday (20th) to Mr. Noel's, and heard Mr. Muncaster, of Manchester, a Congregationalist, one of the clearest, ablest, and most theologic sermons I ever heard. The singing was delightful; precentor and [Lowell] Masonic plain-song. My soul was melted within me by the fellowship of so many unmistakably devout persons. Mr. Noel sat below in his pew; an American face strangely reminding me of my father's, at the age of forty. Blessed Sabbath—blessed gospel—and blessed England still! More than "the ten" are found in London. Prayers for Indian brethren very touching, and infinitely better than the "prayer in War and Tumult,"[2] which we have been hearing. To get away from printed prayers and repetitions, is like Alpine air after a chapel full of torch-smell and incense. The Dissenters in England have universally abandoned standing in prayers, so far as I see. As I cannot consent to irreverence in worshipping God, I am as frequently an object of note as in our prayer-meetings at home, where grown men pray sitting, and sometimes staring. Two-thirds of the Episcopalians also sit. The Germans and Scotch all stand. To such as kneel I feel much respect. I heard Mr. Noel in the evening, (Philip. i. 23.) Lan-

---

[1] "Then was our mouth filled with laughter, and our tongue with singing." "The Lord hath done great things for us; whereof we are glad."

[2] In the "Book of Common Prayer."

guage simple but masterly, half an hour without a gesture, but very bewitching; voice that of a parlour-talk; perfect English, delivered with an absolute absence of all alien intonation. In this respect he is a study. A holy gentleness, with an almost death-bed solemnity; experimental, mature, evangelical, and spiritual; very fervent towards the close. No manuscript. When he stopped, I was like Adam with the angel.[1] His dulcet notes remind me of the Bruges carillons. I think Noel's idea of preaching the right thing; just talking over the Word. My own father was not more simple. Only deep and long experience could have brewed such a sermon. The only man I ever heard preach with so little clamour was Dr. J. P. Wilson.

After what I deemed adequate knowledge of London fog, I am this morning (21st) surprised; perhaps I ought to call it smoke, for it is not wet; it fills the street so, that I see every object through a medium the colour of weak rum and water. Over the top of this fog, the sun is brightly reflected in the three-pair windows opposite. I record with feeling, that for now 118 days I have not lost an hour or a meal by sickness.

I saw a young lady driving a carriage through the jam of High Holborn and Oxford street, with a liveried servant by her side. The shaded sun and autumnal temperature, without any decay of verdure, are just the thing for me. Sun comes out fine. I just missed the annual exhibition of the Blue Coat school and its 900 boys. I was actually within the cloisters, but could get no ticket. The subject of one of the scholar's hexameters was *Funis Electricus*.

After viewing so many Gothic buildings, I have this result: My interest in them is scarcely that of beauty in form; it is the dim association of history. Look at the matchless row of painted windows in the south aisle of Brussels cathedral, or the minute finish of Freiburg—how intense, how continued, how widespread the sentiment which could produce such results! The greatness of the mechanism is often astonishing. Above all, the English cathedrals are wondrous. Carlyle says, what I often think of in reference to better and Christian things and ages, which seem barren from want of record, " greater men have lived in England than any of her writers; and, in fact, about the time when these writers appeared, the last of those was already gone."

American affairs are as much in men's mouths as Indian; and the comments are not always courteous. Renewed reading of the newspapers renews my opinion, that those who have only

[1] " So charming left his voice, that he a while
Thought him still speaking, still stood fixed to hear."
Paradise Lost, VIII.

this way of judging (that is, nine-tenths of the English) cannot but despise America. The articles inserted are about Kansas, Slavery, Repudiation, Burdell, Walker, and especially the Mormons. *N'importe,* we are a century ahead of them. The Times shows up the fogyism which has ruined India. Even now they are waked up to no real energies of reparation. Louis Napoleon must laugh in his sleeve. I believe no court in Europe is so lullabied with Lord Chamberlainism. Large numbers are perpetually busy about the pleasures of the Queen and Prince Consort.

YORK, *September* 24, 1857.

We took the Great Northern Railway at 11, and arrived at 5 15'—191 miles. The points which most interested me were Marston Moor, Newark, and Scrooley, where the little group lived who went to Holland and then to New Plymouth. For twenty miles around York all is flat as a prairie. Glimpses of this pure white Minster, which you would say was built yesterday. But I am sick of what they call Christian Art; it is all an inferior stage of progress. This is the shooting season. At every station hares, grouse, and hampers of game were handed in or out. The number of hares one sees in the fields is surprising. Every day my provocation increases at the tone in which English people speak of and to Americans: it is ignorantly patronizing; they think of our advancement, precisely as we do of that of Liberia.

The Minster shines with a sort of celestial grandeur and beauty after the continental cathedrals. The east window, the chapter-house, and the side-aisles are unique.

MELROSE, *September* 25, 1857.

We left York at nine, and steamed through Newcastle and Morpeth to Berwick. Here we left the main line, and ran up the Tweed to this place, passing Kelso, an enchanting spot. We saw the Abbey with a glory of sunset breaking through its West window. At Abbotsford we heard a robin-red-breast sing.

EDINBURGH, *September* 26—30, 1857.

Prince's street, where we are, looks right across the green ravine to the lofty houses of the Old Town. I never saw any thing more novel or beautiful than the play of thousands of lights as seen in the populous hill-side from these front windows of ours, flinging themselves not into right lines, but constellations. The Sabbath quiet is almost beyond belief. Only one vehicle has passed this house in the three hours I have been in our sitting-room. Blessed be the Lord God of our fathers, whose truth abides here, and who has made this the happiest great city on the globe! We have had great comfort by the way in reading good tracts, the varieties of which are very remarkable, both in England and Scotland. One finds here much more frequently than with us, those views in print which were so much our fathers' views, and which are so little prominent in some Old-School preachers; I mean views combining sovereign freeness of gospel grace with inward spirituality and rest of soul.

On the Sabbath I heard Dr. Bruce at Free St. Andrew's. Sermon on Christ's two quellings of storms in Matt. viii. and xiv. General doctrine, that afflictions are ordered not only to try our faith, but to try our utmost faith; in the second case, Jesus let them go alone. It was a profound piece of experience, viewed philosophically; strong meat; dense, witty at times, unexpected turns like Foster; no elegance of manner, but immense impression. The prayers were almost inspired. Ah here is the true *Eutaxia*, without printed worship! At 2 I went to Free St. John's. Strangers (how truly I comprehend the term!) are admitted only after the first singing. I found myself waiting in a basement with about 500 others. At length I was dragged through a narrow passage, and found myself in a very hot, over-crowded house, near the pulpit. Dr. Guthrie was praying. He preached from Isai. xliv. 22, "Return unto me, for I have redeemed thee." It was fifty minutes, but they passed like nothing. I was instantly struck by his strong likeness to Dr. John H. Rice. If you remember him you have perfectly the type of man he is; but then it is Dr. Rice with an impetuous freedom of motion, a play of ductile and speaking features, and an over-flowing unction of passion and compassion, which would carry home even one of my sermons; conceive what it is with his exuberant diction and poetic imagery. The best of all is, it was honey from the comb, dropping, dropping, in effusive gospel beseeching. I cannot think Whitefield surpassed him in *this*. You know while you listen to his mighty voice, broken with sorrow, that he is overwhelmed with the "love of the Spirit." He has a colleague and preaches only in the afternoon. As to manner, it is his own, but in general like Duff's, with as much motion, but more significant, and less grotesque, though still ungraceful. His English, moreover, is not spoiled so much. The audience was rapt and melting. It was just like his book,[1] all application, and he rose to his height in the first sentence.

I disliked the singing at Dr. Guthrie's; a choir, with twiddling

---

[1] Either "The Gospel in Ezekiel," or "The City, its Sins and Sorrows: a series of Sermons from Luke 19 : 41."

tunes; a clear retrocession towards the way which is becoming unsavoury even to New England. The singers were in pews near the pulpit, and I saw an advertisement in the lobby for a tenor singer. They sing well with precentor at Free St. Andrew's.

It is worth while to come here to learn how a Sabbath may be kept. This great inn (Royal Hotel) has table d'hôte at 5, to give rest to servants. The beautiful avenues of the New Town are thronged with grave but cheerful people, evidently with their faces Zionward, and most of them with Bible in hand. I have a great desire that H. should some day spend some months in Scotland to learn how to preach, catechize, and do pastoral duty. Gladly would I forego for him all that the continent has to offer, for the sake of this.

In reflecting on the two great and precious sermons of yesterday, I wonder at the beautiful diversity of gifts. They were as unlike as an apple and a pine-apple. I have no remembrance of any preaching so analytically experimental as Dr. B.'s, except my own dear blessed father's. At each step he seemed to *assume* all that an ordinary preacher would have preached, and to go on beyond that. His prayers were the same; so searching in confession that I winced, and so paternal and pastoral in intercession, that I could not but fancy his hand feeling all around and gathering sorrows out of every heart to bring before God. His sternness in no degree modified the graciousness of his gospel freedom, as I have too often seen to be the case with rigorous casuists in America. The Bruces have been ministers ever since the famous Bruce, who rebuked King James.

Mr. Dickson's house [see p. 156] is a museum of Sunday School illustrations. His garret is filled with matters from Palestine, beautifully arranged and with appropriate Scriptures. As a single instance, you see in one series flasks of water from Siloam, and four other places, a bunch of wheat from Zion, and one of barley, a plate of vine-leaves, a pomegranate, a phial of oil, a pot of honey from Jerusalem, a loaf, iron and copper ore— then the passage Deuteronomy viii. 7—9.[1] He has a hortus-siccus of Palestine plants; minerals picked by himself, and 400 views, which he sketched; enough being finished in oils to line his back parlour. In a tour of two months, he left no spot west of Jordan without a sketch. Dr. Guthrie is the link between evangelical religion and the aristocracy. People of all sects go.

[1] " A land of brooks of water, of fountains, and depths that spring out of valleys and hills; a land of wheat, and barley, and vines, and pomegranates; a land of oil-olive and honey . . . . A land whose stones are iron, and out of whose hills thou mayest dig brass."

Nobility coming down from London and stopping here, cannot pass without hearing him. They are willing to pay any sum for pews, in order to secure an occasional hearing. Dr. G. called on me, and was very cordial. Look at the "Fortunes of Nigel" and conceive him telling the story of Richie Moniplies' brag concerning Edinburgh to George Heriot; telling it too in broad Scotch, and· at a window overlooking the *Nor' Loch,* or ravine. Dr. G. tells me he was sent in his youth to the Sorbonne for education.

Americans might well be amused to consider that the United Presbyterians, who joined very invidiously in the cry *send back the money,* (of the slaveholders,) should now be the only body which has slaveholders in its communion; a fact concerning their Calabar Mission.

I have seen twenty times as much drunkenness here in a day, as in the wine-countries in ten weeks; indeed I saw but one such in them, and he was only merry.

EDINBURGH, *October* 1, 1857.

Auld Reekie[1] indeed, but the sun is breaking out in a way that is peculiar. I regard Scotland as the flower and crown of all our tour. I could contentedly and profitably have spent my whole time in Britain. Emerson says you can't see England in a hundred years; and I have often told Stewart that the grand requisite for travelling successfully would be to live as long as Methuselah. One great advantage here, is the short distances. Much as you have read of the country, you would be surprised at this. Thus you go from Liverpool to Manchester in an hour; from Edinburgh to Glasgow in an hour and a half; and everywhere towns and other localities, often famous, follow one another with rapidity. Every nook and brook and hill and mansion has its name, and in Scotland these are embalmed in ballads and legends. The position of a "minister" here is high. I remember something of similar observance, when New York and Philadelphia were smaller, towards Dr. Mason, Dr. Green, and Dr. Wilson; but Guthrie, Candlish, Bruce, Lee, Bonar, Tweedie, to say nothing of residuaries, are looked at all the length of Prince's street.

The institution of the *dinner* is potent in Great Britain, and Edinburgh has a traditional geniality of intercourse, after the day's work is done. There is a free and happy mingling of copresbyters here, like nothing known to me elsewhere. Both Guthrie and Lee (before the Committee of the House of Lords)

---

[1] Scotch for smoky.

have formally ascribed the " canny " character of the Scotch, not simply to their being trained on the Scriptures, and to their reading Solomon, but particularly to the custom of using the book of Proverbs as a reading-book. The Anglo-Saxon words and short sentences, where books are rare, made it the thing for the children. There is a pious weaver mentioned in Guthrie's " Gospel in Ezekiel " as a man of prayer. The Doctor said to us " this man prayed, not as one going to heaven, but as one just come out of heaven. He would sit in his loom and super-intend our education. And what we read was such pith as ' he that hateth suretyship is sure,' &c."

The deep, I may say awful impression, made by the events in India in their religious aspect, is very observable in the pray-ers. Generally Scotchmen do not give free vent to their inward experience in talk. I hardly ever was more solemnly wrought on by a prayer, than by Bruce's about this distress; and not least by his tender thanksgivings for the spiritual good already done to bereaved and other suffering persons.

I like the Free Church Tract and Book arrangement. They publish nothing, but keep up the machinery of supply from all sources, colportage, &c. They have, for example, 6,000 different tracts, including the American.[1]

[1] The same day on which this letter was written, Dr. Alexander, with his wife and child, left Edinburgh for Glasgow. A short tour in the highlands, which was in their plan, was prevented by bad weather, and a week was spent in Glasgow in delightful Christian intercourse with many of its princi-pal clergymen and others. They then proceeded to Liverpool, and em-barked in the steamship Baltic for New York.

It is no more than a proper testimony to the liberality of the congrega-tion to their pastor to state, that of the sum placed by them at his com-mand for this journey, nearly three thousand dollars remained untouched.

CHAPTER XIV.

LETTERS DURING THE REMAINDER OF HIS PASTORATE IN NEW YORK.

1857—1859.

New York, *October* 26, 1857.

THROUGH the tender mercy of our God, we reached the wharf about 5 yesterday, and home about 7. Our passage was short for a return, being eleven days, but very rough and even stormy, so that our wheels were all but denuded of paddleboxes on our arrival. The "Baltic" and her captain (Comstock) are all that could be wished. The vessel is staunch and noble, and I have seldom had more sublime emotions, than when standing on the high poop I watched the plunge of the fore-parts, and the succeeding rise, with a spring and buoyancy of motion that seemed to mock at the roaring ocean. I caused our little boy to observe how apt is the Bible figure Ps. xciii. I preached yesterday, the first time since May.[1] How deeply grateful we ought to be, that during six months' absence, no case of indisposition has occurred in our circle here; all alive and all well; let the God of our salvation be exalted! I was everywhere a most reluctant traveller, and drew a lengthening chain. My own general health is almost robust; and yet I have the same catch in my throat. I had not seen an American paper for a long time, and very seldom at all, so that I had much to learn on my arrival. In our ship's company of 160, we had some pleasing characters. A Major Copeland of Boston was with us, returning from Sebastopol, (which he calls Sāy'-vast-ō'ple,) after contracting to raise the sunken ships. I knew of only one Englishman. Major Wm.

---

[1] This was in the ship. The text was 1 Peter iv. 3. On the next Lord's day (Nov. 1) he preached to his own congregation, at both services, from Habakkuk iii. 17, 18.

Preston of S. C. was also a passenger. Beyond all expectation, our boys were waiting us, one having come from Princeton, and the other from Freehold. On looking at the papers, I find myself sadly behindhand, and in church-matters quite unable to enter into the spirit of the fight. Say some words of sincere kindness from us both to our A. friends. I do not know whether they got any account of my very delightful visit to their kinsman, the Rev. Charles Livingston, rector of St. Lawrence's, Ventnor Cove, Isle of Wight, one of the best men I saw during my exile. He is rather proud of his North River connexions, and asked numerous questions about them. Several deaths have occurred during the six months; among them were Mr. Rufus Davenport, perhaps our oldest man, and Mr. James Struthers, who was an elder elect, and so far as human judgment goes, one of the most spiritual Christians in our church. The people have generally returned, and are in a promising state, as to attendance; I even hope for more, as there is a marked reviving of religious interest during the six months of our absence. It will take me some days to get the heavy roll of the ship out of my brain; I don't remember ever to have felt it so much. *Paix it soit!*

NEW YORK, November 3, 1857.

I am glad you think of coming this way. After fast-day, preparatory lecture and communion, (next Sabbath,) I shall feel a little more ease of mind than now. I hitched at once into the old rut, wrote two full sermons last week, and have been hard at visiting ever since my return. I am fleshier than need be, and harder than my wont, having roughed it in all weathers, and borne twice as much fatigue as in '51; but the ring of irritation, phlegm, and strangle in my pipes remains much as before; I mean D. v. to speak, &c., exactly as if it wasn't there, till something decisive stops me.

November 4th.—Good democratic turn in the election here. The new law, prescribing glass globes for the ballots, and forbidding ticket-booths within 150 yards, has wrought much quiet; yet our plebs is very much in ferment. London amazed me more than ever by its size, being a sort of world. People of one part have no knowledge of people in another. This, however, is much the case in New York. To-day my walk lay by the intersection of 4th and 10th streets; I suppose thousands would be surprised to hear that these parallels meet.

The clergy here seem all to be in good case, notwithstanding complaints of hard work. In Scotland, and I suppose in England too, the dinner-institution, always at six, when work is over, with the free, hearty converse of numerous friends, *non sine Baccho*, tends to give a corpulency and a crimson, which make American clerks seem slim in comparison. Pastoral visiting in the cities is less practised than with us, but elders' visiting much more. Deacons were nearly obsolete at the Disruption; the Free Church has made a point of reviving them, but the Kirk remains as before, and many in the United Presbyterian Church formally rejected them as needless. At baptisms, the fathers stand in a row, before the minister; the mothers sit in some neighbouring pew; the children are kept behind the pulpit-stair, or in a room hard by, till the moment of affusion. Very sensibly, a napkin hangs over the rail. The above is an induction from two particulars. The reading of sermons has greatly increased among the Scotch, and greatly decreased among the Evangelicals in England. Sitting in prayer is all but universal among the Dissenters, and widely prevalent in the Church, though under pretence of kneeling. In Scotland, the prayer after sermon is usually as long as the one before, dwelling on intercession, &c.

NEW YORK, *November* 16, 1857.

Lonesome, indeed, is this habitation, as my wife and children are in the Jerseys, and the dreary easterly rain makes egress undesirable for sore throat folks. Natheless, I have spent most of the day abroad, as the arrears of visits (occasioned by my absence) to cases of trouble are very large. If[1] I had received your queries anent Maidenhead during my first and longest sojourn in London-town, I think I should have run down to see it, as many trains go every day; it is 22½ miles W., up the Thames, from London 27 by railway, right bank, in Berkshire, and in 1851 had 3,607 population. It is partly in Bray parish, (vide Vicar of ditto,) and partly in Cookham, and is reached by the Great Western Railway. The living is in diocess of Oxon. It is one long street, neat, paved, and like all English towns of thrift, lighted with gas; it is not exactly on the river bank, being on the Bath Road. It used to be called South Ealington, and between the bridge and town you find a relic of antiquity in almshouses for eight poor men and their wives. The aforementioned bridge has seven stone arches, and three smaller arches of brick at each end. The railway crosses Thames at Maidenhead, by a magnificent viaduct. The market is on Wednesday, chiefly for corn. The scenery just above, is beautiful. Near are Cliefden, seat of the Marquis of Stafford,

---

[1] What follows was in answer to inquiries I made of him, (for the history of the Trenton church,) as to the town in England from which the old name of the present village of Lawrenceville was taken.

and Taplow Court, seat of the Earl of Orkney. At the Greyhound Inn, Charles I. took leave of his family. Shortly before arriving at Maidenhead, you pass Salt Hill, famous for the Eton Montem, which was abolished in 1848, and after clearing the town, you go through Maidenhead Thicket. I ought to say Maiden*hithe* is the transition-name; *hyth* or *hyd*, as a termination, denoting a landing, or accessible bank. My nearest approach was at Windsor and Eton, and I dare say I saw it in both visits from the top of Windsor Castle. Of all these towns and villages in the valley of the Thames, the same general observations will hold good; they are in summer embowered in green, with a moist delicate look about trees and herbage, which strikes an American as peculiarly enchanting; and though all the trees are plantations, they are so dexterously placed, and often so ancient and cherished, that the full, round " bourgeoning " of their heads affords a noble relief to peeping towers and spires. The old towns, if irregular, are romantic and quaint, and you see numerous buildings of which the pattern at least is as old as the Conquest. Instead of *Ealington*, I note that some give *Arlington* as the former name. In the 26 of Edward III. it was, nevertheless, incorporated by the name of the " Fraternity or Guild of the Brothers and Sisters of Maiden *Hithe*." When coaching or riding were the modes of locomotion on this great highway between London and Bristol, Maidenhead-thicket was infested by footpads. The story of the Vicar of Bray (between Maidenhead and Windsor) is found in an old song, and in Fuller; he changed his religion four times regno Henry VIII., Elizabeth, James I., and Charles I., living and dying " Vicar of Bray." (For above valuable facts, we are indebted to Black's Picturesque Tourist in England; Knight's Geogr. of Brit. Empire; and Hughson's London and Neighbourhood, 1808, 6 vols. 8vo.)

I continue to cough, and begin to think I shall as long as I preach, yet I am well up in colour, fat and paunch, eat well, drink kindly, sleep so-so, and altogether am in good case to retire on a pension, turn president, go to Congress, or negotiate a loan in Europe.

NEW YORK, *December* 14, 1857.

I scarcely recover from the stunning effect of the tidings.[1] In such cases the mind falls back on former impressions, and I find my ties with the Doctor closer than I had thought. I knew him as a child, and then on, during many years, including my

[1] Of the sudden death of our mutual friend, one of the elders of the Trenton church, Dr. Francis A. Ewing, several times mentioned in the first volume.

residence in Trenton. His early religious experience was revealed to me in detail.

NEW YORK, *January* 1, 1858.

I and we wish thee and thine a happy New Year in every
high and good sense. There were sixty murders and one hanging in this city in 1857. My motto text is: "Thy kingdom
come." I have been reading a lately found account of Bossuet's
last days, by his private secretary. It appears that for years the
Bible was his chief study. His secretary read the gospel of
John again and again to him, and the seventeenth chapter sixty
times, when the bishop was on his death-bed.

Lying, stealing and bribery, perjury, covetousness and rapine,
make things sometimes look to me like some prophetic tableaux.

The —— churches are using terrible blast-bellows to get up
artificial heat in our city and neighbourhood. Our light materials catch, and I am often anxious in the attempt to hold on our
regular way. I know twenty young people, whom I could
foment into any given amount of excitement in two weeks.
What amazes me is, that the men who apply these methods, at
set times, are at other times as little raised above worldly
thoughts and deeds as common folks.

NEW YORK, *February* 5, 1858.

Yesterday I was invited to survey a clerical class of gymnasts,
beating the air, &c., under Prof. Langdon, an Englishman.
There were seven, viz., Drs. Hutton, Hitchcock, H. Smith, Chambers, Cook, Field and Ganz.[1] It was funny; coats off, and all
together, sometimes so—sometimes so. [Here were outline
sketches of the postures.] Part of it would have answered
Spurgeon's description of a male dance. They laboured (as the
Shakers say) for an hour: it was evidently fine exercise. A blind
woman is playing the fiddle very well in the streets; we saw
one lead an orchestra in Switzerland. It is dreadful to observe,
after all our glorying contrast of Protestant with Catholic countries, how deep is the popular degradation of London and Edinburgh. Pauperism in our own cities is becoming an institution.
The number of books in France on the subject is amazing. If
Colwell [page 166] had given us what he knows in this department
of literature, without his crotchets, he would have done great
service. I am in great doubt whether the doctrine against casual
alms (*e. g.* at the door) is not sacrificing plain scripture to
doubtful theories of economic science.

[1] He afterwards himself practised the "Langdonics."

NEW YORK, *March* 1, 1858.

March comes in like a wet, half-grown lamb. I record with a sense of dependence that the last sign of my cough has left me for about three weeks, and that I am more fleshy. An undue and irregular beating of the heart, though lessened, remains. I am nearly fifty-four years old, (March 13.) In the serious retrospect of life, I see nothing so dark as my sins ; nor did they ever seem more hateful. We admit seven on examination, and eight on certificate. Preaching is assuming a more prominent place than heretofore. A great danger is lest a go-ahead, joyous, auction-like, unreverent elation take possession of the [daily] prayer-meetings. Up town this has been very much avoided by the lead which ministers have taken. Did I write of visits I am paying every day or two to the Roman Catholic Hospital of St. Vincent de Paul ? A young medical student, a pay-patient, is there recovering from typhoid fever, and was baptized by me. There are twelve sisters of charity, and 120 beds. This young man has been nursed in the best manner conceivable. I have seen five or six of the ladies, including the superior. They have treated me with a very graceful courtesy, and are altogether a winning generation. The tidings of the revival on every side certainly tends to set people a-thinking about their souls ; which is a point gained. I feel it overshadowing my own mind, and opening ways of address to the careless, as well as shutting me up to the most important class of subjects.[1]

NEW YORK, *April* 2, 1858.

I have generally discredited people who say they have no time to write, but lately I have been tempted to plead that excuse. Though I have aimed to keep down and regulate excitement among us, and have had no additional service but an exhortation on Monday to such as seek instruction on points connected with conversion, I perceive such a degree of inquiry as has never met me in my ministry. The number of declared inquirers is not more than twenty-five, and most of these have dates a good way back ; but the feelings of communicants and the indescribable tone of assemblies, are new to me. From the start I have held myself ready to adapt measures to emerging demands ; I however feel glad I have pursued the repressive method ; which, by

[1] About this time he wrote " The Revival and its Lessons," a series of eleven tracts, published by Randolph. A large number of these were distributed at the police stations. The one addressed to firemen was sent to each of the engine houses in sufficient number to furnish a copy to each member of the department. A late Edinburgh paper advertises the fifth thousand of the " Revival Lessons." See page 237.

the way, has lost me sundry good opinions even among my own
flock. Study I cannot, being run down by persons, many of
whom I never knew, in search of counsel. The uptown prayer-
meetings are very sober and edifying. I am told that the general
tendency in all is to increased decorum. The openness of thousands to doctrine, reproof, &c., is undeniable. Our lecture is
crowded unendurably—many going away. The publisher of
Spurgeon's sermons, says he has sold a hundred thousand. All
booksellers agree, that while the general trade is down, they
never sold so many religious books. You may rest assured that
there is a great awakening among us, of which not one word
gets into the papers; and that there are meetings of great size,
as free from irreverence as any you ever saw. I have never
seen sacramental seasons more tender and still than some meetings held daily in churches in our part of town. The best
token I have seen of revival was our meeting of Presbytery. I
never was at such a one. Brethren seemed flowing together in
love, and reported a great increase of attention in all their
churches—and this within a very few days. The inquiring condition among ourselves is strange, and all but universal; God
grant it may be continued, or exchanged for true grace in them
all.

We are just setting up a daily (nightly) prayer-meeting in
our Mission Chapel for the poor, (really not nominally.) It is
superintended by a Committee of about ten leading gentlemen,
under sanction of the session. Among the numerous cases of
persons seeking me as pastor, most of the inquirers have been
inquiring long. Numbers are often given rashly; no man knows
how many are convinced; perhaps thirty such are known to me;
I lay little stress on registration in this matter, and deprecate
publicity. I have found it a good way to appoint a certain hour
every day, for persons willing to be talked with. Never have I
felt so much the need of plain elementary instruction as to the
simplest matters in religion. The greater the excitements around
us, the more I see the absolute necessity of knowledge. People
come to me, who have not even the meaning of justification.

NEW YORK, *April* 15, 1858.

The attendance on the union meetings here is not lessened.
Last week the meeting, which embraces Potts, Van Zandt, Hutton,
Prentice, A. D. Smith, &c., was at our church. The house was
filled. Every day but one it was as solemn and tender as most
communion seasons. Constant attendance for weeks leaves my
judgment unaltered, that it is bad to throw the meeting open for
whomsoever to speak and pray.

NEW YORK, *April* 29, 1858.

While it is in my mind I will jot down something about Finney, whom I heard last night at Cheever's. Assembly mid dling. F. looks sound and well, but, of course, older. He preaches in spectacles, and with a "brief," which he mentions: "my little brief, here." Manner much subdued. Voice ringing and capital, but with Yankee twang and nasality. Perfectly colloquial and lawyerlike; avoiding every big word, and as plain as any one could be talking to children. Says the same thing over and over and over, sometimes pausing between, with a singular effect on attention and memory. Doctrinal and argumentative, but not hortatory; with numerous anecdotes and illustrations. Text was: "This is the record," &c. His sermon (exceptis excipiendis) might have been preached by the Erskines or McCheyne. It was all about Christ and believing. *E. g.*, "All you have to do is to *believe.*" "There is the *record:* God has *given his Son.*" "He says not 'I will give so and so, *if* you do so, &c.,' but *God hath given.*" "You are all looking inward for feelings and experience, before believing. Believe first. Believe the record. Then you will have feelings." Figure: A New York beggar. Steamer bring news of a great donation to him; £10,000. Certificate of deposit in Wall St. put in his hands. But he does not believe it. 'I am no rich man; rich men have fine clothes, money, coach and horses, my experience is all the other way.' " "Belief of the record brings soul into union with Christ, and experience ensues." He was able and tremendous against infidels. The interest, though intellectual, was intense. I find his plan and all the details graven in my memory. He keeps up the obsolete custom of an Inquiry Meeting, after sermon.

Seriousness prevails among us. I have had no extra meetings, except four exhortations on doctrines connected with conversion, &c. The best means I have alighted on is an hour given out to receive persons seeking direction every day. This has brought many, and some very often; and the interviews have been sometimes long and always private. I expect to take in on examination more than thirty-five, and less than fifty. The daily prayer-meetings are unabated in interest. Long attendance in no degree reconciles me to the license given to A B or C, to teach or pray; nor to the advertisements requesting prayer. The presence of numerous ministers in fraternity, and their frequent remarks and expositions, produce a good impression.

NEW YORK, *May* 7, 1858.

I am on the Committee of Examination of the Senior Class

in Princeton,[1] and expect to go thither on Tuesday. During
that sojourn I wish to run down for an hour or so to your me-
tropolis. I feel it almost necessary to interrupt the tension of
thought and feeling. Our Session has admitted fifty-seven on
examination, and four on certificate.[2] The majority are persons
with whom I have been dealing for years.[3] I know of no abatement in religious interest. The noon-day prayer-meeting (this
week in the 1st Church) was crowded. There must have been
twenty ministers yesterday; still, solemn, and tender; more like
a communion than a prayer-meeting.

May 10.—The whole lower floor of our church was filled with
communicants yesterday. Dabney's sermon (by appointment of
the Board of Foreign Missions) was a marvellous one, for logic,
weight, and scholarship. Mary S., one of the loveliest of our
new converts, died on the morning of the communion.

NEW YORK, *May* 19, 1858

Last night [Tuesday] I concluded my series on Acts; sixty-
eight lectures. I have never put any one in my place, and never
substituted any other passage. The attendance has constantly
increased. In no instance have I ever penned a line in preparation for them. In the latter parts I have been unspeakably aided
by Addison's Commentary. Professor M. is here under medical
care, but one of those cases religiously which refresh the soul.
A Jeffersonian-infidel, then a Channing-Unitarian, now I doubt
not (though *he* doubts) a childlike Christian. He is a silver-
haired old gentleman, of the true school.

I have no plans for the summer. My brain needs rest.
Spurgeon's fourth volume shows improvement. The selection
is made here, out of the " Pulpit," which contains all he ever
utters. He preaches out of doors everywhere but in London,
where he fears the tumultuous consequences.

NEW YORK, *May* 26, 1858.

In three days I have had three funerals. One was our
penultimate African, æt. 97¼. Funeral in Black church. Sang
four verses of a Long Metre to " China," [Common Metre.]
The entire congregation effected synalæpha and ecthlipsis of the

---

[1] In 1851 he was elected a trustee of the College of New Jersey. Thus
his name stands on the catalogue as a student, tutor, professor, and trustee.

[2] The whole number of new communicants received in the years 1858–'9,
was 125 on examination; 32 on certificate. These numbers include those
who worshipped at the Mission Chapel.

[3] Among those who came to their first communion on this occasion, Dr
Alexander had the happiness of receiving one of his sons. Another son
had lately received his license as a probationer for the ministry.

redundant syllables with great skill, and the singing was delightful. The General Assembly dissolved on Tuesday. The impression on New Orleans was favourable. A young Cuban has just called to get advice about religion, previously to his starting for Paris, where he will learn physic. Great numbers must have their views of religion modified by residence here. I fear, however, often with skeptical results. The Cesarean simplicity of Thiers's histories increases as he goes on. What point-blank lying he convicts Napoleon of!

New York, *June* 7, 1858.

Having passed through a winter of unexampled employment with perfect health, I am seized with a severe cough upon the accession of summer. A conspiracy was detected yesterday of the " Forty Thieves," East River Mohocks, to break up a mission school by sending rowdies to make a noise, and then having a gang without. The captain of the police had wind of this, and placed the entire force of the ward in the station-house, and undress detectives in every neighbouring lot and resort; so they were dispersed.

P.'s discourse at —— pleased numbers, not including " P. P. of this Parish." His speech was commonplaces garnished with sophomore rhetoric; no method; no force, except in terms; no tincture of letters, and every here and there a demagogical lugging in of the dear *demos*, and their wrongs at the hands of science, &c. It was well delivered.

Henry returned to-day from a very useful trip to the extreme North, where he has been fly-fishing in Moosehead Lake. Even after Adirondack and Lake Superior, he gives these mountains and lakes the palm. He lay out, *i. e.* in birch shanties, five nights, and brought home (with young Auchincloss) eighty pounds of trout in ice. The largest brook-trout was three pounds.

New York, *July* 10, 1858

Addison is somewhere in town; but he takes his carpet-bag and determines during his walk whether and whither he shall go. During his vacation he is all the time moving. My congregation is almost all gone, but the church will not be closed. Samuel's and my flock will lie down together. We shall to-morrow receive one on certificate, and sixteen on examination. When will an American Statesman furnish three such volumes, as those of Gladstone on Homer?[1] Herodotus is also coming

---

[1] "Studies in Homer and the Homeric Age," by the Hon. W. E. Gladstone, member of Parliament for Oxford University, and Chancellor of the Exchequer.

out, under the Rawlinsons, with all the elucidations of Egypt
and Nineveh. The sea-breeze has made the evenings and nights
perfectly comfortable all this month, though the days were broil-
ing a fortnight ago.[1]

PRINCETON, August 9, 1858.

Affairs at the Branch went on much as usual after your exit.
I preached at Redbank; a very nice little church. I have not,
for a long time, seen so much talking and laughing in church.
Religious revival has not much visited that country.

During our period of epistolary commerce, now $=x+2$
years, no event has occurred so startling as the Oceanic-cable. I
am stupefied. Yet, after all, the practical results may be less
momentous than is said. I hope V. R. will send a religious
sentiment, for it will be in every one's mouth. Still more do I
pray that it may augur and promote everlasting peace in the
English-speaking world.[2]

Weary, weary, am I of these [theological] controversies de
lana caprina. I have a peculiar position; being in favour of
strict subscription, but to a very short creed. If at any time
you would like to inspect the views of the Plymouth Brethren,
or Darbyites, I can lend you some able and pleasing tracts of
theirs. Gosse, the naturalist, and Tragelles, the biblical critic,
belong to them.

NEW YORK, September 7, 1858.

Almost for the first time in our lives, we old folks are Darby-
and-Joan-ing it at home, without any progeny. It happens,
without plan, that all our young are at Princeton. I stayed at
Saratoga, after I had become more than conviva satur. The
Daily prayer-meetings prevail there; and, from the great conflux
of clergy and laity, the good and evil of that institution are very
prominent. I met there Drs. Woodbridge of Hadley, Bullock
of Kentucky, Fowler of Utica, Parker of China, Worcester of
Salem, Cook of Boston, Magoon of Albany, Ludlow of Po'keep-
sie, Chauncey of Highbridge, Buddington of Brooklyn, and Cleave-
land of New Haven. At our house lodged ——, the gambler
of New York, McCormick of the reaping machine, and Christy
of the Minstrelsy. The last is a well-behaved, grave-looking
man, who drives a pair of milk-white Arabian horses, the gift of

---

[1] The correspondents met, during this month, at Long Branch.

[2] The Queen's Message was a mere congratulation upon "the successful
completion of the great international work;" but the English directors of
the company had added to their magnetic announcement of the supposed
union of the two countries by telegraph, the quotation: "Glory to God in
the highest: on earth peace: good will toward men."

some potentate to our President. I have been very well. Our
church is very thin, most of the hearers being strangers. We
have been very much stirred up and entertained lately, by the
visit and speeches of Jno. McGregor, Esq., of London, on the
Open-air-preaching, ragged-schools, and other philanthropies of
England. He is a barrister of the Middle Temple, a downright,
rapid, witty, merry speaker, whose description of low life in
London and the means of dealing with it, was sometimes almost
in the Dickens vein. It appears from his statements, that
hundreds of open-air discourses are delivered simultaneously in
London, by laymen, who do not sing, or pray, or even take off
the hat. He lays great stress on all these particulars. Has
himself spoken about five hours every Sunday, for several years.
From his own mode, and the incidental specimens, these discourses, in the endeavour to gain attention, are in great danger
of losing all reverence, tenderness, and unction. They are, however, a good deal like Latimer's preachings at Paul's Cross.
Many of the plans would require great modification for America,
in regard to such differences as these: the immense over-peopling
of Britain, the homogeneousness of the upper and lower classes
as to nation, all being English, (and this applies to all such efforts
as "Hearts and Hands,")[1] and the certain and complete protection
afforded by London police. Yet his appeals were awakening in
a high degree. After I am dead and gone, I feel sure our cities
will have large and elegant free churches. I would not object to
sumptuousness, if it went to elevate, solace, and enrich the poor.

Trench's book on the authorized version is delightful. Our
communion is coming on, with only three on examination. My
volume of sermons is nearly printed, but will not be out I
suppose, before November.[2] I have never sent a book to press
with as little self-gratulation. What a purgatorial spot is Staten
Island, "where every prospect pleases, and only man is vile."[3]
The governor fulminates on paper, but I do not see what good will
come of it. The Bench, which used to be our resource when the
populace was corrupt, now lets the ringleaders slip through. I
have little hope even of tardy justice in the way of mulct. I have
been halting on one foot several weeks; perhaps sprain—perhaps
rheumatism—I guess no further. My brother's East River
mission school has grown entirely out of their accommodations.
A number of the most prominent children, who sing hymns

[1] A recent book on duties to the humbler classes.

[2] "Discourses on Common Topics of Christian Faith and Practice," published by Scribner.

[3] The allusion is to the repeated burning of buildings in the course of
erection for a public hospital for contagious diseases.

about Jesus, are Israelites. I heard them sing the ditty, "Where, oh where are the Hebrew children ? "

I most earnestly wish that these frequent prayer-meetings, which have now grown into regular feasts and fasts, could have infused into them some scriptural instruction.

NEW YORK, *October* 7, 1858.

South [Sermons] has always been a stand-by of mine ; a powerful accuser, even to gall, and as un-Christlike in temper as if no gospel had ever appeared. By an association of contraries, I think of A. N. Groves, a Plymouth-ist, a missionary on his own hook, whose life is out by Nisteel. I do not think I ever came across a holier, lovelier, less worldly person. I do not think I ever was so much rebuked by a human composition. We admit twenty-two on examination, from Mr. Rowell's Mission work ; two Germans, three Dutch, three English, the rest Scotch and Irish ; all promising, all respectable working-folk. He must have gathered some sixty thus. I think J. A. A. has excelled in his commentary on Mark. I await completion, before I make a sermon out of the cable.[1] Our sham Crystal-Palace is no more. The greatest loss [by its destruction] is probably that of poor inventors. No wonder ships may burn, when a building of iron and glass is consumed, with a hundred workmen and two thousand visiters in it, a reservoir next-door, and crack fire-engines all ready inside.

NEW YORK, *November* 23, 1858.

The weather is dismal. On Sunday night it seemed very much against our Opera-house service ; but the door-keeper estimates the attendance at 3,000.[2] No doubt, on a clear night, the applicants will be 6,000. Numbers sat in the lobbies and saloons, of the very class who are never seen in church. The collection covered the whole expense, with 15 per cent. over. I wish I could see a free church to hold just as many, and as easy to speak in. Our fault-finders, however, who spy the evil in all plans of others, and suggest none of their own, find objection to this night-meeting also. Carlyle's book[3] is very funny in parts, but as a whole is as unreadable as a bill in chancery. The daily prayer-meetings down town keep up with great spirit, having an influx of strangers ; our uptown ones have no

[1] Several clergymen had preached and printed discourses on the Ocean Telegraph, upon its first promise of successful operation.

[2] " The Academy of Music " was opened on the evening of November 21st for a series of religious services. Dr. Alexander preached on that occasion from Rev. xxii. 17.

[3] " Frederick the Great."

revival character, but simply the grave and occasionally tender character of an ordinary large meeting of Christians. Sawyer's translation reads like a travesty : "And after breakfast Jesus says to Simon Peter, Simon, son of John, do you you love me? And Simon replied, Yes, Lord, you know that I am your friend." Σκανδαλιζεται is always rendered " offended *with* me," &c. The tendency in our churches here is to gather enormously in a few favourite spots. I have never succeeded in getting a single man to leave us, for the purpose of building up weak churches, and I have had every occasion to ask it and press it. As population moves up, each of the lower churches in its turn dwindles. It is just the same with the Baptists and Methodists. The old John street *incunabula* cannot be cited as an exception, as that house is kept as a sort of relic. The Episcopalians are the principal free-churches, since the Methodists went over so largely to pews-yism. I observed in London that the parish system does not prevent this evil in towns ; the great throngs being generally at some newly erected shrine.

NEW YORK, *January* 4, 1859.

I wish you and yours a happy New Year. Ours always begins laboriously;[1] and as it came in on Saturday, there was not much rest. My reins, by occasional suffering, instruct me, with regard to weakness and mortality ; and at this moment I am ailing—though unusually well in general health. I read a MS. by a Liberian minister, in which, not content with mentioning their "ladies," he speaks of them as "fair ones." My sentence for 1859 is : "God, my exceeding joy ; " *Hebrew*, " the gladness of my joy ; " *Greek* and *Vulgate*, " the gladdener of my youth ; " *French* (of Ostervald, giving the force of אל) " le Dieu fort de ma joie et de mon ravissement." May He be such to us all ! I have just read 200 MS. pages of a journal kept by Williams, secretary of the China legation, during all the proceedings which resulted in the famous treaty. Thirty-two vessels were there. One is led to pity the poor Chinese ; and W., as a missionary, is very much on their side. They were, as you know, very near Peking ; in the Peiho River, 40° N. He speaks of the British as selfish and surly, and is very severe upon the opium matter. Our negotiations were materially furthered by the wisdom, kindness, and peaceful tendencies of the Russian ambassador, Count Poutiatine. Williams thinks China will at once be flooded by Jesuits from France. They number their Catholic natives at 800,000. He also thinks it doubtful whether

---

[1] Alluding to the custom of general calls on New Year's day.

Protestant missions will be greatly benefited. The timidity of the people, in their greatest masses, is made more striking than ever. Their forts at the mouth of the river, were demolished almost instanter, and 3,100 were slain.

NEW YORK, *February* 11, 1859.

I have just come in from our Mission Chapel, where nineteen have been admitted on examination, making nearly 70 in the Chapel, during the year. A very able paper is struggling here, called the " Saturday Press," a really dignified literary print. Why does not Everett [in the N. Y. Ledger] give us his reminiscences of Germany, Greece, St. James's, or even the Socinian pulpit ?

NEW YORK, *March* 4, 1859.

Mr. Everett is now speaking, [Oration on Washington.] I had an offer of the devotional performance. This part of ministerial duty has always been very revolting to me. I really miss Walsh,[1] and few perhaps do. About six months ago, I sent to the " Journal of Commerce " an article on Walsh, with, *inter alia*, some account of his " Appeal." How yearningly one's thoughts go after the destiny of a soul like his ! He had noble, rare moral traits ; his patriotism seemed never chilled by expatriation ; he was always the American, and of an old time type. Good, worthy, equable, honest Dr. Carnahan is gone ; *abiit ad plures*.[2]

Till your direct testimony came into court, I would have almost made oath to the statement of the preface.[3] It has been

---

[1] Mr. Walsh died at Paris, February 7, 1859. Many passages in preceding letters show the high regard in which Dr. Alexander held the literary character of Mr. Walsh. He attributed to the daily reading of the " National Gazette," while yet a young writer, some of the prominent peculiarities of his own style. Perhaps this influence caused him to sacrifice somewhat of ease and fluency to the exact and classical stateliness demanded by his model. He himself called it (in Walsh) "twists of diction."

[2] Dr. Carnahan died March 2, 1859.

[3] I had corrected a statement in the preface of his " Revival Tracts," which mentioned that the celebrated stanzas by his brother Addison, entitled " The Doomed Man," inserted in one of the tracts, were then published for the first time with the author's consent. I informed him that the poem had been sent to me by Addison, and was inserted in the " Sunday School Journal," (April 5, 1837,) and that the original had a stanza which, at my recommendation, was omitted as being too horrible. It was the sixth, and read thus :

" But angels know the fatal sign,
And tremble at the sight ;
And devils trace each livid line
With desperate delight."

the common *on dit* in the family for years; he has talked of himself as "the doomed man" constantly, seeing the reprints, &c. I will try to alter the stereogram.

You doubtless have received the "Prescott Memorial," and have read the alleged dictum of P. that Robertson's "style was that of a schoolmistress." But see Philip the Second, i. 356. "Robertson . . . recommended . . . by a classic elegance of style which has justly given him a preëminence among the historians of the great emperor." I am, (as I suppose we shall say,)
truthfully yours.

NEW YORK, *April* 4, 1859.

The signs look like war in Europe; who can estimate the awfulness of such a conjuncture! I find four or five letters from Walsh, chiefly about the Review. The last "Knicker-bocker" contains some irreverence to the manes of our quondam friend, Dr. McHenry.[1] My irritation of the larynx has been on me annoyingly for about two weeks. I have, for the first time, to treat a case of spiritualism. A man, well educated, sound health, good habits, strong mind in every other direction; but perfectly hag-ridden by spirits of his wife, his father, and Robert Hall. He sits up sometimes whole nights, writing; or rather his hand is used by the spirits; the character varying with the spirit. He himself is willing to believe it demoniacal possession; but I have not felt clear to take this ground with him. I have had a heavy stroke of indisposition these last few days, and was unable to preach yesterday afternoon. Mr. Jenkins [of Phila-delphia] preached last evening [in Academy of Music] with great acceptance; Plumer comes next. A member of my church talks of building a church for some poor congregation in the West.

NEW YORK, *April* 19, 1859.

For the first time in my life I have been attacked with some-thing like chills—now about a fortnight. The beginning was a tremendous shake, which made all quake again; since then, crawls, or whatever be the name of those simulations. During these the feeling of "misery" has been very great. I have spoken to very few persons of it, but since the beginning of the year, I have lost all power in the middle-finger of my right hand. The finger *stutters* in writing; indeed, I cannot use it at all. Whether this is paralysis I know not, but I regard it as a Divine

---

[1] Editor of the "American Monthly Magazine" in Philadelphia, for which we had written in 1824.

monition. I am under regular and active treatment. Writing, which was a solace, has become a very burdensome task.[1]

[1] On the 26th April he wrote : " I have to preach a Sunday School sermon next Sunday. My chills are suspended. Deo gratias." On the 1st of
May I heard him preach the sermon referred to, which was delivered with
what struck me as an unusual and unnecessary power of voice. He preached
again on the following Lord's-day, (May 8, communion ; 1 Peter ii. 24,)
which proved to be his last sermon. On the 9th he wrote to me, " My
health has steadily gone down : yet, through mercy, I was enabled to get
through the communion services. I expect to sail for Richmond on Wednesday. I shall probably be addressable at Drake's Branch, Charlotte
County, from the 14th to 21st, and afterwards at University of Virginia till
29th." On the next day (10th) he wrote : " A change in the signs of Providence has changed my plans. So obviously my cough has increased, and
my flesh decreased, that Session and Trustees, *motu proprio*, last night ordered me to vacate from now till October 1. I propose to go to Virginia in
about a fortnight. Don't stay at home an hour ; but if it be fair I will try
to drop in *chez vous* some day this week." On the 12th his report was " No
changes." On the 25th—" though all packed up, and on the eve of starting, we are forbidden by the doctor to go, in consequence of my severe
cough, but more particularly a fever which comes on at night. Plans uncertain. I have not gained any. I endeavour to cast my burden on the
Lord."

In the correspondence of this month he wrote, (in dissent from my opinion that it is better for ministers to prevent actual invitations to new posi-
tions which they know they would not accept) as follows: " All my little
observations confirm me in the judgment, that such things should not be
crushed *in ovo ;* though my own practice has been different. A man runs
before Providence, who answers a question before it is asked. The case
cannot be before him, till he knows the vote, &c. He has a right, as Christ's
servant, to the testimonial in his favour, even of an appointment which he
declines. His congregation have a right to the credit derivable from his
preferring them, in case of refusal. The simple, natural method is the
best."

It was also during the low state of his health in the middle of this May,
that he wrote for " The Presbyterian " an affectionate notice of the Rev.
Henry V. Johns, D. D., of the Episcopal Church, then recently deceased.
From that article I extract a paragraph of biographical interest :

" The first person with whom I ever talked freely, respecting the infinite
concerns of my soul, was Henry V. Johns ; and he has told me that a like
remark would be true of himself. It was in Nassau Hall, then the principal
edifice of Princeton College ; and in No. 27, in the 'second entry ;' a locality fresh in the memory of old Nassovians. We were boys of sixteen ;
though I was about to commence bachelor of arts. Such conversations
begin, one scarcely knows how ; in a short time we had unbosomed ourselves to one another, and entered upon a close and tender friendship which
I trust in God is never to cease. During the days in which Henry was
under the work of the law, and humbly doubting whether indeed he had
attained to justification or not, he used to walk in the grove behind the
college, which, alas! with other forest shades of my boyhood, has long since
vanished away. As he strayed, musing, his eye was attracted by a small
folded paper upon the ground ; this he picked up, and afterwards showed
to me ; it contained these words : ' And they that are Christ's have crucified

NEW YORK, *May* 28, 1859.

As I am ready to catch at any little straw of amendment, I feel cheered by being very slightly better to-day, though after a bad night of vexing dreams and wakings. My cough is in abeyance; the disguised chill and consequent fever return every evening. I have taken a refreshing drive for three successive days.

Upon any fair calculation of probabilities, how likely is it that a promiscuous assembly at Indianapolis will decide a question aright for the whole church? I have long looked in vain for any scriptural or rational foundation for supreme " courts," having half a continent for their scope. This feeling of mine does not extend to Presbyteries.[1]

UNIVERSITY OF VIRGINIA, *June* 7, 1859.

Your alternative of a tour to the West [in preference to the South] would not have suited me at all. I know nobody there, and conveyances and railroads are not what I need. In Virginia I have mountains, numerous friends, at whose houses (as here) I can be sheltered, with sweet, rural quiet, and daily horse-exercise. I could not have come even here, if Dr. Cabell, with considerate kindness, had not gone to New York for me. At the time Dr. Delafield arrested my trip, my cough and expectoration were excessive. I had night-sweats, and my pulse was at 120. It has come down to 84. The journey has done me good, though I have very bad nights. The weather here has been almost cold; the hills and mountains are beautifully clad, but the corn is not so high as in Jersey. Strawberries still linger, of fine quality, and plentiful. We shall probably remain some weeks here, and at a magnificent farm of Mr. Franklin Minor, about five miles off.

After having written and printed a good deal about sickness, health, &c., I find there are pages of experience to turn over, which are quite new. Especially do I see that we may be brought into stumbling and stripping dispensations, of which

the flesh with the affections and lusts, Gal. v. 24. *Try yourself by this!*" The incident made a deep impression on us both, carrying to our apprehensions at that time something of the supernatural. We have talked it over in later years, and there is reason to believe that it had a moulding influence on Johns's experience and life. Soon after this we became communicants, at our respective homes."

[1] May 30.—"I have had a somewhat refreshing night's rest, which I have not had before during some weeks." In a few days (June 2) he set out with his wife and youngest child for Virginia. All his arrangements indicated that he thought it probable he should never return; and as the train passed Princeton his emotions gave unequivocal signs of his reflecting that it was likely to be the last view he should have of that endeared place.

during their continuance we cannot comprehend the nature. I
never felt more perfectly resigned to God's will, or more disposed to justify all his dealings, be it life or death, or disability.
This is my strong permanent feeling. Nevertheless, with this,
and perhaps from physical depression, all things seem sad. The
chords are unstrung, and the instrument relaxed. Give my
love to all yours, and to inquisitive friends.[1]

UNIVERSITY OF VIRGINIA, *June* 23, 1859.

By a dispensation very merciful to me, the summer heats
have been held off thus far. The harvest is in full blast—what
a cheering sight! I presume I saw during a drive this morning
several wheat-fields, of 300 acres each, under the process.
McCormick's reaper is largely used. The improvements here
are great, and still going on. To the Rotunda they have added a
great projection with a new Corinthian prostyle on the North
front. Their great room is very noble, and has a full-size copy
of Raphael's School of Athens. At great expense they are now
working to convey water from a neighbouring mount to every
part of the precincts. A charming parsonage has been built for
their chaplain, on a green hillside, among trees. One of the
best-placed and finest buildings is an Infirmary for sick students.
It is supplied with every convenience, aired throughout by Emerson's ventilator, hot and cold baths, English water-closets, &c.
They have a professional teacher of gymnastics, and two gym-
nasiums, one for summer and one for winter. Russian vapour-
baths are on the grounds, which Dr. C. takes every few days,
leaping from the sweating one into a very cold plunge. Their
" public day " is the 29th, when every thing breaks up. Dr.
Gessner Harrison, now their oldest professor, has resigned. The
demand for schools is truly surprising. I suppose there are a
dozen country-grammar boarding-schools in this county. Gentlemen's sons are very glad to take such places.

If they did not keep saying so, I should not know that I was
any better than a month ago. I lie awake most of the night
with slight fever, and seldom fail of a chill during the twenty
four hours. A slight dinner is the only meal for which I have

---

[1] On the 9th June Dr. Alexander wrote to his intimate friend, James M.
Halsted, Esq., of New York—" Since our arrival here, I have on the whole
been a gainer. While I cannot say that my cough is gone, it is wonderfully
lessened, and quite suspended for long periods. My nights are bad, and I
suffer from a dyspeptic colic, which makes very strict diet necessary. My
appetite is good, and I am riding on horseback every day. My friends
think I shall recover, against the fall. That is as God pleases, unto whom
I desire to submit myself."

any appetite.   Quinine in large doses makes me for days as deaf as the late excellent " K. H." [1]   They begin to let me have raspberries and ice-cream. [2]

[1] The newspaper signature of the Rev. Richard Webster, of Mauch Chunk, Pennsylvania.

[2] The last letter but one, ever written by this faithful hand, so far as I have been able to discover, is the one I subjoin, from the Warm Springs, addressed to his brother Addison, in Princeton.   Like the preceding letters from Virginia to myself, it was written with a pencil, but with no signs of debility.

"BATH COURT HOUSE, *July* 13, 1859.

" Writing costs me so much, that this must go for an answer to A.'s and J.'s letters.   We arrived here on the 13th, perhaps the hottest day of the season.   Though feeling the heat, we are all benefited by the marked change to mountain air.   The bath agrees with me; it is 38 feet diameter, 5 feet deep, and 98° Fahrenheit; being moreover clear as crystal. The waters are also drunk, being weak Epsom salts, and a dash of sulphur. The hotel is well kept, the mutton is delicious, and venison is on the table twice a day.   The guests do not number more than forty.   This place is in danger of being left out of the fashionable range; it is no longer on the way to the White Sulphur and Sweet Springs, and is accessible only by very heavy mountain staging.   It is nevertheless, for picturesque scenery, above all the others.

" Since coming here I have felt better in several respects; better sleep, excellent appetite, and a slight accession of strength.   I am taking no physic, except Dr. Delafield's tonic prescription of *Citr. Ferri cum Cinchona;* it comes mixed chemically.   My absolute strength is small: I was in error about my weight; it is 142 lbs. . . . . . I think the heat must be very great in the plains.   Drought prevails here; there has been no shower for three weeks.

" If my aunt and cousins are still with you, remember me to them kindly. I was so utterly unfit for visiting, that I did not fulfil my purpose of going to Staunton and Lexington.

" This is a very wild country; venison, however, rises in price; it is now six cents a pound.   A buck is brought in, on an average, once a day. Partridges and pheasants abound.   A fox crossed right before our horses' heads on the Warm Spring mountain.   We shall probably remain a week, and then go for more permanent quarters to the Red Sweet Springs.   I neglected to say, that I feel quite free of my intermittent, neither have I any regular cough."

The final effort of his letter-writing was to address some lines to a young nephew in New York, who was suffering with a broken arm.

CHAPTER XV.

CONCLUDING NOTE.

1859.

WITH the letter of June 23, this long, regular, and most affectionate correspondence terminated on the part of my faithful friend. I wrote to him on the 7th and 21st of July, informing him in the latter, that I should leave home on the 27th for a journey of some weeks, and begging him to send me word to certain points on the 5th and 10th of August, of the state of his health. I had been desponding of his recovery from the time of our last personal interview, May 2 ; but was not prepared to receive the tidings of his departure so early as it came ; for before the first date I had fixed for his writing to me he was in his grave.

Nothing, therefore, remains of my present undertaking, but to furnish a narrative of the events of these last few weeks; which I am able to do in the language of those who had the privilege, providentially denied to myself, of being with him in the closing scenes.

At the University of Virginia he had his home with his wife's brother, Dr. James L. Cabell, Professor of Comparative Anatomy and Physiology, whose sympathies and attentions as a companion, friend, and physician, supplied every thing that either his domestic or religious wants could require.

" During the first few days after his arrival at my house," (I quote the words of Dr. Cabell in letters to myself and others,) " he allowed himself to be distressingly exercised on the subject of his relations to the congregation, but letters received almost simultaneously from two of the Elders, in which they requested him to dismiss that subject from his mind until his health should be fully restored, had the desired result; and from that time forward I had no reason to think that the subject ever disturbed him again. The remainder of his days was spent in tranquil enjoyment, evidently at peace with God through faith in Christ, and in love and charity with all men.

"Leaving the University at noon of July 12, we reached Millboro' station at four, and there took a chartered coach for the Warm Springs. The afternoon was exceedingly sultry, and when we reached the Bath Alum Springs, nine or ten miles from the station, and five from the end of our journey, it was found necessary to stop for the night. We made a fresh start at daybreak, (July 13,) and crossed the Warm Spring Mountain before breakfast. It was a fine bracing morning. He had enjoyed good rest during the night, and was in excellent spirits. When we drove up to the Warm Springs Hotel, he got out of the coach with a more elastic step than he had shown for months, and averred that he felt like a new man. After a day or two this feeling of buoyancy deserted him, and was succeeded by an expression of tranquil resignation which puzzled me. On the one hand, the absence of a painful expression was gratifying, in contrast with the previously frequent indications of bodily and mental distress; but, on the other hand, the ordinary signs of convalescence in improved appetite and buoyant spirits, were lacking.

"The suspension of some of his most distressing symptoms soon after his arrival in Virginia, gave me for a time pretty sanguine hopes of his ultimate restoration; but my mind gradually received the impression that despite the abeyance of such symptoms, no ground previously lost was ever recovered. The flesh and strength he had lost were never regained; and more than this, his weakness and emaciation increased progressively, though slowly. By insensible degrees my hopes were lessening and my fears were increasing. He himself never wavered in his conviction that he was not only hopelessly disabled, but that his end was much nearer at hand than others thought. He left New York early in June, six weeks later my house, in the firm conviction that he would see neither place again. Still he was impatient to get into the mountains. You know the force of his æsthetic susceptibilities. In his daily drives, his enjoyment of our mountain scenery, which is unsurpassed for its varied beauty and grandeur, was almost rapturous. It had never before, he said, been half so great. He would repeatedly say that he had no language of his own adequate to the expression of his feelings, and could only exclaim with the Psalmist: ' Oh that men would praise the Lord for His goodness and for His wonderful works to the children of men.' Similar exercises were manifested on our journey to the Warm Springs, and especially at that spot of exquisite beauty, where we lingered a week. It must have been the effect of such mental exercises that produced so marked a change in the expression of his countenance, by removing the traces of suffering, as to cause both ourselves and strangers to mark the change, and to imagine that he was much better. But I recall the fact that he several times said to me : ' I have a strange feeling of increasing debility.' On learning from my sister that he slept better than he had done for months, that he was entirely free from pain at night, and that his appetite and enjoyment of food were keen, I could not attach much significance to a feeling, which is temporarily experienced by most persons who take a warm bath daily. He was impatient to go on to the Red Sweet Springs, (Alleghany county,) his favourite resort in these mountains. Waiting for a rain to lay the dust and cool the air, we left the Warm Springs on the 20th July, the day after a heavy shower had produced this twofold change, on a bright and beautiful morning. But we had not gone many miles before we found, to our great regret, that the clouds of the preceding day had not extended far in the direction of our road, and we were greatly oppressed by the heat and dust. Towards noon he requested me to stop the coach at the nearest house as he was suffering extreme pain. In about a quarter of an hour we reached an obscure country tavern, where we remained four or five hours, and then proceeded eight miles further to a more comfortable house, where well-ventilated rooms and good bedding could be obtained. Here, during the night, symptoms of dysentery appeared, but were relieved by prompt remedies to such an extent as to admit of his travelling the next morning over the remaining eighteen miles of his journey, which brought us to the Red Sweet Springs. Having here more comforts, conveniences and appliances for gratifying his tastes, than could have been brought together elsewhere, both he and my sister made it a subject of thanksgiving that he was permitted to reach a spot endeared to him by its rural and quiet charms and many pleasant associations.

" Our determination to continue our journey was based upon the fact that the tavern at which we lodged, though in many other respects quite comfortable, was rendered unfit for invalids by reason of its being the night-stand for the enormous travel to the White Sulphur Springs. The stages were coming in or going out nearly all night, and there were not two hours of quiet during the entire night. He passed over the eighteen miles with so little discomfort, and with so frequent manifestations of delight as he recalled the familiar objects along the road, that I really thought the disease must have been extinguished. The symptoms returned, however, after our arrival at the Springs, but with so moderate a degree of intensity as to awaken no alarm. The immediate cause of death was an uncontrollable diarrhœa supervening upon an attack of dysentery. His system responded readily enough to the remedies employed, and this circumstance induced us to indulge very sanguine hopes of his recovery until a few days before the termination ; but his physical constitution had been so completely wrecked that he had no recuperative power in reserve for such exigencies. On Wednesday morning, July 27th, after a night of fever, I sent telegraphic communications to his friends respecting his condition. From this time till his death I did not leave his bedside, except to take my meals. Wednesday night the fever was scarcely perceptible, and his sleep was so refreshing that on awaking at dawn of day, he said to me : ' I slept delightfully and am much refreshed.' An hour or two later he said to my sister : ' I must be better—I feel entirely comfortable.' This delusive appearance of amendment continued all the day, and slightly revived our hopes. But Thursday night the fever recurred, and again on Friday night. On the latter occasion a collapse ensued on the subsidence of the fever, which looked like the final sinking. He rallied, however, but the fever recurred early Saturday night, and by midnight he was evidently and unquestionably sinking, though he continued to breathe till about five o'clock on the Sabbath morn.

"Much of the time before his strength entirely failed, was spent in sending messages of farewell and comfort to his congregation and the absent members of his family. He said : ' I have not been in the habit of talking much on the subject of my own spiritual states of feeling. With respect to my subjective religion, I have often disappointed people who look for manifestations of a certain kind. But I have frequently made known to Elizabeth [his wife] the grounds of my hope.' It was now suggested to him that he was exhausting himself, and needed rest, but he added, ' Let me say one word more with respect to the solemn event to which you have called my attention. If the curtain were to drop now, and I were this moment ushered into the presence of my Maker, what would be my feelings ? They would be these : first, I would prostrate myself in an unutterable sense of my nothingness and guilt ; but, secondly, I would look upon my Redeemer with an inexpressible assurance of faith and love. A passage of Scripture which expresses my present feeling is this : " I know whom " (with great emphasis) " I have believed, and am assured that he is able to keep that which I have committed to him against that day." ' In quoting this sentence he remarked, " some persons read it ' in whom I have believed,' but there is no preposition. Christ himself was the direct object of the Apostle's faith." This took place about twenty hours before his departure, after which he fell into a sweet sleep, which continued till the last.

"We are apt to think of sickness and death at a public watering-place as peculiarly distressing. It was far otherwise in this case. Our party had the exclusive occupation of a large isolated cottage, with abundant attendance by excellent and sympathizing servants, and the kind-hearted and liberal proprietor (Mr. Bias) spared neither trouble nor expense in procuring every comfort and luxury which could be had."

It increases our cause of thankfulness for the perfect peacefulness and serenity of this passage through the valley of the shadow of death, to know that Dr. Alexander expected to suffer some severe spiritual conflicts before his release. In view of such a trial he had deliberately prepared the minds of those who might be expected to be most deeply moved by it; reminding them of the nature of such temporary temptations of faith, as sometimes occur in Christian experience before the final triumph, and bidding them not to be disturbed by what might take place in his own instance. But no such darkness, doubt, or trouble came, even for a moment. His countenance, even in silence and sleep, bore such a happy and transported expression, that it was remarked by one who witnessed it that he was already looking into heaven. In this respect, those prayers appeared to be answered, which were intimated by his speaking of the comfort he found on his death-bed in such stanzas as these, (translated from German:)

> Forsake me not, my God,
>   Thou God of my salvation!
> Give me thy light, to be
>   My sure illumination.
> My soul to folly turns,
>   Seeking she knows not what;
> Oh! lead her to thyself—
>   My God, forsake me not!
>
> Forsake me not, my God!
>   Take not thy Spirit from me;
> And suffer not the might
>   Of sin to overcome me.
> A father pitieth
>   The children he begot;
> My Father, pity me;
>   My God, forsake me not!
>
> Forsake me not, my God!
>   Thou God of life and power,
> Enliven, strengthen me,
>   In every evil hour;
> And when the sinful fire
>   Within my heart is hot,
> Be not thou far from me;
>   My God, forsake me not!

Forsake me not, my God!
  Uphold me in my going;
That evermore I may
  Please thee in all well-doing;
And that thy will, O Lord,
  May never be forgot
In all my works and ways—
  My God, forsake me not!

Forsake me not, my God!
  I would be thine forever;
Confirm me mightily
  In every right endeavour.
And when my hour is come,
  Cleansed from all stain and spot
Of sin, receive my soul;
  My God, forsake me not!

I place, here, principally on account of the interest now associated with it by the unexpected decease of the writer himself in less than six months from its date, an extract from a letter addressed to me by Dr. J. Addison Alexander, on the day after his brother's death, but before the intelligence had reached New York.

"NEW YORK, *August* 1, 1859.

" MY DEAR SIR,

" I left town on Friday for a day or two, and on returning to resume my work [writing Commentary] this morning, find that James's sons set off that same day for the South, having heard unfavourable news from their father, and that my brother Samuel followed them last night after receiving a despatch saying that James was rapidly sinking. He was seized with dysentery on his way from the Warm to the Sweet Springs, where it seems that disease is epidemic. I hear indirectly through a member of Dr. Cabell's family, that at the beginning of this new attack he suffered nothing, but seemed nearly insensible. We are now in hourly expectation of later news, which will determine my own movements. In the mean time I think it right to let you know what we know, if you have not previously heard it. I cannot yet abandon all hope, though I stand prepared to hear the worst."

In a letter a month afterwards, and in reference to another

bereavement, Dr. J. A. A. says : " I have no doubt you have
often turned in thought to our departed ' son of consolation,' as
if he were still living. With a strange but not unnatural forget-
fulness, I find myself looking to him for support even under the
irreparable stroke of his own death. I had no conception of
my intellectual dependence upon James, until I caught myself
continually laying things aside to tell him as the person who
could best appreciate and enjoy them. All this says very
loudly ' cease ye from man whose breath is in his nostrils,' and
shows the grace and wisdom of that constitution which reserves
the office of comforter for a divine person. The circumstances
which you mention certainly go far to reconcile us to his death
at this time; but I feel now and then a disposition to repine at
the circumstances themselves. I have no doubt that he shortened
his own life by morbid anxieties, connected not merely with his
health, but with his duties. I find it hard to acquiesce without
a murmur in the loss of such a man from such a cause, or to
reflect, without a momentary pang of discontent, that he might
have preached for many years with ease and pleasure, but sunk
under the weight of other cares.[1]

" It seems an argument in favour of the old Puritan arrangement, which provided both a pastor and a teacher in such cases.
But I have already said too much, and check myself."

Ten days afterwards, referring to the modification in his
Seminary duties, Dr. J. A. Alexander wrote : " The change in my
employments is exceedingly agreeable, and none the less so from
its having been a favourite plan of James's, without whose influence it never would have taken place. This is not the only
point in which he lived to see his hopes fulfilled in reference to
his nearest relatives—another instance of the loving-kindness
which arranged the circumstances of his death."

The decease took place early on the morning of the Lord's
day, July 31, 1859. After a proper interval, the body was
taken to Princeton, and the interment was made on Wednesday,

[1] The writer alludes to his brother's extreme, almost morbid consci-
entiousness, which led him to attempt an amount of labour beyond his
physical ability, and which oppressed his mind when he found he could not
overtake his work.

August 3d. The religious services connected with it were held in the First Presbyterian Church, and were conducted by the Rev. Dr. Thompson of New York, Dr. Magie of Elizabeth, Professor Hope, (since deceased,) of the College, and Dr. Hodge, the last of whom preached a discourse from the words in Matthew xxv. 34, "Then shall the King say unto them on his right hand, Come ye blessed of my Father, inherit the kingdom prepared for you from the foundation of the world."

The sympathy felt by Christians of all branches of the church, in the removal of Dr. Alexander from their communion, was strikingly displayed in a meeting which took place on the 5th of August, at the most largely frequented of American summer-resorts—Saratoga. At this assembly clergymen of the Episcopal, Congregational, Baptist, Methodist, and Reformed-Dutch, as well as the Presbyterian churches, expressed a common sentiment of brotherly affection and high esteem.

The Session of the bereaved congregation in New York, appointed the second Sabbath of October to be observed with special reference to their affliction. It had been expected that the church would be closed during part of the summer and until that day, with a view to some extensive changes in the building to assist the voice of the pastor. But upon the reassembling of the congregation, a marble tablet, inserted in the wall near the pulpit, was the only change to be noticed. That tablet bears the following inscription :

IN MEMORY OF

JAMES WADDEL ALEXANDER, D.D.,

FOR THIRTEEN YEARS THE BELOVED AND REVERED PASTOR OF THIS CHURCH;

WHOSE SINGULAR NATURAL GIFTS, RIPENED BY GENEROUS CULTURE,

WERE SUCCESSFULLY GIVEN TO HIS SACRED WORK ;

AND WHO, BY HIS FERVENT PIETY, PURE LIFE, TENDER AFFECTIONS,

LARGE BENEVOLENCE, AND UNSPARING LABOUR, SO ENDEARED HIMSELF TO

HIS PEOPLE, THAT THEY MOURN

AS FOR A DEAR BROTHER AND BELOVED FRIEND.

HE WAS BORN MARCH 13, 1804,
HE DIED JULY 31, 1859,

DECLARING, AS THE SUM OF HIS FAITH AND HOPE,

"*I know whom I have believed, and am persuaded that he is able to keep that which I have committed to him against that day.*"

With the services on the Sabbath alluded to, were connected in the morning a sermon by Professor Hodge of the Princeton Theological Seminary, from the words, (Acts ix. 20,) "He preached Christ;" and in the afternoon a sermon by the Editor of these volumes, from 2 Peter i. 15, "Moreover, I will endeavour that ye may be able, after my decease, to have these things always in remembrance."

From the former of these, I extract a few paragraphs:

"Dr. Alexander united in himself gifts and graces rarely found in combination. God had endowed him with a retentive memory and a perspicacious intellect, with great power of application and acquirement, with singular delicacy of taste, with a musical ear, and a resonant voice. These gifts were all cultivated and turned to the best account. Probably no minister in our Church was a more accomplished scholar. He was familiar with English literature in all periods of its history. He cultivated the Greek and Latin, French, German, Italian, and Spanish languages, not merely as a philologist, but for the treasures of knowledge and of taste which they contain. To this wide compass of his studies is in good measure to be referred many of his characteristics as a writer, the abundance of his literary allusions, his curious felicity of expression, and the variety of his imagery.

"It was, however, not only in the department of literature that Dr. Alexander was thus distinguished. He was an erudite theologian. Few men were more conversant with the writings of the early fathers, or more familiar with Christian doctrine in all its phases. He embraced the faith of the Reformed Churches in its integrity with a strength of conviction which nothing but the accordance of that system with his religious experience could produce. * * * Theology and philosophy are so related, that devotion to the former involves of necessity the cultivation of the latter. Dr. Alexander was therefore at home in the whole department of philosophical speculation. His last publication was an able exposition of the views of the metaphysicians of the middle ages on one of the most important questions in mental science.[1]

[1] " The doctrine of Perception, as held by Doctor Arnauld, Doctor Reid,

"Thus richly and variously was your beloved pastor endowed. These gifts, however, were but accomplishments. Underneath these adornments, in themselves of priceless value, was the man and the Christian. He was an Israelite without guile. Probably no man living was freer from all envy and jealousy, from malice, hypocrisy, and evil-speaking. No one ever heard of his saying or doing an unseemly or unkind thing. The associations connected with his name in the minds of all who knew him, are of things true, just, pure, lovely, and of good report. No one can think of him without being the happier and the better for the thought. He was a delightful companion. His varied knowledge, his humor, his singular power of illustration, rendered his conversation, when in health and spirits, a perpetual feast. Having been brought early in life to a saving knowledge of the truth, his religious knowledge and experience were profound and extensive. He was therefore a skilful casuist, a wise counsellor, and abundantly able to comfort the afflicted with the consolation wherewith he himself had been comforted of God. He was evidently a devout man, reverential in all his acts and utterances, full of faith and of the Holy Ghost.

"The pulpit was his appropriate sphere. There all his gifts and graces, all his acquirements and experiences, found full scope. Hence the remarkable variety which characterized his preaching; which was sometimes doctrinal, sometimes experimental, sometimes historical, sometimes descriptive or graphic, bringing scriptural scenes and incidents as things present before the mind; often exegetical, unfolding the meaning of the word of God in its own divine form. Hence, too, the vivacity of thought, the felicity of style, and fertility of illustration which were displayed in all his sermons. He could adapt himself to any kind of audience. * * * He preached Christ in a manner which seemed to many altogether peculiar. He endeavoured to turn the minds of men away from themselves, and to lead them to look only

and Sir William Hamilton," in the Repertory for April, 1859. As I have, in the progress of the volumes, indicated Dr. Alexander's articles in the Repertory, as far as I can identify them, I will mention that in the course of 1858 his contributions were, 1. "Ancient Manuscript Sermons;" 2. "Sprague's Annals."

unto Jesus. He strove to convince his hearers that the work of salvation had been accomplished for them, and was not to be done by them ; that their duty was simply to acquiesce in the work of Christ, assured that the subjective work of sanctification is due to the objective work of Christ, as appropriated by faith and applied by the Holy Ghost. He thus endeavoured to cut off the delays, the anxieties, and misgivings which arise from watching the exercises of our own minds, seeking in what we inwardly experience a warrant for accepting what is outwardly offered to the chief of sinners, without money and without price. He was eminently successful in his ministry, not only in the conversion of sinners, but in comforting and edifying believers. The great charm of his preaching, that to which more than to any thing else its efficiency is to be referred, was his power over the religious affections. He not only instructed, encouraged, and strengthened his hearers, but he had, to a remarkable degree, the gift of calling their devotional feelings into exercise. In his prayers there were those peculiar intonations to which the Spirit of God alone can attune the human voice, and at the sound of which the gates of heaven seem to unfold, and the worshippers above and the worshippers on earth mingle together, prostrate in adoration. Your religious services, under his ministry, were truly seasons of devotion, the highest form of enjoyment vouchsafed to men on earth. The man who can give us this enjoyment, who can thus raise our hearts to God, and bring us into communion with our Saviour, we reverence and love. This is a power which no one envies, from which no one wishes to detract, which surrounds its possessor with a sacred halo, attracting all eyes and offending none.

"Dr. Alexander's preëminence, therefore, was due not to any one gift alone; not to his natural abilities, to his varied scholarship, to his extensive theological knowledge and religious experience; not to his divine unction, or to his graces of elocution. It was the combination of all these which made him, not the first of orators to hear on rare occasions, but the first of preachers to sit under, month after month and year after year."

[The last letter ever written by Dr. Alexander, as referred to on page 290, was as follows :]

"WARM SPRINGS, *July* 19, 1859.

"MY DEAR LITTLE CHARLEY.—We have all been very much grieved to hear of your trouble; your mother's letter is all we know, but we trust you are by this time over the worst. I am weak, and cannot write much, but I beg you to consider that it is your Heavenly Father who sends this affliction on you, for your good. And if you are patient and resigned to the will of God, it will please God as much as if you did the most laborious works. We were pleased to hear how manly you were, after you were hurt. This was God's gift; and he will take away your timidity, if you ask him, and make you strong and courageous.

"Willy has a letter begun to you, but he is a poor writer, and every thing draws him away. Give my love to your dear parents, to my sweet little Netty, to Archy and Sam, also to your Uncle Sam; all join in this. A letter is a great treat up here. Our address will be : Red Sweet Springs, Alleghany Co., Va. ☞ Please let this be known to our friends. We expect to leave here to-morrow in a chartered stage. Mrs. Cabell is better. Your aunt is well; so is Will. My own troubles are chiefly from extreme weakness. I gain little.

"God bless you, Charley !
"I am your affectionate uncle
JAMES."

APPENDIX.

No. 1.

PRESBYTERIAL CHARGE.

1841.

[It will not, I think, be considered an inappropriate addition to the friendly counsels contained in many of the foregoing Letters, to insert the public CHARGE addressed by their writer to his correspondent, as part of the prescribed services at his Ordination and Instalment. This took place, August 11, 1841, in the First Presbyterian Church of Trenton, the same over which Dr. Alexander was installed, February 11, 1829.]

Invested as you have just been with the most sacred office known among men, you feel it, I doubt not, to be the most solemn hour of life, one to which you will look back with profound interest during all your pilgrimage—perhaps in your dying moments—and certainly from the eternal world. And whether the retrospect be one of joy or grief will depend on the manner in which you shall have fulfilled these vows. If you perform the duties of a gospel-minister with faithfulness, to the end of your course, you will shine as a star in the firmament of glory ; but if you turn aside, seduced by sloth, fear, pleasure, literary or professional fame, ambition or lucre, your account will be as dreadful as your privilege is great.

Consider what it is that you have vowed. To be zealous and faithful in maintaining the truths of the gospel, and the purity and peace of the church, whatever persecution or opposition may arise to you on that account ;—to be faithful and diligent in the exercise of all personal and private duties which become you as a Christian, and a minister of the gospel ; as well as in all relative duties, and the public duties of your office ; endea-

vouring to adorn the profession of the gospel by your conversation; and walking with exemplary piety before the flock over
which God hath made you a bishop. And, finally, and specially,
to discharge the duties of a pastor to this congregation.

These, my brother, are the duties which you have just now
recognized as yours; and I am appointed to charge you, yea in
God's name, solemnly to charge you to persevere in them. But
why need I enlarge upon them? It is not the knowledge of
our duties which is most needed, but the heart to perform them.
We all know more than we do, and little would be gained if I
were to rehearse to you the contents of all the volumes on the
pastoral care. These you might know, and yet be a cast-away.
But to *do* them is what only the Spirit of God in your heart will
ever ensure. There is only one thing which will make you, and
keep you a faithful pastor, and that is the new nature in vigorous
life; evincing itself in love to Christ, and love to souls. Take
heed, therefore, to *thyself*, as well as to all the flock over which
the Holy Ghost hath made thee bishop, to feed the church of
God, which he hath purchased with his own blood. Take heed
unto *thyself*, and unto the doctrine; continue in them; for in
doing this thou shalt both *save thyself*, and them that hear thee.
Though you are a minister, it does not follow that you are a
member of Christ. I am sure I speak your own convictions
when I say, that all ministerial activity and success is hollow and
deceptive, which does not flow from inward experience of the
divine life. Without this, vanity is stamped alike on the tongues
of men and of angels—on prophecy, mysteries, and all knowledge, on self-impoverishing alms and martyrdom itself. If you
ever really preach Christ Jesus the Lord, it will be because God
who commanded the light to shine out of darkness, shall have
shined into your heart, to give you the light of the knowledge
of the glory of God in the face of Jesus Christ. Have you, my
dear brother, beheld that glory? Having the same spirit of
faith with Paul, can you say I believed and therefore have I
spoken? Does the love of Christ constrain you? Beware of
preaching an unknown Saviour. It is He who is to be the theme
of all your ministrations. Make sure of an interest in his death;
and not only this, but strive to keep the fountain full, rather than
to multiply the streams; cultivate the graces of the closet, in
order that you may come forth in public and private, fresh from
divine communications.

It is, after all, personal piety which makes the able minister.
It is a mournful fact that the holiest services may degenerate
into a routine, and we may preach and pray with hearts as dead
as those of our hearers. Even the measures supposed to indicate

the extremest zeal may be conducted in utter coldness and hypo-crisy ; and the preacher may come reeking from the heats of fanatical parades, to show in the domestic circle a frivolity and asperity, a sensuality, or a cupidity, at which even his unconverted hearers blush. O watch the fire within doors !

My brother, this is a true saying, If a man desire the office of a bishop, he desireth a good work. A bishop, then, must be blameless, the husband of one wife, vigilant, sober, of good be-haviour, given to hospitality, apt to teach, not given to wine, no striker, not greedy of filthy lucre ; but patient ; not a brawler, not covetous, one that ruleth well his own house, having his children in subjection with all gravity. Be thou an example of the believers, in word, in conversation, in charity, in spirit, in faith, in purity. Meditate upon these things ; GIVE THYSELF WHOLLY TO THEM.

If these precepts be observed, you will the less need rules as to the details of duty. Love is wiser than rules. Love is wisdom, nay love is power. The particular measures to be adopted as to the communication of divine truth, I leave to your own Christian discretion. Love is inventive and will find out ways. Live in the Word of God ; be mighty in the Scriptures ; turn what you read into experience ; and you will save the souls of those who hear you.

And now—May the blessing of God rest upon you, and the Spirit of Christ fill your heart ! *Amen.*

No. 2.

ADDITIONAL LETTERS FROM EUROPE.

1851.

[No more extracts from the correspondence were inserted in Chapter XI., than were sufficient to furnish a general outline of the first European journey, without giving those few months a disproportionate space in the memoir. The following additional selections have been made as not only entertaining in themselves, but eminently characteristic of the observer.]

LONDON, *June* 9, 1851.

As I am bent on *old* London, I caught at the coachman's say-ing this morning, that we might see Greenwich Fair. Down the New Road in an omnibus to the *Bengk*, (so is " bank " hight,) thence to Temple Bar in another ; thence to London Bridge in a third, (always on top,) seeing Bow church, Guildhall, Mansion House, &c., to the stairs by the bridge. Hundreds on hundreds of vans laden with country folk. Scores of steamers, some for a penny, for the Fair. Such masses of heads I never saw. Yet the ever-present police prevent the slightest jam. Off we go, under London Bridge, seven miles downward to Greenwich. Such a sight! Streets cleared of animals and vehicles for miles. All one raree-show. Thousands on thousands. Here is a mountebank; there a Highland piper in tartan, and boys dancing the fling; then theatres, with Hamlet and Ophelia begging the people to come in, price one penny. I saw three several Punch and Judys. Like ten old commencements [of Princeton College] in one. Yet among a hundred thousand people we saw no disorder, heard no oath, and met but one tipsy man. They get warm toward night.

Then to glorious Greenwich Park, acres of green turf, and trees centuries old. We supposed the number of separate stalls or places must have been several thousands. All laughing, all merry, all kindly, all rosy, all plebeian, and all Cockneys. We saw not one gentleman or lady. From time immemorial, the people at this Fair use a little noisy wooden scraper-wheel, called the "fun o' the fair." Everybody scrapes everybody's back unawares. Hundreds of babes in arms, and all this in a smart rain. But, as I said, London rains are play-showers.

LONDON, *June* 10, 1851.

Holidays continue. Hundreds of people will come from all the railways. I am writing early at the south-east window of the house, four-pair back. Through one pane of glass, without moving, I count fifteen churches, including St. Paul's, over which the sun is trying to colour the black London smoke, but for which I could perhaps count forty steeples thus. I look down into the court of Somerset House, without rising from my chair. All about are chimney-tops, but by going to the flat roof, I see all this quarter—the Tower, Abbey, Lambeth, bridges, river, &c. It is what brought me here. [142 Strand.]

The wonder of wonders is the police. There are 900 added. They are so protected as to feel their respectability. A few days ago, an uppish Captain of the Coldstream Guards, connected with the Duke of Devonshire, struck a policeman. Notwithstanding his extreme flouncing, he was sentenced to ten days' imprisonment. These policemen are to the great machine of London exactly what our fifty engineers were to the engine of the Arctic. I have seen but one tipsy man, and heard but one oath in England, yet I have been in the most populous parts. No

crowding is allowed. There is ten times as much collision at
Fulton street, New York, as at the East end of the Strand, or
London Bridge. I have a passion for getting lost in odd streets,
and have done it to my heart's content here, resorting to policemen for aid. It is believed any 'bus-man, or officer, would be
dismissed instanter who should be uncivil to a stranger.

Our host came yesterday, 97 miles in two hours and a
quarter. Yet it was smooth as a sleigh. They are adopting
some bars of solid iron, with no sills or sleepers between them
and the gravel. All along the sides of road [railway] it is at
this season like a parterre.

A 'bus which I used was marked 6365. As many a-top as
in. The 'bus coachmen are far above ours; being often coachmen driven from the roads by the railways. They never chew,
talk low, or behave surly. The one who last drove me to the
Bank is a genuine Mr. Weller, Senr.; was twenty-eight years
coaching; came out of Hessex—" did ye never 'ear of Hessex?
Many convicts in America? I has a nevoy in Adelaide." He
helps me up, holds my umbrella, calls other 'buses, and covers
my legs with a cloth when it rains. He knows me again and
engages to take me up. This is true of all. Two can sit each
side of coachman. He has nothing to do with the money, but
drives from 7½ A. M. to 12½ night. Some days, the Paddington
says, he takes in his ten pounds, often only two. Price is sixpence.

Having been at Greenwich Fair yesterday, and seen all
Cockneydom in glorious delight, I went *up* stream to-day to see
the other extreme, viz., Windsor Castle. The contrast is extraordinary between this dead-level garden (like a magic prairie)
of matchless green, and the frowning fortress, which you see
for miles, and which you almost skirt in arriving at it. Its
towers are a hundred feet high. All my ideas of castellated
strength were quite feeble, compared with the reality. Outside
it is a giant hold; inside it is a scene of luxurious art. All my
conception of Gothic churches being from drawings, I was struck
dumb when I first entered St. George's Chapel. It is vain to enlarge on it. What I cannot get over is the glorious airy loftiness,
lightness, and sweetness of this edifice, *without one idea of gloom.*

One of the very prettiest things I have seen was a string of
Quaker girls at Windsor, no doubt wealthy, but uniting the
innocency of the pale Philadelphians with the British roses. It
requires some little historic knowledge to survey such galleries
of art as these at the castle. One room is filled with the works
of Van Dyck, and one with those of Sir Thomas Lawrence. The
view from the top of the castle has often been described, (see
Gray's Ode,) but it seems endless, and may, for extent, be com-

pared with Monticello, [Virginia.] The number of pedestrians is astonishing. Every one drinks the light malt liquor of the hostelries, but none seem excited. Games of cricket on the greens are often in sight. The boats on the river seem wholly gala-boats, and chiefly rowed by boys. The number of the boys' boats at Eton is surprising.

June 11.—Before breakfast I surveyed Covent Garden Market near by, and saw the matchless flower and fruit emporium of London. Scores of large peaches, forced in hot-houses, and selling for 2*s.* 6*d.* a-piece, [55 cents.] After breakfast across Waterloo Bridge to the South-Western Railway. It is Hampton Races. This caused a multitude to be going the same way. This also showed us every variety of sporting character. The course is a mile from the Palace. (As a proof of English exactness, 1*s.* 7*d.* is this moment sent in from the Post Office, to be returned to an unknown person in this house, which has been over-paid.) The palace of Hampton Court is on the north of the Thames, ten miles up the river, near Richmond. Way very lovely ; green lanes, winding pathways, cricket parties, green winding banks of the gentle Thames, pleasure-boating, (the only use of wherries now,) amazing swiftness of the four-oar boats, rowed by amateurs. At length get out at Hampton. Roads full, full ; nobles, gentry, jockeys, pony-phætons, donkeys saddled for races, grooms, postilions, men in every livery, and colour of breeches. As they turn off to the left, we turn off to the right, to the palace. The elms were planted by Wolsey, who planned this immense structure. The glory of the building is its paintings. For the first time I beheld works of M. Angelo, Corregio, Murillo, Guido, Titian, and the original Cartoons of Rafaelle. We visited thirty-two apartments and saw 1,026 pictures.

June 13.—I was much gratified with the law-courts. Lord Chancellor Truro was on the seat of equity, and Mr. Wood was speaking, in that hurried, clipping way common to all about St. Stephen's. Lord Campbell and Coleridge at Queen's Bench. Benches crammed with sergeants and barristers, in wigs, bands, and gowns. I also entered the court of the Vice Chancellor, Sir J. Knight Bruce. I hardly expected to see so many wigged ones on the benches ; they filled them like pews. Then dash out, and lose myself in the city—in the London of C. Lamb. After all my study of the localities, I can hardly believe my eyes. Such dark, dim, tall, narrow, winding ways, such labyrinths, plainly just so for ages. People stare as I drive into the courts around St. Mary Aldermany church, Bow-lane, and peep into Friday street, Bread street, Old Change Alley ; often have to get into a doorway to let a single cart pass. Come out suddenly on St. Paul's Church-yard; go round it, among the shops; survey the Religious Tract Society, their beautiful committee-room and library. Portraits of Burder and Bickersteth. Invited to meet their Committee. See Arnold's face [portrait] in a shop, and go in; it is Fellowes's, his publisher. Greatly struck with Newgate street and Old Bailey. Wonderful old courts opening into Farringdon St. Without. Down from High Holborn to Fleet street. O the throng! Think of Johnson. Fleet street becomes the Strand, and in this I am now at home.

A wondrous eating and drinking folk are the Cockneys. Pastry-cooks and chop-houses seem to be a fourth of the shops in some parts, and you can hardly look up without seeing bright pots of ale carried about. Yet nobody seems to be drunk in the streets. I begin, however, to be aware of desperate lazars, and see pallid, begrimed children. I have no time for telling of the ancient churches, which are numberless. Their names carry me back to Foxe's Records. Bow church I pass daily. St. Mary le Strand is very near me; so is St. Dunstan's in the East, and St. Clement's. St. Sepulchre's (St. Pulchre's) is near Pie Corner, where the great fire stopped. In another direction I found myself at the Seven Dials. I owe much to the cuts in the "Penny Magazine" for my familiarity with these spots.

June 14.—I went out before breakfast to revisit Covent Garden market, which I suppose is the greatest flower market in the world.[1] I could smell the rich odours long before I got into the street. I bought a moss-rose, a damask rose, a bud, a geranium, and a bunch of pansies, all for sixpence. You must know that no rose will any longer grow in the close air of the "City." After breakfast I went to the Horse Guards, traversed the St. James's Park, and enjoyed the green grass, the water, the swans, the song of birds, and the play of a thousand children. These three great parks open into each other. Don't think of them as little patches like those in New York. In the middle of these parks you are out of sight of all the great city, but with gigantic trees, velvet turf, copses, thickets, artificial rivers, even with miniature ships on them; thousands of people gently sauntering or resting, and children without number playing, romping, rolling, flying kites, and fishing. I pursued my way to St. James's Palace, and found the Foot Guards just proceeding thither from Buckingham Palace with music. I followed them into the quadrangle of the ancient palace. There these noble red-coats formed a hollow square, and the band played for an hour the choicest operatic airs. I need not say a Queen's band is

---

[1] He afterwards had to acknowledge the superiority of the Paris market, page 144.

no mean affair. I then proceeded to another court, and approached one of the stiff sentinels. I showed him Mr. T.'s letter to his brother. He presented arms, and accompanied me to the right door. I rang and was admitted to the palace—to an ante-chamber. Four servants were in waiting. Mr. T. had not arrived. It was about eleven, and all the court-people had been up till four at a masquerade ball at the palace. I was ushered into his office, which was full of great ledgers about levées, drawing-rooms, presentations, &c. The servant brought me a fresh "Morning Post," which is the Court paper. Presently T. came in. I told him I had thus far failed to see the Queen. He directed me to go to Buckingham Palace, near Constitution Hill. Crossing Green Park I did so, and took a seat looking towards the Palace Garden. Presently there was a sensation. A coach, with four elegant outriders, approached with the Queen and Prince Albert. I saw both distinctly. They were coming home from the Crystal Palace. The people observed dead silence, and the general raising of hats was quiet and momentary.

In the afternoon I went into Hyde Park, to see what I con-sider the greatest display in England. Every day before dinner (5 to 6½) all the aristocracy appear, either in carriages, or on horseback. The drive is miles round. All the wealth and beauty of England is here represented. Coachmen, footmen, postilions, all in livery, all in white cravats, breeches and stock-ings, and many powdered. In Rotten Row the equestrians appear. Our Virginians stand aghast at the bold riding of the ladies. Such horses and horsemanship cannot be matched. Among this multitude I did not hear a loud word, or giggle, or see an arrogant or bold look. Very few of the women are beautiful in face, but the figure and port are incomparable. Nothing was apparent to distinguish noble persons, unless it were studied cleanliness and plainness. All the finery is on the horses and servants. The most graceful dressing was on the French ladies, of whom there are many.

June 16.—Clear again; but it will rain before night, as it has done every day. You don't see one in a hundred, even of women, with an umbrella. The water here is good, and so are the milk and butter. Such mutton and beef I never saw. Bacon (as they call it) differs from ours, and is very melting and delicious. Cherries have just come. No cheap strawberries yet. English eat cheese with salt. Their Cheshire is about like our Goshen. The Stilton is rich and altogether peculiar. The cream cheese and the sausage are better than we have at home. The bread is not always good. It is not dark all night now. I waked at two, and could have read large print.

To-day at Westminster Hall; saw the Vice Chancellor on the Bench. In the Common Pleas saw the Lord Chief Justice, Sir J. Jervis, and Sir T. N. Talfourd. In Exchequer, heard a funny case about tobacco samples. Lord Chief Baron, Sir J. Pollock, displayed much keenness in bridling Mr. Humphrey, Queen's Counsel. Sir James Park, of the same bench, spoke often. In Queen's Bench again saw Lord Campbell. The lawyers wear not only the wig, with two rows of curls and two queues, and the gown, and very long bands, but also the strait coat of a century ago. I sat among them some time in the Exchequer court.

The house next door to me, (No 141,) is that in which Jacob Tonson kept shop, and where were published Thomson's Seasons, Tom Jones, and the histories of Hume, Robertson, and Gibbon.

June 17.—I again visited Covent Garden market to see the matchless fruits, and flowers, and vegetables. Here are things which cannot be described. I passed by the old Hummums. Revisited the Temple; entered the house where Johnson lived and Lamb was born, and Johnson's house in Bolt court. Thence to the neighbourhood where the " Boar's head in Little East-cheap " once was; now occupied by the statue of William IV. Then to the American Minister's, [Mr. Abbott Lawrence;] great style; he has an excellent manner, very English, and keeps up the American style. Then for the fourth time, to the Crystal Palace. This time I must say there was a crowd. There must have been hundreds of school boys and girls in uniforms. Whenever I see a well-dressed woman, I know she is French. The riding of the ladies in Hyde Park is a beautiful sight.

Mr. Lawrence had given to Major Preston and me an order to enter the House of Lords. Being a little too early I passed some time in Westminster Abbey, just opposite, among the tombs. Then I went out to see the Lords assembling. The day was fair, and it was a fine sight. The common mode was on a noble horse, with a groom on another, who immediately rides off with both horses. Some came in coaches. Some walked, and I even observed some getting out of very or'nary cabs and paying the fare. I had the uncommon pleasure of seeing the Duke of Wellington, for the second time. He was on horseback with a groom; white trowsers; much of Dr. Miller's look. He dismounted with much difficulty. I did not see him afterwards in the House. The Chancellor, Lord Truro, was on the woolsack. I saw Brougham, Grey, Sir J. Graham, (in the gallery,) Lord Lansdowne, Earl of Anglesea, (with one leg,) Archbishop of Canterbury, Bishops of London, Norwich, and Oxford. The bishops waddle up and down in their full robes. The judges have their gowns and wigs. The Lord Chancellor has a wig with immense ears. The rest of the Lords are dressed in ordinary morning trim, generally in frock coats, very plain, but scrupulously clean. The Chancellor left the woolsack and made a very warm defence of Chancery. Lord Stanley made a powerful attack on the ministry in regard to the navigation laws. Every other sentence was about the United States. He was answered by Lord Grenville, of the Board of Trade, and when I came away at 7½ (still dinnerless) Lord Hardwick was just speaking. I thought the debate most able. Stanley is a truly eloquent man.

PARIS, *June* 20—*July* 9, 1851.

From London to Dover we went like lightning, flying through Kent, too fast to see much. It was about like going from New York to Trenton. O the wretched little steamer across the channel! They are half an age behind us in steamboats. We tossed like an egg-shell. The sea broke over us, so that the deck was soaking, and the spray like rain. Below—one pavement of emetic ladies. As for me, except the ducking, I never enjoyed any thing more. I could not stand up, but I felt perfectly triumphant as we cut through the waves. Calais in sight. What a change for two hours! Now for the customs. A little Frenchman, indescribably quick and *habile*, spies out the Americans in an instant; attaches himself to us as commissionaire; carries every thing; takes us to office to show passports; then to bureau to change our sovereigns for French money; then to a room, where coffee and luncheon; then to an office to get our ticket stamped; then to the cars to secure a separate carriage for ladies, &c.; then to weighing place (of trunks); then to another office where baggage-tickets are given; then to cars to see us locked in. All this (which we could never have done ourselves) little Mons. Marguerite does for one franc. At four we are off on the newly-opened railway. Our carriage is as sumptuous as the finest coach, roomy and soft, in every way luxurious. We had 235 miles to go after 4 P. M. I can hardly collect my thoughts to tell about it. All the trees, even in what seem to be woods, are planted in rows; all trimmed, except the innumerable poplars, which look like green pillars. Perpetual sight of peasantry. As they stop to look, the scenes are for a painter. They wear the boldest colours, and seldom less than four; high caps; groups in the deep-green hay and barley, look beautiful. Dear little children, in hues of the rainbow, held up by fathers in blouses from the hay-fields. Villages on villages; all of one story ; all either tiled or thatched, and some both at once. At Amiens the beautiful sun was going down in the western plains, and casting a blush on the ancient cathedral. How indebted I am to the " Penny Magazine " for its cuts and descriptions ! At Douai (where the Bible was translated) the whole neighbourhood is cut up into ups and downs by the fortifications, and the green sides of the moats and ramparts were filled with people. They gathered around us, but in the most civil way. The peasant women are as coarse as men. It was still daylight when we passed Lille, and these scenes were repeated on a larger scale. Arrived at an enormous station-house in the north of Paris, we take an omnibus for the Hotel, and roll through lighted streets. Thousands sitting out in the *rue de la Paix*, &c., even at midnight.

After breakfast next day, I took a drive in a cab ; stopped to deliver my letters to Dr. F. Monod. The concierge says : " to the left, second floor." I ascend ; see door marked " Monod, Pasteur." I send in my name ; instantly I am seized and kissed on both cheeks, not by good Dr. M., but by Mr. Bridel, who remembers me in an instant. Adolphe Monod lives opposite.[1]

Besides our general view of the President [Louis Napoleon] at the review of the Champ de Mars, [p. 142,] we had two several occasions of looking him closely in the face, at corners where our pushing driver drew up. We were enveloped in the enthusiastic crowd, who began with *Vive la Republique*, and ended with a universal shout of *Vive l'Empereur!* Women ran like mad among the tramping of the horses. The cortége was preceded by guards holding cocked pistols, and followed by the carabiniers in brazen helmets and cuirasses, which sounded as they rode. All the troops were regulars. I never expected to see such a review, as they commonly fall on Sunday. All the fine equipages seem English, as do all the beautiful children. The creatures that go about in sabots, and run after you with bouquets, or carry great panniers on their backs, are brutally hideous. The grisettes in shops, and the trim little women in caps, that trip along every moment, are well-dressed, and graceful to a degree. There is nothing in England like the Avenue des Champs Elysées, or the Concorde, or the Louvre, or the fortifications, or the middle age piles of the Cité, or the quays, or the Arche de Triomphe. This last fills my eye more than any thing architectural I have seen. But I love London more. I miss the ever-present police, always kind and ready, giving you a sense of protection wherever you are. And then there are not ten men in France whom I could care to go ten miles to see ; whereas I can name a hundred in London.

---

[1] Dr. A. Monod died April 6, 1856.

On the 23d, I passed through lines of soldiers to the south side of the National Assembly. Place assigned me in the gallery, opposite the tribune and President's chair. Assemble at two. President has an enormous bell, which he rings to keep order. Heard a speech from Leroux, and a long one from Laurent. Then for a long walk, along the matchless Avenue, through the Tuileries, among hundreds of statues, deep shade of trees, and thousands of flowers to the Champs Elysées. Scores of amusements among the trees. All the working-people of Paris seem pouring into these artificial forests. Punch and Judy. Cripples with music. Flying-horses and circulating boats. Dancing dogs. Two little open-air theatres, with numerous singers and large orchestra. These immense forests, called gardens, are used by the Parisians as nursery, smoking-room, and study. The people live out of doors. All the men seem to be either priests or soldiers, so the women keep the shops.

In the *pays Latin* I was in a little rapture. The Hotel Cluny gave me impressions for life. These old black, grim, fimous, conic-topped towers, fill all my mental blanks *au sujet* of the middle ages. In the *rue St. Jacques*, that long, long, tumble-down street, I began to breathe afresh, as in the Old Jewry, &c., but with more hoary and romantic souvenirs. The inside of French churches is stable-like, compared with St. George's, Windsor, or Henry VII.'s chapel.

One morning I took my early coffee at a *laitière's*. Saw the sale of milk, and the perfect courtesy and elegance of the servants who came for it. I have learnt to bow to the lady when I enter a café; this was, however, a plebeian shop, the cafés were not open. On returning, I found that Mr. Rives had called in person, and afterwards had sent me his silver medal to admit me for the day to the diplomatic tribune, the best place for seeing and hearing; so I shall go again. I have seen the chief notabilities of France in the Chamber. Soldiers are just as numerous as bees in a hive. The red-legged regulars are the meanest creatures, singly, I ever saw. The enthusiasm for Louis Napoleon is great. I am sick of seeing on every church, house, and wall, " Liberté, Egalité, Fraternité." It is positively babyish. I miss the noble English policemen. It is advised not to ask the soldiers; they are provincials, and know nothing. I find the priests most *suave* and agreeable, and they speak such French; for much of the jumble of the *badauds* is incomprehensible. French *men* do not compare with the English, but for one good-looking, graceful English woman, there are 800 French. I observe two marked classes of women : the peasantry, who work like horses and walk like oxen, and the Parisians, who are light,

graceful, and *bien mises*. French children are no touch to the
little angelic things of Kensington Gardens.

I wish you could get one glimpse of the Boulevards. Conceive of a curved street, a bow, of which the Seine forms the
bowstring. Make this twice as wide as Broadway. Line it with
lofty houses; set two rows of large trees in a sidewalk twice as
wide as the widest in New York; illuminate this like daylight;
fill it with thousands on thousands of holiday-people; imagine
cafés and restaurants with fronts all plate-glass, and interiors all
marble, mirror, and gold; then add chairs filling almost all the
space on the sidewalk, occupied by well-dressed people, eating
and drinking, and this nearly all night. Even the poor do every
thing in public view. Before a bit of a shoe-shop, the man,
woman, and children cut their loaf and hand about their bottle,
and clack, and bandy compliments, as if no mortal were near
them. This is repeated during this ambrosial weather every
few paces for miles. In the old quarters, near the Pont Neuf,
or Hotel de Ville, (town-house,) where the streets are about as
wide as a bed, the swarms of people look, I suppose, just as five
hundred years ago. They live on bread and wine. The bread
is weighed in the shops. I even see broken crusts sold. The
people live miserably inside of their houses. A tailor, for
example, has a bedroom up eight pair of stairs, and over the
river, and no sitting-room. His shop is all glass and gold. His
wife keeps a brilliant café, as idol or presidente; *i. e.* if she is
very handsome. After work-hours they are all the time in the
public gardens and places, breakfast and dine in the open air, and
look like Ahasuerus and Vashti; as Cobbett says: "pigs in the
parlour, peacocks on the promenade." Still these funny creatures
are full of "Monsieur" and "Madame," and full of gesture and
smiles. The genteel French people are perfectly graceful.
When I go to while away an hour over an ice, always accompanied by a whole decanter of ice-water, frozen around the inner
surface, I study the groups of three, four, and ten. They are
dressed to a marvel, as to fit, colour, and *mise*. They never
stare at you, or seem to know you are near. They have no
formal bows or motions. I observe nothing which would be
unusual in a first-class New York parlour, except a certain
smirk, arising from a feeling that one must always speak with a
smile. The people look American; for we get our fashions
here. The better sort, as in the Chamber of Deputies, (Cavaignac,
Lafayette, Lamartine,) are like very plain American gentlemen;
only some have a scarcely visible show of crimson ribbon in the
second top button-hole—the decoration of the legion of Honour.
Dr. Monod wears one. A. Monod is a beautiful, saintly man,

for elegant, primitive simplicity. Every Thursday he has a general reception, and probably does more good than by preaching. Prayers in French before tea. Fine singing from the " Chants Chretiens." I could not help thinking, at one of these soirées, I never saw so much simplicity, so much polish, and so much affection, mingled. My father would have been pleased with the sweet quietness of the girls. Almost all the conversation was religious.

Parisians hear music every hour for nothing, which it would take large sums to procure in America. I calculated that one might hear gratis thirty orchestras and 150 singers, any evening in the Champs Elysées. The music in the Madeleine, St. Roch, Notre Dame, St. Etienne, Notre Dame de Lorette, and St. Vincent de Paul, is *rococo*, and probably equal to any out of the Pope's chapel. The solos of a distant, lamenting female voice, *tremolo, minore, diminuendo,* contrasted with a crash of a hundred instruments, and then a hundred voices like Russell's, [deep bass,] and the interspersed *canto fermo,* or austere Gregorian chant, centuries old, combine with the *tableau vivant* of a priestly pantomime of purple and gold chasubles, (the mantle with cross,) and the yet more imposing long white flowing robe of cambric over pink, girt with pink—the young priests being picked for their figure—to make a bewitching show, which intoxicates poor female worshippers into a trance of ambiguous rapture, which they deem religion. I think the magic of anti-christian pomp has attained its acme. Poor Puseyism, compared with what it imitates, is but pewter to gold and rubies. They have made a separate *art* of the dressing and marshalling of hundreds of officiating persons, who move or stand with the height of solemn grace, and the overpowering combination of costume, the prelates, the priests in heavy purple or crimson, gilt—the younger clergy, imitating the white-robed angels of their pictures, the nuns, (most of them seemed crying, with swollen eyes,) the little boys in pure white, and the innumerable girls, in veils. I observed that men, who looked like emperors at the distant altar, were canal-men and bravos, when they passed me in the procession.

When an eminent speaker in the House of Commons said, this week, that none of the Dissenters went over to Popery, adding that the existing plan of Oxonian training tended to rear up Romanists, he uttered what any eye may see confirmed in Paris. Who would not, if he goes pomp-hunting, prefer the real old middle-aged mummery to the would-if-I-could-ish simulation of it? Frequent visits to Popish celebrations, must lead truly Protestant minds to doubt the possibility of giving any aid whatever to genuine worship, by the appliances of costly architecture, graphic representations, and elaborate music. "Christian Art," in the sense of the modern art-mad school, there is none. The highest philosophy of *cultus*—if the phrase may be allowed —leads to the most simple and apostolic rites.

It is high time that America and Britain were bestirring themselves to send light and leaven into this continent. M. Gasparin has lately given some frightful accounts of once evangelical Germany. Among his statements are these : Public worship is disregarded. In Berlin, out of four hundred thousand souls, there are three hundred thousand who never attend any of the thirty-two churches. Dr. Tholuck declares that, a few months ago, at Halle, in the principal service of the cathedral there were present fourteen persons ; in another church six, and in a third five ! Next day he attended a sermon, of which he was the only auditor ! The theatres are as full as the churches are empty. Is it wonderful, when we regard the tendency of German philosophy ? The papers of the tailor Weithing are published by the state authority of Zurich. Delecke makes fun of poor timid Voltaire and Diderot, "who never were prepared to look on man as the culminating point of existence." Marv and his fellows say :—" The *idea of God* is the key to the dungeon of mouldy civilization. Let us away with it. The true road to liberty, equality, and happiness, is atheism. Let us teach man that there is no God but himself." Wichern testifies that emissaries are out, that schools of atheism are founded very widely, under the guise of reading clubs and singing societies.

M. Thiers has made a speech against free trade, which, independently of the topic, is considered the greatest speech of the session. All the left side, his opponents, joined in the acclamation. I don't believe that Demosthenes ever showed more tact in "wielding the fierce democracy." His triumph as an orator is complete, though the question may go against him. This government feels itself in great danger. These amazing gatherings of soldiery show it. They are from distant provinces. Everywhere you see *casernes* taking the place of other buildings. People feel the mortification of this under a Republic. Two spies attend poor Mr. Close's little chapel ! The police is three-fold : 1, soldiers ; 2, police without uniform ; 3, unknown spies, (waiters, guards, valets, drivers, &c.) Thank God for our gospel and our freedom !

In the number of animals the Garden of Plants is surpassed by the London Zoological Gardens ; but what surpass its gardens, trees, walks, buildings, museums, fountains, and free lectures ? Constantly open to the people. Every tree of every climate ; all flowers of the world in numbers of enclosed gardens, with paths between; every plant labelled with the botanical name, and all arranged by families. The museums of natural history, the mineralogical and geological and paleontological collections of Cuvier, Hauy, and Jussieu, the collections of fossils and comparative anatomy, kept me perpetually wondering. The buildings are numerous and extensive. The Cedar of Lebanon, which is a colossal tree, repaid me for all my weariness. It is ten feet round, near the branches.

The palace of Versailles might occupy a volume. It would take a month to see it well. In my ignorance I thought all these palaces, with their grounds, not a hundredth part so extensive as they are. I did not figure to myself miles of avenue, trees of all zones, thousands of statuary, spaces so ample as to remind one of American forests and prairies, and chambers so numerous that the foot wearies before they are half traversed.

I attended a lecture on history in the College of Sorbonne. Entered the library, filled with quiet students reading; a priest presides. Library of St. Genevieve; what a place! Transcendent loftiness and beauty; 200,000 volumes; 100 reading; copy of Rafaelle's School of Athens as large as the side of a house.

On the 5th (July) I went to church, expecting to hear Monod. The old psalms did me good. The old Huguenot look was in some of the Frenchmen. Just before the second singing, a sparrow tried to get into a window over the pulpit. Immediately they sang Psalm lxxxiv. 3. The preacher was M. Enfoux, of Geneva. I dined at the table d'hôte; nineteen changes of plates. On my right, a Russian lady and four daughters; they spoke English, French, German, and Russ. On my left a party of fine English. I love to meet decent English people; you look in their faces and believe them. In the evening I went to Wesleyan chapel, and heard the minister, young Mr. Close, preach a beautiful orthodox sermon; full and able on original sin. About a hundred were there.

I sicken at the everlasting sight of bayonets and swords, and the feeling of espionage. There never was a stronger police under an autocrat. I am weary of speaking broken French, though the courtesy of every class passes description. So do the vastness, beauty, and keeping of public institutions. Fifty thousand persons are maintained in these charities. Under a polish, which reaches almost the lowest of the canaille, there is a godlessness which is horrible. Leaving out a few names in Sardis, blessed ministers and people, whose love seems the greater for insulation, this beautiful, matchless, glorious capital is Satan's seat. Words fail—paper must not aid—to report the moral rottenness of a generation brought up in bloody infidelity. The fear of God, producing truth, is lacking. Yet of ceremonious religion there is vast increase. The priests, in black garments, go about the streets. Yet evil as popery is, it owns a Saviour, prayer, a heaven and hell, and a God. There is a school growing rampant, which denies each or all of these.

The chief thought I had in these fairy-land palaces and Eden pleasaunces, was of the monarchs, and great ones, who had been violently torn from them; Louis XVI., Napoleon, Charles X., Louis Philippe. The chief thought as I gazed from the north balcony of St. Cloud on the incomparable view of Paris and the great spaces around and between, was, will God's justice suffer this wicked country to remain unvisited? The chief personal reflections were, I love American simple nature more than ever, and American freedom of religion more than any words can utter. I love and covet these matchless and incredible wonders less than my dear fireside; 1 less than ever wish ornaments for my church, or ornaments for my house. O for the purity and peace of Christ's religion for all I love!

DIJON, *July* 10, 1851.

To-day I have been in a fairy-land all the while. O la belle France! It is just the word. By stage I can understand how it might be very tedious, but by luxuriously rapid and well-appointed rails, it was just the sliding of one ravishing picture over another. A few elements in bewitching combination—this is the secret of French landscape. The time is favourable. Every thing is in its glory. The early part of the day we were almost always dashing through the valley of some river. The valley is a prairie exactly; we see the gentle barrier on each side. Towards evening we began to be sensible of a great change. The scene became rugged. We went through tunnels of thousands of feet. Bare rocks expose themselves, and at length the basin (in which we seem always to be) shows around its further edge mountains and beginnings of what we are going to have anon. We pass the watershed, and are in a new world; every thing is changed. Geology, houses, dress, almost sky, seem new. I have come into the land of St. Bernard! I am in the heart of Burgundy, a dukedom greater than many realms. Every village has had some memory, all day long, but now we are nearing the central region of a country most famous. France is as green as England, and along here as much of a garden; but O how pensive from the total absence of cottages! Every inch is tilled except where perpendicular. No forest, but tens of millions of trees, all planted and very scattering, now in clumps, now in rows. I have certainly this day seen a hundred miles of poplars.

In the boundless champaign of tillage, they seem as necessary to the scene as the spires of Holland. Why am I so often reminded of Old Virginia? I will tell you. In England, or even New England and New York, the eye would behold the plain cut up by hedges, &c. Here, as in Virginia, though for a different reason, all is open. Yonder is a view of rolling land, descending rounded towards the river we are skirting. Ten thousand acres lie over the round haunch of the broad swell, as perfect a garden as I ever saw, but so mottled that every one of us compared it, over and over, to a bedquilt; a patch of wheat, a patch of rye, a patch of mustard, a patch of broom, a patch of walnuts, the ground of all being vineyard, vineyard, vineyard, in a green like distant Indian corn. Vineyards are exactly like pole beans of a certain height. In certain situations they are very beautiful, as to-day, when ever and anon they hang over the round bank of land next the horizon, like hanks of green yarn over a hedge. Observe, the prospect is so vast, and so unobstructed by trees, that fields look like squares of chess, only oblong, and no division breaks the continuity except a sweet, fairy-road, winding away among vines and wheat, with, it may be, a cart load of girls, all colours, under broad brims of straw, with pitchforks. We have seen miles of hay-making, with five hundred groups, no one of which would disgrace a picture of Claude. You know all the people live in villages. These villages, at this season of deep verdure, seem always to be nestling. You wonder how the houses can squat and huddle so. They cluster around the little church, like sheep around the ram, as close, as irregular. All are of a colour, rusty russet red, tops are same as sides. In themselves ugly and mean, as parts of a rapid landscape very snug and beautiful. What remembrances crowd in during 200 miles of road carrying one deep into the ancient feudal soil! Here were the Gauls; here was Cæsar; we have passed several towns named by him. Here were the barons and monks of the middle ages. Here were Burgundian princes, who were all but kings, and yonder are their castles, black with age and awfully frowning over the sweet peaceful soil. Here, as you approach Dijon, were the walks of Bernard's and of Bossuet's childhood.

Dijon! I now understand what an old rocky French town is. I never can describe it. Everybody here as fresh as Irish. I wonder at the hale, happy look of all. But we are high up; all the way from Paris to this vicinity, we have been going up the streams. Every thing in the air is like Lexington, [Virginia,] or Schooley's Mountain, [New Jersey.] At a glance we see we are in the old Burgundian capital. Quiet, pleasant old town. Our first visit was to the celebrated Museum. Men and girls are copying in the galleries. Among the signs of decreasing population, several churches are perverted to other uses—one is a corn-market, another a fruit-market, a third a fodder-market.

GENEVA, July 13—17, 1851.

The complexion, though we go south from Dijon to Geneva, gets clearer and clearer as we ascend, and I see many a blue eye, reminding me of the Germanic origin of the Burgundian stock. The ploughs have a wheel and four horses, and they plough very shallow. Great industry. Nobody looks unhealthy or suffering. Roses abound, and many times I meet peasants in the road, carrying each a rose in his mouth. The houses, as we gradually rose, assume a trace of the Swiss cottage, so that when I saw a real châlet, I was not surprised at all. The great wooden shoe looks crippling, especially on children. Thatch on almost every house, about nine inches thick, often covered with a deep moss. Thus must these higgledy-piggledy towns have looked 500 years ago. These plains are rich, and tempted warriors. Therefore the houses are thick and defensible. Therefore also the people gathered in villages. We began to see single cows led by a string, to crop along the road's edge. Cattle generally a reddish dun. Oxen yoked from the horns. The expanse of hay-fields or prairies amazed and delighted me. The swell of the land increased as we advanced, and with it the beauty of the prospect. "That great mountain" Jura, which we thus approached, is very long and very broad, made up of parallel ridges, together shaped like the back of a mighty ox. At certain turns we saw the peak of Mont Blanc, like amber. It is beyond Switzerland, being in Savoy.

We breakfasted at Champagnolle, having left Dijon at 3½ A. M. I am perpetually asking myself "can this be France?" when I look at the beautiful skins. True the hard workers burn nearly mulatto, but the children and some women are of perfect red and white, and even the men show such blond that you wonder to hear French out of their mouths. In descending these sides, the valleys and gorges begin to assume more and more an amphitheatrical shape, and we found ourselves running sheer round the shoulder of great cliffs, with the depth opening green and solemn below, often with herds and cottages in the very fundus. How little did I expect to be so long crossing Mt. Jura, or to ascend it at a canter and almost a gallop. Ghylls or becks, little foaming streams, dashed across our way. Greater streams, white with rage, ran beside us. I remember one cascade of snow, which poured out of a field of emerald. It was young hemp. Every inch is rescued where a hoe can enter.

One sees hay-making girls, under broad flats, in a little rug of land, away over among the inaccessible rocks. The valleys have a green, which is black ; the very air seems changed ; the effect is not melancholy but an awful serenity. As we get more among proper mountaineers, cut off from the rest of mankind, it is pleasing to observe how the family feeling becomes more manifest. Fifty times I saw what I thought a family, on some knoll, by some spring, down some well-like plunge of green with a house at the bottom ; three sisters with broad Leghorn flats, and haymakers under a tree ; babies held by others little bigger, that the mothers might hoe or drive. No poetry or fiction can reach the reality of such scenes, occurring every moment, and amid such sights and such air.

On the beautiful evening of the 12th, we drove into lovely Geneva, a beauty in the midst of sublimity.[1] We have been greatly favoured in weather, for it is said that there are not more than fifty days in the year which furnish a perfectly clear view of Mont Blanc, and we have had three of them, and seen the full moon rise above it, which could only happen with great southing. As I now see it, it is rose-colour in one part, while, as the sun declines, the left-hand portion assumes a ghastly bluish pallor, which must remind every one of death. I had never thought much of this thing of hues. This very day (the 14th) as I was walking along the delightful avenue, skirting the south side of the lake to Dr. Merle's residence in Eaux Vives, I suddenly found the perspective ending in the placid Leman. But what a play of hues ! The foreground avenue all deep-green ; the nearer water pea-green ; the tilled lands just below, a veil of lilac ; the mountains beyond that a crystalline hue, shading off into pearly clouds and blue heaven.

Who would have thought, that Geneva could have been turned into such a stamping-ground ![2] The park or wood on the northern eminence is full of booths, stalls, shows, and gambling tables. The variety of gamblings is great. Women generally keep the tables, and children are inducted into the mysteries. Some are rolling balls for eatables ; some shooting a cross-bow at a target, over which a rude Liberty rises, on each shot, with the appropriate information that she purposes to go round the globe. Here are flying-horses, more rapid and comical than in Paris or anywhere else, having one row of whirlers within another, going not merely on horses, but on

[1] Dr. Alexander found great pleasure and assistance, during his Alpine travels, and to Heidelberg, in the company of the Rev. J. W. Newton, chaplain of the U. S. Navy, and formerly of the Edgehill School at Princeton.
[2] The *Tir Fédéral :* see page 148.

swans, sleigh-bodies, and so on. Here are lotteries, " ou l'on ne perd pas," and dice-playing, where you get gingerbread or knives. Here are booths of cirques, and jugglers, and posture-makers, most primitive in kind, and outvying Greenwich Fair. I never could have expected to see two such displays of un-American sportiveness.

Swiss politics is in much commotion about these times. Enjoying freedom for ages, except when the French had them under, they are nevertheless practised on by every sort of French and Italian refugee. What is in the mouths of every one about aristocracy, is very much like the same talk in France, during the years preceding the reign of terror. Yet, when I think of the past, when I look on the face of nature here, and especially when I contemplate the thousands of mountain men and women now in Geneva, so fresh, frank, hearty, honest, and Protestant, I hope strongly that God has something better in reserve for the sons of Tell, as they love to call themselves.

I have seen four priests going about in the black robes of their detestable order. There is a rookery of Jesuits here, and they have set the sisters of Charity a-going, as most likely to win our Protestants by acts of real humanity. The number of papists in Geneva is about 10,000. The more I see of the pomp of Romanism—and I have seen perhaps as much as could be seen out of Rome—the more I am in love with simple archi-tecture and simple worship.

GENEVA, *July* 19, 1851.

I have just returned here, fifty-one miles from Chamonix. It is summer, and European summer, without summer-clothes, summer debility, or summer insects. Geneva is full of English. Sir R. Peel is near me, and Lord Vernon and Lady Vane prob-ably in the house. Lord Vernon put twenty balls in the centre of one of the targets the first day of the shooting match. The distant mountains interest me most; near by they are too cold, cloudy, and frightful. The sights one sees are somewhat, but nothing to the millions of thoughts which the sights awaken. The sights are only the keys; the thoughts are the music. Many a mark is in E.'s Bible of spots, where I have read God's words under the tremendous shadow of mountain walls reaching to heaven, and by torrents pure and beautiful, leaping and foaming down the perpendicular but broken sides of deep vales. The dark, but clear atmosphere, caused by the elevation, the un-paralleled verdure, the shadow of giant mountains, and the play of altogether novel lights and shades, affect me even more than the summits of the great Alps. I could slightly imagine the latter; the other is entirely beyond every descriptive power. I have thought of an eclipse; but there is no melancholy. It is a serene, heavenly awe. The very potato blossoms look pearly, and shine like some sort of brilliant exotic. This shows that it is the air and light which produce the effect. The imminent and terrific passes and paths make even the horse and mule different from ours. In precipitous ascents, when the driver dismounted, the stout muscular horses took the carriage up as well without him. As to the mules, their footing is next to a miracle. They always take the outside edge, and go boldly along places more difficult than the bowsprit of a ship.

It was almost like home when I reached Geneva. With its lake, its suburban parks and *campagnes,* its nearer hills, and its Alps in view, it is the loveliest place I know. Mr. Newton and I united in thanking God for the wonders of these three days, and for good tidings from home. " Let the God of my salvation be exalted."

The horrible priest-riding of the kingdom of Savoy, smites me everywhere. The priests are the largest, finest, and fattest. The churches are solid and often modern.

O how a bell resounds in the green Alps! The crosses are as frequent as milestones. If the Virgin could weep, it would be to see the puppets and frights which represent her in the wayside shrines. Swiss families seem to love one another with intensity. They love all their little livestock. What a blessed land do you and I live in, where poor woman is not turned into a beast! I am sure I have seen girls of fourteen, carrying as much straw or green branches as would fill a cart. Their heads are used for this. I saw one woman carrying thus a closed umbrella, and another a heavy pick-axe. My soul is weary of soldiers. The sight of a soldier or a priest makes me first angry, and then sorrowful. As I surveyed the boundless arable lands on the slopes of the mountains, which contain the lower Arve, all one map of varying meadow, garden, and harvest, unincumbered by fences, dotted with sweet cottages, sprinkled with trees and vines, without a square foot in a state of nature, I remembered the numberless wars between Savoy and Geneva. And when I looked at the soldiers, and listened to the fierce, radical politics, and the sounds of rifle-shooting at the grand national match, I was made sure that unless God interpose, all this sweet land will be given up again to fire and blood. Yet these Swiss of the great cantons are a noble race. It was doubt-less the best of them I saw here, during the great democratic celebration. The mountain-girls, in costumes of every cut, were fresh as roses and brawny as boxers. The middle of the streets was their walk. Not a loud word, nor a disorderly gesture. To tell the truth, they looked American to me, and I laid it to (1) Republicanism, and (2) to Protestantism; but rather of their fathers than their own.

Here the wheat-harvest is in its glory. I looked out on rising, and saw a company of young men and lasses going a-field. Their sickles were all fantastically ranged around a staff, surmounted with a grand bouquet, and borne aloft by one in the middle. They make a play of every thing.

VEVAY, *July* 21, 1851.

We arrived at Vevay by steam from Geneva on the 19th, in order to spend the Sabbath in one of the loveliest, quietest towns in Europe. From the bank here, we look into the rounding of the lake, and see the castle of Chillon. We took a calèche, and visited it on Saturday. Without an interval this road is walled the whole way. It has on the right the lake-shore, vineyards to the very edge, and on the left, the swelling round mountains, vineyards to the very top. So populous is this region, that it is like one village all the way. Vevay is celebrated by Rousseau as the most enchanting spot on earth, and I see no reason to the contrary. The old cathedral is the chief Protestant church. The building bears date 1498. Alas! the gospel of the Reformers who occupied it, is not preached there in French, but in English. I heard one of the most blessed gospel-sermons, of the Simeon sort, from an Anglican chaplain, Mr. Cleves; John v. 42. About sixty English were present. It was a refreshment to my weary soul, which I shall remember all my days. When I came out, and looked from under the perfect shade over vineyards, town, lake, and nearer hills, to the silvery, heaven-like Alps, on a day of great clearness, with temperature making cloth dress indispensable, I trust my heart experienced some of God's sure mercies, and I was reminded that his covenant is more durable than the Alps, which must crumble away. The people are in great contrast to the mountaineers of Savoy. They are a ruddy, industrious, teeming, happy generation. The illusory view of a tourist is that they know no care.

On Saturday evening, at dusk, the streets and neighbouring roads were full of people, coming in from the vines, and sitting at their doors. A most wonderful *yodler* sang in the court, in the Alpine manner. It is as indescribable as inimitable, and does not sound like a human organ. The peasantry drink wine as freely as we drink water, but intemperance is very rare. Bread and wine are the universal meal. I am surprised to see how little flesh is used, even in twenty courses, at table d'hôte.

Indeed I think the air and climate lessens one's taste for it.
There is no end to the confections. Their cakes are always dry,
crisp, and macaroony. I am sure I have tasted 200 kinds in
France and Switzerland. Warm bread is unknown.

LUCERNE, July 25, 1851.

From Vevay I went to Berne, a stern old Protestant town,
more noble in my view from my having just come out of Freiburg, the chief Catholic canton. The Jesuits are in full blast
there. I have no expectation of ever seeing. such farms, such
crops, such peasantry, such houses, and such babies as I saw in
Berne. The châlets equalled all my best forethoughts, and
erased the ill impressions of the Savoy Alps. Millions of bee-
hives in these vales and heights. Morning or evening the honey
is never absent.

We entered Lucerne the 24th. The country people of Lucerne
are not to be compared with those of Berne, whom I continue to
think the finest yeomanry I ever saw. We took a little steamboat yesterday, to survey the lake Lucerne, which, in the opinion
of Sir James Mackintosh and others, is the noblest lake in Switzerland, i. e. in all the world. I read Schiller's "William Tell"
among the very scenes it describes. The spirit of liberty waked
up in me very strong at Rütli, the green ledge, where in 1307
the three Swiss conspirators met to free their country ; at
Flüchen, by Altorf, where Tell shot the apple ; at the chapel
where he leaped ashore out of Gessler's boat ; and in view of
Küssnacht, near which he slew Gessler. Five hundred years
have not taken away the interest of the Swiss in these mighty
deeds. At least three men, of whom two were quite common,
indicated the localities to me, and the third told me the whole in
English, with tears in his eyes. The music of the Lucerne
church-bells is beyond any thing I have yet heard. Many of
the people speak Italian, but most a horrible German patois.
The Jesuits have a college here, and go about like princes.

ZÜRICH, July 26, 1851.

Here I am, Deo favente, in the old Protestant city of Zuingle.
We came from Lucerne in about 7½ hours across the Mt. Albis.
We went through the canton of Zug ; all Papists : but I saw no
such horrendous life-size images of our Lord crucified as abound
and stare at you in Lucerne. Crossing this little canton, we
entered the sweet, rich, green, Protestant land of Zurich. The
road went round and round the mountain (Albis) in successive
platforms, for a length uncommon even in Switzerland, so that
this enchanting paysage was every moment coming up afresh,

all lying flat and long and wide before us, so as to remind me of what they tell concerning views from a balloon. I begin to feel quite German since I slept under a feather-bed, and paid my bill in Gulden and Kreutzers. Our removes were nine : Soup ; bouilli and carrots ; trout ; tripe with oily mashed potatoes ; cherry fritters, with the stems sticking out ; volaille with lettuce ; strawberries dressed with wine and cinnamon ; cherries, cakes, &c. ; a bottle of white wine at each plate.

On Sunday I went to the cathedral where Zuingle preached. The church is awkwardly divided by a rude ill-painted screen through both nave and aisles, and is seated with deal forms, with backs, marked and numbered but unpainted. There is no paint, except some daubing at the pulpit end. I saw and heard no organ. About 200 persons seemed little where 2,000 might have been. I saw one man besides myself in the nave. A few old men sat along the side walls. One gentleman was near the platform. Two men were on it at the preacher's right ; about six singers at his left ; these were led by a blind young man, who read the hymn from a large book with raised letters. He is an admirable singer. They sang twice, but only one tune. The peasant women, who made up the assembly, sang almost perfectly. Every one had her black and gilt book, with a folded white handkerchief. The tune was ancient and slow. All sang, and all stood up in prayer. The preacher was in gown and bands. The sermon was on the fear of God, and seemed to be an attempt to be very pathetic upon mere moralities. The women almost all slumbered and slept. I saw whole rows thus exercised. The service was one hour ; viz. : 1. Hymn, (sitting.) 2. Prayer—read by the preacher standing. 3. Sermon, (he stopped at each head, turned round and employed a blue handkerchief.) 4. A prayer read, (Lord's prayer at close of both.) 5. Hymn. Minister then immersed himself in a hat, and people retired. I recognized no benediction. On retiring, some of the poor women bought fine cherries at the foot of the steps. A deader service, out of Quaker meeting, I never saw. No wonder they have forgotten Zuingle's name. The University here has about forty professors and more than 300 regular students ; but the *Cantonalschule*, like a [German] Gymnasium, has 400.

HEIDELBERG, *July* 31, 1851.

I left Zurich on the 28th for Basel. Some of the villages on the road were the worst I have seen. Dunghills all along the streets. They are just in wheat harvest, and the valley of the Rhine is one sea of corn and sheaves ; the more striking from the absence of fences and roads. All the people seem to be out. Old men sit among the sheaves. There are more women than men at the work, and babies lie about in abundance. The approach to the Rhine naturally awakened me. At first sight I compared it with the Passaic at Newark, but I soon thought it more like the Shenandoah. The flow of the stream is majestic. We entered Basel as the eclipse of the sun declined. It was my first view of mighty walls of the middle ages, though I have seen many walled towns. The first stork I saw at the place where we dined.

We left Basel in omnibus, and took rails at Heiltingen for Freiburg. Crossing the Rhine takes me out of sweet Switzerland into Germany—the Grand Duchy of Baden skirting the east bank of the Rhine. I now go fully into German-speech. At Berne it began, but it has been mixed, everywhere the two languages and always English at the inns. The headman at Lucerne spoke English, French, Italian, German, and Dutch. He is a Hollander, and says he learned them by grammars, in order to be a waiter.

Freiburg is a Romish town with a small University. It borders on the Black Forest, which, in truth, is a mountain-range, covered with firs, some of which are 120 feet high. The cathedral greatly impressed me. The sculptures exceeded my thoughts. The tower, 380 feet high, all of stone, looked like a delicate and graceful nothing against the mountains or the sky. Living water flows in wide streams through all the streets. It is a healthy but wintry place. We left it (on the 30th July) by railway to Kehl ; by omnibus to Strasburg Cathedral ! Leaving S. in the afternoon, we passed Rastadt and Carlsruhe, and entered Heidelberg just after dark.

Kenilworth is a plaything compared with the mountain-castle of the old Electors. Old ruins and new erections ; walls twenty feet thick in places; twenty rooms at least with shrubbery full-grown in them ; vaults and dungeons; towers, half fallen, where you have the city under your very feet, and a champaign country all gold and green, now falling before the mowers and reapers. There are about 650 students here. They swagger through the streets with little caps of every hue. The rowdyism of the boys passes belief. An apprentice let loose is a feeble comparison. The number of professors and lecturers is seventy. Many of these get not more apiece than a New York coachman. In the Medical Faculty some zeal is apparent. There are two courses of Medical Jurisprudence ; one for jurists, and one for medical men. There are lectures on the History of Medicine, on diseases of the aged, and on many subdivisions of anatomy and therapeutics.

I left Heidelberg on the 1st. Tnough nominally at Frank fort, I did not really see any thing of the place. I saw a good many troops, and one corps in white uniform, who were prob ably Austrians. Biberich, where I took boat, may be called the port of Wiesbaden. When I got to Cologne about 10 P. M.. my trunk was missing. All inquiries proved fruitless.[1] A gentleman condoled with me, and offered to lend me from his wardrobe. I afterwards found it was Lord Dudley Ward. Visited the cathedral; more than a hundred men are working in sheds at the costly carvings. That which most struck me in the interior is its awful grandeur, its vast extent. The Papists grow zealous in proportion as the Protestants have become erroneous and indifferent, and are regaining their hold on the young. In the cathedral I saw rows after rows of girls deeply engaged in devotions, in the side chapels. I dare not give the proofs I have of lax morals in the towns; the natural consequence of forsaking God.

The streets of Cologne are narrow, crooked, dirty, and without sidewalks. The filth of German inns is inexpressible; yet the linen and beds are fine. Bread is capital, so is butter, which I have never seen salted in Europe.

Since I left Paris, I have seen no painting that moved me so much as one at the Museum here—" the Jews at the willows of Babylon," by Bendeman, of Dresden. Cologne delights me with its Roman ruins and inscriptions, its labyrinth of old lanes, toppling houses, indescribable courts and markets, and quaint edifices. Yet I long to see our own fresh and progressive cities; to see a land where there are no guards, watch-towers, passports, and over-worked women. Poor things! their furrowed mahogany faces, their gray hair streaming from whimsical head-dresses, often make me muse sadly.

I was in the great cathedral on a high day. The vaulted roofs resounded with an orchestral mass. A great number of instruments, joined with a grand organ, performed one of the most learned masses. But by far the most impressive part was purely vocal, and plain chant, all in one part, often by boys; the performers being visible in stalls around the choir. I was very near the Archbishop of Cologne, who is also a great prince. The Priests' seminary, near by, has 400 young priests. I was at the Jesuits' church, which is fine; also at St. Peter's, chiefly remarkable for an altar-piece, the apostle's crucifixion, which Rubens esteemed his best work. The only Protestant church,

[1] The trunk was not recovered until August 8, at Rotterdam.

borrowed from the Romanists, is for the soldiers here who happen to be Protestants. I saw yesterday (the Sabbath) a wonderful procession around St. Martin's church. It was St. Martin's day. Purple and gold, incense and tapers, chanting and mummery. I cannot describe the agony of devotion I often see in German Catholics, especially in old women and young girls, with their rosaries, &c. In my humble view a generation is growing up most craftily trained in every popish delusion. The German popery is altogether a different thing from that of France and Italy. The very advertisements on church-doors breathe a spirit of profound tenderness. God grant that some of the poor priest-ridden souls may find the true cross!

I attended the Episcopal service at the British Consulate. There were sixty present, apparently people of some mark. It was Puseyitish. The priest backed the people, had an Oxford cap, moved here and there, and had much mumming over the elements of the offertory. Twenty-one communed.

AMSTERDAM, *August* 5, 1851.

From Cologne in steamer Rubens for Arnhem in Holland —the charmingest town for elegant neatness. We really know nothing of interior Holland in America. The East India trade enriches hundreds of men, who live at home, in a quiet grandeur, like Quaker princes. The fronts of some houses are just like white porcelain. The landscape gardening is English. The windows are the most chastely elegant; adorned with little screens of Berlin-work, embroidery, or costly Japan. Apropos, the Japan trade is all with the Dutch. Of Java tin, a sale was yesterday made, (two million guilders,) all to a fellow-traveller and acquaintance of mine. The Dutch complexion is even better than the English; and the people are quiet and happy. The seaports are indeed like others, and Amsterdam is filthy; its canals smell like bilge water; but Utrecht is like an island in a sea of tranquil academic verdure. I spent some delightful hours (in U.) traversing the China-like streets, the water-side-walks, and the cool still University and Library. Mr. Ader, the librarian, was all attention; spoke English, German, French, Dutch, and Latin. All the theological lectures in Holland are in Latin; the medical in Dutch. Utrecht is the seat of so-called orthodoxy. Leyden and Groningen are liberal. There are about 5,000 Jansenists in Utrecht. Of the 200,000 population of Amsterdam 30,000 are Jews. There are 600 windmills. The Philadelphia "State House" is plainly a reminiscence of the palace. The very name is the same. I feasted my eyes at the Museum with paintings of the Dutch school, which gave me the same pleasure in comparison with Guido and Rafaelle, that Boz does in comparison with Milton. The country we passed is a perfect flat. Think of the meadows near Newark, [New Jersey;] make these perfect green or yellow velvet; remove all fences; intersect with narrow and broad canals full to the green edge; cover them with myriads of cattle, always black and white; dot them with low white houses; extend this plain till the windmills all along the horizon look like chessmen; add flowers, clean peasants, and storks, and you have Holland. There is no country but America so belied as this. It is the only country I have thought I could live in. Arnhem, for example, is a little city of trim, lovely houses, pure streets, green parks, ramparts turned into promenades, and an appearance of wealth among the retired East India merchants which was new to me. But Utrecht gratified me yet more. Its hotel meets every demand of the most fastidious quietist. Though very large, it is so quiet that I never saw or heard another guest in it. The women going by were all dressed like a play, in clean caps, longish short-gowns, and black petticoats. All looked like toy milk-maids.

In Holland people smoke at the dinner table, smoke while eating melons, smoke while setting the table. In Leyden nothing moved me more than the remembrance of Boerhaave. I came away with reluctance from his speaking portrait. It has some traits of our Franklin, but more heart and more love. I stood by his simple memorial in St. Peter's.

"SALUTIFERO

BOERHAVII

GENIO

SACRUM."

On a basrelief medallion likewise the legend *Sigillum veri simplex.* We were shown about the University by Prof. Dozy, to whom Dr. Robinson had letters. They have only one term and the holidays are now. The library has 1,631 oriental MSS., exclusive of Hebrew. Dozy has published one volume of a catalogue of these MSS. At the University I ascended the desk where Witsius often held his acts. But the Senate Hall is a place which, Niebuhr says, has no equal for academic memories. It contains 108 portraits of Leyden professors.

We visited Siebold's Japan Collection, the only complete one in Europe. He was eight years in Japan, and one of these in prison. The " Museum van Oudheden " carried me back to Egypt, Carthage, and Etruria. Mummies of babies, who died 3,000 years ago. The Museum of Natural History has a world-wide fame. In ornithology and comparative anatomy, it beats Paris. Whole droves of skeleton genera, from an elephant to a mouse. The rector of the Leyden University is Dr. Nicholas Christian Kist. The Theological Professors are Kist, Van Hen gel, Van Oordt, and Scholten. Add, from the Philosophical Faculty, Rutgers, who reads on Exegesis, Antiquities, and San scrit ; Juynball, on Hebrew and Arabic, and Stuffken on Logic. According to a hasty enumeration the Professors amount to thirty-three. Both at Utrecht and Leyden, the libraries are in buildings devoid of all costly display. At Leyden the accommodation for books is altogether insufficient. Leyden is the only place where we have seen bills advertising students' rooms, in Latin ; several windows held out *cubicula locanda*. But the medical lectures are already in Dutch, and the theologians will soon be forced to follow the example of Germany. Customs, however, take deep root in Holland, and one sees many usages which are known in Bergen and Somerset [New Jersey]. In our inn at Utrecht—the neatest and most home-like I ever entered—five footstoves were in our breakfast room ; and there were at least twenty in a pile beside the door of the great lecture-room. In one of Wouverman's celebrated paintings at the Hague, we observed the same implement, of the same fashion, even to the rhomboidal cup for the charcoal, which always belongs to the *Vuur Stoof*. The same persistency might be exemplified in window-mirrors, storks, health-bulletins, and the clerical-looking undertaker, who invites to funerals in a dress as dignified as a bishop's. Take it altogether, Holland, in its rural portions, gave me such unexpected pleasure, that my chief regret is that I had only a passing glance.

Of the moral and religious state of Holland, I must refer you to more authoritative statements, which may be expected at the Evangelical Alliance next week, in London. A hurrying visit, like mine, to inns and galleries, does not give much insight beyond the surface ; every word I write on this head must be subject to correction. We were of one mind in thinking that evangelical religion had not sunk in Holland so much as in Germany and Switzerland. A pious and intelligent officer, high in the service, declared to me his belief that the persecution of the Separatists was at an end. They abound in the province of Groningen, where also lax divinity is most rife. The Heidelberg Catechism is too much supplanted by abridgments, but is still regularly preached on. Many good people in the National Church contribute to the support of the pious Separatists. My informant himself does so ; and further expressed his belief that thousands of the common people hold fast to the divinity and atonement of our Lord. At the same time great coldness and formality are prevalent, as in Scotland under Moderatism. But the churches are full, and the people have that Protestant and

Presbyterian look, which is in contrast with what one sees on the upper Rhine. The works of the great poet and historian Bilder-dijk are read with affection. His admirer and friend Dacosta is well known as an evangelical believer. Yet the book-shops reveal a portentous preference for German, and especially for French literature, and the days of vernacular Dutch theology seem to be over. Many versions of English practical works are for sale; and at the Hague, in an open market, we found a tract-man vending Christian broad sheets and little books, of which I will show you a sample. Hopes are entertained that measures will soon be taken to restore in part the freer action of the Classical and Synodal Courts.

THE HAGUE, August 6, 1851.

I do wish I could for one instant show you a Dutch town. You will never believe me if I describe it. Broeck, as every-body knows, is the cleanest place on earth; we failed to reach it, but know that there is neither horse nor cart road, that every pipe must have a stopper, that the pavements are in figures like mosaic, and the gutters running with pure water. English comfort is not so cosy, nor so universal. The Dutch of this city are the best-dressed people I have seen; fashion without finery, and plainness without dirt. Positively, whole rows of houses look more like china-ware than bricks and mortar. The Hyde Park of Haag is called the Bosch. It is a forest, two miles long, with a square green parade in the middle. For imitation of nature it surpasses the English parks. Dr. Robinson says it beats the Thiergarten of Berlin, and that of Munich. What music I have heard there just now at sunset! All the better sort of people seemed to be walking there, but orderly and com-posed. Holland is not seen to advantage by Americans who hasten up the Rhine. All my days shall I remember Arnhem, with Vevay, Eton, and Heidelberg. True, I felt the contrast more after three days in Cologne, of which Coleridge says—

> "Ye nymphs who reign o'er sewers and sinks,
> The river Rhine, it is well known,
> Doth wash your city of Cologne;
> But tell me, nymphs, what power divine
> Shall henceforth cleanse the river Rhine?"

The Hague, as a royal residence, adds a subdued splendour to the Dutch neatness. I do not therefore take it as a sample of Hol-land. The streets are clean. The canals are not so intersecting as at Amsterdam, which is cut into 95 islands. The houses are peculiar, but neat. Much marble is used for the whole pave-ments of halls, and for the trottoirs in a few places. The bricks are so thin, and the white pointing so exact, and the paint of the wood-work so redoubled and polished, and the plate glass so large, that the fronts have an indescribable porcelain look. It is like the quietest parts of Third street [Philadelphia] thirty years ago, with a great addition to finish.

The Hollanders drink tea, which is very fine, and comes from Java. The quantity of East India furniture, japan-ware, &c., in Holland is very great. The little frames, which lift up with the sash, are very pretty. They conceal the people spying out of the *spions*, or mirrors. I used one of these mirrors at Leyden, and could sit and see a great way up the street. They have an admirable linen curtain, which a simple cord pulls up, in fanfolds; very cheap and pretty. Every parlour-window looks beautiful from outside.

LONDON, August 19, 1851.

I arrived here in the night of the 9th, in twenty-two hours from Rotterdam. The English being poor sailors avoid this by preferring Ostend, or even skirting along to Calais. I would not have missed the voyage for much. As soon as I got to the noble Boompje of Rotterdam, and saw the Indiamen, and flags of all nations, and the " General Washington of Alexandria," better-looking than them all, I began to take courage. A sniff of sea-air revived me after the unutterable stench of the canals, and every breath of the German sea did me good. We had more than 100 passengers, besides 108 calves. N. B. The veal of Holland is peculiar and a rarity. They serve it as the *bonne-bouche* ; it is as white and delicate as chicken. I could not say with Voltaire, " Adieu canards, canaux, canaille ! " I shall always love Holland ; the more for that it took me unawares. Amsterdam and Rotterdam are all over like Chatham St. [New York] and South street [Philadelphia] combined. Amsterdam is alive with Jews, who seem the mobile part of the population. Erasmus's statue at Rotterdam is in the very midst of a throng, not one whit above the Market street [Philadelphia] fishmarket, and we could scarce approach it for the folks taking down their movable stalls. Boats lie almost touching the really grand old image. The immense cathedral, frowning over the whole, is begirt with dark, musty shops, such as America has none of. The Boompje, or great maritime street, is a wide quay on the Maes, (the Rhine has here lost its name,) and is lined with such trees as are in the Philadelphia State House yard. But the heaviest shipping penetrates by canals into the very heart and bowels of the city, and is unloaded at the doors of stores.

What most pleased me in Holland, was to see how different

the lot of woman is from that of the sex in France and Germany.
Here are no women carrying heavy loads, or doing men's work.
Indeed, the Hollanders have a hundred devices to save the very
men.   Horses and carts abound in their fields.   There are thousands of dog-carts ; and wind and water are levied on for every
kind of work.   In Holland.the chief reading, if I may judge by
the bookstores, is first of French, then of German, then of
English.   This is unfavourable.   Col. S. says the Separatists are
no longer persecuted ; that the people would not bear it.   He
thinks most of the poor country people retain sound doctrine.
The rationalists are city-men and professors, and even these do
not openly impugn the doctrines of grace.   The churches are
largely attended ; which differs from Germany.

Here, in the thick of old London, a stone's throw from
Milk street, in Cripple-gate Within, it is as quiet as a New
England village.   In the evening after my arrival, coming by the
little old church of St. Mary's in the street (Aldermanbury) of
our first lodgings, I saw lights and could even discern the preacher,
whose motions indicated earnestness.   I slipped in near the further door.   The preacher, a middle-aged man, was very warmly
engaged on Hebrews i. : "Thy throne, O God," &c.   He had
not uttered many sentences, before I found him to be evangelical.
His third point was on the perpetuity, his fourth on the glory
of Christ's Divine kingdom.   He read part, but added much ex
tempore, reading his numerous and fervent citations from a little
Bible lying beside his MS.   The application was full of point and
unction.   Coming just from the depths of popery and neology,
and from the tossings of the German sea, I enjoyed as much as
Jonathan when he found the honey-comb, and my eyes were
lightened.

On the 13th we got into very good snug quarters at 34 Great
Ormond street, Queen's square, Lamb's Conduit street.   I went
to survey Billingsgate.   It is well, for they are putting up a lofty
pile to supersede the old classical place.   The fish-people were
more decent than I expected.   Crossing several vessels, I boarded
one of the oyster-sloops, and got acquainted with the skipper.
He ordered up some oysters for me to taste, such as sell for
thirty-two shillings a bushel.   They have a high flavour, and are
small, round, flat, and not clustered.   Larger ones, for nine
shillings, are coarse and repulsive.

As I walked up Cheapside I met a school of little girls,
belonging to some old foundation; brown petticoats, white capes,
caps and pinafores ; little old women of a former age.   One can
scarcely walk about in London, without seeing some token of the
numerous charities of a better day.   The supply of churches in

the " City " unquestionably surpasses that of any town on earth.
You sometimes pass a dozen in a five minutes' walk, almost
every one bearing a name of history. To-day I came all of a
sudden on St. Swithin's lane and church, and looked about for
London Stone. I came near missing it, for an idle fellow, lean-
ing against the wall of the church, entirely covered it. I feel a
strange interest in the very old part east of the Monument, i. e.
the part untouched by the fire of 1666. Some of the houses
look as if Wiclif and Chaucer might have lived in them. I
went to St. Paul's, and heard some of the cathedral singing.
Then I perambulated the great precincts. Two statues held me
long, and I went back to them—Dr. Johnson and John Howard;
and both are by John Bacon, the pious sculptor. Johnson's is a
noble work of art, though the idea is ancient, being neither more
nor less than a Hercules. As to the rest, I grew weary of
attempts to ring the changes on Victory supporting a dying hero.
Emblematic and allegoric sculpture has done me no good.

The corner house opposite our lodgings is a gin-palace, brilliant
as day. The next, a vintner's. The next, opposite to us, is a
sweet dairy shop. Most of the other houses in this Sansom-like
[Philadelphia] street, are private. I have scarcely been able to
write for the delicious street music. No music has given me
such soothing pleasure, as what I have heard by chance. The
gin-palace has a stream from dusk onward—boys, women with
infants, smart young women, errand people. I see sad signs of
drink in London, on a closer inspection. No drunkards abroad
—the police see to that—but men and women muddled, and in
that sleepy state which daily imbibing secures.

There is, in my judgment, a rancorous envy of America
very general in a certain English class, and that a very large one.
They lose no chance of laughing at the American part of the
Exhibition, and ringing changes on Mexico, Slavery, &c. This
is mingled with a certain dread and respect, which is flattering
to us, but only implied. They think our cleverness amazing.
Mr. Bull is somewhat slow to take an idea. Certain things in the
American Exhibition will run all over England before they have
done funning at us. For example, McCormick's threshing-
machine will cut down hundreds of English harvests. A ruling-
machine sets the stationers aghast. In the care of the soil and
the housing of crops, and the saving of land and produce, we
are very far behind them, but as far before them in tools and
quick work. The American cradle is itself a century in advance
of the old corn-growing countries. I travelled hundreds of miles
through actual harvests. The sickle was universal, (so here also,)
and the work slow, though neat. Ploughs and harrows were going

for the next crop, while the wheat was in the shock or wagon; but nine-tenths of the ploughs I saw on the continent were shallow things, drawn by oxen or cows, and with a wheel. In Holland, things are more as in Somerset and Bergen, [New Jersey.]

The Christian Evangelical Alliance meets on the 20th, and lasts twelve days. I do not expect to go, after their acts concerning American slave-holders. I declared to Dr. Hamilton that whatever my private opinions were on slavery, I would sit in no body where my Southern brethren were excluded, and that I would not submit to any inquisition by English Dissenters.

LONDON, *August* 22, 1851.

It is impossible to give an idea of the way the street-people talk. It is not this or that word, but all the words; and hardly a name fails of some change. "Go by the Fondlin' sir, ye'll see no turnin' to put ye out, till ye git to Lamb's Cundick"—"theng' ye"—"hit's a good 'apenny"—"ye'll bean American." Mr. ——, when I ask after his family, always says: "Nicely! I assure you."

I am now familiar with the sight of liveries, uniforms, and odd costumes. Postmen, servants, soldiers, proctors, bishops, some clergymen, coachmen, beadles, charity-scholars, wagoners, appear in a dress peculiar to each. The low population is very vile.

The opening of the Evangelical Alliance on the 20th was the most elevated season of devotion I ever attended. I stayed from ten till two. It was a great prayer-meeting at Freemason's Hall. I had some delightful chat with Noel. Dr. R. Buchanan, of Glasgow, read an address of an hour, full of Presbyterian good sense. The Rev. Ed. Bickersteth (the son) made an address so full of modesty, humility, and love, that every one felt like embracing him. He is pale, small, and plain, but so simple, John-like, scholarly, and winning, that I rejoiced that the church of England had such men. When he alluded to his father, all the house was in tears. In this the English assemblies are just like the Virginians. There were three hymns and three prayers. The first hymn was,

"Come, let us join our cheerful songs."

Another was Psalm 133, old version. The whole look of the assembly is English. So many stout, ruddy men; more [than English] uncouth, peculiar faces; more ugliness, greater strength, health, and play of countenance. Occasionally I would see a swarthy, sour-looking one, like me; he was always a Frenchman. Sir Culling E. Eardley, Bart., was made President. He stepped up gaily; a fresh, smiling little man; youngish; green frock, yellow waistcoat, white trousers, checked neck-cloth, brown gloves, and umbrella under arm while he spoke. The meeting was more familiar than with us. The speeches were numerous, and generally short; kindly, but often poor and sometimes very awkward. The sing-song tone of some was comical enough. The more educated and gentleman-like spoke most like Americans. A churchman, who offered an extempore prayer with open eyes, is the only Englishman whom I have heard say *kyīnd* and *gyīde.* Sir Culling says "urgin', givin', utterin', also *illustret, vindikēt.* The meeting, which was very long, was one of animation, devotion, and many tears. There was much clapping of Bickersteth, and some " hear ! hear ! " Next day (21st) I heard Mr. Noel's address at the Alliance. His manner is very easy, quiet, and perfectly colloquial. But he was never animated, and seldom made a gesture.

My ticket at the Tower showed that I was the 4,002d visiter yesterday. At the Alliance to-day I entered the house when they were discussing a paper of Dr. Baird's, which I have not seen, but which is said to have been sound and patriotic. My name was mentioned by the President, Sir Culling E. Eardley, and I was suddenly asked whether I would consent to meet a Committee on the subject. Much surprised, I nevertheless replied as follows:

" ' I have been present, Sir Culling, only as a respectful and affectionate visiter, and am under obligations to leave town to-morrow.'

" *Sir Culling E. Eardley.* ' At what hour ? '

" ' That question, let me answer, seems to imply that there is some hour in which I would engage in such a discussion. We, Sir Culling, who have preached to the slave, and stood by the slave in his dying moments, know too well the agitations which a question so complicated with other interests can produce. I have joined in the prayers, and at a remote part of the circle, in the praises of this festival of Christian love ; and for one I am not willing to introduce an element into these conversations, which, happily, has been thus far absent; and not willing to engage in any gladiatorial exhibition on the subject of American slavery.' "

The spirit of certain Independent and Baptist members of the Alliance is quite offensive. I would not give place to such, by subjection; no, not for an hour. Some of the Church of England men and the best heads of the Free Church, are willing to hear the facts and to discuss the matter candidly and fraternally.

Lime-street, famous in theology,[1] is a narrow, crooked alley. The number and closeness of the old churches is surprising. The day was when great regard was had to the spiritual wants of London. If the Non-conformist Reformation had not been quenched by war and by Cromwell, this home-missionary zeal would have made London the glory of England, and England of the world. As it is, the star has gone westward. It is in America that the genuine principle of English Protestantism has expanded itself. The spirit of slumber has fallen on the titular Church of England, which has neglected God's poor. Little is to be hoped from the fiery fanaticism of political dissenters, who are constantly fevering themselves with some new excitement. God grant that American Christianity may go forward, with that life which I know so much better how to prize, after seeing the symptoms of moribund society here!

Street-shows and street-wonders would take up a book. This morning we had—1, a venerable gray-haired man, without hat, led by a dog, cantillating his woes; 2, a trio, Hindoo man and two children, one beating a drum-keg with his hands, and singing his ills; 3, a show of unknown contents, like a Swiss char-a-banc. Accompanied Dr. Robinson to the British Museum, the great object of my curiosity. We made at once for the antiquity gallery. Here are Layard's things. Most are figured in his books: the perfectly Caucasian and fine profile of the chief figures. The Egyptian faces show the Hindoo eye, unmistakably. Elgin Saloon! Models of the Parthenon as perfect, and as in ruins; representing even the friezes, metopes, and internal statue of Minerva. This is indeed the consummation of sculpture-art. Tangled, rumpled drapery, from the age of Pericles. My mind is made up in an instant. I am glad they are here. Here they are safe, and only here can they be examined nearly. Wonders on wonders in the Egyptian saloon, taking one back to the times of Moses.

On the 17th, I heard Dr. Hamilton on Col. iii. 16. Service 1 hour 45 minutes. Prayers long, before and after. Order thus: 1. Singing part of Ps. cxlvii. 2. Prayer. 3. Reading Col iii., ending with "The Lord bless his word." 4. Singing of Psalm cxlvii. continued. 5. The Lord's Prayer. 6. Sermon. 7. Singing of remainder of Psalm cxlvii. 8. Prayer. 9. Notices. 10. Blessing. The sermon was about an hour; was exuberant in similitude, and full of pathos. Altogether different from the one in June. Just like his "Mount of Olives." Manner warm; sermon read, but with interpolations. Gown and

[1] "The Lime Street Lectures," by Non-conformist divines, 1730–'31.

bands. Bible carried before him into pulpit. One of the deacons
acted as precentor. All sang, but in bad time, and amazingly
slow. I sat in a high pew, back, called the " Elders' pew." In
it was Dr. Brown, Greek Professor at Aberdeen, former Moderator of the Free Assembly. The house was built for Irving.
Some painted glass, on which the Scotch thistle and the burning
bush. Seats in the aisles, and rush of people after the first
prayer. Next day had good chat for an hour with Dr. Hamilton
at his house, and thence with him to the British Museum.

This morning I went to Westminster Abbey for a leisurely
survey. My more mature thoughts differ from what I expected.
In no view that I can get of it does the outside of Westminster
present itself as one idea, like Freiburg, Strasburg, or Cologne.
As works of art few of the statues in the wilderness of tombs,
redeem the English school from the common censure. Chantrey's, even, are not all I hoped for. The best in my humble
judgment is a bas-relief by Flaxman, representing a sister prostrate in all the effusion of hopeless woe upon a brother's tomb—
that of George Lindsay Johnstone in the north aisle.

BERWICK UPON TWEED, *August* 26, 1851.

Before leaving Cambridge yesterday, I found the rooms of
Martyn and Kirke White at St. John's. The chambers of Milton,
at Christ's, are no longer known. We were warmly invited to
dine with the Fellows of Trinity, but we had already dined in
King's by invitation of the new Vice Provost, Mr. Heath.
There are about sixty Fellows at Trinity College; about eight
get £300; about eight £250; the rest £200. King's about £250.
Not necessary to reside. Thorwaldsen's statue of Byron, which
had been refused at Wesminster Abbey, is in the library of
Trinity. I am yet to behold any thing so enchanting in its
mixture of antique art and perfect nature as King's College. The
grounds are like green plush, without even a daisy, or an extra-
neous leaf on the smooth-rolled turf. This extends over many
acres to the river, and is encircled and broken by majestic trees.
The Fellows live like princes.

In six hours from Cambridge we reached Lincoln. We saw
the noble exteriors of Ely and Peterborough cathedrals, the surpassing tower of Boston Church, and more fully Lincoln Cathedral and York Minster. And here we are on the edge of Scotland, England, Tweed, and the German Ocean. We are one day
ahead of the Queen, who is to sleep at Doncaster to-morrow on
the way to Edinburgh. I never saw so much wheat, even on
the Rhine, as I have seen harvesting during a week. It is matter
of unspeakable thanks. This I feel when I see often fifty persons

gleaning in a stubble field. The country gets tumbled and rumpled as you get into Durham. They most awkwardly cut the wheat with a scythe. But their stacks and ricks of immense height are worth going to see. Berwick is a fine old town ; the clear, black situation, with hillside, Tweed-vale and sea, took me by surprise. There is no railway known to me, which goes so long by a river of picturesque beauty. Is there any lovelier valley than that of Tweed ?

EDINBURGH, August 30, 1851.

The way from Berwick was along the Tweed by Kelso to Melrose. Every name recalled Border history, Burns, and Scott. How often has poor Sir Walter's pony crept along the sweet, shaded lanes, through which I went to Abbotsford! I was in his superb library, and the study ; saw Chantrey's bust, with abundance of the things named by travellers. We crossed the Gala Water again and again. It is generally said this borderland is the loveliest in Scotland. The little rivers, pure as crystal, and winding in green vales, come purling in every now and then, and each is known in history ; and here and there a castle or abbey 800 years old rises majestically among the verdant fields. The only trees are planted. The round hills are treeless, but green or purple with heather, and the eye runs over such waves of this green ocean, that the distant herds and flocks look like specks. We came near Flodden-field and saw Dryburgh Abbey, where Scott lies. When we got to the quiet little inn at Melrose, and had lunched on broiled salmon-steak, the host said : "There is an American here, who has been walking over the hills." Presently he came in ; it was Major Preston. I had already given him two adieux. He accompanied us to Abbotsford.

How soon we lose the Northumberland burr on crossing Tweed, and what a different look in everybody! The children talking broad Lowland Scotch seem so funny. I hear some boys flying kites—" Jamie, I bate ye 'till be ower heevie—ye'll hae it agen the brae." This is not as stumping as the Yorkshire "He maxum pikum," (he makes them pick them ;) and "Sneck yett" is "shut the gate," for they have no article.

We are at 20 George's square. Mr. Dickson met us at the terminus with a cab and real Scotch hospitality. I enjoy a Christian house more than you can know, till you have been three months in hotels. Queen Square is a private street ; no horse or vehicle passes. Sir Walter Scott passed his boyhood in this row, No. 27. Back of us is Watson's Hospital, with the meadows, as the fine avenue is called, which leads to the green outskirts. I cannot note a tithe of the sights. The University-rooms of Chalmers', Wilson's, and Hamilton's Lectures. Statue of Burns, by Flaxman, his last work. The Harrow, where Hogg lodged. Houses of Hume, Blair, Knox, Cardinal Beatoun. The Wynds; the Tolbooth; Grey Friars Church. The Castle. The Antiquarians' Museum. The Advocates' Library, where the librarian showed us a letter of Charles I., when a boy, a Mazarin Bible, and the autograph of Waverley. I find Edinburgh, as often described, " beautiful for situation," beyond all cities. It has eminences, valleys, architecture, mountains, water, wide prospects, and thronging memories. Surely Scotland is " a field, which the Lord hath blessed."

The intelligence, culture, and warmth of the excellent persons I meet, is delightful. They are the quickest people I ever saw, and this is united to great piety. I have fallen into the very circle to which McCheyne's friends belong. Hewitson (his life is published in America) was an intimate of Mr. Dickson's, whose name occurs often in it. The piety of the Free Church folks of this school runs in the vein of exceeding tenderness and humility. Among many others, I must remember the Rev. Andrew Cameron, editor of the Christian Treasury ; the Rev. Mr. Gould, of the Reformed and Presbyterian church, editor of the new edition of Owen's Works ; Mr. Johnstone, of the house of Johnstone & Hunter, chief publishers for the Free Church ; Dr. Hetherington, the historian ; Dr. W. Lindsay Alexander, the Independent ; Mr. James Bonar, editor of the Assembly's Proceedings ; Mr. Hackett, of the Advocates' Library.

On the 28th the Queen entered about 4 o'clock, through the Dumbiedykes to Holyrood. I had a close view. Prince Albert was by her in an open carriage. The next carried the Prince of Wales and Princess Royal. Instead of receiving the Queen in the narrow streets, the body of the population poured out and spread themselves in a broad, green valley, between Holyrood palace and the range of hills including Arthur's Seat, Salisbury Crags, &c. This ravine was covered by tens of thousands, not in a level mass, but stretching up the sides of the hills on the clean turf, higher and higher, till the remote groups were almost too small for vision. The crags resounded with enthusiastic acclamations and the roar of cannon. So happy a multitude and so sublime a gathering I had not seen. If the Queen has any heart, she must have been overcome. She looked hearty, though she had come 250 miles that day. Lord John Russell was very much cheered, but I heard some Popish hissing. He visited the New College of the Free Church. The people love to speak of the Queen's punctuality and energy. On the night of her arrival she went out to see Lady Buccleuch, who is ill, and the next morning she went to Donaldson's Hospital before her early start northward at 8 o'clock. At the Hospital provision is made for the instruction of 300 boys. The building is so grand, and the grounds and prospects so delightful, that it is thought of for a palace.

At the "Ragged School" we saw 300 children, all without means of living. They come every morning and go home every night. When they come they strip off all their tatters, go into a bath, put on school-clothes, learn, work, have three meals, then put on old tatters and go home.

On the 1st of this month partridge-shooting began. The number is surprising of gentlemen with gun-cases, &c., that one meets. They have regular dog-tickets on the railway.

At the College of the United Presbyterian Church we saw the Library, and the beautiful Hall in which their Synod meets. They have about 130 students. Their professors are all pastors, and their session is only seven weeks! It is common for the ministers to live several miles out of town. Dr. Eadie comes here every day from Glasgow to his lectures. Almost every pastor is away at this season.

BRIGG OF TURK, PERTHSHIRE, *September* 2, 1851.

Dr. Robinson and I left Edinburgh yesterday morning. I sit at a window of my bed-room in this lonely mountain inn, just at the opening of the Trosachs, or pass to Loch Katrine, to which I expect to walk after breakfast. All day yesterday and all to-day, it is the scenery of "the Lady of the Lake," and this is really what draws people here; for there is grander scenery in Europe, but men love to go where poets have been. On the way from Edinburgh were Linlithgow Palace, Bannockburn, and Stirling Castle. If I had got to Stirling a day sooner I should have seen the Highland Sports, such as pitching the stone, tilting, broadsword, highland-fling, wrestling, &c. As it was I saw plenty of beggars and barefoots, and part of the 79th regiment in the castle, all bare-kneed, but mighty brawny and big. I began to see the Celtic visage and hear the Gaelic, which is a sweet language and very like Irish and Welsh. This morning the sun rose beautifully over a mountain. The air was Alpine. Huts in the distance had low roofs, and sometimes no chimney, the blue peat-reek coming out of the door. Wherever you looked, all was tumbled up and down in fantastic hills and dales, but perfectly soft and perfectly green, except where the purple heather covered the sides. An old Highlander sat in the fog, wrapped in his plaid, with his shaggy dog, watching a herd. Hay was making in some little patches far off, and through my glass I saw a little girl using her hands for pitchfork, and a baby propped up in the hay. We got into a vehicle, without cover, and drove through the Trosachs to the Loch. While we waited for the steamboat I mounted a hill, and lay down in the heather. It is soft and fragrant, and the flower is beautiful. It is not unlike clover at a distance, but taller, and far more uneven, and when viewed closely, is a beautiful bushy flower. I can well understand now how people might sleep on it, and how the fleeing Covenanters, in hiding, could escape by means of it. No wonder it is the darling growth of Scots. Almost every one travelling carries some heather-bloom somewhere about him. On the boat we had a Highland piper. Why did he not play " Hail to the Chief," which was made for this lake? He played " Roy's Wife," and " the Campbells are comin'."

We got out in sight of the house where Rob Roy was born. We then rode five miles to Loch Lomond. No woods, no farms, no cultivation ; all hills and muir-land, and peat-bog ; all green, with thousands of fern and heather ; and mountains before us to the north and on both sides. I saw peat or turf burning for the first time. They cut it in the moors, and pile it in stacks. It makes a nice, gentle fire, and the smell is pleasant. The people have little tillage, and live by their cattle and sheep. Almost every man wears a plaid around him, and so do half the gentlemen tourists. Stunted trees of tangled growth sometimes appear. Stone fences run irregularly up and down, often surmounted by scrubby dwarf-oak hedge, and with every crevice full of mingling fern, broom, and heather. Black cattle and black-faced sheep roam over the muir-land. The whole scenery is wild and novel, but thus far less lofty than I expected. The trip in a cart from Katrine to Lomond was very jolting, but O the singular, dream-like wildness of those hills and moors, where a man would be lost in half an hour, if he left the only road, and yet no forest ! Look on every side, and see the horizon shut in sometimes by rocky mountains of every varied contour which primitive granite can take, but seldom bare, and for miles together gently blushing with the flower of the heaths now in their glory. Within this bounding rim, see the country tossed up and down, as if the ocean in a long roll had suddenly been turned into green land ; for everywhere the green is perfect, and the matted grass is short and thick like moleskin. Mark the silver rill that meanders on the left to join Lake Artlet to Loch Lomond, showing that we have passed the water-shed, and go down. Observe the low piles of granite rocks, without mortar, without window, thatched or turfed, the smoke coming out of the chimney or door, and the truncated pyramid of black peat standing by. Do not neglect the million gay flowers with which God has beautified these solitudes, nor the fantastic mists and clouds that roll about the eminences of Ben An, Ben Venn, and Ben Lomond.

GLASGOW, *September* 10, 1851.

At Balloch, on lake Lomond, we took rails for Dumbarton; saw the wonderful castle, but did not hear " Dumbarton drums beat bonnie O." I had seen many castles, but for singular prominency this exceeds. The twin mount, on which it is built, rises out of the river beach, as if a gigantic elephant had pushed himself half way out of the flats. This, like Stirling, is kept garrisoned, by provisions in the treaty of union. Here we took steamboat for Glasgow, and ascended the broad Clyde. Every mile showed us the approach of a great commercial and manu- facturing city. It is a noble town, is Glasgow, (as the English express it.) The college is of the grand stone common here, and has some massy houses and quadrangles. The professors have quite a street of academic mansions. The Hunterian Museum is rich in MSS., printed incunabula, and medals. A Virgil of 1470. A Golden Legend, Caxton, 1483. An Antho- logia, by Aldus, 1503. A Plotinus, ed. princeps, 1513. A stereotype plate, used by Ged, in his Sallust, 1744, long before Didot. Principal Macfarlane preaches in the old cathedral. The beautiful choir is the place of worship; behind this is a Lady Chapel; then a Chapter House, used as a vestry. The crypts are very old and in good repair. Here Scott makes Rob Roy to have listened to the long sermon. The Green, or Common, a lawn with a drive of 2½ miles, was swarming with poor, drying clothes, and young folk playing and lying on the grass in a smart rain. The Bridge Gate, full of wretched poor, such as I have seen nowhere else. The Tron Church and St. John's, memorable for the labours of Chalmers. The new parts of Glasgow are better built than Edinburgh; though the site is far inferior, yet equal to almost any other place. Houses of the finest sort rent for £100 to £120. They are built of a dark solid stone laid in large pieces. The smoke of factories keeps the town in such a smoke as I have not seen before. The Mitchells are full of hospitable warmth. Mr. Andrew Mitchell lives at Helensburgh, twenty-nine miles down the Clyde opposite Greenock, but comes up daily to his warehouse in Virginia street.

I attended, at Grey Friars Church, the ordination of Mr. Leach, the missionary for Madras, by the United Presbytery. Dr. King preached a great sermon from 2 John 8. It was memoriter, and eloquent in a high degree; polished, ingenious, and faithful. They had a choir, and artificial music, but all sang.

Dr. Symington, of the Reformed Presbyterian Church, (brother of the theological professor of Paisley,) showed me an original of the Solemn League and Covenant. I breakfasted with the Rev. David Brown, of Free St. James's—the writer on the Millennium. Went to Paisley and saw the Abbey and Dr. Witherspoon's old church.

The 7th was spent in a visit among the Highland lochs, with the Mitchells, Rev. Mr. McEwen, &c. The great characteristics of Scottish scenery were here apparent. The granitic hills come down everywhere to the water, leaving little laps of land for towns and seats. They run down in such wise to the great estuaries that they are all cut into indentures like glove-fingers. These run up among the highlands, and are girt with soft hillsides, beyond which mountains rise and peep. I was among these lochs, sometimes in steamboat, sometimes in row-boat, and often on foot. On every hand were towns, churches, mansions, noble seats, but generally wild walks for cattle and sheep. We saw Loch Long, Gare Loch, Loch Goil, and Holy Loch. In so doing, we saw Greenock, Gourock, Dunoon, (of which Dr. Mackay is minister,) Ardentinny, Roseneath, (where is the Duke of Argyle's seat.) The population of Glasgow fly to these seaward slopes. Some of the towns are made up of villas. Plenty of Gaels, with kilt and mull and guttural but soft language. The nestling churches and manses of Presbyterians differing only in name, and the cheerful aspect of a pleasure-taking yeomanry, gave me an unwonted delight.

The 8th—a lovely, placid Sabbath—was spent in Helensburgh. Such places and such scenes must have been in the mind of Grahame when he wrote his "Sabbath." The hills lie softly on every side of the frith and around the neighbouring lochs. Small towns twinkle in the half-veiled sun across the water. The harvests, only partly cut, shine over the rounded fields. There is a perfect stillness. The temperature just admits, but does not demand fire. The town seems about the size of Princeton, and has an Established Church, a Free Church, a United Presbyterian, and an Independent. I worshipped with the third of these. The assembly was about equal to yours in Trenton. They were plain people in general, with a considerable sprinkling of gentry. A sister of the Duke of Argyle is a frequent hearer. Mr. McEwen preached in the morning on Col. iii. 17, the next verse to what Dr. Hamilton preached on in London. I preached in the afternoon from Jude 20, 21. It was like a revival meeting all day, for earnest hearing, looks of fire and affection, and psalmody that I never can forget. In the evening at Mr. Mitchell's, some one suddenly observed that every man in the room was a minister's son; and we soon discovered that four of the five were ministers' grandsons. One of the company was Mr. Hugh Moncrieff, a descendant of the original Seceder. The Secession body gave more than two-thirds to the United Presbyterian Church. They are together the most liberal of the Scotch Presbyterians. They have much of the best pulpit talent in Edinburgh and Glasgow. The prayers affect me more than the preaching.

The Duke of Argyle's domain is very large, and I passed on foot through that part of it which lies between Loch Long and the Gare Loch. I passed the solid, modest new Free Church, with its tent for sacraments, and visited the Established Kirk of Roseneath. Turning into a green lane, I found about twenty-six low stone cottages close side by side. Then came the ancient grave-yard, overhung by trees, with walled enclosures for noble families, &c. Outside of this is the parish school and schoolmaster's house, very well built and snug. The dominie showed me the church, which stands in the midst of the grave-yard. It is on a very narrow parallelogram, by far the narrowest church I ever saw. The pulpit and pews are unpainted, and the stone floor is cold and even wet. The sacramental table was longitudinally the whole length. Quality folks use the gallery, and the Duke's pew is just opposite to the pulpit and singularly near it. Going out of the grave-yard, you enter a park belonging to the kirk, with the most extraordinary avenue of yews within, and limes without. They mingle for such a length, that in the remote perspective it is almost night-like. This charge of perhaps £180 cannot have more than forty hearers. The manse is a beautiful cottage, overgrown with vines, about half a mile off. From here you look over the Loch to Row, famous for the " Row heresy."

We were accompanied on our return to Glasgow by Mr. James Smith of Jordanhill, who, at 70, has his yacht-pea-jacket on, and talks freely about Greek antiquities. He presented me a copy of his learned monograph on Paul's Shipwreck. He is of the Establishment, [Presbyterian.] More walks over the city. Called on Dr. Runciman of St. Andrew's (Established) Church. He does well here, and has filled his church from the wynds. His reception of me was cordial and elegant.

My mind, as you would expect, has been much on the Presbyterianism of Scotland. The surface-view, which a mere guest takes, is perhaps worth little, but I am seeing much and hearing

more in answer to my queries. In general, the absolute state
of religion in Scotland is higher than I thought. The events
following the Disruption have wrought more widely and deeply.
The effect on the Establishments has been to make them better
and not worse. There is not a parish [Established] preacher,
who would not resent the charge of being Arminian. They
have noble charities, and the Normal schools, &c., are palatial.
The Free Church is striving hard to keep up at the speed which
they began. Nowhere, except in some new-measure spots of
old, have I seen such signs of universal working, by Bible-classes,
tracts, books, hymns, domiciliary visits, care of poor, Sabbath
schools, &c. They cannot help remembering their undue zeal
against Voluntaries, and burden themselves by claiming to be the
Kirk, and so by planting a church beside every national church all
over Scotland. Their mighty man is Hugh Miller. He is hot,
excitable, and on occasion implacable. I see much to make me
believe that the power of Scotch Presbyterianism is in the United
Presbyteries. They have no hypotheses *in petto*. They are more
like us. They have acquired a status by the Disruption, and work
heartily with the Free Church. There never can be any vital prelacy here. The Episcopalians here are about as often mentioned as
the Moravians with us. The clergymen of the Free Church whom
I have seen are exceedingly well-informed as to our American
churches, and acquainted with our literature. The education of
the rising ministry is going forward with great zeal. In acquaintance with all the modern works of German interpretation, the
new race of ministers will be much before those of the Anglican
Church. When I speak of the Free Church, I mean that the
remark should apply to all the Dissenters of Scotland, between
the different classes of whom there is an increasing fellowship.
Even the Reformed Presbyterians appear to be separated by a
scarcely distinguishable interval from the others. The angriness
of the controversy concerning the Atonement seems to have
departed ; whether with any sacrifice of old Calvinistic tenets in
any quarter it would not become a passing stranger to determine.
   Both in Edinburgh and Glasgow the eye is continually saluted
by Presbyterian structures. Many of these are in the modern
Gothic style, and some are florid in a high degree. Their interiors,
however, are less airy and ornate than with us. All the Scottish
churches have vestries, and all the ministers wear the Geneva
gown or cloak, which has come down from the days of Knox.
In some churches the preacher pronounces the Lord's Prayer
immediately before the sermon. The old version of the Psalms
is universal. The prayer after sermon is uniformly longer than
with us, and the service varies from an hour and three-quarters

to two hours. At this season the usual hours in town are eleven and two. The custom of "turning up" the passage remains in all its strength, and hundreds of Bibles are rustling at once. So far as I can learn, the topics which fill the pulpits are just those which fill the Catechism; and the general strain of preaching is not so much alarming as persuasive. The person and work of our Lord form a prominent part of public discourses. Great diversities, of course, obtain among men of various gifts and temper, but in general there is much earnestness in public addresses. In the cities many sermons are read from the manuscripts, but the country parishes scarcely tolerate this.

BELFAST, *September* 16, 1851.

If you knew that my letters are generally written on my knee, you would wonder that there is any handwriting about them. I write this, that you may know of my safe arrival in the land and province of my progenitors, after the dangers of the North Channel. There is something very solemn in approaching a new country by morning twilight; both my views of Ireland have been such. As this is the great mart of the linen trade, one of my visits was (with Dr. Maclean and Mr. Thomas Mitchell) to the Linen Hall, where we saw the article in all its varieties. An English Quaker gave us many explanations. He showed us the different bleached and unbleached fabrics. Sometimes a linen-house pays a thousand pounds in a week to hand-loom cottage-weavers. But cottage-spinning, so famous in the days of my great-grandfather, has been done away by machinery. We saw how gaudily the shirtings are put up for the American market. Also the difference of the linen for the British trade, which has less starch and less "beetling," as a pounding is called, which flattens the thread. The British fabric looks as well after washing as before. No person whom I have questioned, knows any thing of the new operation for dressing flaxen thread, so as to remove the "cold feel" which distinguishes linen from cotton goods. It was boasted that this would make flax take the place of cotton. American flour is largely used here, as also in Glasgow; at about £1 1*s.* the barrel.

A jaunting-car took us to Cave Hill, where we had as good a view of the Lough and surrounding country as this hazy atmosphere allows. The Divis and other hills are fine. Abundance of water comes down from these heights. The country houses look well, but every thing lacks the trim finish to which my eye has been accustomed. The hills are without heather and often bare. In and near the town I see numbers of ne'er-do-weels, half-naked children, and canal-digger-like men, but no tokens of absolute distress. I am surprised that things are so familiar. It arises from the American look of the brick houses, the imperfect keeping of the lawns, and the Scotch-Irish countenance of the peasantry.

The drive along the sea-shore to the Giant's Causeway was delightful. The beach is not sand, but generally beautiful rock, often limestone, which keeps the water from being muddy. It is as clear as a spring, and the mottled bottom has a novel appearance. The curves of the bays are beautiful. But every thing derives its character from the cliffs and mountains, which were always on our left, rising high and magnificent, with basalt columns and wonderful freaks of the igneous rocks, giving premonitions of what appears in its perfection at the Causeway. The whole north-east shore derives its picturesque loftiness from the primitive and basaltic rock, which girdles the inner limestone and other stratified rocks of the island. When we began to turn inland, we had beauties of a different sort; mountain prospects, long winding treeless glens, hill-sides covered with the chequered oat-fields and pastures, occasional moors with peat, cottages and flocks, browsing goats and merry peasants. On leaving Ballycastle, where is a fine old ruin, we found a highly cultivated country. The church of Ballintoy seems almost in the sea, and the manse is a cold, white solitary house looking over the water to Rathlin. I saw the sun go down, a disk of molten gold, over the foreland of Bengore. About nine in the evening I saw a beautiful Aurora Borealis—well so called at this point. It was a zone arched over a chord of about sixty degrees of the horizon, having Arcturus in the centre, with bright radiations striking up from several points.

The prints generally represent the scene about the Causeway, so as to give the neighbouring *precipices* as the Causeway. These precipices are grand, and are likewise columnar, but they are nothing to the main object. The Causeway is well named. It is a platform jutting out in three capes into the sea, toward which it inclines. It is not very high above the water. It is made of columns, side by side, perfectly dry and close. You cannot thrust a knife between some of the junctures. These columns go down unknown lengths. They are exposed on the hill-sides, so that you can see them joined together in pieces. Where one end joins another there is a concavity fitting a convexity, which is as wonderful as any thing. It is on the tops of these joined pillars that you walk. The surface is a little uneven, but in general may be described as plane. The columns are of dark gray basalt. They are polygonal prisms—hexagons, pentagons, a few heptagons. I saw one nonagon, one square, and one rhombus. The little concavities in some hold sea-water, which leaves salt; and on most of them are numerous lichens, and even small flowers. Piles of these blocks are taken away, even to America. Our guide delivers a set at Liverpool for about £4. There are two famous caves. I entered one of them, Port Coon. The effect is awful. You have at your back a cavernous depth of dark, and in front the wild ocean roaring in to your feet.

DUBLIN, *September* 18, 1851.

My first stage from Belfast was to Armagh, a fine old town, where the Papists are building a cathedral, which Dr. Cullen says shall surpass the Anglican one. Here we coached it across the county to Castle Blayney. The country has the same undulations, but looks worse; smaller patches, ruder hovels, more wastes, later oats, and dirtier folks. At Blayney we took cars for Dublin. Drogheda is a seaport, and has a brisk commerce, fine edifices, a stern, middle-age gate, but we drove through long streets of blank, ugly, stone, one-story thatched hovels, and were infested with beggars. From there southward through the counties Louth and Meath, the beauties increased every mile. Often we were by the sea, and at Malahide Bay were carried over its noble arm. Howth Head is a grand eminence, and the approach to Dublin is famous. Its capacious bay, its broad river, its eight bridges, and its superior public edifices, tell of grandeur, which is every day decreasing.

Saw the poplin-looms at Atkinson's, Sackville street. He sells nothing but poplins, and only to retail-buyers. Got a sample of a dress worn by the Queen, fifteen dollars a yard. Phœnix park is seven miles round, and contains 1,760 acres.

I made a trip to Inch to inquire about the relatives of our servants at home. Their mother had gone to America, but was directed to a brother. I went there. Poor man! he denied his name, and was afraid to come out, fearing no doubt some proctor or landlord's agent to turn him out. At this point I made known my purpose, and a great change came over them. As many as seven persons, old and young, came out of the cottage-door, and gathered around my jaunting-car. They asked many questions about the girls, and said all here were well. When I rode away, the blessings of the whole group followed me in most hearty Irish. The country around Thurles, Drum, and Inch, is very beautiful and the roads are like a floor, with walls or hedges. Indeed I can no longer say Ireland is without levels, for we were in a stretch of flat land most of the way from Dublin.

But then on our right we had the blue ridge of Sliebh Bloom, which we flanked, and took its south-west on our right in going to Limerick. At Thurles we got out. The most of it is of white rough-cast stone houses thatched; with irregular streets and a little dirty market-place, where a score of women have piles of excellent potatoes on the earth. Beggars and tattered hordes of lazzaroni, more ragged than those of Drogheda, roamed in the ways. Thurles is a very churchly little town, and was once a great one. Three castles in ruins, a monastery, two nunneries, a college, an English church, a chapel, barracks for the soldiery, barracks for the constabulary police, poorhouses, (here as elsewhere fine edifices, and lately containing 1,700 poor,) female schools, and other charities. Here the great Popish Synod met some months ago.

I inquired at Inch for L.'s father, and saw him. He bears a good character, but is very poor, and patched to a mournful degree. He had heard nothing from L. for eighteen months. The poor old man has no longer any work at the college. Great numbers have gone to America from Tipperary. Twelve cottages were desolate on a mile of road. Only one tenant is left on Mr. Trant's estate, which is six miles long. This is the worst county in Ireland for shooting landlords and proctors. The land is good, but the people look dogged and unhappy. From Thurles to Limerick we had broad pastures and romantic hills. Take it altogether, Ireland is a land of unsurpassed charms of the green, wild, and quiet sort. You are hardly ever out of sight of some ivy-crowned ruin, castle, church, or abbey, telling of the power which has gone by.

Roman Catholic Ireland is depopulating in some sense. Small cottage-farms are disappearing, large estates are growing larger, fewer hands are required for pastures and sheepwalks; better cultivation will make this beautiful, this enchanting island, more beautiful and enchanting; the Celtic race will be increasing in America and Australia, and the over-stocked priesthood of Ireland will lose its slaves and its supports. Ulster is in a different case. It smiles with agricultural, pastoral, and manufacturing wealth, and has spots unsurpassed on earth.

I found that our Minister, Mr. Abbott Lawrence, had been at Limerick and at Galway, and was down the river with Lord Monteagle and others. As to Limerick—50,000 population— the new town is beautifully built, no place of it size is more showy. The people in the good streets are handsome and elegant; but the masses in the over-crowded lanes and along the quays and noble bridges, beat all I ever beheld for abandoned, rowdy, jovial, beggarly appearance. Such rags, such stench, such impu-

dence, such almost naked, though often ruddy and handsome
Irishism, I find not even in Ireland. The grand old cathedral is
begirt with offensive smells and fearful sights. I doubt whether
Venice is more full of license than Limerick. Here popery
revels. The new part of Limerick is more fair and regular
than Belfast, with streets like Chestnut street somewhat vulgar-
ized. But who can describe the gangs of wretched, wanton,
roystering, impudent women and children, half-naked, tattered
and foul, who sit, sprawl, lie, squat, bluster and laugh about the
cathedral, the bridges, and the quays!

The mountains on our left after quitting Dublin, were no
doubt part of the Wicklow cluster. Kildare was an interesting
point. Its ruined abbey, and tower 130 feet high, are grand objects. Portarlington is noted as the place of Wellington's
education. A French colony till lately had French preaching
here. There are many boarding-schools, and we saw a bevy of
fine young girls going to the capital. All the country scenes
rich; much pasture, heavy hay, some oats, occasional bog with
piles of turf, few cottages, few labourers in the fields, and these
were more haggard and woe-begone than in even the middle
counties. This whole vale is more wooded than usual. As we
entered Tipperary the land looked flatter and more neglected,
but with more numerous broken-down castles and some good
mountains towards the south.

GALWAY, *September* 21, 1851.

On the 20th I left Limerick on the top of an old-fashioned
mail coach, of which there are more remaining in Ireland than
in England. The roads were fine, and perfectly smooth all day,
and as the country is limestone, and rocky, were without exception lined by stone walls for all the sixty-four miles (Irish) to
Galway. Castles and abbeys in ruins were scarcely ever out of
sight. The country grew poorer and rockier as we went on, and
the small dust of the limestone roads was exactly like rye-flour.
At Clare, a small wretched town, with a beautiful site, we saw
hundreds of young women and girls on the river bank. I was told
their mates have gone to America. The fields look stony and
poor, and the whole country is marked up by the ugly stone
dykes. Moors or bogs are not very frequent. The roads abound
with foot-people; they are squat, flat-faced, homely, and often
brown. At Ennis we left the coach for a jaunting-car. Ennis
is the chief town of the county Clare. It is made up chiefly of
one-story hovels, thatched. It was market-day, and the peasantry
were crowding the market-place. This day, it seemed to me,
that I saw more asses than in all my previous life. The same

poor, barren, stony, white land, prevailed all the way to Gort; but when we came near to Gort, we arrived at the demesne of the Viscount Gort, extending some miles. We drove through it. Though he is poor, the castle is fine, and the grounds are in a fine style of landscape-gardening, with parks, deer, avenues of ash and beech, dark and romantic; glimpses over the lovely lake Cootra of sloping mountains, and exit by a grand carved portal. A little beyond we got out to see a great natural curiosity. A river, called Blackwater, runs out of the lake, and then goes under ground, and reappears in a wonderful manner in a deep place fifty feet down like a goblet, and called the Punch Bowl. We are now in the county Galway, Province of Connaught. It was market-day at Gort also, and from the inn where we dined we looked out on the broad but irregular market-place. Here we were among the aboriginal Irish. The women wear a dark blue cloak and hood, and red petticoat. The scene was novel and lively. Crowds and groups, stalls, booths, and tents. One was selling kitchen stuff by auction. A woman had four hats on a board, and another two. One had *dulse*, [an edible sea-weed.] There were carts of buttermilk packed in straw around kegs. Stalls of shoes, and of nails in little parcels. A woman brings a hen or a dozen eggs for a mile. A girl had a donkey to sell, and held it by a straw rope. Pigs, washed clean, were conducted by the same sort of line. Potatoes, of course, abounded. Hay in bundles; heather brooms; sacks of oatmeal. Plenty of rags and little appearance of dress. Red coats here and there predominating over the sport, Connaught-men, and a good many in the constabulary uniform.

We took another car, and posted to Galway. The same scene; walls, ruined cottages, roads full of women in hoods, and groups of travellers from the market. Occasionally, a " plantation " announced a rich estate. Ruined cottages, with only walls. All gone to America. An English clergyman tells me he counted 114 such ruined cabins in eight miles in Mayo. Galway and Mayo suffered more than any other counties. I passed a hut, and saw the woman on the straw-bed, her only seat. All speak Irish. Two poor little boys, about four years old, came to beg. The larger one said, apologizing for the silence of the other, " he has no Inglis."

Galway is the fifth city of Ireland, and has about 20,000. It has some fine buildings. The Queen's College is magnificent. There are also the two court-houses, the Union or Poor-House, the usual barracks, several monasteries, and several Catholic chapels. But whole streets are of one-story hovels, close to-gether, dark and thatched. The noble estuary and neighbouring lake give dignity to a place which is far, far beyond all I ever dreamed of for squalor, filth, and poverty.

On the Sabbath I found the principal street crowded with people even more than Princeton in an old-time Commencement. All talking Irish. Not one well-dressed person. Even the female sex shows no care for finery or cleanliness. Dark cloaks and broad-ruffled caps, without bonnets or shoes or stockings, and with red petticoats. Women carrying babies in their cloaks behind them. It is difficult to get through the throng in the mid-street. Women in red wrappings. Lines of women sitting on the ground. Little appearance of drink or gaiety. No good faces, but many open, funny ones. I am reminded of squaws. I never saw such rags, holes, fringes of tatters, filth, combless black locks, and babies half exposed and shamefully uncovered. I saw a thousand such. These are Irish of the Irish. Men in knee-breeches. Beggars follow you for a furlong full of wit, comic entreaty, and prayers for your welfare. A gentleman, who has been at Connemara, says their car was surrounded by a hundred at once. The stench of the ways is horrible. Near the chapels the crowds are indescribable. The English church was a Catholic one till the time of Edward VI. It is of fine stone, a regular cross, with a lady-chapel added to the west side of the south transept. Since the twelfth century it has had a foundation for a warden and six vicars, who still reside. The service was going on, and I heard the conclusion of an evangelical discourse (to the military) from Mr. D'Arcy, who is a Galway man. He kindly showed me over the house. The nave is walled up, and the service is in it and the choir and south transept. Mr. D'Arcy preached again (to the congregation proper) extempore, on Rom. v. 1, a right Calvinistic sermon upon justification by faith and imputed righteousness. I never heard better organ-playing. It was almost a cathedral service, and two voices in the choir were transcendent. I had not gone to the Presbyterian church, having heard that it was Arian; but finding I had been misinformed, I went there in the afternoon, and heard a young man preach to twenty-five hearers. The Protestants are increasing, and are about one in twenty.

Billingsgate is a paradise to the fish-market of Galway. A chatter rises from it to the bridge above, which is unlike all I have met with. Though so overcrowded and underclothed, these Connaught Irish seem peaceable. During the famine it was indeed otherwise. As I looked at an ass with panniers of bread, the post-boy said " a year or two ago that load could not have gone by here without an escort." As we entered the walled hill-road, which leads into Galway, we met cart after cart for miles, all full, having more women than men, and in some cases all drunk. We met gangs of the same sort on foot in the road. The post-boy said robberies were frequent not long since along here, and that he should stop in Galway all night.

An optical phenomenon was observed by Dr. Maclean, Mr. Mitchell, and me, near the Queen's College. Persons in some numbers, walking on a quay, or river-promenade, looked so much taller through a scarcely perceptible mist, that we all agreed the same appearance would, in ordinary circumstances, indicate a stature of thirty feet. It was fearful.

The poor people are all emigrants in intention. I never talked with one among hundreds, who did not speak of America as of Paradise. The population still seems to an American eye immense. The priests walk among them like a superior race, elegantly dressed, and with an air not unlike that of our own clergy. I rejoice to add there is a work of God going on among these lowest of European Papists. Last month in Connemara alone, 1,900 Papists were " confirmed " under church-missions. In Mayo there is persecution. The Rev. Hamilton Townsend was thrice shot at in his own house. After all, my general conclusion is, from repeated conversations with the most informed gentlemen, that a better day is coming. The very famine has tended to improve agriculture; the very depopulation also has thrown thousands out into a new soil, and at home has aggregated innumerable ill-tilled patches barely sustaining life into large farms or sheep-walks requiring fewer hands, and gradually filling with new tenants. But this involved in part a change of race. Nowhere has the pure Celtic blood been energetic. Unlike as are a Highlander and a Connaught man, they are as to unthrift and idleness, identical. Large numbers of English labourers are coming into Mayo. In the east of Ireland the mixture of Celtic with Anglo-Norman blood has produced the finest physical result on earth. The better class at Dublin and Limerick, the people you meet in carriages, are by all odds the very handsomest people I ever saw. In Galway one has the population of a city with the squalor and brutality of a hovel. I dare say there are a thousand houses in the town without a floor. The contrast between these and the palaces of the regiment, the police, and the priests, tells a painful tale. I dwell thus on Galway, because it is the worst place I have been in.

DUBLIN, *September* 23, 1851.

Leaving Galway, we came directly eastward by the Midland Great South-western Railway, 127 miles across Ireland to Dublin. The first part of our way was stony like the road from

Gort. The number of ruinous cabins was great. Castles were numerous. As we advanced through the great limestone plain, the country constantly improved in verdure, houses, and crops. After leaving Cranmore we were in quite a plain. We were some time in the county Roscommon, formerly the most turbulent in Connaught. Athlone is an important central point, but its glories are in ruins. Great fortifications, and signs of military force. The British government pursues a policy like that of the Romans, laying out vast sums on public works, which will last for ages; these show Ireland to be a conquered province. Now, on leaving the Shannon again, we came into gentle wooded regions, which, nearer to Dublin, became perfectly English, with lodges and trimmed trees, and neater cottages. Great numbers of emigrants were in the trains, and we saw bitter partings outside. The people look far better in Leinster. But everywhere, those who have the least pretension to gentle blood are the best-looking people I ever saw. A Spanish gentleman in the train told me he would have taken me for a Spaniard; he and I looked like mulattoes among the lily and rose of Jerne. Mullingar and Maynooth were passed. The grounds and colleges of Maynooth are stately, with an old castle and fine trees. Well-dressed, important-looking priests, were pacing, with the never-absent breviary, on the green banks of the canal.

All over the island Ulster is spoken of as a happy model, and even in the mouths of the priests " Ulster-tenure " is a common word; it amounts almost to fee simple.

So many things crowd on me, that I am utterly unable to say what I wish on any one. As to the government policy—for some years I am fully convinced government has seriously intended the good of Ireland. The problem has been almost insoluble. It was perplexed by the potato rot, fear, dysentery, and cholera. If Providence had not opened the new world, the results would have been awfully worse. Mr. D'Arcy told me, that at one time he saw 130 putrefying corpses above ground in a field near Galway. The power of the government has been put forth to an extent which no man can estimate without being here. Let me hint at some of its indications. In the numberless towns and villages through which we passed, the majority of houses being hog-pens, and the people like beggars, there were always three or four noble structures of the finest building stone in the world. You need not ask what these were. The largest is the Poor House; the next is the jail; the third is the regimental barracks; the fourth is the guard-house of the Constabulary, who are in great strength, wear uniform, are fine picked men, always from a distance, and armed. Here we see the conquered Province, but who can say what else England could have done ? Again, government has lent vast sums to the railways of Ireland, and these given (not to flourishing Londonderry) but to Drogheda, to Enniskellen, to Cork, to Galway. They are fully equal to the best English roads. The stationhouses, as a whole, are superior to the generality in England, being such as will abide for ages, to speak for England as the ruined roads and aqueducts do for Rome. I know England has sought her own power in this, but she has no less served the interests of Ireland by her recent policy. Even this matter of evictions has two sides, just as slavery has with us. The Presbyterians of Ulster are perfectly satisfied with government. Truth is no doubt hard to be got at among such differences. That the tenant-tenure and the absenteeism have wrought iniquitously and murderously no sane mind ought to doubt. Yet on this very head matters tend in the right direction. Under the Encumbered Estates Act (which is named every hour in Ireland) titles can be made good to purchasers. The beggared nobles of Ireland are selling to rich merchants, gentlemen, &c. In the long run this helps the populace, notwithstanding proximate evils. Just as you know how much more miserable are the slaves of a poor planter, or a bankrupt. Emigration (blessed be God !) has allowed hundreds of thousands to go to a country, where they may be happy. The priests have had their day. They are phrensied just now, under the Ecclesiastical Titles' Bill, and the ultramontane zeal of Dr. Cullen. But my belief is their time is short.

OXFORD, *September* 27, 1851.

Leaving Liverpool day before yesterday, the train came by the beautiful Trent valley again, and I caught a glimpse of Lichfield Cathedral and Lord Lichfield's park. The first few stages I was alone in my carriage. From Blatchley to Oxford my companion was the Hon. ——, son of Lord S., going to Eton. He was constantly opening his hat-box, which contained a pair of trousers, and his carpet-bag, which was swollen so as to be tied with twine. He was very offish and affected, till the sky was covered by a rainbow of uncommon beauty, and then he was so carried away, and so lighted up, that he lost all sense of his rank, and submitted to be taught the word *vibgyor*.[1] My gentleman had risen very early to take the train, and, I fear me, had not washed his hands; and his beautiful hair streamed in the wind like elf-locks. At Oxford he furnished himself with a Benjamin's

---

[1] The mnemonic initials for the primitive colours.

portion of tarts and cakes, which he attended to while I dined, keeping his hat on; (boys here all wear hats.)

The Oxfordshire peasantry talk more like New Englanders than any I hear, but not in regard to their *Us*. My guide might pass for a Massachusetts man, in his very intonation, were it not for the pains he takes with his "aches." He industriously says "hentrance," "Hoxford," "Hariel College," "hinner closhters." I employed a guide, and visited the exterior and grounds of Christ Church, Magdalen, University, Balliol, Merton, Exeter, Queen's, New, Lincoln, All Souls, Jesus and Pembroke Colleges, and Magdalen Hall. Happily the verdure is as yet untouched. I rejoice in these genuine old English streets and yellow house-fronts, gables, square casements, oriels and projecting stories. They first won my affection at Eton. I foresaw that Oxford would take all the colour out of every thing else; because I knew there was nothing like it on earth. I should like to be here again in term-time, yet I would not miss the solitude, silence, and memorial ghastliness of such haunts as New College Garden, Christ Church Meadow, Maudlin Walk, Quadrangle of Jesus College, place of the martyrs, &c. King's at Cambridge greatly surpasses any one thing here taken singly, and Trinity College, Cambridge, is fully equal to any one structure here; but all Oxford is immensely above all Cambridge. Things which strike me:—Christ Church Meadow, walks, and trees. The avenue is nowhere so perfect as that of Trin. Coll., Cambridge, but is vaster, wilder, and if not so pensive, more captivating. The sunset meanwhile was American. The tower of Maudlin, from which Dr. Phillips's church [Fifth Avenue, New York] is derived, as the Lenox Hall, [Princeton Seminary Library,] from Magdalen chapel. The walks of Magdalen, especially Addison's walk. New College, antique and massy; its gardens and trees *sans pareil*. Deer were at the very doors in Mag. College Park. The Bodleian. The Clarendon. The Theatre. The Radcliffe Library. "Manners makyth Man," over the gate of New College. Jesus College, only for Welshmen; its physiognomy like its namesake at Cambridge. The reading of my childhood was strangely and eagerly about the Universities, and it left deeper traces than I knew of before. These English boys have some peculiar and winning points. Being sent so early from home they gain a certain manliness. They abound in a slang idiom, which would be almost unintelligible in America.

LIVERPOOL, *September* 30, 1851.

From Birmingham to Liverpool is five hours. There was much to please, in the winding of little rivers, the verdant pastures, the universal hedges and planted trees trimmed in an odd slender way; the fine cattle, the thatched cottages, with roses; the hayricks as trim and smooth as vases; the rosy children; the winding country roads and lanes; the peeping spires, and mighty substructions, viaducts, and tunnels of the Great North Western Railway.

On the Sabbath I proceeded to make a new trial to hear Dr. McNeile. His beautiful new church is in the country suburbs, far from houses, among gardens and villas, with abundance of well-kept ground about it. The congregation was very large, many being strangers, whom the gowned vergers led up. The assembly looked plebeian, but devout. The organ was simply played; no interludes, no intoning, no musical Kyrie Eleison, only the Gloria was so given. The people all bowed at the name, but McN. not perceptibly, if at all. The hymns were of Bickersteth's collection; a hymn opened the service and all the people sang loud and well. Dr. M. read the lessons well, but rhetorically. He has two voices, and his baritone voice is incomparably rich, but he makes too much of it, barely shunning the theatrical. He is tall and thin for this country, florid, with noble aquiline face, and hair very gray. He prayed extempore, both before and after sermon. He preached in the gown. The text was Matt. xi. 25, 26. He preached without manuscript, holding a small Bible in his hand throughout. His oratoric art was seldom apparent in preaching. His manner is the elevated colloquial. His discourse was clearly unstudied, but clearly unwritten. There was no hesitation, nor any infelicity of expression, while he went often to the very edge of familiarity. He had no occasion for the pathetic, but was awfully solemn in places. His plan is evidently to be a teacher. He opened most familiarly from ver. 26, "Thou hast hid these things:—what things?" His introduction was an answer to that from a perfectly plain, natural, simple, concise, but elegant exposition of ver. 16—24. He spent about half the body of the discourse in showing that some things were not hid from "the wise and prudent." He exalted the man of worldly wisdom, quoting largely from Sir John Herschel, and reading from two bits of paper, which he held up just as if at his fireside. He showed how much the great philosopher may learn of God. Here he horrified me by a most pernicious doctrine, viz., that God's benevolence cannot be inferred from creation and providence. I could scarcely keep quiet in my pew. He was clear and able on the incapacity of a carnal mind to see the spiritual objects. I have seldom heard this great but ticklish point more cleverly touched. Illustrations from the senses. Inter alia– "It is a peculiarity of spiritual light that it carries

its own evidence with it. At this instant you perceive in this
house a great variety of colours. (At the moment the sun was
breaking in very radiant, and even shining on half his face.)
You need no proof that the objects have these hues. You possess the senses for it. The light that appeals to these senses is
self-revealing. Now suppose a blind man among you should say,
' there are no such colours—there is no such beauty—the per-
ceptions of these people are delusive and their admiration is
enthusiastic folly '—would this disturb your persuasions? Not
for an instant. But many of you lack another sense. You see
no excellence in the Gospel; you discredit the witness of those
who do. Why are some born with four senses instead of
five? born blind? (then with scarcely audible tones and a manner of unparalleled abasement) ' *even so Father, for so it seemed*
good in thy sight! ' And why are some born again with six
senses instead of five? new born? (then with the same pause
and eloquent subduing of tone,) ' *Even so Father,* &c.' " This
was his transition to the second part, which was to refer all to
Divine sovereignty. He was thorough-paced in his Calvinism,
and ended most abruptly with one of the very boldest demands
on every hearer to bow and become a babe and believe it.

I regard McNeile as a prince among extempore preachers.
He escapes several evils to which such are very prone. He is
very dense; he says what he means, and goes on; yet he lodges
his meaning completely, by a happy choice of words and by
avoiding poetic terms, technical phraseology, and language unusual among common people. Though singularly happy in
illustration, he is very sparing with it. The staple of his
discourse was exegesis, and argument on the exegesis. I have
said his voice is perfect. He never employs effort, or breaks
into spouting tones. When most effective, he is most colloquial
and least loud. At the warmer and more rapid places his
native Irish broke forth most distinctly, never in pronunciation,
which is classically English, but in the accent and cadences.
As compared with Dr. Cook I note as follows: Cook is past his
prime, being perhaps 65—68. Cook has a trifle of conventional
pulpit tone, and becomes a declaimer, so far as management of
voice goes. Cook's sermon [p. 158] was much more articulate,
and built up Presbyterian-wise. Cook plays the orator more,
and soars into imaginative pictures and showers of similitude.
I apprehend nine out of ten would give the palm to Cook. I
am not sure but that I also should do so, when I get over the
immediate impression of McNeile, as the last heard. Cook
preached 69 minutes; McN. 50. They are by a long way the
most eloquent men I have heard in these climates. Up to a

certain point I thought Dr. King such. He is indeed a great preacher. But he has one set of faults inseparable from a Scotchman, and another set inseparable from a memoriter preacher. He cantillates, and more and more as he gets on; never uttering one sentence as he would at his table. He writhes, and brings his right arm around, as if he were reaping. He makes you sympathize with his pulpit sweats. Then his whole sermon, though learned, ingenious, and richly original, smells of the lamp. There is an artful reserve of pungency for the last part of the sentence, which is often antithetical. This surprises and gratifies, but it hinders the great effect, and is a mannerism. Few can attain it, but those who do fall below the highest style. Dr. King abounds, even in prayers, in a cunning citation of texts so apt and so curiously tesselated, that it has almost the effect of wit; it is an outgrowth of Seceder textual preaching, as cultivated in a soil of elegant literature. Yet it sins against nature, and so against eloquence.

The best *speakers* I have heard, are Coquerel and Adolphe Monod. In no single word, gesture, or tone, do they ever transcend nature. I think McNeile sometimes does in regard to that deep organ-note which he cannot help using out of place. If I could hear Monod in a regular sermon, I should, perhaps, regard him as the nearest pulpit perfection. At present it lies between Cook and McNeile; and as to matter, the praise is greatly on the side of Cook.

I would not think of naming Dr. H. among "the first three," yet he is a great man in his way. In spite of his pronunciation and tone, he is an eloquent preacher. His flowers deceive and betray him, but he has more than flowers; he has argument, original thoughts, and a pathos which redeems his metaphors and apologues. A few years hence he will probably be a far greater preacher than he now is.

Next to all these above named I place Mr. Scholefield of Cambridge; but he is as simple as a child, and as plain as a farmer, and not an orator at all.

STEAMSHIP "ATLANTIC," October 1—15, 1851.

October 3.—We loosed from moorings at 1 15, P. M., on Wednesday the 1st inst. At eleven on Thursday night the piston rod broke, and after stopping an hour we got under way with one engine. The repairs will require immense labour, and many of the passengers wished to return to Liverpool, or put into Cork. It is a mercy that the wind is not as high as it was, though the sea runs fearfully high. I occasionally hear a sea shipped over my head, running off the fore-deck like a river.

October 7.—For several days and nights it has been impossible to write. Indeed the place where I now sit has been filled with water during part of the time. We have now been six days going in the teeth of a gale, which, during many hours of Thursday, and especially that night, was a dreadful storm. It is a mercy to be remembered that our piston was repaired before the worst came; for with one engine we could not have kept our head to the wind, and so should have gone into the trough of the sea and been submerged. As it was, the irruption of waters was fearful. The seas which followed us were as high as the pipes. The forepart plunged into mountains of water, which swept the decks, floating the water-casks and making it deep enough to swim. It broke through four bulwarks or break-waters, one of which was four inches thick. The sound of the labouring, creaking, smashing seams was like going to pieces every moment. The seas shipped forward came down the hatch-way, breaking the thick glass, and making it knee-deep in some state-rooms in an instant. Our own was floating. High as is the stern of the "Atlantic," the sea broke over the hurricane deck, and came through the dining saloon, and into the main saloon below. The thumps upon our counter were like tons of metal falling from a height. This lasted for part of a day and night, and even when it remitted on the morning of the 3d, we were still in a terrible gale. Anxiety was increased by a man's falling from the mast. We made only four or five miles an hour most of the time. During these awful hours every eye was turned towards Capt. West. His tall, noble form appeared everywhere, but for whole nights he was drenched. In the terror of that memorable night I believe many of us thought we should never get to land. It was too violent and noisy for prayer in common. Bishop Otey[1] and I prayed in his state-room, together with my room-mate, (Capt. Cullum,) who was wrecked in the Atlantic, when Dr. Armstrong was drowned, [page 59.] We talked the matter over during the height of our tempest. Perhaps those suffered least who were deadly sick, as scores were.

On the 5th, the Lord's Day, it was so far abated that I read the 107th Psalm, and prayed in the dining saloon. Soon afterward it abated further, and we had quite a passable night. Yesterday it was very rough again, but not so horrible. About midnight the wind and sea were comparatively quiet. "O that men would praise the Lord for his goodness, and for his wonderful works to the children of men!"

October 8.—At noon we had an observation, and found by

---

[1] Of the Episcopal Church, Tennessee.

dead reckoning, that we were 1,212 miles from Liverpool.
Yesterday, during a blow a white bird alighted on our vessel,
and was caught by the cabin-boy. It must have been driven out
six hundred miles from the Summer Isles.

SONNET,

WRITTEN ON THE STEAMER ATLANTIC,

October 4, 1851.

Tossed like an egg-shell on the heaving main,
Our ship, that looked a giant at the quay,
Shivers and groans a frighted babe on sea,
As the wind roughens all the watery plain;
Till oak and iron own the wrenching strain.
So weak is man's work in the mighty hand
Of him who gives the howling surge command,
To lift the wrestling waves that foam with pain.
But yet the force which drives the wreck to land,
Or whelms whole squadrons near some treach'rous strand,
Or forks the lightning in the helmsman's face,
Or shoots the waterspout in column grand,
When gulfs.lay bare the deep uncovered sand,
Is power all wedded to triumphal grace.

October 10.—We approached the banks of Newfoundland,
but the wind is stiff ahead, and it rains almost all day. Great
gloom prevails in the company. Some are not yet come forth
of their chambers. Some are lying about in the cabins, both
day and night, wretched with a sickness which has no parallel.
In the upper dining-cabin, on the quarter-deck, much of the day
is occupied with meals; breakfast from 8 to 11; luncheon at
noon; dinner at 4; tea at 8, and supper at 10. Towards evening the rain abates, and at 9 the full moon shines beautiful over
the whitening sea. For the first time, in this gloomy voyage,
the young folks gather in the dining-saloon for games and merriment. Every morning Bishop Otey and I have prayers in his
state-room.

October 11.—We are on the banks of Newfoundland. We
had tremendous heavings, and one sudden pitch, which many
thought greater than any during the gale. It threw down a
sailor into the forecastle companion, and greatly injured him.
Towards night a dead whale hove in sight, escorted by porpoises
and birds. Grampuses are seen to spout, and sea-birds become
numerous.

October 12.—Lord's day. Divine service in dining saloon at
10½. Bishop Otey preached. The attendance was very good.
After tea I preached in the same room on the prayer of the
publican. The saloon was entirely filled, and the company was
attentive.

October 13.—Fog. We blow the steam-whistles now and then, to give warning to poor fishing-vessels, which might be overthrown by our tremendous weight of 2,900 tons going fifteen miles an hour. We passed not a great way from Halifax. The bad weather, by preventing ventilation, has made many of the state-rooms quite offensive, so that when you pass by the doors you sniff a variety of odours, like the wards of a lazaretto. These ships are spoiled by the addition of new berths filling up what used to be the fine open space of the forward cabin. Not only are these state-rooms all along the sides of the vessel, but a compact village of rooms fills the interior, leaving only some insignificant areas, where the stairs and skylights are, and some narrow entries. These rooms are close and dark, and here the rush of waters was greatest during the gale. The gay fellows have names for several parts, such as Cavendish Square, Pall Mall, and Rotten Row.

October 14.—Shortly after breakfast it became evident that there was some cause of alarm. Presently we began to perceive breakers on our starboard bow. How beautiful are these deadly enemies! It becomes apparent that we have missed our reckoning, and have run too near Nantucket shoals. The engine stops, and steam is let off. It is hard to think of peril under this clear sun and amidst this beautiful blue sea, and from those snowy surges that dash up and twinkle in the sun. We heave the lead twice, and find about 24 fathoms.

October 15.—The wooded, flat shores of Long Island are in view. We soon pass the Narrows. It is an incomparable morning, making one think meanly of European skies. Sun and moon are both visible. The grand bay with islands and shipping is in sight. We come to at the foot of Canal street, about 6 30 A. M.

No. 3.
SUPPLEMENT TO THE EUROPEAN LETTERS OF 1857.[1]

LIVERPOOL, *October* 9, 1857.

You will have learned from other sources, that the 7th of October was observed throughout the British Isles as a day of Humiliation and Prayer, in regard to the present Indian calamities. There is good cause to think that it has been a day of spiritual good to many thousands. The daily newspapers of yesterday from one end of the land to the other, are filled with

[1] This is taken from Dr. Alexander's correspondence with "The Presbyterian."

reports of the sermons preached; and from these, it is plain that the talents and piety of the best men were employed in this work. In Glasgow, where I was at the time, the shops were closed, and there was no appearance of business in any one of the numerous streets through which I walked or drove. In some churches, the services were of a freer character, familiar to us in America, and prayers were offered alternately with addresses. This is true of the United Presbyterian church in Wellington Street, of which the excellent Dr. Robinson is the pastor. He was assisted by the Rev. Dr. Archer of London, and from both we heard faithful and memorable exhortations, addressed to a very large assembly of solemn and sometimes deeply affected worshippers. I accepted it as a token of confidence in American sympathy and Christian love, that these good men and esteemed brethren forced me into the service, which as a foreigner I scarcely knew how to undertake, especially after twenty weeks of silence, but which they were pleased to recognize as a tribute of unfeigned regard for the testimony which we uphold in common. On that, as on other occasions, my soul was melted within me at the thought of these beloved missionaries of our own and the Reformed Presbyterian Church, who, I fear, have fallen asleep amidst the assaults of the murderous Sepoys. After the service of two hours, I saw the adjacent lecture-room, where the late venerable Dr. Mitchell, pastor of this church, for more than half a century, used to instruct the theological students of the Secession Church. His portrait and those of two ruling elders adorn the walls. According to my best recollection the communion numbers about thirteen hundred.

Not to confine myself to a particular body, I went in the afternoon to the Barony Church, belonging to the Establishment, in order to hear the Rev. Norman McLeod, who is at this time second to no preacher in Scotland, for what may be called a catholic popularity. Accustomed as we are in America to consider the Establishment and Moderatism to be much the same, we ought to rejoice and be thankful for the tidings that there are not a few ministers in that body who preach Christ, with a fulness, fervour, and spiritual unction, which no denomination can surpass, and which would have been stigmatized a century ago as ranting Methodism. On this occasion I heard only the second of two discourses, which was on Lam. v. 16, "The crown is fallen from our head; woe unto us, that we have sinned." Other topics had occupied the forenoon; he was now upon the sins to be bewailed, and the hopes to be cherished. Mr. McLeod has every advantage of external gifts, in stature, face, carriage, and gesture; and in regard to voice, I have never

heard any more flexible, rich, and controlling ; I cannot suppose
that in popular address our Dr. Mason was either more strong
or more pathetic than Norman McLeod. I had not heard him
utter two sentences of devotion, before I ceased to wonder why
crowds attend upon his ministry, while I less than ever was
tempted to crave any liturgical crutches in the way of printed
prayer. Let men pray thus, and we shall hear of no deviation
from the way of our fathers ; and with a rubrical imposition of
forms men cannot thus pray. I have no quarrel with " our
excellent liturgy ; " I have gratefully joined in its best parts
almost every Sabbath for months; I believe it to be the best
compilation from the Latin offices that has ever been made,
nevertheless I hold on in our primitive and more excellent way,
and should be pleased to read an answer to famous John Owen's
tractate on Free Prayer. Apropos of this matter, I have heard
one of the most celebrated ministers in Scotland, eminent alike
for the gift and the grace of praying, interlard his devotions with
passages from the prayer-book. I cannot but make reclamation
against this, on grounds of unity and sacred composition. Those
collects, which I had often joined in with reverential admiration,
seemed out of tune amidst the inspired breathings of David and
Jeremiah, which were legitimately and beautifully introduced at
the same time. I could not help wondering at the gifted utterances of the very minister to whom I here allude, and who is
known in more lands than one.

But to return, Mr. McLeod's sermon was a noble piece of
free argumentation and passionate eloquence. He spoke like a
senator on this occasion, and you may judge in how untram-
melled a manner, when I add that he read from several volumes,
and even from Tuesday's *Times*. The secret of the effects produced by this preaching is, that his heart is bursting with the
very emotion which he seeks to cause. I need scarcely add
that he used no manuscript; sometimes he does so ; but this
was one of the discourses which cannot be written. There were
several generous allusions to our own country in this delightful
sermon, which gratified me all the more as contrasted with the
crude, ignorant, and fiery attacks of many, on what they think
American toleration of sin. Mr. McLeod's vindication of Missions, his plea for national mercy, and his retorts upon the infidel
party, were triumphant. But most of the time I was too near
breaking out into tears to sit as a critic. When, on another
occasion, I heard Mr. McLeod preach on a Sabbath afternoon,
I was really lifted up to consider that God had still a testimony,
in a large school of the younger churchmen, for the most evangelical doctrines and experience. This, however, need not be said

to any one who has read the "Earnest Student," which is his work, or the "Footsteps of St. Paul," by another minister of the Kirk, in Glasgow.

It would be very presumptuous in a passing stranger to pronounce upon the ministry of a great people, or to characterize their pulpit. He can at best hear only a few, and these may not be the representative minds ; I shall, therefore, indulge in no sweeping remarks, but content myself with saying, that so far as I can learn, there is no country on the globe, which is better furnished, in its rank and file, with a thoroughly orthodox and earnestly evangelical ministry than Scotland. How entirely exceptional all but the Presbyterian element is, may be gathered from the fact, that in Glasgow alone there are more than a hundred Presbyterian ministers. I am not very far astray, when I say that of these the Established Church has thirty-four, the Free Church thirty-three, and the United Presbyterian Church thirty-one. On the National Fast, it is to be supposed, all these, and many others, were engaged in leading the minds of their hearers to penitent reflections suited to the present crisis. In a word, the national mind has been thoroughly waked up to the religious aspects of this portentous theme. One mighty dictator of British opinion, the *Times*, though sometimes admitting letter-writers who take the other side, nobly vindicates Christianity and Missions from the charge of having provoked these hostilities. It is honourable to the British people, that everywhere the most candid confession of national sin is fairly uttered. The opium business has especially come in for its share. I acknowledge that our British brethren, who often say hard things of our government, are just as ready to say hard things of their own. This is a land where free speech and a free press are high in influence ; nowhere more so. I felt the fellowship of the old Presbyterian temper, when I heard a pastor from his pulpit protest against the terms in which the Queen *commanded* the Fast to be observed ; a protestation which the venerable Dr. John Brown also made very prominent in his discourse in Edinburgh.

As I sat in the gallery last Sabbath, when Mr. McLeod referred to a passage by chapter and verse, a thousand pocket Bibles instantly turned up the place ; it is so everywhere in Scotland. The practice of using a reverent posture in prayer is universal here ; and I have never found myself the only person, besides the minister, who was standing, as has often happened to me among the indolent worshippers of England and America. The Presbyterians of this country, that is to say, the great body of the population, love the house of God, and are attached to their own particular forms. Churches are built for use, and in most cases are very closely seated, so as to be full even to packing. I was delighted to observe that on an evening when I heard a Glasgow clergyman preach, the house, which had aisles and even pulpit-stairs crowded, was occupied largely by those classes of hearers who in some of our cities have so much left us for other denominations, or for none at all.

If my experience is worth any thing, there is not a more hospitable land than this; people talk of Highland welcomes, but you are met thus to Gretna and the very Tweed. A minister in Rosshire, whom I never saw, gave me a warm and cordial invitation to tabernacle with his family all summer, beside his lochs; and no doubt would have given us Gaelic treats of salmon and grouse. What Emerson says, concerning England, of "full dress and dinner at six," as a national influence, is just as true of Edinburgh and Glasgow; and I question whether what Mrs. Hannah More said was already going out in London, to wit, *conversation*, is anywhere more nobly upheld than in the better circles of the cities. Some of the most instructive and entertaining—let me even add, edifying lessons I ever received, have been in such circles, as well six years ago as now.

While so many of our young men go annually to Germany, year after year, bringing home no practical good that I can comprehend, it is sincerely to be wished that some of them might go to Scotland, to see the Presbyterian machine really worked, by congregations having from twenty to thirty ruling elders each, and as many deacons, and to limber their academic sermonizing by a hearing of several commanding preachers, who unite athletic bodies with well-furnished, determined, and fervent minds. Some things I honestly believe they might learn of us, but in the faculty of carrying gospel truth with interest to promiscuous assemblies and the common people, they excel us. With hardly any exception, all the preachers of Scotland, who are much followed by the multitude, are as remarkable for purely evangelical preaching, as for intellectual power and impressive elocution. Few of them are what we should denominate good speakers.

With thanksgiving to the God of our life, who has preserved me and mine through many changes, I record my desire to return to the land which I admire and love the more by reason of all contrasts and comparisons, and to the labours for which I trust I am in some slight measure better prepared in body, though not yet wholly relieved.

INDEX TO VOL. II.

———◆◆◆———

THE END.

LaVergne, TN USA
01 October 2009
159627LV00004B/8/P